CROWN
INSIDERS'
GUIDE™
TO JAPAN

Also in the series:

CROWN INSIDERS' GUIDE™ TO JAPAN

Robert C. Fisher

Crown Publishers, Inc.
New York

Copyright © 1987 by Crown Publishers, Inc.

All rights reserved. No part of this book may be reproduced or transmitted in any form or by any means, electronic or mechanical, including photocopying, recording, or by any information storage and retrieval system, without permission in writing from the publisher.

Published by Crown Publishers, Inc., 225 Park Avenue South, New York, New York 10003 and represented in Canada by the Canadian MANDA Group.

CROWN and CROWN INSIDERS' GUIDE are trademarks of Crown Publishers, Inc.

Manufactured in the United States of America

Library of Congress Cataloging-in-Publication Data

Fisher, Robert C.
   The Crown insiders' guide to Japan.

   Includes index.
   1. Japan—Description and travel—1945–   —Guidebooks. I. Title.
DS805.2.F57 1987   915.2'0448   86-23941

ISBN 0-517-56545-5

10 9 8 7 6 5 4 3 2 1
First Edition

CONTENTS

List of Maps

EDITOR'S NOTE

There's a Native American saying about walking in another person's moccasins before you can understand his or her feelings. That advice fits any discussion of visiting Japan, I think. Long a victim of stereotyped attitudes, Japan has passed through a whole range of images, from hermit empire to home of "the Yankees of the Orient," as Teddy Roosevelt allegedly called the Japanese. Then they were said to be a nation of nothing but cheap imitators, knocking off copies of Western products.

Pearl Harbor surprised the world, not only because of its daring (or cunning, if you will), but because the Japanese were regarded as weak and inefficient, yet somehow brutal. At war's end, in a stunning turnaround, and aided by history's most benevolent military occupation, Japan began to rebuild. Less than 40 years later, she had the great empire she once longed for, but now it was to be measured in dollars, not square miles of conquered territory. Many experts believe she will surpass the United States in gross national product by 1990, becoming the world's leading economic power.

All the books about Japan's systems of management, her homogeneous population, even her fencing (Miyamoto Musashi's *Book of Five Rings*) help the curious to understand what makes this nation tick. But there is nothing like seeing for yourself, and if you travel to Japan with your eyes open, your prejudices left at home, and an inquiring mind, you may learn more than all the books can teach you.

The Crown Insiders' Guide™ Series

Knowing Japan inside out isn't enough to make a good travel guide writer. You have to be an outsider who thinks

like an Insider, almost a well-meaning spy. Good jour-
nalists are born, they say, and the best learn to think like
the people they are writing about, just as the savviest
policemen and criminal lawyers imagine themselves in the
shoes of their quarry or client. In this series of books, the
authors try to show the reader what each country looks
like to a trained observer, one who knows the ground but
isn't blinded by tradition, connections, or misplaced loyal-
ties. Our Insiders have to be outsiders for the very reason
that natives of the country have too many obligations, too
much cultural baggage of their own, too little knowledge of
what American readers want.

You'll learn from an Insiders' Guide the perils and
pitfalls of travel, items most travel books tend to ignore.
We'll make it a point to highlight the good things, too,
calling attention to special finds, such as free English-
language telephone service for tourists.

The Authors

The Crown Insiders' Guide authors have all lived and/or
studied in the countries they write about. In the case of
Japan, I am a lifelong student of the people and their
culture. I was first introduced to Japan by a junior high
school teacher who had never been there, but was
nonetheless infatuated with the land and its inhabitants.
Even during World War II, this strong-willed instructor,
Vida Annegers, taught her Burlington, Iowa, pupils to
respect the Japanese, while condemning their government's imperialistic policies. At Harvard, I studied international relations and worked part-time at the Harvard-
Yenching Institute, where I came into contact with such
academic notables as Edwin O. Reischauer, later ambassa-
dor to Japan, and Serge Elisseeff, the grand old man of
Asian scholars in Cambridge. Taking leave from college, I
served in the U.S. Army after the Korean War, being
attached to the British Commonwealth Forces headquarters near Hiroshima as part of a Counter Intelligence
Corps unit. After graduating from Harvard and entering
Columbia University's School of Law, I took a leave of
absence (again) and enrolled in Tokyo University's Gradu-
ate School of Social Sciences.

Besotted with Japan, I never returned to law school,

staying in Tokyo to work as a consultant for a Japanese politician, Takeo Miki, who later became prime minister. At the same time, I began travel writing and editing, putting together the first Fodor guide to Japan and eventually replacing Eugene Fodor as president and editor-in-chief of the company. After 20 years with the firm, I left to write and edit other guides, of which this is one. I return to Japan constantly; I've lost count of the number of trips.

THE INSIDERS' RATING SYSTEM

The authors and the editor jointly award 1, 2, 3, 4, or 5 crowns to hotels, restaurants, and such places as museums, monuments, temples, shrines, and other sights or sites that seem important to them. Here is our interpretation of the awards:

Hotels and Restaurants

♕ ♕ ♕ ♕ ♕	Best in the country
♕ ♕ ♕ ♕	Outstanding
♕ ♕ ♕	Excellent
♕ ♕	Very good
♕	Recommended

Sights and Sites

♕ ♕ ♕ ♕ ♕	Once-in-a-lifetime
♕ ♕ ♕ ♕	A "must see"
♕ ♕ ♕	Worth a considerable detour
♕ ♕	Important
♕	Interesting

Become an Insider

Nobody's perfect, and though our Insider has tried to include everything worthwhile, omit the tourist traps, and maintain up-to-date prices and other information, the ever-changing aspects of travel ensure that something in this book will change between the time we wrote about it and the time you visit. Let us know, by writing to the author and/or the editor at Crown Insiders' Guides, Crown Publishers, Inc., 225 Park Avenue South, New York, NY 10003. We'll be grateful for corrections, suggestions for new listings, or any comments you care to make.

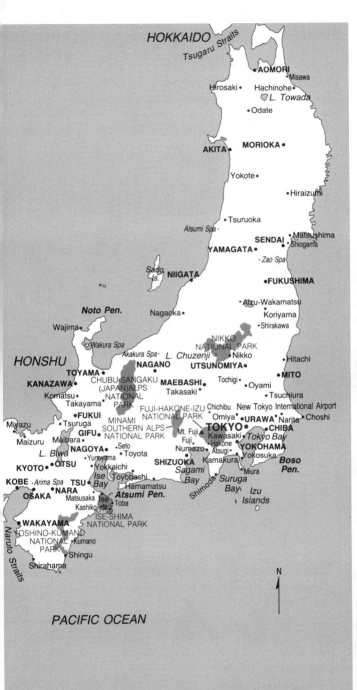

INSIDERS' INFORMATION

BEFORE YOU GO

WHY VISIT JAPAN NOW?

If you want to see modern Japan in its purest state, go now. The old cliché about it being the Land of the Rising Sun is passé, because Japan's place in the sun has come, and with a vengeance. The second-richest nation (after the U.S.), it is at the peak of its status as the country that made it big, that's sitting on top of the world. Why do I emphasize this? Well, being at a peak implies a downhill slide, and one way or the other, some things in Japan are not going to remain the same for much longer.

It's not the cherry blossoms or Fuji-san that will blow away, though the flowers do just that every spring, and Mt. Fuji last shed its top in 1707. It's not even the *geisha* girls or public bathhouses I'm worried about, though there are signs of immutable transition for both those institutions. What may be disappearing sooner are two aspects of Japan which can be seen today at their finest—booming Japan, preparing to lead the free world into the 21st century, and refined Japan, clinging proudly to its cultural and artistic heritage.

Travelers may not worry much about seeing boomtown Japan lose a little steam. There is a long line of angry Americans waiting to prick the balloon of Japanese economic success if given the chance. As more American factories close and the trade balance grows worse by the minute, few tears will be lost if Japan slows down a bit. This in fact has begun to happen, and it's not just because of the weaker U.S. dollar against a strong yen. For the first time in 11 years, the GNP in Japan fell in the summer of 1986. The signs had been apparent for quite a while. The latest generation to go to work wonders what all the fuss is about. Why do their parents work so hard? Why all this talk about how "poor" Japan really is, in terms of natural resources and public facilities? (The same talk, by the way, that subconsciously prevents many foreign products from ever gaining a foothold in Japan, because the "poor little Japan" argument has millions of supporters in every aspect of society here.) Young people, raised in relative affluence, have no fears about Japan ever being poor. Lacking a sense of history, and with the optimism only the young can flaunt, they now ask a potential employer the "Three Dreaded Questions": (1) How much vacation time do I get? (2) Do we have to work on Saturdays? (3) What is the average bonus you expect to pay twice a year?

A good Japanese never used to ask these questions. He or she never took all the vacation time coming, anyway. And if the office or factory was open on Saturday, everyone came in, even if it was only to spend the obligatory half day reading the newspapers and making tea. If you do want to see the rip-roaring Japan portrayed in all the "how-to" executive books so popular in the United States, come now before the nation succumbs to the ills caused by affluence—sloppy workmanship, decreased service in every aspect of commerce, and "what's in it for me" as a philosophy of life. Despite all the talk, Japan is headed in this direction, the direction long ago taken by Britain, northern Europe, and the United States.

More important to the traveler, of course, is the loss of old Japanese cultural and artistic attitudes. Take food, for example. The best of true Japanese *haute cuisine* is, with a very few exceptions noted in this book, getting to be so pricey that only executives on expense accounts can afford it. At the opposite extreme, American fast-food emporia can be found everywhere, driving out small restaurants in the neighborhood. And, as happened in the U.S. and is now also happening in France, the middle-priced decent restaurant is finding it impossible to compete. Though the traditional arts are still fostered, attendance at the *kabuki* and Noh theater are way, way down (foreigners are now offered discount tickets, for just one example of how bad things are), and young people are scarcely seen at traditional vaudeville-type shows. The *geisha* themselves are a dying breed, as few girls want to go through the long apprenticeship, wear the cumbersome clothes, or apply the cloying makeup to their hands and necks, as well as faces.

But all the attributes of old Japan are still very much in evidence, if you don't delay too long. You can still attend imperial court dances, dating from the 7th century, at the emperor's palace in Tokyo. You can watch the Noh theater by torchlight in the garden of a Buddhist temple in Kyoto, cruise a river with cormorant fishermen, whose birds pluck sweet trout from the moonlit waters, or photograph a fertility festival featuring "obscene" floats that would offend practically everyone back home.

JAPANESE NAMES

Throughout this book, we have given Japanese names with family name first, given name second, as is customary in Japan. The author known to Americans as Yukio Mishima, therefore, is referred to herein as Mishima Yukio, and so forth.

HISTORY IN A HURRY

Here is a list of cultural periods and major events in Japanese history:

Before 7500 B.C.	Pre-Jomon Culture
7500–3000 B.C.	Jomon Culture, 1st and 2nd stages
3000–2500 B.C.	Jomon, 3rd stage
2000–1100 B.C.	Jomon, 4th stage
1100–400 B.C.	Jomon, 5th stage
660 B.C.	First emperor, Jimmu
400–100 B.C.	Early Yayoi Culture. Capital moves with each emperor, no permanent base established.
100 B.C.–A.D. 100	Middle Yayoi Culture
100–250	Yamato from Korea invade Japan. Late Yayoi Culture
250–400	Early Tumulus Culture
360	Empress Jingo invades Korea.
400–500	Middle Tumulus Culture
405	Writing imported from Korea.
538–645	Asuka Culture (first reigning empress, Suiko)
538	Buddhism imported from Korea.
645–794	Nara Period
710–784	Capital in Nara
784–794	Capital in Yamashiro

794–1192	Heian Period; flowering of early Buddhist art
794–1868	Capital in Kyoto
860–1167	Fujiwara Culture. Japan's noblest family guides the emperor.
1159–60	War between Heike and Genji. Taira and Minamoto families vie for power.
1167–90	Heike Culture
1192–1331	Kamakura Period. Shoguns leave emperors isolated in Kyoto, as capital deteriorates.
1192–1219	Minamoto shoguns and Hojo family as regents. Heyday of *samurai,* code of *bushido.*
1226–52	Fujiwara shoguns and Hojo regency
1252–1338	Imperial princes as shoguns and Hojo regency to 1333
1274, 1281	First and second Mongol invasions. Kublai Khan retreats when bad weather threatens first landing. Typhoon, or *kamikaze* (divine wind), destroys second fleet of 150,000 men.
1331–92	South North Period (Nambokucho Jidai) also called Yoshino Period. Ashikaga Takauji betrays Kamakura shogunate, which is destroyed. Rival emperors crowned, two courts lasting until 1392.
1338–1573	Ashikaga shoguns (in Kyoto)
1338–1358	Ashikaga Takauji
1358–1367	Ashikaga Yoshiakira (abdicated)
1367–1395	Ashikaga Yoshimitsu (abdicated)
1392–1573	Muromachi Period; the zenith of Japanese art, including architecture
1395–1423	Ashikaga Yoshimochi (abdicated)
1423–25	Ashikaga Yoshikazu
1428–41	Ashikaga Yoshinori (assassinated)
1441–43	Ashikaga Yoshikatsu
1449–74	Ashikaga Yoshimasa (abdicated)
1474–89	Ashikaga Yoshihisa
1490–93	Ashikaga Yoshitane (abdicated)
1493–1508	Ashikaga Yoshizumi (abdicated)
1508–1521	Ashikaga Yoshitane (returned)
1521–45	Ashikaga Yoshiharu
1542	Portuguese arrive, introduce guns.
1545–65	Ashikaga Yoshiteru (assassinated)
1568	Ashikaga Yoshihide
1568–73	Ashikaga Yoshiaki (abdicated)
1573–1603	Azuchi Momoyama Period
1573–1615	Momoyama Culture
1573–82	Oda Nobunaga ruler of Japan (assassi-

	nated). He toyed with idea of opening country to outside world.
1585	Toyotomi Hideyoshi made chancellor, prime minister later
1587	Hideyoshi bans Christianity.
1592–98	Hideyoshi invades Korea, troops leave on his death.
1600	Tokugawa Ieyasu victor at Battle of Sekigahra; Will Adams arrives in Japan ("Anjin" in *Shogun* book and film).
1603–1868	Edo Period (Tokugawa Period)
1603–05	Tokugawa Ieyasu (abdicated)
1605–23	Tokugawa Hidetada (abdicated)
1609	Ryukyu Islands conquered (including Okinawa). Dutch allowed to establish Nagasaki base.
1623–51	Tokugawa Iemitsu
1623	Greatest persecution of Christians
1651–80	Tokugawa Ietsuna
1680–1700	Tokugawa Tsunayoshi
1700–12	Tokugawa Ienobu (1701–1703); 47 Ronin in Chushingura Incident
1704–1868	Edo Culture
1712–16	Tokugawa Ietsugu
1716–45	Tokugawa Yoshimune (abdicated)
1724	Death of Chikamatsu, "the Japanese Shakespeare"
1745–60	Tokugawa Ieshige (abdicated)
1750–1800	Apogee of the *ukiyoe* (woodblock print) artists
1760–86	Tokugawa Ieharu
1786–1837	Tokugawa Ienari (abdicated)
1792	First Russian explorer reaches Hokkaido.
1801	Japanese explore Sakhalin.
1837–53	Tokugawa Ieyoshi
1837	First U.S. ship, *Morrison*, visits Edo Bay.
1853–58	Tokugawa Iesada
1853	Commodore Perry arrives at Uraga.
1858–66	Tokugawa Iemochi
1859	Start of foreign trading in Yokohama
1866–68	Tokugawa Keiki (abdicated)
1867	Emperor Meiji ascends throne.
1868–1912	Meiji Period
1868	Tokyo chosen as new capital.
1870	Commoners allowed to take surnames.
1873	Adoption of Gregorian calendar, end of ban on Christianity
1874	Conquest of Formosa
1877	Satsuma Rebellion defeated.
1881	Political parties formed.
1894–95	Sino-Japanese War won by Japan.

1902	Anglo-Japanese Alliance, first between European and Asian powers
1904–05	Russo-Japanese War. Japan wins, first defeat of European power by Asian power.
1908	Gentleman's Agreement limiting Japanese emigration to USA
1910	Annexation of Korea
1912–26	Taisho Period
1914	Japan enters World War I on Allied side.
1915	Japan presents "Twenty-one Demands" on China.
1918	Japan and Britain send troops to Siberia to fight Reds.
1920	Japan assumes mandate over former German islands in Pacific.
1923	Great Tokyo Earthquake
1924	U.S. abrogates Gentleman's Agreement, cutting off emigration.
1925	Diet legislates universal male suffrage.
1926–present	Showa Period
1927	First Japanese intervention in Chinese civil wars, Shantung, followed by more over years
1931	Outbreak of "Manchurian Incident"
1932	Japanese create puppet state of Manchukuo.
1936	Attempted coup d'état by some army units, Tokyo
1937	Outbreak of war with China, *Panay* bombing (U.S. gunboat on Yangtze)
1938–39	Canton, Hankow, Hainan captured.
1940	Creation of puppet Chinese government, invasion of Indo-China, alliance with Germany and Italy
1941	Continued expansion in Indochina, attack on U.S. at Pearl Harbor, start of "Great Pacific War"
1942	Greatest expansion of Japanese Empire to India, Java, New Guinea
1943	Fall of Tarawa
1944	Fall of New Guinea, resignation of Tojo; U.S. bombing begins.
1945	Fall of Manila, Okinawa; atomic bombings; surrender and demilitarization
1946	Emperor denies own divinity. New constitution, labor unions, land reform.
1947	Socialist premier (lasts only 1 year); Tojo and 6 others executed as war criminals.
1950	Korean War starts, Japan becomes arsenal.

1951	MacArthur dismissed; peace treaty signed between Japan and most nations (not USSR)
1952	U.S. occupation of Japan ends.
1956	Japan admitted to United Nations.
1960	Japan launches "high economic growth policy."
1964	Tokyo hosts summer Olympic Games, ends trade and exchange controls.
1972	U.S. returns Okinawa to Japan.

JAPANESE CULTURE IN A CAPSULE
Architecture

The single most important feature about Japanese architecture is its intimate relationship with nature. Striving at all times to be open to the outdoors, the typical Japanese building is made from wood, paper, and earth. Everyone is by now familiar with the paper *fusuma,* or sliding doors, and paper *shoji,* on doors and windows in a latticed pattern. The ubiquitous wooden house, with its raised verandah, sliding storm doors, and polished *tokonoma* alcove, is featured in every film about Japan. The roof of many a thatched house is made of tiles, clay in the old days, tin for cheaper buildings today.

Though the Japanese have four distinct seasons to weather, including very cold winters and very hot summers, the houses are constructed as though this archipelago were in the South Pacific. There is very little insulation in traditional homes, only the wooden walls, paper partitions, and sliding doors at night to keep out cold, light, and wind. Many anthropologists cite the method of building these homes as evidence the race had some of its origins in the South Seas.

Japanese are also aware that wooden houses burn easily, killing hundreds of thousands in conflagrations such as those which followed the Great Earthquake of 1923 and the March 1945 firebombings by American B-29s. On the other hand, wooden structures are easy to put up again, and cheaper than brick, stone, or concrete. Most of all, though, the Japanese feel closer to nature in a house made of wood. The construction is always designed, moreover, to bring the garden indoors by sliding an entire wall back.

Traditional architecture expands horizontally, not vertically, with few exceptions.

A traditional dwelling would have, in addition to the wooden doors and paper screens mentioned earlier, a floor made of *tatami* (mats woven from rush grasses). These mats are always the same size (approximately 3 feet by 6 feet) and are used as a basis for computing rooms size. A *yojo-han* (4½-mat room) is adequate for a child's bedroom, for example, and a *rokujo* (6-mat room) is the minimum for a living room or parents' bedrooms (usually the same).

In addition to gardens (often tiny) for homes, the Japanese architect plans traditional-style buildings (and some modern ones, for that matter) with a garden in mind. Look for the different types, such as *karesansui*, as in the famous rock garden at Ryoanji Temple in Kyoto. This is a dry garden, using sand or gravel to represent rivers or the ocean, and even a boulder to represent a waterfall, a boat, or a mountain, depending on its shape. The Tsukiyama-style garden attempts to portray nature in miniature, with a pond, small hillocks, and little bridges. Next to teahouses is the third major style of garden, the *chaniwa* (lit. tea garden), featuring a stone basin, lantern, stepping-stones, and a bamboo water pipe.

In Buddhist temples, each building has its own definite purpose, such as the Kondo, where images and statues of Buddha are protected; the Kodo, where the scriptures are read; the pagoda, where relics are preserved; and the gates, where evil fortune is warded off. The Kodo is sometimes called the Hotto; the Kondo is sometimes called the Butsuden. Note the small details, such as a post with a kind of acorn on it—actually an inverted lotus flower. Windows in a kind of bell shape are also designed after the lotus blossom. From the round tiles on the end of the ridge poles on temple roofs, you can tell the period when the roof was built, if you know the complicated code.

Shrine architecture, dating back hundreds of years before Buddhism came to Japan, is less colorful most of the time, with wild exceptions (Heian and Kasuga shrines come to mind, not to mention the mausoleum to Tokugawa Ieyasu at Nikko). Shrines were built at places where the gods were thought to have come down to earth, and the objects of veneration are things inside which the spirits dwell. (The sacred mirror, one of the three imperial regalia, is a good example of one such holy object.)

Sculpture and Painting

As you may expect, most premodern sculpture is inspired by religion, and in Japan, that means Buddhism. Although Shintoism and Buddhism coexist in most Japanese hearts and souls, Shintoism has no tradition of art, and no need to depict religious dogma in wood, bronze, or colored pigments. As Buddhism was imported from China, via Korea, so too came the interest in images of the Buddha. Many of the most famous are discussed in this book, and a remarkable number of wooden carvings have survived the frequent fires which have plagued Japan, not to mention dampness and rot, wet or dry. Few examples of the rich polychrome which covered most wooden statues remain, of course, thanks to the climate.

Bronze works have survived better, and examples of great works range from those in the Tokyo National Museum to the giant images at Kamakura and Nara. Sculpture reached its height in the 13th century and declined thereafter. The creators of many such works are anonymous, and sculpture has never been an important art in Japan, to this day. What counts, this country seems to say, is painting.

When you visit Nijojo Castle in Kyoto, to mention only one place, you will realize how important painting is here. With vast expanses of sliding paper doors, plaster walls, and standing screens calling out for decoration, painters had a field day throughout the centuries. Lacking much furniture, save cushions, lamps, and low tables, the Japanese room came alive with whole walls of tigers,

---

JAPAN'S FIVE BEST MUSEUMS

Kyoto: Kyoto National Museum
Nara: Nara National Museum
Tokyo: Horyuji Treasure House of Tokyo National Museum
　　　Nezu Institute of Fine Arts
　　　Tokyo National Museum

peonies, bamboo groves, flights of wild cranes, and landscapes. The golden age of painting, which came to Japan with Buddhism in the 6th century, came in the 16th century, with the Kano school in Kyoto. Look for works by members of this school, and of the later Korin school.

Music and Dance

The earliest forms of native music related to Shintoism and used mostly percussion instruments (blocks of wood and gongs, as well as drums). The *kagura* dances stemmed from a desire to bring back the dead, and can be traced directly to the folkloric tale of the sun goddess, Amaterasu Omikami, being lured from her cave (where her pouting had blacked out the world) by slightly indecent dancing, whatever that means. Wooden flutes—the sonorous *shakuhachi* are a later derivation—came along later. With the introduction of Buddhism in the 6th century came influences on Japanese music from Korea, China, and even India. Some of the world's oldest dancing and music can be heard in the occasional performances of *gagaku* and *bugaku* (court orchestra and court dance) given in Tokyo, Kyoto, Nara, and sometimes Miyajima Shrine. You can enjoy recitals on the *koto* (harp) and *samisen* (a kind of banjo or guitar) wherever *geisha* perform and in occasional concert-hall appearances.

Japanese folk songs have influenced modern music, which is heavily derivative of Western modes. Genuine folk music is hard to come by, and is being preserved on records and tape as fast as the scholars can get it down, as the young people of Japan are totally uninterested. At festivals, some old songs have been modernized, and the blare of the loudspeaker is heard throughout the land. You might enjoy an evening in a *karaoke* bar, singing along to accompany a taped background. A few places have Western songs on tape. In some bars, an applause meter is hooked up to the system, so you can see whether you're intended to be a star some day.

Western classical music is very popular, Tokyo alone having five symphony orchestras and three opera groups. As anyone who knows about the Suzuki method of teaching the violin is aware, the Japanese are among the world's best musicians, at least in a technical sense. You can hear the Western classics all day long on the state radio, NHK, or pop into a coffee shop to soak up Brahms, staying for hours if you wish, for the price of a cup of mocha.

In addition to ballet, which Japanese adore, several innovative troupes have become popular recently. The Juku group, which has toured America and Europe, used to specialize in dangling nearly nude performers from building tops (until the death of one in Seattle) and squiggling around the stage like worms, among other daring ventures. A Butai group features huge drum accompaniment to its dancers' efforts, with flute and small drum on the side. The costumes of the musicians are as dramatic as those of the dancers. The development of the Japanese as dancers has proceeded with the advancement of their diets, and sleeping in beds, sitting on chairs, and otherwise getting away from squatting on *tatami* mats all day and tucking the legs under the body every sitting moment. Lincoln Kirstein used to despair of the classical Japanese body, which had a torso as tall as that of a Westerner, but legs quite a bit shorter. This seems to be a thing of the past, as average height here rises each year (up about 3 inches in only 30 years).

Theater

As I mention several times in this book, *kabuki* is a grand experience, and every attempt has been made to make it easy. There is simultaneous translation (at Tokyo's Kabukiza), there are English-language programs (there and at the National Theater in Tokyo), rented opera glasses, discounted tickets (see page 72), English-speaking reservation clerks, and even books describing each plot in great detail. If you're in Tokyo for 3 days and don't see *kabuki*, you're not trying hard enough to experience Japan. (See page 102 for a brief description of *kabuki*'s background.)

The Noh theater dates back to the performances of acrobats and jugglers of China, who came over to Japan with the Buddhist religion after the 6th century. By the 14th century, under the influence of *bugaku* and *gagaku* court music and dance, it had evolved into a form of mime, wordless and slow, a long journey covering perhaps a few feet on the stage, but taking several minutes. Considered too cerebral by many Japanese, who attend performances with translations of the archaic language employed by the reciters, Noh is heavily subsidized by the government and by temples in whose compounds open-air performances are still given. Interludes of comic dancing or miming, called *kyogen,* break up the slow pace of an evening of Noh. It was from these *kyogen* dances that innovation led to the *kabuki* in the 16th century.

The magnificent *bunraku* puppet theater can be seen at its home base in Osaka, and on occasional visits to Tokyo. Many of the best plays now performed by *kabuki* troupes were written originally for *bunraku* by "the Shakespeare of Japan," Chikamatsu.

Modern theater forms, including *shimpa* (19th-century origins) and *shingeki* (today's theater), require a knowledge of Japanese, so I will skip them here. The public wants, and gets, up-to-date theater from abroad, too, and some group somewhere is always performing *Death of a Salesman* or Shakespeare.

You can still see old music-hall performances, Japanese-style, with conjurers, comics, and even animal acts, but again, knowledge of Japanese is pretty important to these activities. (See page 172 for details.)

Literature

Japan can claim the first novel, *The Tale of Genji,* written by Murasaki Shikibu in 1001. Long before, of course, had been poetry, the first of which was the *Manyoshu* (c. 760), and collections of folklore and mythology, the earliest of those being the *Kojiki* (c. 712). Because the written language, using Chinese characters and two kinds of native syllabary (similar to the Western alphabet), conveys images in the shape of the writing as well as just letters, literature in Japan, whether prose or poetry, can be almost impossible to translate with the same feeling. The written language has been borrowed from the Chinese, who began their form of writing with ideograms—picture words in which the word for tree looked like a tree, that for water looked like a flowing river, and so forth. Each character can convey a whole battery of images, not just the "word" or part of a word it represents. Even the syllabary, based on Japanese sounds, was derived from these *kanji* ideographs imported from China and grafted onto the spoken language.

Since the Meiji Period, writers have been influenced by European and American literature, so that narration and dialogue have become more important than in the past. Names to watch out for include Mishima Yukio, Natsume Soseki, Nagai Kafu, Dazai Osamu, and Kawabata Yasunari (the only Japanese to win the Nobel Prize for Literature, in 1968). All are dead, all have had significant parts of their work translated into English. Also available in English are some contemporary writers, the most famous of whom are, to mention only a few, Oe Kenzaburo, Endo Shusaku, and Ooka Shohei.

Movies

The film industry is in a slump in Japan, and the great directors are dead, dying, or in financial trouble. The great Kurosawa had to finance his latest triumph, *Ran*, in France, for example. With the advent of television, the Japanese are deserting the movie theaters, so the producers of movies have turned to cheap detective stories and soft porn to keep going. I believe you can stay away from Japanese movies for the time being and not miss a thing.

Folk Art and Handicrafts

The exquisite lacquerware of Japan is one of its national glories. Made in slightly varying form in different parts of the country (see page 232), it relies on the abundance of lacquer-providing trees throughout the country. It's not for nothing the Europeans referred to "Japanned" work in the recent past when describing lacquerwork. Kanazawa is the best place to obtain lacquer, followed by Kyoto, then any other major city. Black-and-gold, red-and-gold, even the plain varieties stand out. Though the art was introduced to Japan from China in the 6th century, Japan outshone its teachers quite early on, and the work here is considered the world's best even today.

Pottery is a delight here, too, ranging from the roughly modern look to the intricate and smooth pieces of past tradition. Porcelain costs more, and factories now produce sets of dishes, car-engine parts, and toilet bowls. Look for antique Imariyaki and Kutaniyaki and for modern Mashi-koyaki (*yaki* = pottery). Some of the more fascinating articles are those intended for export to Europe, such as coffeepots from the mid-19th century.

Handmade paper is the best in the world, one of its makers having been declared a Living National Treasure some years ago. Paper and dolls of every shape and description are on sale in the many Handicraft Centers that local governments have erected around Japan, and in private shops as well. Cloisonné, called *shippo*, is a good buy if you like brightly decorated vases, cigarette cases, and the like. Like collapsible paper lanterns, cloisonné articles are light and easy to pack.

The dolls are charming, but workmanship on the Hakata variety has declined recently. The Hakata dolls are made of clay, those of Kyoto of china with cloth costumes; the *kokeshi* dolls, found primarily in Sendai, are usually just a wooden cylinder with a round head.

Items made of bamboo can be found everywhere, and for a conversation piece, you could do worse than to buy a cricket cage, for example.

Woodblock Prints

Regarded as throwaway art by the Japanese until the 20th century, when admiration of American and European connoisseurs forced them to look again, *ukiyoe* came to the attention of the public in the 17th century and reached its height in the 18th. Beware of reproductions and imitations. You can bet the price should indicate something. If a reputable-looking shop says something is a Hiroshige and it costs only a few hundred dollars, you should know that it is at best an old copy. Originals of the famous artists run into the thousands today. The biggies include Hiroshige, Hokusai, Sharaku, Harunobu, and Utamaro.

A DAY IN A LIFE . . .

Though the Japanese lead daily lives similar in many respects to those of people in any industrialized nation, the differences are of enough significance to mention, even in a travel guide. Although the feminist movement, for example, is light-years behind America's, Japanese women have far greater authority than outsiders commonly believe. A majority of husbands give all their earnings to the wife, getting back an allowance for personal spending. They shouldn't come back home too early from the office, either, as neighbors might think they have unimportant jobs. This partly accounts for the large number of men entertaining each other in the cheaper bars and restaurants in the evening. (It usually ends up on some company's expense account.)

Getting to work means public transportation for most Japanese, and that means being squeezed into trains and subways, often by men hired for just that purpose—"pushers," they're called. The apartment in which the urban Japanese live is small and relatively cheap, and these days is a mixture of traditional *tatami*-matted rooms and hard-floored Western-style rooms. Although most Japanese still sleep on a *futon* placed on the *tatami*-matted floor, each year sees a significant rise in the number of beds ordered, as well as chairs. The Japanese have discovered the comfort of the Western-style toilet, too; it surpassed the old squat-type trough in popularity quite recently. The Japanese have long believed that sitting cross-legged on the floor and ignoring chairs has made their legs shorter than those of Westerners.

At work, the famed "extended family" syndrome becomes apparent. There are few private offices, an entire division of clerks, with their bosses, occupying a gigantic space, with no dividers, no cubicles. The boss sits behind inferiors, always watching. Among the hundreds of rules, regulations, and customs, a few are all-important. Don't make waves, don't take all your vacation, don't take long lunch breaks, don't be late. Come early, stay late, polish the brass and the apples. Despite all the talk about company loyalty, fear is still the chief motivation driving the Japanese work force. It may not be fear of unemployment, but it is fear of ostracism, of losing out on promotion, of being shunted aside, off the treadmill and into oblivion.

Meanwhile, at home, the children study long hours with private tutors, their parents not being content with the ordinary schooling, good as it is. To get into Tokyo University, for example, your chances are better if you attend a certain high school. To get into that school, you should attend a particular middle school, and so on down the line until you have, so help me, tutoring for preschool! And yes, you have to pass an entrance exam for each level, from preschool on up to university. Once you enter Tokyo University (or any other, for that matter), you can relax, as the worst is over. Nobody gets thrown out of university, short of murdering a professor. Your university, of course, determines your choice of jobs, as graduates scheme to hire their successors at the same school. The old-boy network may be famous in other countries, but it is critical in Japan.

The extended family in a genealogical sense is breaking up these days. No longer can an elderly parent expect to move in with his son and daughter-in-law and become the tyrant of the household. The Japanese, having conquered the world in cash-register terms, are just beginning to come to grips with their own social problems. Living in what one French economist called "rabbit hutches," with inadequate municipal sewage systems, few parks, and almost no facilities for the aged, the Japanese will have a rather bumpy ride in the next decade or so. Younger job applicants are beginning to ask questions never previously heard: "Do we have to work on Saturdays?" "How many weeks vacation do we get?" "Is promotion based on seniority, as has been customary, or on results?" Some men and women are even changing jobs, hopping from one company to another as pay and benefits increase. Some, horrible though the thought may be, even suggest that the Japanese work too hard and should take a break now and then. Amazingly enough, Prime Minister Nakasone, at the suggestion of the United States, is one of the advocates of slowing down, of living a life with better quality.

Having plenty of money, and being unable to spend it on big-ticket items such as buying a house (land being so dear and changing hands so rarely in Japan), the average consumer buys nice clothing, the best in sports equipment, and frivolous luxury items, from rare Scotch whiskies to Italian leather, from German cars to American grapefruit (about $20 each). Living in a society with practically no violence, no graffiti, few strikes, little public rudeness, and only carefully restrained individualism, the Japanese has an easy life. It is one which can lull the average person into complacency, and allow the ambitious one to succeed without much effort, if he or she remembers but one rule: To get along, go along.

THE MOOD OF THE PEOPLE

Japan is in its most golden age right now, with prosperity, peace, and few apparent troubles. Everyone is having a good time, from the young people boogying in the park to young salaried women spending lots of money on shopping trips to Hawaii (where, incidentally, they think things are cheap, compared to Japan). Groups of farmers visit India to see Buddha's birthplace, middle-aged male office workers go on "sex package tours" to Bangkok, Manila, or Seoul. With a lot of disposable income and no hope of buying a house, the Japanese are having one big party.

You can get a little bit of an inferiority complex about the way things work in America when you visit Japan. You'll ride a quiet, clean subway train, and there's an electronic board which tells you where the next train is, how soon it will arrive, what track it's on. Each station has signs (in English as well as Japanese) showing the station name, plus that of the station next in either direction. There are system maps everywhere, often bilingual. The trains are graffiti-free, and you never see rowdy kids, not to mention muggers-in-training. The trains are on time, without a Mussolini ordering them to be, and the civil servants are civil to everyone. In shops, the salespeople wait to serve you instead of chatting with each other, and phone calls are not given precedence over you, the live customer at the counter. Everything works, or seems to. There are times, some visitors claim, when they would like to see a little disorder to remind them of home. (Not me; I like trouble-free travel.)

The old feelings about America of the postwar period are a thing of the past. In this land of higher educational standards than the U.S. (with 99 percent literacy), they know a lot about the outside world, more than *gaijin* know about them. There is a regular television program on one channel called "New Yorking," which keeps the citizens up to date, for 30 minutes, on young artists, the drug problem, and even politics in the Big Apple. So nobody loves or hates the Americans anymore. Like the British, Italians, and Dutch, the former conquerors are taken for granted. (The Japanese intelligentsia still love the French, and everyone hates the Russians. The Americans, who occupied Japan, are forgiven because their hegemony was so benevolent, and the Japanese figure that the atom bomb more than made up for any guilt about Pearl Harbor. On the other hand, Japan had a nonaggression pact with the Soviet Union, and the latter broke the agreement, invading Japanese territory north of Hokkaido after the atom bombs had fallen, at the last moment of the war. The Russians still haven't signed a peace treaty with Japan, or given back the captured islands.)

HOW MUCH WILL IT COST?

With a weaker dollar, Japan is more expensive than it was just a while ago. That's the bad news. The good news is that Japan will run you only about $64 a day per person for room and board, if you're careful, and $100 to $110 if you're not. If you want to go deluxe, it can be $200 or more a day. If you want to live the life-style of the rich and famous, that can be arranged, too, but only with the proper introductions. (It's actually hard to throw your money around in Japan!)

Anything imported will be pricey, such as Florida orange juice or Scotch whisky. But buy local, as, of course, the Japanese do most of the time, and you'll find prices quite comfortable. Japanese hotels, for example, are far cheaper than those in the larger American or European cities. The average deluxe hotel room in Tokyo is $140, for example; moderate hotels average $96 and inexpensive ones $60 for a double (two persons). Furthermore, there's no tipping in Japan (with a couple of exceptions noted in the text), hence no surprises.

Taxis are priced about the same as those in Los Angeles, somewhat higher than the American average. But public transport is otherwise cheap, the minimum subway fare in several cities being ¥120 (about 70¢). A local telephone call is only ¥10 (about 6¢), a big bottle of beer (= 3.5 U.S. cans) ¥500 ($3). Postcards can be found readily for ¥60 (35¢), soft drinks for ¥100 (60¢). A subway pass in Tokyo for all day is ¥600 ($3.50); a bus pass in Kyoto is ¥890 ($5.40). Foreign visitors are given discounts at the *kabuki* theater, and there is toll-free information and assistance, in English, from the Japan National Tourist Organization. In addition, you can buy a Japan Rail Pass, which works like the Eurail Pass, allowing you first- or second-class transport on the JNR trains (including the famous Bullet Train), buses, and ferries around the nation. You even get tax-free shopping on many items the natives must pay luxury tax on (see page 71).

TYPICAL DAILY EXPENSES
(Hotel and meals, per person)

	Deluxe	*Moderate*	*Inex-pensive*
Western-style hotel (half of double-room price)	$70	$48	$30
Breakfast	18	11	9
Lunch	42	20	10
Dinner	65	31	15
Total	$195	$110	$64
Alternatively:			
Japanese *ryokan* (inn), with breakfast and dinner included	167	80	NA[1]
Lunch out	42	20	NA
Total	$209	$100	

Note: These are prices for larger cities, such as Tokyo, Kyoto, and Osaka. Elsewhere in Japan, prices for restaurants are about 10 percent lower. On the other hand, because of fewer hotels, room prices are about 10 percent higher, though no single hotel or *ryokan* will be higher than those found in the larger cities.

[1]Inexpensive *ryokan* also averages about $30, but without meals. (Frequently, simple breakfast is served, at very modest charge.)

THE BEST TIME TO GO

Late October and early November are my favorite times, because the air is clear and the temperature just right. Spring is second best, with its gorgeous blossoms (plum in February, cherry in March or April). The climate of Japan is very similar to that of the eastern United States coastline, from Maine to northern Florida, with Tokyo at about the Washington, D.C., level of climate, and Kyoto at that of Philadelphia. From Tokyo west along the coast, there is not much snow, but in the mountains it's like the Rockies. The Japan Sea side gets weather similar to that of North Dakota and Montana in winter, and the same is true for Hokkaido. In charts below, I include New York and London references for sake of comparison.

AVERAGE TEMPERATURES NORTH TO SOUTH, FAHRENHEIT

	January	April	July	October
Sapporo	21	40	70	47
Sendai	33	48	73	56
Kanazawa	37	52	77	60
Tokyo	39	56	77	62
Kyoto	37	54	78	61
Hiroshima	38	54	76	61
Kagoshima	44	60	79	67
New York	34	52	75	54
London	40	49	63	50

AVERAGE RAINFALLS IN INCHES AND (HUMIDITY %)

	January	April	July	October
Sapporo	4.6 (75%)	2.5 (68%)	3.5 (80%)	4.0 (74%)
Tokyo	1.9 (57%)	4.8 (66%)	5.5 (79%)	7.9 (74%)
Kyoto	2.2 (72%)	5.7 (67%)	9.3 (76%)	4.8 (74%)
Fukuoka	3.0 (69%)	5.2 (74%)	9.9 (80%)	3.9 (76%)
New York	3.1 (66%)	3.8 (60%)	3.9 (67%)	3.1 (66%)
London	2.2 (81%)	1.5 (63%)	2.3 (65%)	2.3 (77%)

Avoid Golden Week (April 29 to May 5), when there are three national holidays and the country closes down for at least 7 days. Everyone travels during this period, too, so every facility is packed. The New Year holidays, January 1 to January 3, are also bad, as everything closes again, but people stay home and call on friends, business colleagues, and neighbors. In the spring, in the second half of March and early April, the schools are out and kids shoot about the country in buses and trains, getting underfoot and pestering foreigners for autographs (for your exotic hometown, not your fame or name as such).

If you want to be sure of seeing Mt. Fuji, come in winter, which is also the season for outdoor hot spring bathing, in *rotenburo* baths carved out of rock and surrounded by piles of snow. Spring is for the flowering blossoms and trips to Kyushu, to catch the sun's warming rays the longest. In summer, sample the beach life if you like crowds. You can also escape them, except on weekends, with a little planning. In summer, hiking in the Japan Alps is the thing to do. Some of the country's best grape-wine producers are here, so if you tire of *sake,* carry a liter of Sadoya red in your knapsack. There are lots of festivals in autumn, the weather being neither too cold (as for Sapporo's Snow Festival in February) nor too hot (as for Kyoto's magnificent Gion Matsuri in July). Best of all is Okunchi, Nagasaki's premier festival.

National Holidays

January 1	*Oshogatsu* (New Year's Day). Most people take off for several days around this holiday, so beware of shop closings, etc. Gorgeous *kimono* on the women, especially in Kyoto.
January 15	*Seijin no Hi* (Coming-of-Age Day). Also called Adults Day, when people reaching the age of 20 can vote, etc.
February 11	*Kigensetsu* (National Foundation Day), commemorating the ascension to the throne of Japan's first emperor, Jimmu, in 660 B.C. (probable date). Also called *Kenkoku Kinenbi.*
March 21	*Shumbun no Hi* (Vernal Equinox Day). The week it falls in is called Higan, and prayers for the dead are offered.
April 29	*Tenno Heika no Tanjobi* (Emperor's Birthday). The real one, not an "official" one as in England. You can visit the palace and shout *"Banzai"* for him if you wish, one of the two days the palace is open to the public. (The other one is New Year's Day). This is the first of three holidays coming within a week, so the period is called *Kin no Shukan* (Golden Week).
May 3	*Kempo Kinen no Hi* (Constitution Day), honor-

ing the basic law of Japan written by the American Occupation professors and outlawing war (it says here).

May 5 · *Kodomo no Hi* (Children's Day). Formerly Boys' Day (the girls had their own; see below). Paper and cloth carp flags are put out or flown over houses where there are boys. The carp is supposed to symbolize strength, as it allegedly does not wiggle when placed on the chopping block. Last day of Golden Week.

September 15 · *Keiro no Hi* (Respect for the Aged Day). No special events, just be nice to Mom and Dad, to begin with.

September 23 · *Shubun no Hi* (Autumnal Equinox Day). Visit shrines and temples and honor your ancestors.

October 10 · *Taiiku no Hi* (Health and Sports Day), a new holiday commemorating the Tokyo Olympics of 1964. Track meets and the like, everywhere.

November 3 · *Bunka no Hi* (Culture Day). Formerly a day honoring Emperor Meiji, but changed after the war. Still, people continue to go to his shrine in Tokyo, and elsewhere, to venerate this former "deity."

November 23 · *Kinro Kansha no Hi* (Labor Thanksgiving Day). A new name for an old holiday in which, before the war ended, the emperor symbolically tasted the first harvest (wine, fruits, wheat, rice) and offered them to his ancestors. No special observances by the public these days.

Other Important Nationwide Holidays

The Japanese used to celebrate holidays on an orderly basis, the 1st day of the 1st month, 2nd of the 2nd, and so forth. Some remnants of that system remain, as in the national holidays above on January 1, May 5, and October 10. Below are some more of these "logical" holidays, and others, which make the everyday scene so much more colorful for the tourist and inhabitant alike.

February 3 or 4 · *Setsubun no Hi* (Bean-Throwing Festival). This is around the last day of the old lunar winter, and people gather at local temples to cast out demons by throwing beans, shouting, "In with good luck, out with the bad." Celebrities, television, chaos.

March 3	*Hina Matsuri* (Doll Festival), also the Girls' Holiday, 3rd day of 3rd month; Boys' Day was on 5th day of 5th month. Rows of pretty dolls are displayed everywhere, in homes and in public. You'll see them in your hotel lobby, department stores, etc.
April 8	*Hana Matsuri* (Buddha's Birthday). Visitors to local temples pour sweet tea over Buddha's head, or offer flowers.
May 1	May Day (English words are used in Japanese), observed by many labor unions. Members and their families parade peacefully, then break up for picnics and the like.
July 7	*Tanabata Matsuri* (Milky Way Festival), honoring the lovers in an old Chinese legend who died and became stars. They meet only on the 7th day of the 7th month. People make wishes on this day, tying the slips of paper to trees in temple precincts or elsewhere. Best celebration is in Sendai, with big parade.
July 15	Approximate date for *O Bon* (Festival of the Dead). Honors deceased ancestors and friends, frequently with O-Bon *odori* dances in temple precincts. Big platform on stilts, big drum, much noise and drinking. Buddhists believe in a hell, and praying for the dead will get them out, so O-Bon celebrates their release.
August 15	Approximate date for O-Bon in the country, closer to the old lunar date when it was celebrated. In addition to the dancing, services are held and sometimes lanterns on small rafts are floated downstream or out to sea in honor of the departed.
November 15	*Shichi go san* (Children's Shrine Visiting Day). Parents take their boys aged 3 and 5 and their girls aged 3 and 7 to shrines to thank the gods for protecting the kids through infancy. Best *kimono* and other costumes are worn, so this is a real photographer's treat.
December 24	Christmas Eve is celebrated as a night out on the town in this definitely non-Christian nation. Have you ever danced to "Silent Night" with a mambo beat?
December 31	The Japanese stay home, visit temples to atone for their sins (108 of them, according to the Buddhists), pay their debts, clean the house, get ready for a fresh new year. Momma doesn't cook the first 3 days of the New Year, so she kills herself in the kitchen getting enough food ready beforehand. The first

3 days are also for calling on friends and business contacts, at home, so food will be needed for them, also. (Always cold food only, called Osechi.)

INSIDERS' TIPS

"March 3, 62" is the way Japanese newspapers might be dated on the next Girls' Holiday. (Actually, it would be 3rd month, 3rd day, Showa 62.) The Japanese frequently use the current-era year rather than the Christian Era year, so if you see a year date of only two digits, add 1925 to it (that's the year before the present emperor ascended the throne). 1925 + 62 = 1987, so there you are.

HOW TO GO

First, look at the package tours available (see page 30). Sometimes that can be the best route for you, but not very often. Decide what you'd like to see, by reading this book and talking with friends, for example, then check out the tours. If they don't fit your needs, plan a trip yourself, but I advise doing so with the help of a reliable travel agent. Much has been written about travel agents trying to steer you to the most expensive packages. If you go to an agent, tell the travel consultant there exactly what you want and how much you will pay. No reliable agent will try to up the ante. If the agency wants you back—and repeat business is the key to a successful company's profits—it won't try any tricks. (For a reliable agent, make sure the firm is a member of the American Society of Travel Agents, ASTA. If you don't have an agent and have no sound advice from friends on finding one, write to ASTA at 4400 MacArthur Blvd. N.W., Washington, DC 20007.)

Good sources of information, in addition to guides and your own collection of newspaper and magazine clippings and advertisements, are the airlines and the Japan National Tourist Organization, whose branches are listed forthwith:

- Chicago: 333 N. Michigan Ave., Chicago, IL 60601, tel. 313-332-3975
- Dallas: 1519 Main St. (200), Dallas, TX 75201, tel. 214-741-4931

- Honolulu: 2270 Kalakaua Ave., Honolulu, HI 96815, tel. 808-923-7631
- Los Angeles: 624 S. Grand Ave., Los Angeles, CA 90017, tel. 213-623-1952
- New York: 630 Fifth Ave., New York, NY 10111, tel. 212-757-5640
- San Francisco: 1737 Post St., San Francisco, CA 94115, tel. 415-931-0700
- Canada: 165 University Ave., Toronto, Ont. M5H 3B8, tel. 416-366-7140
- England: 167 Regent St., London W1, tel. 01-734-9638
- Australia: 115 Pitt St., Sydney, NSW 2000, tel. 232-4522

There are other offices in Hong Kong, Bangkok, Paris, Geneva, Frankfurt, São Paulo, and Mexico City.

Documents You Will Need

You'll need a passport, of course, to enter Japan, and a visa, unless you're from one of those nations with which Japan has reciprocal agreements waiving them. (Among English-speaking countries, Britain, Ireland, and New Zealand are the only ones.) Citizens of the U.S., since it requires visas of the Japanese coming to America, must have a visa. There is no charge, and you will get, if you ask for it, a visa good for 5 years, but for stays of only up to 90 days at a time. Your travel agent can arrange for visa applications, as can professional services in some major cities. One good agency (with many celebrity clients), for example, is Passport Plus, 677 Fifth Ave., New York, NY 10017, tel. 212-759-5540 or 800-367-1818. Cruise ship passengers staying less than 15 days and airline passengers in transit for less then 3 days do not need visas, but are granted shore passes at the port or terminal (airline passengers should apply through an airline representative).

No health certificates are required in Japan if you are arriving from anywhere except an infected area where cholera is endemic.

Currency

You may bring in or export any amount of foreign currency, but only ¥5,000,000 (about $30,000) in Japanese currency in or out. You will note that this is six times what the American government allows in or out, without reporting, that is.

PERILS & PITFALLS

If you like Japan enough to want to stay, be careful, as the regulations about working are as strict as they are in America, and it's a lot harder to get lost in the crowd there than it is in New York, for instance. If your visa is good for 3 months, as are most tourist visas, you can get an extension by going to the Immigration Office, 3-3 Konan, Minato-ku, tel. 03-471-5111; or World Trade Mart, Sunshine City, Ikebukuro, tel. 03-986-2271.

If you have the money, it's easier to leave the country and come back in, perhaps by making a side trip to China, Korea, or Hong Kong. Don't take a job without having a working visa, even though there is plenty of work available. In addition to teaching English, which the Japanese think anybody can do (how wrong they are!), there are jobs as doormen, bartenders, and nightclub hostesses, all paying quite well. Models are much in demand, too. The Daisho Creamy Co. of Osaka even wants children, "aged 0 to 18 only," for TV and other commercials. The company's liaison, Michelle, says that "the best agency offers you the best jobs and memories."

WHAT TO PACK

You can buy almost anything in Japan, but you'll want to bring what you need, of course. Pack as you would for a normal trip, but note that Japan is more formal than America, and loud colors are considered low-class and vulgar, unless you're actually on the beach. Women in pants are the exception, not the rule. You should dress as you would for a Western European city, like London or Paris, not for the Caribbean or some other resort. Japan's weather is pretty moderate, similar to America's East Coast, so pack accordingly.

Bring comfortable walking shoes that slip on and off easily, as taking them off is part of the ritual of visiting many places, including temples, palaces, and restaurants. Carry a shoehorn to make things easier. Bring a flashlight for dark temple interiors; thick socks for winter travel, as you'll be shoeless much of the time; moisturizing lotion to fight air conditioning in summer; sunglasses and bathing suits in summer (many hotels have pools). You can buy good Japanese film here, as well as Kodak, and many British and American medicines are on sale at places like the American Pharmacy in Tokyo. Laundry and cleaning facilities at Japanese hotels are expensive but excellent, 1-day and even faster service being common. Local cosmetics and tobacco make good substitutes for your own, but buying clothing is a good idea only if you have a Japanese-style figure (ditto for shoes).

INSIDERS' TIPS

The Japanese have expanded on the courier system, as it is known in the U.S., and you can have your luggage or other packages sent around the country for much less than it costs back home. If you want to travel around Japan, you can keep sending a suitcase ahead, or back, and parcels of purchases as you make them. They'll even take golf clubs or skis. A suitcase from Kyoto to Tokyo, for instance, arriving the next day, will cost about ¥1,200 ($7.27). The packages are assembled in Tokyo overnight, and as they enter on a conveyor belt are directed by voice command (no hands, Ma) to the appropriate truck or plane.

The ABC Baggage Service System in Tokyo will transport your suitcases between airport and hotel (or wherever) for ¥2,000 ($12.12) the first 30 kilograms (about 66 pounds), ¥1,000 ($6.06) each additional bag. On arrival, if you don't need your bags until the next day, go to the ABC counter (there's one in each wing) with the bags still on your trolley. For departure, phone ABC 2 days before departure, to be sure, and then get your luggage on the departure floor (again, a counter in each wing). You can also do this at the Tokyo City Air Terminal (tel. 03-284-2525), which also ships throughout the country, as do Kuronekko (Black Cat) and Perikan (Pelican). For the latter, ask your hotel concierge or bell porter. Say you want to send it *takuhaibin* or *tokyubin*. The desk will even wrap things for you if you have no container.

HINTS ON YOUR HEALTH

If you're on medication, don't count on being able to get a prescription refilled at the pharmacy. You may have to see a doctor to get it done, but not always. Japan has excellent medical facilities (see below), but you may wish to prepare by having an ID bracelet if you have a life-threatening disease or allergy. You may also wish to join the International Association for Medical Assistance to Travelers (IAMAT), a nonprofit charitable organization, which issues a booklet listing English-speaking doctors around the world (including Japan), as well as hospitals, etc. The doctors listed have all trained in America, Canada, or Britain, and agree to charge no more than a fixed fee (indicated in the booklet) to patients. As IAMAT needs contributions, you should send something when you ask for the free booklet (I suggest $25). Write to IAMAT, 736 Center St., Lewiston, NY 14092, or in Canada to 123 Edward St. (725), Toronto, Ont. M5G 1E2. In Australia, it's St. Vincent's Hospital, Victoria Parade, Melbourne 3065. (Declaration of self-interest: I am on the board of directors of IAMAT, serving, as do other board members, without compensation of any kind.)

Here are some clinics and hospitals with English-speaking doctors in Japan:

- Tokyo Medical & Surgical Clinic, 3-40-30 Shiba Koen (No. 32 Mori Building), Minato-ku, tel. 03-436-3028
- Kyoto Baptist Hospital, 47 Yamanomoto-cho, Kirashirakawa, Sakyo-ku, tel. 075-781-5191
- Osaka Yodogawa Christian Hospital, 1-57 Awaji-honmachi, Higashi Yodogawa-ku, tel. 06-322-2250
- Kotani Dental Clinic, Hotel New Otani Arcade, Kioi-cho 4, Chiyoda-ku, tel. 03-265-1111

TRAVEL FOR THE HANDICAPPED

There are several organizations which promote travel for handicapped people, a leading one being the Society for the Advancement of Travel for the Handicapped, 26 Court St., Brooklyn, NY 11242, tel. 718-858-5483. A good book to read is *Access to the World*, by Louise Weiss, published by Facts on File, 460 Park Ave. South, New York, NY 10003. Japan is pretty far behind in providing facilities that are accessible, such as ramps, wide doorways, special toilet cubicles, railings, etc.—perhaps where the United States was 10 or 20 years ago. Neither country comes close to having the facilities now available in Western Europe, especially in Scandinavia, Germany, Holland, and Britain.

The Red Cross publishes *Accessible Tokyo: Guide for Wheelchair Friends.* Free of charge by writing to Japanese Red Cross Language Service Volunteers, 1-1-3 Shiba Daimon, Minato-ku, Tokyo 105, or telephoning 03-438-1311.

GETTING TO JAPAN

PACKAGE TOURS

Are they best for you? They aren't the best in the sense of allowing you to see what you want, but they may be best in terms of price. Some travelers also like to travel with a group, making friends and sharing experiences. Estimate your own costs from this book and your phone calls to airlines, then compare with the tour package. If you select modestly priced hotels and are not an expensive eater, you may do just as well on your own.

If you do take a tour, consider some of those described below for starters.

Japan Travel Bureau, the nation's most experienced, has tours originating at Narita Airport, running from 5-day to 16-day itineraries, priced from ¥96,600 to ¥441,000 ($585 to $2,673), some meals included, and all hotels, transport, etc. Here are the 7-day and 14-day itineraries:

Seven-day Sunrise Holiday: ¥133,100 ($807), including 2 lunches. Arrive in Japan, transfer to Tokyo Prince Hotel for 2 nights.

- Next day (in afternoon) tour Imperial Palace Plaza, Asakusa Kannon Temple, and Pearl Gallery and have a boat ride on Sumida River.
- Day 3, drive to Hakone via Kamakura, lunch at Lake Hakone, take a cruise. Stay at Hotel Kowaki-en.
- Day 4, take Bullet Train to Kyoto, lunch at New Miyako Hotel, visit Nara in afternoon, where you see Todaiji Temple, Deer Park, Kasuga Shrine. Stay at International Hotel Kyoto for 3 nights.
- Day 5, tour Nijojo Castle, Gold Pavilion, Old Imperial Palace, Sanjusangendo Hall, Heian Jingu Shrine, Kiyomizudera Temple.
- Day 6, free in Kyoto.
- Day 7, to Osaka and its airport, where tour disbands. Daily throughout the year.

Fourteen-day Sunrise Holiday: ¥384,600 ($2,331), 8

lunches included. Operates Monday, Wednesday, Friday from late February through late November.

- Days 1 and 2, same as 7-day tour, above.
- Day 3, excursion to Nikko, seeing Toshogu Shrine, Futaarasan Shrine, Kegon Waterfall, Lake Chuzenji, Tachiki Kannon Temple. Lunch at Kanaya Hotel in Nikko.
- Day 4, drive from Tokyo to Hakone via Kamakura, lunching at Hakone Hotel, then sightseeing. Stay at Kowakien Hotel.
- Day 5, take the Bullet Train to Nagoya, where you have lunch. Then train to Toba, and cruise on bay. Stay Toba Hotel International.
- Day 6, visit Pearl Island, lunch at hotel, then drive to Ise Jingu Shrine and train to Kyoto, where you stay at Kyoto Hotel for 3 nights.
- Day 7, excursion to Nara for Byodoin Temple, Todaiji Temple, Deer Park, Kasuga Shrine, Kofukuji Temple, lunch at Nara Hotel.
- Day 8, visit Nijojo Castle, Gold Pavilion, Old Imperial Palace, have afternoon free.
- Day 9, take Bullet Train to Hakata and do an afternoon tour. Stay at Hakata Miyako Hotel.
- Day 10, by bus to Beppu for lunch at Hotel Seifu and afternoon city tour. Stay at Suginoi Hotel.
- Day 11, drive to Mt. Aso via scenic highway, then to Kumamoto to see the castle and stay at the Hotel Castle.
- Day 12, drive through Unzen National Park to Nagasaki. Stay at Tokyu Hotel.
- Day 13, morning sightseeing of city, then the limited express to Hakata and Bullet Train to Osaka, where you stay at Tokyu Hotel.
- Day 14, transfer on your own to Osaka International Airport for departure.

JTB has several offices in the United States and other foreign countries. They include:

- Chicago: Suite 1220, 625 N. Michigan Ave., Chicago, IL 60611, tel. 312-943-9300
- Honolulu: 2270 Kalakaua Ave., Honolulu, HI 96815, tel. 808-923-8744
- Los Angeles: 624 S. Grand Ave., Los Angeles, CA

90017, tel. 213-623-5629
- Newport Beach, CA: 5000 Birch St. (200), Newport Beach, CA 92660, tel. 714-476-8566
- New York: 45 Rockefeller Plaza, New York, NY 10111, tel. 212-489-1904 or 800-622-1106
- San Francisco: 360 Post St., San Francisco, CA 94108, tel. 415-986-4764
- Canada: Suite 2794, Four Bentall Centre, 1055 Dunsmuir St., Vancouver, BC V7X 1L3, tel. 604-688-0166 or 800-663-0229
- England: Canberra House, 10-16 Maltravers St., London WC2R 3EX, tel. 01-379-6244
- Australia: 25th Level, CBA Centre, 60 Margaret St., Sydney NSW 2000, tel. 02-27-5210

Globus Gateway Tours, a British firm with strong American representation, has an excellent "Best of Japan" package, lasting 15 days and costing $1,395 plus airfare. (The firm quotes basic round-trip fares from $882 to $958 out of Los Angeles, $1,121 to $1,197 out of New York.) This is about what you'd spend as an individual if you traveled very carefully and watched every penny. On a tour, you have nothing to worry about. Includes 13 breakfasts and 8 lunches and dinners, the works. The first day is lost in midair, but you get it back on the return flight, thanks to the international date line.
- Day 2, arrive Tokyo and stay at Hilton International.
- Day 3, sightsee Tokyo, including Meiji Shrine and Asakusa.
- Day 4 is free in Tokyo (you might want to pay for a trip to Nikko).
- Day 5, to Kamakura and Hakone by bus, seeing Great Buddha and cruising Lake Ashi, plus a cable-car ride up Mt. Komagatake. Stay Kanko Hotel.
- Day 6, to Nagoya and Takayama, where you stay at Hida Hotel.
- Day 7, to Shirakawa for its *gassho-zukuri* houses, then to Noto Peninsula, a place of wild beauty. Stay overnight.
- Day 8, to Kanazawa, visit Kenrokuen Park and *samurai* houses, stay Tokyu Hotel.
- Day 9, to Hiroshima via Kyoto. Stay ANA Hotel.
- Day 10, to Miyajima Island, a highlight of any Japan trip.
- Day 11, to Kurashiki, the museum town, staying at

Kokusai Hotel.

- Day 12, to Kyoto, staying at the Grand.
- Day 13, see Heian Shrine, Nijo Castle, Gold Pavilion.
- Day 14, free in Kyoto, a side trip to Nara suggested on your own.
- Day 15, to Osaka and flight home, arriving before you left Japan if you live on the U.S. East Coast, the same day on West Coast, gaining the day you lost before. This tour includes some of Japan's best hotels. Operates March through November.

Minshuku tours. Japan Travel Bureau (in Japan, *not* overseas, unfortunately) will arrange a *minshuku* tour for you if you'd like to experience homelike accommodations

---

FOLLOW THE *SAMURAI* ROAD?

Unlike Germany, which has a Romantic Road of castles and walled towns, or Britain, which boasts of its stately mansions, Japan does little to exploit its most famous product, the *samurai*. Extolled in American books about business ethics, worshiped by lovers of the martial arts, the *samurai* stands tall on overseas tour, but isn't a hot property back home. There isn't a *Samurai* Road, there are no tours for foreign visitors to Search Out the *Samurai*, there is, in short, a general lack of interest. "*Samurai*," say modern Japanese, "well, they're just like the knights of yore in Europe." There are many *samurai* heroes, but no single name commands adoration. Even Miyamoto Musashi, considered by many to be the most famous and author of the *Book of Five Rings*, isn't a household name. (He's not listed in the *Historical and Geographical Dictionary of Japan*, for instance.)

The closest thing to a *samurai* tour I can find is the half-day or evening program arranged by Joe Okada in Kyoto. For about ¥6,000 ($36.06), he picks you up between 6:30 and 7:10 P.M. and takes you to his "Momoyama Castle Theater," where there are demonstrations of *karate*, *kabuki* theater, *kendo* (swordsmanship), *koto* music, Kyoto dance, tea ceremony, flower arranging, and a wedding costume show. All this in 90 minutes! Phone Joe at 075-241-3716. His Homes and Countryside Tour, in the afternoon, makes three stops at private homes and farms near Kyoto. Joe himself wears formal *kimono* and a *chonmage* hairdo at all times, so if you've never met a *samurai* look-alike, now's your chance.

in Japan. You'll stay with families in the *minshuku* they operate, sleep on the floor, wear the *yukata* if you like, live like the Japanese in many respects. The tours are also cheaper, a 14-day all-Japan visit coming to ¥147,850 ($896), for instance, compared to the deluxe Sunrise Holiday tour staying in Western-style hotels, described earlier, which comes to ¥384,600 ($2,331). In some places, you will stay at a hotel—in Tokyo, for example, on the first 3 nights at Shiba Park Hotel.

- Day 4, to Shimoda, where you stay at a *minshuku.*
- Day 5, to Mishima and Nagoya by rail; hotel is Terminal.
- Day 6, to Toba, stay in a *minshuku,* and have day 7 free there.
- Day 8, to Nachi and Katsuura, where you stay in a *minshuku.*
- Day 9, to Osaka, Toyo Hotel.
- Day 10, to Nara, staying at a *minshuku.*
- Day 11, to Kyoto, stay at New Kyoto for 3 nights. Depart from Osaka for home.

There are three other 14-day courses, for about the same price, and a 21-day route. Sightseeing is not included, and you make your own way around, seeing what you like, paying your own (small) admission fees to temples, etc.

You have to remember that you won't have a private bath or toilet, that Japanese baths and toilets are built differently, that there is no key to a sliding paper door, and that you might have to sleep with strangers (though segregated by sex). Also, Japanese breakfasts are the same every day, just as typical American breakfasts are the same every day.

Ask your retail travel agent to book through JTB (in Japan, *not* in U.S.), or contact Nippon Travel Agency, 551 Fifth Ave., New York, NY 10176, tel. 212-986-7393, which organizes similar tours.

Choosing a Tour

In choosing a tour, you should consider, first of all, whether it takes you where you want to go, or allows you enough free time to visit your own personal destinations. Then think of the cost. Most operators now quote land costs only, but the good ones tell you what fares you can expect to pay. In general, you can expect to pay, for *everything* on a tour, just about the same amount you'd spend on room and board alone if you travel independently at the first-class level. (The JTB tours I've listed run from about $115 per day for tours up to a week, about $165 per day for longer trips. The JTB *minshuku* tour runs only about $65 per day. The Globus Gateway tour costs about $100 per day, even though it's 14 nights.) So, on a tour, you'll save the cost of all domestic transport, sightseeing, admission fees, and even a few meals (not all of them).

Maupin Tours has some of the best tours for travelers used to luxury, and there are always garden tours, study tours, and other special-interest programs given by about two dozen operators in the United States. Organizations such as the Japan Society and the Asia Society, not to mention the Bronx Zoo and the Boston Museum of Fine Arts, have tours for their members, as may a similar group in your hometown. Here are just a few more commercial operators that have recommendable tours to Japan:

- Abercrombie & Kent, 1420 Kensington Rd., Oak Brook, IL 60521-2106, tel. 312-954-2944
- Guides for All Seasons, P.O. Box 917, Carnelian Bay, CA 95711, tel. 800-457-4574
- Hemphill Harris Travel, 1600 Ventura Blvd., Encino, CA 91436, tel. 800-421-0454
- Japan & Orient Tours, 250 E. First St. (912), Los Angeles, CA 90012, tel. 800-421-0212
- Journeys East, 2443 Fillmore St. (289), San Francisco, CA 94115, tel. 415-931-2509
- Maupintour, 408 E. 50th St., New York, NY 10022, tel. 800-255-4266
- Mountain Travel, 1398 Solano Ave., Albany, CA 94706, tel. 415-527-8100
- Nature Expeditions International, 474 Willamette St., Eugene, OR 97440, tel. 503-484-6529
- O.C. Tours, 1366 San Mateo Ave., San Francisco, CA 94080, tel. 800-227-5988
- Off the Deep End Travel, P.O. Box 7511, Jackson, NY 83001, tel. 800-223-6833
- Orient Visitours, 120 E. 56th St., New York, NY 10022, tel. 800-221-4616
- Overseas Adventure Travel, 6 Bigelow St., Cambridge,

MA 01139, tel. 800-221-0814
- Pacific Delight Tours, 132 Madison Ave., New York, NY 10016, tel. 800-221-7179
- Pacific Select, 551 Fifth Ave., New York, NY 10176, tel. 800-722-4349
- Questers Tours, 257 Park Ave. South, New York, NY 10010-7369, tel. 212-673-3120
- Thomson Vacations, 401 N. Michigan Ave., Chicago, IL 60611, tel. 312-467-4200
- Travcoa, 875 N. Michigan Ave., Chicago, IL 60611, tel. 800-621-8260
- Wilderness Tours, P.O. Box 807, Bolinas, CA 94924, tel. 415-868-1836
- World Adventure Travel, 2836 78th SE, Mercer Island, WA 98040, tel. 206-232-2700

AIRLINES

They're all the same, you say? I don't agree. Getting there is no longer half the fun, as the old slogan went, not even a smidgen of fun now that economy-class travel resembles a long bus trip. (Sometimes the stagecoach comes to mind.) But there are slight differences in the type of service handed out, even back in steerage, and quite considerable differences in business or first class. I've always recommended using the national airline of a country when you're going there, by which I mean that if you can arrange it without losing money, you should fly to Japan, for example, on a Japanese airline and return to the United States on an American airline. Going, you begin to get the flavor of your destination, and returning, the comforts of home, as it were. If you're on certain types of round-trip fares, you can't do this, of course.

At the moment, 14 airlines provide *direct* service from the United States and Canada to Japan. They are:
- All Nippon Airways (ANA). From Honolulu, Los Angeles, and Washington, D.C.
- British Airways (BA). From Anchorage, nonstop.
- China Airlines (CAL). Taiwan. From Honolulu and San Francisco, both nonstop.
- Canadian Pacific (CPA). From Toronto and Vancouver, the latter nonstop.

- Japan Air Lines (JAL). From Atlanta, Chicago, Honolulu, Los Angeles, New York, San Francisco, Seattle, and Vancouver, all nonstop.
- Malaysian Airways (MH). From Los Angeles, nonstop.
- Philippine Air Lines (PAL). From San Francisco, nonstop.
- Northwest Orient Air Lines (NWA). From Dallas/Ft. Worth, Honolulu, Los Angeles, Minneapolis/St. Paul, New York, San Francisco, Seattle/Tacoma, Tampa, and Washington, D.C., some nonstop.
- Sabena Belgian World Airways (SN). From Anchorage, nonstop.
- Singapore Airlines (SQ). From Los Angeles, nonstop.
- Scandinavian Airline System (SAS). From Anchorage, nonstop.
- Thai Airways (TG). From Dallas/Ft. Worth and Seattle, the latter nonstop.
- United Air Lines (UAL). From Boston, Chicago, Denver, Honolulu, Los Angeles, New York, Portland (Oregon), San Francisco, Seattle/Tacoma, and Washington, D.C., some nonstop.
- Varig (RG) (Brazil). From Los Angeles, nonstop.

From Australia, Qantas and JAL have direct flights, and from New Zealand, it's Air New Zealand and JAL.

From Europe, 12 carriers offer direct service, many of them nonstop flights from such capitals as London, Paris, and Rome. From London, try British Airways, Cathay Pacific, JAL, or (for the adventurous) Aeroflot. There are 19 airlines that provide service from various points throughout Asia, including, of course, JAL.

At press time, the lowest fares from the United States to Japan, advanced-purchase 14–60-day excursion (APEX) on Japan Air Lines, United, or Northwest, was $1,299 low-season round trip New York to Tokyo, $1,305 high-season. From Los Angeles, San Francisco, or Seattle, the same fare structure was $851 low-season, $927 high-season. Unless you insist on a nonstop trip from the East Coast, you'd be well advised to purchase one of the cheap coast-to-coast domestic flights and board your plane on the West Coast.

Cheaper fares are often to be had from so-called bucket shops, which advertise regularly in such newspapers as the *New York Times, Los Angeles Times, Chicago Tribune,* and elsewhere. Here you'll find seats several hundred dollars cheaper, but you always have to realize the bucket shop may go broke and leave you with a worthless ticket. It may also issue you a fancy ticket to a different destination, such as Hong Kong, warning you not under any circumstances to let the airline see any unused portion when you check in for the return flight. It does make one a bit nervous, it does. Many such shops book seats for tourist groups which never existed or do not materialize, and this is why you get the discount. They buy at the wholesale tour operator's price, and fudge over the fact that you're not part of a package. One or two airlines (libel laws forbid saying which) even discount illegally, wanting half a loaf as better than none. The bucket shops will probably put you on a less-famous airline, or one requiring a little dogleg on the journey perhaps. But the plane is still a 747 or DC-10 or some other thoroughly reliable piece of equipment.

SHIPS AND CRUISES

There is no scheduled transpacific passenger service to Japan, but you can always jump a freighter if you've time and the stomach for it. The only scheduled boat services to Japan are from Korea by ferry and the Soviet Union. As part of a Trans-Siberian Railway journey, you may wish to top it off with a Soviet liner from Nakodhka (near Vladivostok) to Niigata, but you could also fly that route.

Cruise ships call frequently at Yokohama, Kobe, and Nagasaki. The ships range from occasional visits by around-the-world favorites like the *QE2* to regular journeys on the *Pearl of Asia,* out of Hong Kong, after its stops in Chinese ports. Watch the newspapers for advertisements of cruises or contact your travel agent, as there are no schedules on an annual basis.

In my opinion, rather than cruise *to* Japan, you should consider sailing *within* the country, perhaps down the Inland Sea, or just through part of it (see Kyushu and Western Japan chapters).

TRAIN

Yes, you can get to Japan by train, or at least most of the way. You start from London or Paris, change in Moscow to the Trans-Siberian Express, and spend what may seem like months en route to one of three places where you must get off in order to fly or fly/sail to Japan. (You can't go to the end of the route, Vladivostok, as it is still one of those closed cities no capitalist is allowed to see.) Most popular are the Irkutsk-to-Japan route (all air) and the Nakodhka-to-Japan route (choice of sea or rail). The sea route takes you to Niigata, air to the same city or Tokyo.

Only the most ardent rail buffs ever say they'd take the Trans-Siberian a second time, and for some perhaps perfectly understandable reasons, a succession of British poets have taken the route, hated it, and written books about it.

USEFUL NUMBERS
(Nationwide, unless noted otherwise)

Police and emergency (Japanese only)	110 (no charge)
Fire and ambulance (Japanese only)	119 (no charge)
Japan Travel Phone	106 (except Tokyo and Kyoto)

ARRIVING IN JAPAN

A LITTLE GEOGRAPHY

Japan's four main islands vary not only in size but in quality of attractions. You will spend most of your time on Honshu, where lie Tokyo, Kyoto, Osaka, Nara, Hiroshima, and other highlights of any trip to this country. Second-most-important is Kyushu, where you might enjoy Nagasaki, Miyazaki, or Kagoshima. Third is Shikoku (though it is last in size), almost unspoiled, where you'll find Matsuyama, Takamatsu, and Tokushima of interest. The fourth biggie is Hokkaido, utterly rural, home to Sapporo, hot springs, and mountain retreats. Okinawa, far to the south, is visited mostly by business people dealing with the American military.

You'll probably want to arrive at Tokyo's "New International Airport," Narita, as the facilities here are best, and most flights come here. (Taiwan's China Air Lines is the only major carrier using Tokyo's domestic airport, Haneda, for its terminal—this for political reasons, as the People's Republic of China carrier, CAAC, uses Narita.) Should you choose to fly "directly" to Osaka or Nagoya, you may face a change of planes at Narita anyhow, and immigration and customs facilities at the other airports (not to mention ground transport) are not as well developed as Narita's. You can even enter Japan at Kagoshima, Fukuoka, or Niigata, if coming from Southeast Asia in the first two instances or the USSR in the case of Niigata, but Narita is still best.

I've selected four itineraries of 1 to 4 weeks, covering the most important in each. A good reason for starting in Tokyo is its familiar facade, looking in many respects like any modern city in the West. After you settle in, you can then begin to look for the increasingly exotic as you get used to the scene.

Numbers in parentheses represent days in city.

One week: Tokyo (1), Kamakura-Hakone-Fuji (1), Kyoto

and Nara (3), Tokyo (2), with day trip to Nikko from Tokyo.

Two weeks: Tokyo (2), Kamakura-Hakone-Fuji (2), Kyoto and Nara (4), Hiroshima and Miyajima (2), Nagasaki (1), Tokyo (3), with day trip to Nikko.

Three weeks: Tokyo (3), Kamakura-Hakone-Fuji (2), Kyoto and Nara (5), Hiroshima and Miyajima (2), Nagasaki (1), Kagoshima and Ibusuki plus Miyazaki (3), Kanazawa (2), Takayama (1), Tokyo (2), with day trip to Nikko.

Four weeks: Tokyo (3), Kamakura-Hakone-Fuji (3), Kyoto and Nara (5), Hiroshima and Miyajima (2), Kumamoto (1), Unzen (1), Nagasaki (2), Kagoshima and Ibusuki plus Miyazaki (3), Tokyo (1), Kanazawa (2), Takayama (1), Sendai (1), Sapporo and Noboribetsu (1), Tokyo (2), with day trip to Nikko.

IMMIGRATION AND CUSTOMS

If you arrive by airplane, you'll pass through quarantine first (which you can ignore unless you're bringing in something strange or coming from a cholera-infected area), then go to meet immigration. There are two kinds of lines, for Japanese and for aliens, just as back home, where it's U.S. citizens and everybody else. You will have your passport and visa scrutinized, after which you pass on to customs. Here the distinction is more subtle, as it's residents versus nonresidents of Japan. No green or red passages here, as yet. The customs officer may ask you what the purpose of your visit is, and it is a good idea to have your passport out so he can easily identify your nationality. You may be asked if you have anything to declare, and as long as you don't have anything beyond the reasonable limits described below, say no. Don't try to use your Japanese language here, if you have been studying up. It will just make the officer think you are a resident alien, and probably up to no good. (Japan is one of those countries where the better a foreigner speaks the language, the less he is trusted. A little Nihongo [Japanese] is considered charming and a sign of good intent, but a lot may mean you have a Japanese spouse, are a spy, or are a smuggler and dope dealer.)

The Japanese dress conservatively, and if the officer

sees sunglasses, long hair or earrings on men, "hippie-style" costumes, or evidence of a lot of sweating and zombielike trances, you will probably be scrutinized carefully. You can't help jet lag, perhaps, but you can dress quietly, the better to pass through customs. (Paul McCartney was jailed, not deported, on his arrival in Tokyo with a little marijuana on his person.) Japan is relatively drug-free, and the authorities are very strict. Long jail terms are the norm here, and though the jailers are humane, the food is the pits.

If you arrive by ship, the procedures are the same, though the facilities will prove less pleasant, and less well organized.

You can make an oral declaration at customs on arrival, except (1) if arriving by ship, (2) if you have unaccompanied baggage coming on another flight, or (3) if you have articles in excess of the duty-free allowance (see below).

MEASUREMENTS

Until the modern era (since 1867), Japan had its own peculiar system of measuring things, in *ri* (for distance), *koku* (bushels), and *sun* (length), for example. Now, like all the world except the U.S., it seems, it has gone metric. Here are a few figures to help you convert things:

40 kilometers are 25 miles, but more specifically:

1 kilometer is .62 mile	1 mile is 1.51 kilometer
1 meter is 3.28 feet	1 foot is .31 meter
1 centimeter is .4 inch	1 inch is 2.55 centimeters
1 kilogram is 2.21 pounds	1 pound is 450 grams
1 liter is .26 gallon	1 gallon is 3.75 liters

In approximate terms, a liter is about a quart and a meter is about a yard. (Well, a miss is as good as a mile in this kind of thing.)

To convert centigrade to Fahrenheit when trying to tell the temperature, multiply the centigrade temperature by 1.8, then add 32, and you have Fahrenheit. (For example, $25°C. \times 1.8 = 45 + 32 = 77°F.$)

Time on Japanese schedules for trains, airplanes, ferries, etc., is measured in the 24-hour system, or what Americans think of as military style. Thus, 1 P.M. is 1300, 2 P.M. is 1400, and so forth. Midnight is 2400, and 1 minute later is 0001.

Any reasonable amount of personal effects and professional equipment may be brought in, the customs officer deciding what is reasonable. Maximum duty-free articles include 400 cigarettes or 500 grams of tobacco or 100 cigars (and only if you're over 19); 3 bottles of booze, each not to exceed 760 cc; 2 ounces of perfume; and gifts or souvenirs whose total market value is less than ¥100,000 (about $600).

Banned from Japan besides drugs are pornography (and that includes *Hustler, Playboy,* and other magazines of that type), guns, weapons, explosives, and certain kinds of fresh fruits, vegetables, and flowers.

GETTING TO TOWN FROM THE AIRPORT

There are several ways to get to Tokyo from far-out Narita, but the best way (short of being met by a friend) is by bus direct to your hotel. At press time, there were 120 buses a day direct to hotels on Airport Limousine (orange buses), and 36 a day on Airport Express (purple). Note that some hotels are served by both companies, others by only one: Airport Limousine to Akasaka Prince, Akasaka Tokyu, Century Hyatt, Ginza Tokyu, Grand Palace, Haneda Tokyu, Hilton International, Imperial, Keio Plaza, Metropolitan, New Otani, New Takanawa Prince, Okura, Pacific, Palace, Shimbashi Dai-Ichi, Shinjuku Washington, Sunshine City Prince, Takanawa Prince, Tokyo Prince; Airport Express to Akasaka Tokyu, Capitol Tokyu, Grand Palace, Imperial, Marunouchi, Miyako Inn, Miyako Tokyu, New Otani, New Sanno, New Takanawa Prince, Okura, Pacific, Palace, Shiba Park, Shimbashi Dai-Ichi, Shinagawa Prince, Takanawa Prince, Tokyo Grand, Tokyo Prince, Tokyu Inn. Cost is ¥2,600 ($15.75) or ¥2,700 ($16.36), depending on hotel (half fare for children). Most Airport Express buses also stop at Tokyo Station. The Airport Limousine company also operates many buses directly to the Tokyo City Air Terminal, where you might wish to go if you are not staying at any of the above-mentioned hotels. This costs ¥2,500 ($15.15). From TCAT, there is a shuttle bus to Tokyo Station for ¥200 ($1.21). If you're lucky, you can get a bus directly from Narita to Tokyo Station, for ¥2,600 ($15.75). The same company also operates direct service to Disneyland, Haneda Airport, Shinjuku Station, and Yokohama City Air Terminal. Both companies claim they can get into Tokyo (as far as TCAT) in only 1 hour, but crawling across town could take up to another hour.

The TCAT bus, if you take it, has recorded announcements in English and a slide show in case the scenery gets boring. (As much of the expressway is now soundproofed, with baffle walls to protect nearby residents' ears, this is not really a joke.) At TCAT, get a cab to your hotel.

Another popular way to get into town from Narita is on the Keisei Skyliner, a private railroad which connects its airport station (a short bus ride from the terminal) with

ACCESS FROM NARITA AIRPORT TO CENTRAL TOKYO

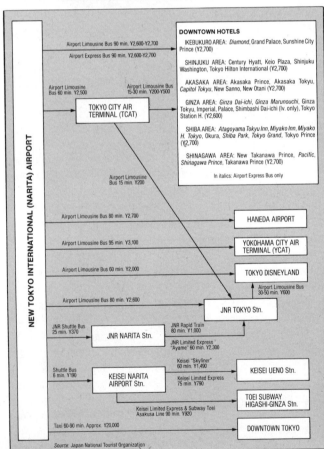

DOWNTOWN HOTELS

IKEBUKURO AREA: *Diamond*, Grand Palace, Sunshine City Prince (Y2,700)

SHINJUKU AREA: Century Hyatt, Keio Plaza, Shinjuku Washington, Tokyo Hilton International (Y2,700)

AKASAKA AREA: Akasaka Prince, Akasaka Tokyu, *Capitol Tokyu*, New Sanno, New Otani (Y2,700)

GINZA AREA: *Ginza Dai-ichi, Ginza Marunouchi*, Ginza Tokyu, Imperial, Palace, Shimbashi Dai-ichi (lv. only), Tokyo Station H. (Y2,600)

SHIBA AREA: *Atagoyama Tokyu Inn, Miyako Inn, Miyako H. Tokyo*, Okura, *Shiba Park*, Tokyo Grand, Tokyo Prince (Y2,700)

SHINAGAWA AREA: New Takanawa Prince, *Pacific, Shinagawa Prince*, Takanawa Prince (Y2,700)

In italics: Airport Express Bus only

Source: Japan National Tourist Organization

Ueno Station, in northern Tokyo. You board the Keisei Skyliner bus at the curb (after buying a ticket in the arrival area at the Keisei counter), then board the Skyliner itself, and about 60 minutes later, arrive at Keisei's Ueno Station (not the Japan National Railway station). From there you must get a cab to your hotel. Cost of the Skyliner is only ¥1,680 ($10.18), and it departs every 40 minutes. All seats are reserved. The same company has Limited Express and Express trains which take longer, cost much less, and run every 20 minutes. Get Skyline tickets at counter, others at vending machine.

A fourth way by public transport is the Japan National Railway, which costs as much as the airport bus and takes longer. Bus to Narita town from airport, then train to Tokyo Station (fastest train is 77 minutes). If you have a Japan Rail Pass, you might want to use this route getting *to* Narita, to save ¥2,500 ($15.15), but it is a lot of trouble.

You can also go by taxi, but it will run you at least ¥20,000 (about $120) and still take 1 or 2 hours, depending on traffic.

The very rich, in the unlikely event they are not being met, can have their minions order a rental car with chauffeur to meet them. This should be around ¥35,000 ($212), or almost twice a taxi's cost.

Having dealt with the wise, the budget-minded, and the rich, let us now turn to the foolish. If you plan to drive around Japan, you could pick up your rental car at Narita and plunge right in, jet lag and all. I wouldn't do it (see page 68 for details).

PERILS & PITFALLS

There are no toilets on the airport buses in Japan, even on the one taking up to 2 hours from Narita airport to central Tokyo, so keep this in mind when making the trip. If you're traveling alone and arriving at Narita, you can push your luggage cart to a restroom before or after buying your ticket.

INSIDERS' TIPS

There are only three occasions on which you tip in Japan, outlined below. Otherwise, *never* tip. Don't get the habit started in a country where the vice is not widely practiced.

Person	Amount to tip
Airport porter	Nothing. There is a ¥200 or ¥300 ($1.21 or $1.82) fee per bag.
Railway porter	Nothing. There is a ¥200 or ¥300 ($1.21 or $1.82) fee per bag.
Hotel porter	Nothing. There is a 10 percent service charge on your bill, covering everything.
Hotel waiter or bartender	Nothing. The service charge on your bill takes care of it.
Room service	Nothing. Service charge takes care of it.
Hotel doorman	Nothing. Service charge includes him, too.
Taxi driver	Nothing.
Restaurant waiter or bartender	Nothing. A service charge of 10 percent or sometimes 15 percent takes care of situation.
Restaurant captain or wine steward	Nothing. Service charge covers it all.
Guide bus driver	Nothing. He'd be offended if you did.
Guide	Nothing. He or she would be offended.
Cloakroom attendant	Nothing. He or she would think you were crazy and might be offended.
Japanese inn room maid (*ryokan*)	¥1,000 ($6.06) a night, if you have had either breakfast or dinner in your room. Put it in an envelope and present it when leaving, preferably at door.
High-class *ryotei* (*haute cuisine* restaurant)	Change. Leave it on tray if you pay by cash. If you pay by credit card leave ¥1,000 ($6.06) per person.
Hairdresser or barber	15 percent.

The service charge added by many establishments, and distributed by the management according to a formula, is usually 10 percent at deluxe hotels, 15 percent at high-class *ryokan* (inns), and zero at business hotels, economy inns, youth hostels, *minshuku*, and pensions.

The Money

Larger than American banknotes, Japanese paper currency comes in two types, as there has been a changeover recently in the faces on the bills.

There are four paper bills:
    ¥500, approximately $3
    ¥1,000, approximately $6
    ¥5,000, approximately $30
    ¥10,000, approximately $60

Then there are six coins:
    ¥1, about half a cent
    ¥10, approximately 6¢
    ¥50, approximately 30¢
    ¥100, approximately 60¢
    ¥500, approximately $3

When you exchange money, you'll note that the bank tellers try to give you as few bills as possible, meaning all large notes. Insist on small change. Also note that on leaving Japan you must change money before going through Immigration Control.

INSIDERS' TIPS

In hotels, there is a local tax applied when the total of room and meal charges exceeds ¥5,000 (about $30) per person per night. The rate is 10 percent but there is a ¥2,000 ($12.12) deduction per person per night.

THE INSIDERS' JAPAN

WHERE TO STAY

Hotels, good as they are in Japan (and they are cheaper than their American or European counterparts), are not the only place to stay in this country. It would be a shame to miss the chance to stay in a Japanese *ryokan* (inn), expensive though many may be, and you should also give consideration to the occasional pension, Buddhist temple, or even youth hostel.

Here's a breakdown of the possibilities:

Hotels

International hotels. These are further subdivided into deluxe and standard. Establishments in the first category are something more than the Western concept, as they are active social centers for weddings and important business socializing. On certain days you'll see the hallways filled with women in gorgeous *kimono* and men in formal morning suits, the sure sign of a wedding. In the afternoon or evening, large cocktail parties and dinners are held, as in the West. In the spring, gaggles of young girls in wildly colored *kimono* turn the lobbies into riotous gardens of moving flowers, at their high school graduation parties honoring teachers. At year's end, companies have their New Year's parties on the premises. The reason for all those strange hotel shops (usually on the second or third floor) with often horrible gifts in showcases is for weddings—but here, the bride and groom and families give the guests the gifts, picked right at the hotel, which caters the reception and, often, the ceremony itself. The standard international hotels are the same, only less plush, less costly.

Business hotels. Often composed of tiny little rooms, yet each is fully equipped, with TV, hot tea maker, direct-

---

JAPAN'S FIVE BEST HOTELS

Kobe: Portopia Hotel
Kyoto: Kyoto Hotel
Miyako Hotel
Tokyo: Imperial Hotel
Hotel Okura

And Two Best *Ryokan* (Inns)

Kyoto: Hiiragiya
Tawaraya

---

dial phone, miniature bathroom, even, sometimes, room service. Small lobby and restaurant, often not much English spoken.

Prices. For two persons in a twin prices range from $40 to $200 per night and do not include the usual 15 percent service charge nor the 10 percent room tax. Most hotels have more than one rate for their twin rooms. When an *even* number of rates are quoted by a hotel (two or four rates for twin rooms, for example), I have taken the average of the prices and listed them in this book. When the hotel quotes an *odd* number of rates for a twin room, I have listed the middle rate. The rates are always for a standard twin, not deluxe, not double, insofar as I could obtain such information. Hotels and inns are listed together, first by town, then by crown rating (number of crowns), then alphabetically.

How to reserve hotel accommodations. The easiest way is to ask your travel agent to do so. Second-best, if you're not using an agent and are flying on an airline with affiliated hotels (JAL and United, for example), is to book when you make flight reservations. Third way is to use a hotel representative in or near your hometown. See the yellow pages of your telephone directory. You can assume that most of the big deluxe hotels in Japan have a representative. In addition, so do many of the chains, especially Hilton, Holiday Inn, Hyatt, Sheraton, and Tokyu.

Ryokan

The classic Japanese inn can provide a fascinating experience, if you're flexible and have an inquiring mind. From the formal greeting as you arrive, the shoes-off shuffle down the polished wooden halls, and the ceremonial cup of tea in your room while you register there, you know things strange and wonderful are going to happen. Your maid, who will be on duty from early morning till late at night, introduces herself, points out the operating details (how to run the bath, etc.), asks if you want dinner that evening and what you want for breakfast the next morning, and briefs you on other important matters. On the question of meals, you can't decide at the last minute, for the inn needs plenty of advance notice, so be ready with your answer.

Sleeping in *futon* on the floor is comfortable and has the added advantage that you never fall out of bed. Your private bath should be lined with paulownia wood (light color), and there should be a shower arrangement as well as the sunken tub. You probably know the ritual by now: Soap and wash outside the tub, reserving it just for soaking. Open that little window down near water level and you'll probably have a worm's-eye view of the garden.

The *ryokan* is the place to play Japanese, to try to savor the restfulness which the slower pace of an inn can inspire. Spend some time contemplating the scroll on the wall, and especially the garden. It may be as rewarding as attempting the same thing at some famous so-called Zen garden (Ryoanji in Kyoto, for example), and certainly quieter.

Ryokan prices range from $55 to $485 per night for two persons, breakfast and dinner included, and all taxes and the 15 percent compulsory service charge as well. If you want to stay at a certain *ryokan* and don't wish to take meals there, you can ask in advance, and if the management agrees, the charge will be reduced, usually by about 10 to 20 percent.

How to reserve accommodations in a *ryokan*. The easiest way is to ask your travel agent to do so. If the agent can't, or won't, or if you are planning your own trip, then write directly to the inn. Hotel representatives usually don't represent inns, as inns are often quite well booked in any case, and are so small the volume of work doesn't make it profitable for the rep. The third way, then, is to book after you arrive in Japan. Again, do so directly by telephoning or writing, or, for cheaper (average $25) *ryokan*, contact the Japanese Inn Group's Liaison Office in Tokyo at 03-364-2534. (Very little English spoken here, however, so get someone to help you.)

Alternatives

In this book I've listed examples of the above four types of hotels and inns. There are other places to stay, which require some knowledge of Japanese and/or readiness to rough it. Here they are, with addresses where you can obtain further information:

Youth hostels. You don't have to be young to stay at a youth hostel, but you do have to take potluck some of the time, unless you plan ahead carefully. Of the more than 500 hostels scattered around Japan, 75 are government-operated and open to anyone. The others are privately owned and open only to members of the International Youth Hostel Federation or Japan Youth Hostels, Inc. If you're a member of the former, you can get information on the location and other details of hostels in Japan from your organization. If you aren't a member, on arrival in Japan, inquire at the Tourist Information Center in Tokyo or Kyoto (or at Tokyo Airport) about hostels open to the public where you intend to travel. The TIC has a booklet, Youth Hostels in Japan (in English), for just this purpose. There are also Youth Hostel Reservation Counters in the following Tokyo department stores: Keio (in Shinjuku branch), Seibu (Ikebukuro branch), Sogo (Yurakucho branch).

Minshuku. The *minshuku* (lit. people's lodgings) is like a guest house, and nearly all are operated by families. A very few have someone in the family who can speak English (often rudimentary). Cost may be as low as $30 per night, breakfast and dinner frequently included. You can't reserve these abroad, but on arrival in Japan, you can contact the Tokyo Minshuku Center at 03-371-8222. Again, have someone who can speak Japanese do the phoning for you. You should note that few *minshuku* are near the touristic centers of cities.

YMCA and YWCA. Contact them after arrival in Japan. The YMCA is open to both sexes and to families. Some English spoken. Tokyo YMCA, tel. 03-293-1911. Tokyo

YWCA, tel. 03-293-5421. They are near each other in the Kanda area.

Buddhist temples. A few temples allow overnight stays, particularly in places like Mt. Koya (Koya-san), where pilgrims come from long distances and the temples make a business of accommodation. Even fewer have short courses in *zazen*, with some instruction in English, for serious students of Buddhism. Obviously, these can be arranged only on arrival in Japan. For Koya-san, even the Japan Travel Bureau can make arrangements for you, but for others, inquire at the Tourist Information Center in Tokyo or Kyoto, and make arrangements on the spot. (See also pages 79, 168, and 232.)

WHERE TO EAT

The Japanese love to eat out. There are said to be about 50,000 places to eat or drink in Tokyo alone (that's one for every 230 inhabitants), compared to 14,000 for New York City (one for every 500). This figure includes tiny little eating stalls in front of rail stations, as well as plush places like the only branch of Tour d'Argent outside Paris (located in the New Otani Hotel). New York calls itself the eating capital of the world, but then what does it know? You'll find all the major cuisines of the world here, from Argentinian to Yugoslav, but you didn't come to Japan to eat *shashlik*, now, did you? In the restaurant listings for specific cities and regions, the section on Food and Drink following this, and the Menu Translator at the end of the book, I go into a lot of detail about all this, so I won't here.

FIVE BEST JAPANESE RESTAURANTS

Kyoto: Hyotei
Osaka: Kitcho
Tokyo: Fukudaya
       Hannyaen
       Jisaku

And Two Best French Restaurants

Kobe: Alain Chapel
Tokyo: Apecius

There are lots of stories about how expensive food is in Japan. This is true if you want French-style cooking, or the most *haute* of traditional Japanese *haute cuisine,* and it's true if you want bacon and eggs with freshly squeezed orange juice, croissants, and coffee brought to your hotel room. But Japan can be a cheap eat if you look for the ordinary places where the locals go. Try those restaurants with the plastic models of food in their windows—with few exceptions, they'll be neat and clean, and though foreign guests will make the staff nervous, smile, point to what you want, and enjoy your lunch or dinner. When traveling by train, I try to arrange the trip so that I have lunch on board. It's not wonderful food, but it's decent fare, it's inexpensive, and you combine sightseeing with lunch.

There are some famous chain restaurants in Japan, usually branches of an outstanding restaurant which demanded franchising. Nadaman is one such Japanese cuisine "chain," with branches in better hotels around the country. Peking is a good Chinese "chain," with branches in Osaka, Nagoya, Sendai, and Tokyo's Imperial Hotel.

Note: Addresses are not given for restaurants in smaller towns and cities, as establishments are well known.

Save money on lunches by looking for the special set meals, often in Chinese restaurants inside hotels. In Sendai on my last trip, I found one such in the basement of the Rich Hotel, offering a 5-course lunch for only ¥730 (about $4). Prices come down to attract the salaried worker for lunch. They go up at night, when the expense-account business people come out to play, and maybe work.

Dinner, too, can be inexpensive if you watch out for special bargains. On my last trip, the Tokyo Prince was offering dinner for only ¥2,000 ($12.12) in its Prince Villa Restaurant, normally very expensive. On Mondays through Thursdays, ladies only (!) could have a 3-course dinner with glass of wine for this price. Appetizer was mixed seafood salad, dessert was frozen yogurt ice cream with fresh fruit, and main course was a choice of curried beef or casserole of seafood (choice of shrimp, abalone, or scallops). At the newly opened Le Normandie in Tokyo, the set lunch was ¥2,000 ($12.12), set dinner ¥4,500 ($27.27); tel. 03-444-7677.

Cost of "Average Dinner"

The cost of an average dinner in this Crown Insiders' Guide means appetizer, main course, and dessert, including service charge and tax, except: (1) If a restaurant features a fixed-price dinner, that is the "average dinner." (2) In the case of restaurants serving only one kind of inexpensive item, such as *yakitori, kamameshi,* and the like, I have estimated a fair number of the items. (3) In *sushi* restaurants, I have used a set meal price where available. I have never included the cost of estimated drinks of any kind.

INSIDERS' TIPS

Readers should be aware that *sushi,* as popular in the U.S. as it is in Japan, is not ordinary fare for the Japanese. It is quite expensive, to begin with, and practically nobody tries to prepare it at home. The fish at the corner shop, fresh as it may be, will never be as fresh as that in a *sushi* restaurant. Add to this the difficulty of preparing *sushi* correctly and you'll see why it is regarded as a treat in Japan, not an everyday thing. *Sashimi,* on the other hand, is often prepared at home, usually as an appetizer.

FOOD AND DRINK

"It's not just raw fish" might be an apt phrase for beginning to describe Japanese cuisine. As in every other country with strong cultural traditions, the development of the art of eating here has its roots in the customs and religions of the people, as well as the bounty of their farms, rivers, mountainsides, and seas. Fish and fowl were always consumed in Japan, though the introduction of Buddhism in the 6th century led to vegetarianism on the part of the monks and scholars, not to be challenged until the 13th century, when one sect began to allow meat. The Zen tradition continues the vegetarian rule, though exceptions are now the rule.

Meat being such an innovation (there is a memorial to the first cow slaughtered for beef, at the temple in Shimoda where America's premier diplomat Townsend Harris resided), dishes such as *sukiyaki* are not considered traditionally Japanese. Importing ideas about food as well as everything else has provided Japan with a thriving dairy industry, its own American-style cheeses, and wines. You can always tell whether something on the menu is traditional or imported, as the latter invariably retain the foreign name—cheese is *chizu*, beer is *biru*, wine is *wain*, butter is *bata*, and so forth.

Rather than narrate the story behind Japanese cooking, I think it more helpful to describe the dishes and drinks you're most likely to encounter, explaining them as I do so. The list includes entries on regional specialties, types of restaurants, etc., as well as on specific dishes. (See also the Menu Translator later in this book for a glossary of words and phrases that may be useful.)

The word *ryori*, which you'll see a lot of, means cuisine, as in *Nihon ryori*, Japanese cuisine.

bento Boxed lunch, usually cold, in bamboo box with rice balls, pickles, a fish or meat "main course," tiny bottle of soy sauce, some ginger. See **eki-ben**, below.

chawan mushi Steamed egg custard, with vegetables, especially ginkgo nuts.

chazuke, usually *ochazuke* Green tea poured over rice in a bowl. A late-night snack, found in bars or *yakitori* stalls and restaurants.

eki ben Lit. rail station box lunch. Good, cheap, and varying according to station. You buy the *bento* right on station platform from hawkers.

Hiroshima specialties This region is famous for *kaki* (oysters), best in winter. You can have a 12-course meal of oysters alone. Try *kaki* in *nabe* (hot pot), out of the shells and with *miso* as *dote nabe*.

Hokkaido specialties This northernmost part of Japan is famous for its *nishin* (herring) and *sake* (salmon). Try an *ikura* (salmon roe) *nabe* (hot pot), flavored with *miso* stock.

Kagoshima specialties This southernmost region of main islands of Japan is subtropical, and fine fruits abound. *Shochu* is used in many dishes, such as *tonkotsu ryori*, pork chops in the liquor and *miso*. A good *iwashi* (sardine) dish is *kibinago*, eaten raw with *miso* sauce.

kaiseki ryori Traditional Japanese *haute cuisine*, stemming from the tea ceremony. Small dishes are featured, with food served in as natural form as possible, yet at the same time artistically. Everything is understated, even the portion of rice put in the bowl. Instead of being filled about 80 percent of the way, as is usually done, the *kaiseki* bowl is filled only 20 percent up, though you will be urged to have several helpings during the meal. In the Menu Translator, several types of dishes are listed.

Kanazawa specialties Seafood is king of this region's cuisine. A famous dish is *jibuni,* a kind of chicken stew served with tiny mushrooms and *wasabi* (horseradish).

karashi Mustard, hotter than usual Western variety.

Kochi specialties Kochi prefecture, on Shikoku, is famous for *katsuo* (bonito), so here is the place to have Kochi *sunomono.* The fish is grilled, then pickled with vinegar, soy sauce, garlic, and ginger.

kushi age Seafood or vegetables breaded and deep-fried, usually served on skewers. Frequently used are prawns, quail's eggs, green pepper, beef, scallops, squid. Can be a full meal, with rice.

maki zushi *Sushi* wrapped in a roll of *nori* (seaweed), then cut into small bite-sized pieces. Favorite ingredients are tuna, pickles, conger eel, cucumber, and *kanpyo.*

miso Fermented soybean paste, and after *shoyu* (soy sauce), Japan's favorite seasoning. Many variations, and used in soup, hot pots, over vegetables. The basic division is between *shiroi* (white) and *aka* (red).

PERILS & PITFALLS

Fugu is pufferfish, eaten in winter only. Also known as blowfish. Russian roulette comes to mind when eating this, as its liver and some other parts contain a deadly poison. Only specially trained chefs can buy the fish and prepare it. Very delicate taste, served in almost transparent slices. Dip in spicy sauce (chives, pepper, vinegar, etc.) as *sashimi.* Can be served cooked. Japanese men claim it is an aphrodisiac. A *kabuki* actor was last known famous victim. He insisted on a little of the poison, for the thrill of it. After he died, the chef committed suicide.

Nagasaki specialties This is the only place in Japan to have foreign contact during the 250 years of seclusion, so food is heavily influenced by China, Holland, even Portugal. The local souvenir most popular with other Japanese is *castera,* a sponge cake brought here by the Portuguese.

Local legend says that a Japanese, pointing to the plate on which the cake was served, asked, "What is that?" The Portuguese diner, looking at the picture of a castle *(castello)* on the plate, replied, "It's a *castello.*" The Japanese not being able to pronounce *l*, the cake became known as *castera*. Nagasaki's most famous dish, which you are encouraged to try if you have a big appetite, is *shippokku ryori*. It contains about ten dishes, ranging from typically Japanese soups to Chinese-style pork, pickled white fish, and fresh fruits. It was intended to be a festival meal.

nigiri zushi Sushi served Tokyo-style, now throughout Japan. Two pieces at a time, vinegar-flavored rice shaped into oblong forms, fish put on top. Order by the *setto* (set) or à la carte. If by set, specify *nami* (regular), *jo* (special), or *tokujo* (super special).

ramen Chinese noodles, made with flour and egg. The cheapest form of fast food and can be a lunch in itself. Usually with pork or chicken stock, and a lot of soup. In summer, ask for *hiyashi chuka*, a similar noodle but served cold, with strips of ham, cucumber, egg omelette. No soup, but nice vinegary sauce.

restoran Western-style restaurant of uncertain type. A French restaurant in Japan serves *Fransu ryori*, a Chinese restaurant has *Chuka ryori*. When something is a *restoran*, it means Japanized Western food, such as that served in a department store. Good food, filling, inexpensive. Plastic models of the food will be found outside, with numbers. You tell the cashier your number, pay for it, get a ticket, find a table, and wait. The food comes, you eat, you leave. No tipping, as I've mentioned many times before. You'll find *hayashi raisu, kare raisu*, spaghetti bolognese, and other cheap dishes here.

robata yaki Lit. hearthside grilling. Cooks prepare many kinds of dishes over open charcoal fires in front of guests, who shout their orders and have it confirmed back by shouts. Noisy and fun. Grilled fish, meats, vegetables, *tofu*. Can be a big meal if you want it so.

ryotei The highest class of eating place in Japan, always a classically styled house, with heavy debt to teahouse architecture. Reservations a must, and may be hard to get without personal introduction. (Sometimes the hotel manager can do this for you.) Never go alone, as *kaiseki* meals served here are intended for a minimum of two guests. Each party has a private room, and there is only one sitting per meal, so singles are discouraged. You will always be served sitting on *tatami* mats in an *ozashiki* (private room) overlooking a garden or other gorgeous view. The price is likely to be astronomical, but there are exceptions (see listings).

sashimi Raw fish, sliced thin and served with soy dipping sauce and *wasabi* (horseradish). At a *sushiya* (*sushi* restaurant), most people order some *sashimi* to begin with, as a kind of appetizer. Among the less expensive fish are *maguro* (tuna) and *ika* (squid), and among the pricier, *tai* (sea bream). There is always some *daikon* (shredded radish) as a garnish.

shabu shabu Hot pot using beef or crab (then called *kani shabu*), in which you dip the meat and vegetables into a boiling stock. (The name is onomatopoeic, from the sound of swishing the food back and forth in the liquid.) Chinese cabbage, mushrooms, onions, and chrysanthemum leaves are used, and the sauces are likely to be at least two—one vinegary, the other a thicker, sesame-seed-based dip.

shojin ryori Vegetarian cuisine. Also called *saishoku ryori*, and a vegetarian is a *saishoku-shugi-sha*. Some Buddhist sects still require that priests eat no meat, so protein is obtained from *tofu*, served in hundreds of different ways. Rice, *miso*, vegetables, nuts, and sometimes eggs are the basics.

shokado bento Lit. dining room box lunch. This is not your run-of-the-mill *bento*, as it is served at ceremonies such as weddings or on other important occasions. A big and beautiful lacquerware box, it contains several expensive dishes, from *sashimi* to *tempura*, with elegantly molded rice (shaped like a cherry blossom or such). The vegetables include *hasu* (lotus root) and *kabu* (turnip), for good luck. You probably won't get this in any restaurant, but look for it if you're invited to some function.

soba Buckwheat-flour noodles. *Sobaya* (*soba* shops) are found everywhere, serving hot or cold *soba*. Most *soba* dishes are served in a stock, and the noodles slurped up noisily, at least by the menfolk. In summer, look for *mori soba*, cold noodles served on a bamboo rack and dipped into separate sauce. *Zaru soba* is the same thing, with *nori* (seaweed) on top. *Tanuki soba* is a hot dish with fried *tempura* batter on top. *Kitsune soba,* also hot, has fried *tofu* and onions on top. If you see a square wooden container on the table, it is filled with the stock from cooking the noodles. You can add it to the dipping bowl after eating all the noodles, making a little soup for yourself.

somen Thin noodle made from wheat flour, always eaten cold after dipping into a soy sauce mixture.

sukiyaki Lit. plow-grilled. A foreign import, but very popular now in Japan. One chain, the Washington hotels, has a restaurant called Sanjusangendo, in each branch, which features *sukiyaki* eaten at low tables on *tatami* mats into which a *kotatsu* well has been carved so you don't have to sit on your legs. Every foreigner loves it, as the combination of beef, onions, *konnyaku* noodles, *tofu,* and chrysanthemum leaves is a sure winner. It tends to be sweeter in Kyoto than in Tokyo, and is cooked differently in the two areas. In Kyoto, meat and vegetables are eaten separately (meat first), in Tokyo all together. If you're told the meat is Kobe beef, it only means it's a better grade than average. Matsuzaka beef, on the other hand, is supposed to be the best in Japan, and if it's Wadakin, you are either at the restaurant of that name down near Ise or are eating the most expensive beef in the world, sold by that establishment, which has its own farm.

sushi Raw fish on vinegar-flavored rice balls. See also *maki zushi, nigiri zushi.* Eat with fingers or chopsticks, as you prefer. Don't eat the bamboo-grass decorations, do eat the ginger. If you order à la carte, see Menu Translator for names of fish. If ordering as a set, see entry above for *nigiri zushi.*

temaki zushi Lit. hand-rolled *sushi.* Instead of being rolled tightly as is *maki zushi,* this is rolled into a cone shape, one end open, the same wrapper (*nori* seaweed) being used. *Kyuri* (cucumber), *takuan* (pickle), and *maguro* (tuna) are among the more popular fillers.

tempura Fish and vegetables battered and deep-fried. Said to have been introduced by the Portuguese in the 17th century. One secret of good *tempura* is dipping the food in ice water before frying; another is to get it from pan to diner as quickly as possible. You usually sit at counter facing cook to eat this straight from the fire. You can eat it with just lemon and salt, or most of the time with a special *tempura* sauce, into which you mix *daikon* (radish) and *shoga* (ginger).

tonkatsu Pork cutlet, an import, now thoroughly Japanized. Fried very slowly in deep oil, then served with a special sauce, different in each restaurant, but using soy sauce or *miso* as a base. Served with mustard and shredded cabbage, rice, and *miso* soup. Inexpensive and filling lunch.

tsukemono Pickles. My favorite is *takuan*, a yellow form of the giant *daikon* (radish), after soaking in salted rice bran. Nearly every traditional Japanese meal has some form of pickle, including breakfast. *Umeboshi* are little plums or apricots, hard and salty, the seed still inside, and are wonderful with rice. The fruit is colored with *akajiso* (red beefsteak plant) leaves. Other popular pickles: *hakusai* (Chinese cabbage) and *fukujinsuke* (sour bits of red radish). Eggplant and turnip, not to mention cucumber, are also popular material for pickling.

udon Noodles made from wheat flour, not buckwheat, as is *soba*. Everything said about *soba* can be repeated for *udon*, but some styles of preparation are exclusively for *udon*, never for *soba*. (*Nabeyaki udon*, for example, with tempura, egg, and vegetables, is never made with *soba*.)

unagi Eel. In Japan eel is almost a cult, and is especially popular in summer. Raised commercially now, and as oily as ever. Usually grilled over charcoal, then brushed with a special soy-based sauce. See *unaju* in Menu Translator. Said to be aphrodisiac.

wasabi Horseradish, but the Japanese version is a pale green color. A friend of mine, now departed, said there are 94 different kinds, but they are all hot, hot, hot. You've encountered it with *sushi*, if no other place.

yakiniku Grilled meat. Many restaurants serve this, often as strips of cheap beef marinated, then grilled over charcoal. Best dipping sauce is *tare*, made of *miso* and *togarashi* (red pepper). Korean restaurants are known for their *yakiniku*, which they call *pulgoki*.

yakisoba Fried noodles, except that the noodles are not really *soba* but *ramen* (Chinese egg noodles). You can have *yakisoba katai* (hard) or *yawarakai* (soft), the difference being in whether noodles are fried alone (hard) or with the other ingredients (soft). Includes pork, shrimp, Chinese cabbage, carrots, mushrooms, bamboo shoots, whatever.

yakitori Lit. grilled bird. Usually chicken cut into cubes and grilled over charcoal with onions and served on a skewer. Sauce is mixture of soy, *miso,* red pepper, etc. and is brushed on before grilling. Many *yakitoriya* (*ya* = shop) advertise their presence with big red lanterns outside. See Menu Translator for information on ordering.

yatai Stall. Food stalls can be found on streets near nightlife districts and rail stations. Intended to catch the reveler on his or her way home, and featuring such fast foods as *soba, ramen, ishiyaki imo* (baked sweet potato), *tomorokoshi* (corn on the cob), and *yakitori.*

yose nabe Hot pot containing wonderfully rich mixture of fish, chicken, and vegetables. Usually served in winter at hotels and some restaurants, and a traditional home dish. Any vegetable you feel like. At the end, best of all, *udon* noodles are added to the broth and you finish up with as good a chicken noodle soup as Mother ever made.

PERILS & PITFALLS

There are other stall foods, none of which I recommend to first-time visitors unless they're into weird foods. Here they are: *Oden,* boiled vegetables and fish paste, all of which taste rubbery to me. *Takoyaki,* grilled octopus cakes, eaten on a toothpick, ditto rubbery. *Okonomiyaki,* a round pancake with lots of flour, nice-tasting but difficult to eat as it falls apart like a taco. Hot dogs. All right, but have the same qualities as those on the streets of London, being made of dubious meats and other materials. Not nearly as good as those found on streets of New York, for example.

Drinks

Biru (beer) and *uisuki* (whiskey) are about the only drinks that you can be sure of knowing what you are ordering in Japan. Best of the beers, in my opinion, is Kirin, followed by Sapporo, then the sweeter Asahi and Suntory. Sapporo's boast is that it lies on the same latitude (between 40 and 50 degrees north) as Munich and Milwaukee. Beer comes in great big bottles, *O-bin* (almost a liter), and in *ko-bin* (smaller ones), and now in *chu-bin* (middle-sized). It also comes in cans similar to those in the U.S., rarely on tap. Draft beer, so-called, is sold in cans and bottles as *nama biru* (lit. fresh or raw beer). The beer industry in Japan was started with help from the Germans, but the beer can best be described as somewhere between the American style and the German.

Whiskey in Japan means Suntory to most visitors, and it is very popular. It can be called, safely, a Scotch-*type* whiskey, and Suntory does import some malts from Scotland. Other popular brands are Nikka and Robert Brown. You can, more or less, anticipate the smoothness by the price. You'll enjoy the fractured English (or Japlish, as some call it) in the bars. My favorite, in days when prices were cheaper, was "Highballs ¥100, low balls ¥50," referring to the quality of whiskey used, of course.

Here are some drinks not so familiar, or the Japanese words for which are not common knowledge outside the country (see also Menu Translator):

awamori Brandy made from sweet potatoes in Okinawa. What Marlon Brando and the fellows drank in *Teahouse of the August Moon.* Harsh and potent.

bancha Green tea made from large leaves picked late in the season. Standard tea.

cha Generic term for tea (note similarity to Hindu *cha,* Russian *chai,* etc.). Always prefaced by honorific *o,* as in *o-cha.* (You can put the *o* in front of almost anything in Japan to make it more polite, even *o-tearai,* honorable hand-washing place, which means toilet, not a hand-washing place as such.)

hojicha Toasted *bancha* leaves brewed as a tea.

ocha See *cha,* above. If you just ask for *ocha,* you're likely to get *sencha,* which see below.

kocha Black tea, or Indian tea. Served with (surprise) *remon* (lemon) or *miraku* (milk).

matcha Tea-ceremony tea, a lovely shade of green and whipped to a froth by what looks like a bamboo shaving brush. Made from very young leaves without stalks. The leaves are protected from sunlight while growing. Surprisingly strong green tea taste.

sake Called rice wine, but it's brewed, like beer. Also called *Nihonshu* (Japanese wine) in some traditional restaurants. Made from fermented rice and water, with about 15 percent alcoholic content. Some drink it cold (out of square wooden boxes with a pinch of salt) in summer especially, but most drink it hot. There are three grades, Tokyu, Ikkyu, Nikkyu (Special, First Class, and Second Class), marked on an oval label near the top of the bottle. *Sake* is usually drunk from *choko* (drinking cups), tinier even than the small *tokkuri* (flask) in which the drink is heated. Five *tokkuri* make up about 1 liter. There are hundreds of different *sake* in Japan, in localities large and small. There is a *sake*-tasting center in Tokyo, but I suggest just asking for the local *sake* wherever you go. (Ask for *jizake*, which means local *sake*, or ". . . [name of town or region] *no sake, kudasai.*") If they ask about size, don't worry, as it always comes in the *tokkuri*. Should you want to buy some on your own, there are two bottle sizes, *issho-bin*, which holds 1.8 liters, and *sho-bin*, half-size. *Sake* is also sold in cans from vending machines. Of the famous national brands, I prefer Gekkeikan, allegedly purveyed to the Imperial Household. Also good is Hakutsuru (white crane).

sencha Most common type of green tea, what you get if you don't specify something else. Young tea leaves picked in midseason are the basis.

shochu A clear liquor made from wheat, rice, or corn, sometimes potatoes. Usually mixed with *oyuwari* (hot water) or in awful combined cocktails. Very harsh. A modern innovation is to mix *shochu* with ice and lemon, the resulting *chuhai* being a bit like vodka and soda. If you want to ask what kind of *shochu* it is, you should know that *mugi* is wheat, *kome* is rice, *tomorokoshi* is corn, and *jagaimo* is potato. Other brands are made from *satsuma imo* (sweet potato) and *awa* (millet).

umeshu Plum brandy. Made from mixing *shochu* and plums, plus sugar. Plums are favored, but you can also use strawberries or apricots.

HOW TO GET AROUND
Train

Japan's railroads are simply marvelous, especially when compared to those in the U.S. They start and arrive on time, the cars stop at designated markings on the platform, they are clean, and onboard service is excellent. The personnel are polite and answer questions instead of shrugging their shoulders and rolling their eyes. Most of the time, you'll be using Japan National Railways (JNR), which covers the country with trains, buses, and ferries. Buy a Japan Rail Pass if you plan to travel much (see box below).

Everyone wants to experience the Bullet Train, called Shinkansen by the Japanese, the world's first supertrains (now the French have faster ones). They range from Tokyo as base to Kyushu in the southwest and Tohoku in the north, and depart every few minutes throughout the day—more than 90 daily on the Tokyo-Kyoto-Osaka route, less on the others. The fastest are Hikari, slightly less fast the Kodama (more stops), and each consists of 16 cars, 2 of them first-class (Green Car); 5 cars are unreserved, 2 are nonsmoking. There is a dining car for meals, buffet car for snacks. Two telephone booths, Western and Japanese toilets, and luggage compartment in Green Car. The Koda-

---

INSIDERS' TIPS

The Japan Rail Pass is a good buy. If you plan to see a lot of Japan, get a Rail Pass, good for either a 1-, 2-, or 3-week period and costing between $165 and $340 for the ordinary pass. A special Green Car (first-class) pass is also available for between $230 and $480. Offered only to nonresidents of Japan, and it must be purchased abroad from Japan Travel Bureau, Nippon Travel Agency, Japan Air Lines, or Pacific Select. Good also on JNR buses and ferries, which means most of the transportation network in Japan, including the Shinkansen (Bullet Trains). Here are New York numbers for the above agencies: JTB, 212-246-8030; NTA, 212-986-7393; JAL, 212-838-4400; Pacific Select, 212-972-8748.

What you get when you buy a pass is a voucher, which you must turn in for the actual pass when you get to Japan. If you have time, it's smart to exchange the voucher for the pass at the JNR counter at Narita Airport on arrival. It is right in the middle of the arrival area, between north and south wings. The Narita counter is open from 7 A.M. to 11 P.M. If you wait, you can exchange the voucher at one of several JNR Travel Service Centers, such as at Tokyo Station, Marunouchi Exit, where the hours are 10 A.M. to 6 P.M. Other centers are in stations at Sapporo, Sendai, Niigata, Yokohama, Nagoya, Kyoto, Osaka, Hiroshima, Hakata, Kumamoto, and Kagoshima.

ma has 11 nonreserved cars, 2 nonsmoking cars, one Green Car. No dining car, but there is a sales counter and a Western-style toilet.

The Tokyo-Kyoto route is 320 miles (513 km) and takes 2 hours 53 minutes, costing (at press time) ¥12,200 ($73.94) or ¥17,600 ($106.67) for Green Car. (Air fare is ¥15,600 [$94.55] and elapsed time is about the same, an hour in the air and at least an hour at each end to city center.) A nonreserved seat is only ¥500 ($3.03) less than a reserved seat on the Shinkansen, perhaps not worth the saving. (On the other hand, making a reservation does take a few minutes of your time.)

You'll have to find out which track your train is on *("Namban sen desu ka")* as you go through the ticket wicket. If you hold up one or two fingers, the ticket taker may take the hint and reply with his fingers held up too, in case you don't catch the answer (*"Ichi ban sen"* for Track 1, and so forth). If you don't ask, don't worry, as the track numbers are posted all over the place, with number of train followed by track number, in English as well as Japanese. Go to the track and find your car number posted on the platform, stand where the arrows painted on the ground indicate, and when the train arrives, your car will stop exactly where the signs say it will.

Regular trains are not so luxurious, and most will have no dining or snack car, but you then have the fun of buying *bento* box lunches on different station platforms when the train stops. You can check luggage on all trains except the Shinkansen (they don't stop long enough to allow loading and unloading of checked baggage). You can also store your luggage at most JNR stations for ¥200 ($1.21) per day up to 5 days, ¥400 ($2.42) after that. You can send luggage ahead, using the *kyuhaibin* (courier) service, not a JNR function (see page 27).

There are *akabo-san* (redcap porters) in larger stations, but they are getting harder to find. Charge is a flat ¥300 ($1.81) per bag, no tipping needed. (Don't tip for anything on the train, either, in dining car or elsewhere.)

There are private railways in addition to JNR. If you use these at all, it will probably be for day trips around Tokyo, Kyoto, or Osaka. The best way to Nikko is on the private Tobu Railway (see page 296). There is an extensive private railway network around the Osaka-Nara-Kyoto-Kobe complex (Kansai), but the terminals in Kyoto and Osaka are not well signed in English, nor are they located as conveniently as those of JNR. The same can be said for Nagoya. References to Kinki Nippon, always amusing to foreign visitors, are to the private railway of the same name, officially Kintetsu (Golden Rail) Nippon. Keihan is a big private railway in Kansai, Nishitetsu in Fukuoka.

Here are some sample rail fares (if you don't have a Rail Pass), one-way. No discount for round trip. Shinkansen to Osaka and Fukuoka, combined Shinkansen and other trains to Sapporo.

Tokyo-Osaka: ¥12,200 ($73.94), Shin Osaka Station on Shinkansen; ¥17,500 ($106.06) on Green Car; 3 hours 10 minutes

Tokyo-Fukuoka: ¥19,400 ($117.58); ¥27,300 ($165.45) on Green Car; 6 hours 40 minutes

Osaka-Fukuoka: ¥13,300 ($80.61); ¥19,400 ($117.58) on Green Car; 3 hours 30 minutes

Tokyo-Sapporo: ¥19,350 ($117.27); ¥33,250 ($201.52) on Green Car; 16 hours 1 minute

---

INSIDERS' TIPS

As Japan gets richer, so do the perks for the well-to-do. Not content with first class (Green Car), JNR now has added private compartments on the Shinkansen trains. At first, this is limited to those between Tokyo and Hakata (via Kyoto and Osaka) 5 days a week (not on Wednesday or Thursday). Car No. 9 will have 4 single compartments and 6 triple compartments (2 can be joined to accommodate 6 persons). Car No. 10 will have 2 single compartments and 1 double compartment (especially for honeymooners, JNR says). Car No. 8 will become a double-decker diner, the tables upstairs, kitchen below. Surcharges, replacing Green Car fare, will be ¥6,500 ($39.39) for a single or double compartment (per person) and ¥5,400 ($32.73) for the triple rooms between Tokyo and Osaka, ¥9,400 ($56.97) and ¥7,800 ($47.27) for Tokyo-Hakata. Total single fare then would be Tokyo-Osaka ¥18,600 ($112.73), Tokyo-Hakata ¥28,900 ($175.15), just a few dollars more than regular Green Car. If a single person takes over a larger compartment, he or she must pay half the surcharge on the empty seats. Each compartment has reclining chair and footrest, small folding wall table, and phone for internal communication on the train.

Air

There are five airlines in Japan, three of them operating major routes. Japan Air Lines (JAL) is best known to foreign visitors because it has been, until recently, the only Japanese flag carrier operating scheduled routes abroad. Within Japan, it flies (at press time) only to Osaka, Fukuoka, Okinawa, and Hokkaido, though other routes are envisioned in the near future. It uses giant 747s and DC-10s. JAL also owns or operates several outstanding hotels. Superseats (like a first class) are available for about 30 percent over usual cost.

All Nippon Airways (ANA) is actually the biggest Japanese carrier, and until recently operated scheduled flights only within the country. (Starting in July 1986, it began a Tokyo–Honolulu–Los Angeles–Washington D.C. route.) ANA serves, from north to south, Sapporo, Kushiro, Hakodate, Akita, Yamagata, Sendai, Narita, Tokyo, Hachijojima, Nagoya, Niigata, Toyama, Kanazawa, Komatsu, Nankishirahama, Takamatsu, Osaka, Kochi, Matsuyama, Okayama, Hiroshima, Yamaguchi, Ube, Tottori, Yonago, Matsue, Oita, Fukuoka, Kumamoto, Nagasaki, Miyazaki, Kagoshima, and 13 smaller places. It uses 747s and Tri-Stars, as well as Boeing 767s, 727s, and 737s and a few Japanese-built YS-11s. It also owns a chain of fine hotels.

Toa Domestic Airlines (TDA) is an amalgamation of several smaller firms, and now flies the European-built Airbus (A300), the DC-9, the YS-11, and the German-built Dornier 200. From north to south, it serves Memanbetsu, Asahikawa, Kushiro, Obihiro, Sapporo, Hakodate, Aomori, Misawa, Akita, Hanamaki, Yamagata, Sendai, Niigata, Tokyo, Nagoya, Matsumoto, Nankishirahama, Okayama, Oki, Yonago, Izumo, Osaka, Tokushima, Takamatsu, Matsuyama, Kochi, Fukuoka, Nagasaki, Kumamoto, Oita, Miyazaki, Kagoshima, Tanegashima, Yakushima, Amamioshima, Tokunoshima, Okinoerabu, and Yoron.

Southwest Air Lines (SWAL), based in Okinawa, flies between there and Ishigaki, Miyako, Shimoji, Kume, Yoron, Okinoerabu, Aguni, Kitadaito, Minamidaito, Tarama, Yonaguni, and Hateruma. Uses 737s, YS-11s, and De Havilland Herons.

Nippon Kinkyori Airlines (NKA) picks up some odd routes, mostly at the northern and southern extremes of the country. It serves, from north to south, Sapporo, Nemuronaka, Shibetsu, Monbetsu, Wakkanai, Rebun, Reshiri, Hakodate, Okushiri, Akita, Tokyo, Oshima, Miyakejima, Hiroshima, Kagoshima, Kochi, Fukuoka, Tsushima, Nagasaki, Iki, Gotofukue, Amamioshima, and Okinawa. Equipment: 737s, YS-11s, and De Havilland DHC-6s.

Some sample air fares at press time (one-way, 10 percent discount for round trips):

Tokyo-Osaka: ¥15,600 ($94.55); 1 hour
Tokyo-Fukuoka: ¥27,100 ($164.24); 1 hour 30 minutes
Osaka-Fukuoka ¥15,400 ($93.33); 1 hour
Tokyo-Sapporo ¥25,500 ($154.55); 1 hour 25 minutes

Airport buses (why do they often call them limousines when they hold 50 people and you have to climb several steps to get in them?) are available from all airports to city centers, the service depending on volume of traffic, of course. For information on Narita Airport at Tokyo, see page 43. Here are a few other details:

Osaka International Airport is a mess now, but when the new one is built, it will be a lot more efficient, and, of course, much farther away from Kyoto. At any rate, if you don't want to taxi to Kyoto—about ¥12,500 ($75.76) at press time—take the bus for only ¥730 or ¥800 ($4.42 or $4.85), three or four departures hourly from either end except from midnight to 6 A.M. The Kyoto terminal is the Hotel Keihan, opposite Kyoto Station's south exit. Some buses go directly on to seven Kyoto hotels and the ANA and JAL offices. Takes 1 hour between air terminal and Kyoto bus terminal. Phone Osaka Airport Bus, 06-844-1124, in Japanese. From the airport to Umeda in Osaka takes only 25 minutes, costs ¥360 ($2.18). Taxi will run about ¥4,500 ($27.27).

Car

If you decide against my advice and want to rent a car, you'll need an international license, or a Japanese one (very difficult to get, considering the written and driving tests). Nissan Rent-a-Car has small vehicles from as little as ¥4,000 ($24.24) per day (the March car), up to ¥12,800 ($77.58) per day (Cedric Gloria). Offices in every major city; in Tokyo, tel. 03-587-4123.

By 1990, there should be many more road signs in English, says the government. Beginning in Tokyo, bilingual signs will be erected first, then throughout the country. So help may be on the way, but driving is still difficult.

PERILS & PITFALLS

Where am I? The address system in Japan is peculiar. In most cities, street names are not used, and buildings are numbered in order of their having been built, though some changes have been made recently. Every Japanese address begins with the prefecture (province), then town (or county), then ward, then village (or district), then area or block, then a number. A typical address reads Tokyo-to, Mitaka-shi, Naniwa-ku, Kita-machi 3-chome, 1-15. *To* (or *fu* or *ken*) means prefecture, *shi* means city, *ku* means ward, *machi* means village, *chome* means area. This is why you need explicit instructions if trying to find some out-of-the-way place, and it explains why so many Japanese advertisements contain little maps.

Taxi

Cabs are costlier, but more available than in most American cities. The ratio for cabs to population in Tokyo, for example, is 1 to 300. Comparable figures for New York are 1 to 593, for Chicago 1 to 652, for San Francisco 1 to 954, San Diego 1 to 977, Los Angeles 1 to 1,978, and Indianapolis 1 to 2,282! As for fares, the meter drops at ¥470 ($2.85), in Tokyo for a medium-sized car, and takes you for the first 1½ miles (2 km), then starts turning over at the rate of ¥80 (48¢) for each 370 meters. All this works out to about $1.90 for first mile, then $2.40 for each additional mile. Los Angeles figures are $2 for first mile, then only $1.40 for each additional mile.

You can hail cabs anywhere, except in Tokyo's Ginza (that city's Fifth Avenue) at night, when you must go to taxi ranks (there was too much unseemly squabbling, plus offering two, three and four times the meter just to get cabs here when the nightclubs closed, all at 11 P.M.). A cab is empty when you see a red light in the lower right hand corner (as you face it). If it's green, it means the night surcharge (20 percent) is in effect. If the light is out, the cab is occupied.

You can phone for cabs, but you have to speak Japanese. They charge from the moment they get the call, but that's usually no more than ¥500 ($3.03) maximum. Big companies include Nihon Kotsu, tel. 03-586-2151; Kokusai, tel. 03-491-6001; Hinomaru, tel. 03-814-1111; and Yamata, tel. 03-563-5151.

PERILS & PITFALLS

You should remember that the rear doors of most Japanese taxis open automatically, so don't stand too close as driver approaches. They also close automatically when you get in, so let the driver do it.

No tipping in taxis! Have a matchbox from your hotel, or business card, so you can get back easily at the end of the day. If you think your destination may be difficult, ask your hotel front desk to write it down for you in Japanese.

SHOPPING

Note: See page 76 for business hours.

Japan can be heaven for shoppers, but cheap it isn't. If you plan to buy such well-known products as electronic equipment, cameras, or pearls, check out prices back home very carefully, lest you pay as much, or more, in Japan. Generally speaking, you should keep your eyes peeled for antiques and fine art, cultured pearls, ceramics, lacquerware, pottery, dolls, handmade paper, and food products like *sembei* (rice crackers). Modern clothing can be fun (see especially Best Shopping list in the Tokyo chapter), and used *kimono* are good buys. (The Japanese don't like to wear secondhand clothing, generally speaking, so a lot of wardrobes end up going abroad.)

Bargaining is not the custom except in Osaka or at flea markets anywhere in the country. It is also acceptable in antique shops, where everything is a one-of-a-kind, who-knows kind of thing. On returning change, the Japanese do not count it out, but thrust it at you in a lump, assuming you trust them. (I've never caught a clerk making a mistake.)

If you want to purchase items duty-free, be sure to have your passport with you, and keep any forms you are given. You will have to show the customs people your purchases when you depart in order to validate your tax-free purchase. Among items on which you can avoid the luxury tax (5 to 40 percent) are:

- Cameras, movie cameras and projectors, including lenses, bodies, tripods, photometers, and flash apparatus
- Furs
- Record players and record concert equipment of ensemble type, including speakers
- Household implements made of fiber
- Hunting guns
- Magnetic tape recorders
- Pearls and articles made of or decorated with pearls
- Radios
- Slide projectors
- Timepieces, including those with cases decorated with precious metals, precious or semiprecious stones, gold, or platinum
- Television sets
- Articles made of precious metals or decorated with gold or platinum, or plated or covered with precious metals
- Articles made of precious stones or semiprecious stones, or decorated with them
- Articles used in smoking
- Articles made of tortoiseshell, coral, amber, or ivory, as well as cloisonné ware

NIGHTLIFE

If you're not worn out from your sightseeing during the day, aim for the traditional Japanese ways of spending the evening. Tops should be the *kabuki* theater, then *bunraku* and Noh, in that order (from most exciting to most cerebral). For music lovers there are *bugaku* or *gagaku* performances (ancient court dancing and music, respectively). I can't really recommend *shimpa*, the old-fashioned Western theater, or even the modern *shingeki*, contemporary theater, unless you know Japanese. Kitsch lovers will want to see the Takarazuka all-girl (count 'em, 500) operetta or revue, featuring ultrasweet song and dance. At the end of the native-arts list would be *rakugo* or vaudeville, where, again, knowledge of the language is a necessity.

Western-style music is extremely popular, as you'll ascertain if you visit a classical *kisaten* (coffee shop) or listen to the government NHK radio. Tokyo has five symphony orchestras at last count, of which the NHK Symphony is best, Tokyo Philharmonic second-best, in my opinion. Three professional ballet companies grace the scene, the best being Nikki Kai. Rarely do these orchestras and dance groups perform music composed by Japanese, but when they do, Mayazumi Toshiro is probably the man whose work is played most. A steady diet of the Big Bs seems to be the bread and butter for the orchestras, and Russian-style ballet for the dance groups.

Traditional nightclubs are getting harder to find, anywhere, these days. See our listings, and bring lots of money, as you are competing with the *shayozoku* (expense-account) system, and the sky's the limit. More fun are the little bars, where you can meet the people, sometimes English-speaking ones, especially in the Roppongi district of Tokyo. Some bars have hostesses (be sure to figure out the system before you jump in, as the pricing can get out of hand, otherwise), some are just for music lovers (especially jazz). Then there are discotheques, which come and go like the bars, will-o'-the-wisps in the *mizu shobai* ("water trade"), as its denizens call it.

The Nihon Kokusai Kanko Kyogikai (Japan National Tourist Organization) offers foreign visitors a 10 percent discount coupon for performances of *kabuki, bunraku,* and *shimpa* at the National Theater in Tokyo and the Bunraku Theater in Osaka. Get your coupons at any JNTO office, such as Tourist Information Centers at Narita Airport, in Tokyo's Yurakucho, and in Kyoto. Take the coupon to the theater to get your discount and ticket.

While planning your night out on the town, you should note that in every city (including Tokyo), public transport grinds to a halt around midnight, resuming again around 5 A.M. Late-night trippers should plan on using taxis, with their nighttime surcharge, between those hours.

In the listings for nightlife spots in Tokyo, Kyoto, and Osaka, I have included only places, unless otherwise noted, where the tourist buses do *not* go.

Many Japanese bars operate as clubs in theory, and any place serving alcohol after midnight must also serve something to eat. Hence all the cooking going on behind the bar in small places. If you're drinking so late, you'll probably enjoy a snack anyhow.

INSIDERS' TIPS

Japanese electric current is the same voltage as that in North America, namely 110 volts AC. East of a line drawn through Shizuoka City, the nation is on 50 cycles (that includes Tokyo). West of the line, Japan is on 60 cycles per second, the same as the U.S. This includes Kyoto, Osaka, Hiroshima, and Kyushu. Most appliances won't be affected by the different cycles, except for things like a record player. Plugs are American-style.

DOING BUSINESS IN JAPAN

Many books have been written on this subject, and you should read them, carefully, before making the plunge. Here are just a few shortcuts, however.

Several major hotels have Executive Business Centers. Outstanding is that of Tokyo's Hotel Okura, and very good those at the Imperial and Keio Plaza. Conference rooms, telex, typewriters, library, equipment rental, the works.

The ISS (Interlanguage Service System) has counters in several hotels, such as Osaka's Nikko, Tokyo's New Otani, etc. Language and secretarial services are its specialty.

Rental Shop Acom in Tokyo, tel. 03-350-5081, or Osaka, tel. 06-315-0727, will rent you the following, from 1 day to 15 days (perhaps longer), from ¥1,400 ($8.48) up: cameras (handy or SLR), golf clubs and bag, overhead projector, projectors for slides, 8mm or 16mm movies, screens, tape recorders, tennis rackets, typewriters, video cameras (including portable ones), and video projectors. Open daily.

Japan Air Lines will get your business cards printed up

in Japanese, and has an Executive Lounge you can use in the Imperial Hotel if you are flying JAL. JAL also sells several books for the business person coming to this country.

TBS, the Tokyo Business Station, will provide you with office space, data service, secretarial services, etc., even marketing surveys, from its plush offices in Shinjuku. 4-2-23 Shinjuku (Urban Shinjuku Building, 3rd floor), Shinjuku-ku, Tokyo 160, tel. 03-341-1112.

Every major hotel in Japan has telex facilities, and most now have fax (facsimile) transmission machines, to send your own handwritten note, if you wish, to any other fax machine.

The American Express Interpreting Service is available from that group's Tokyo office, 4-3-13 Toranomon, Minato-ku, Tokyo 105, tel. 03-459-6155, with other branches, including one in Osaka.

TELEPHONE, TELEGRAPH, AND MAIL

Telephones come in all colors in Japan, but the service is always the same—outstanding. If you want to make a simple call, head for a red phone, which takes the basic ¥10 (6¢) you need to call anywhere locally. Blue phones are a little rare, same as red but taking more coins if you want to talk longer. If you want to talk a long time, go for yellow, which takes up to 10 of the ¥10 coins and 9 ¥100 (60¢) coins. Now, for international calls if you're in an airport or some such place, look for a green phone. If you happen to have a Japanese phone company credit card (which I doubt), you can put the card in the slot and dial anywhere in the world. The meter tells you how much you're spending. If you run out of the card's credit, you insert coins, up to 5 ¥10 and 4 ¥100. This means if you want to use cash and call the U.S., you can talk for only about a minute. Cards can be purchased in limited amounts, but you're better off calling from your hotel. (No surprising surcharges as in Europe, and certainly not if you're using your own international calling card or calling collect.)

You can dial directly to most of the world from your hotel phone in most modern hotels, using your credit card, reversing the charges, making conference calls, and the

---

INSIDERS' TIPS

A great help to foreign visitors is Japan Travel Phone, operated by the Japan National Tourist Organization, for those times when you need English-language assistance or just plain information. Phone the following numbers:

Except Tokyo and Kyoto, 106 toll-free. Insert ¥10 (6¢), which will be returned, tell operator in English, "Collect call, TIC."

In Tokyo, insert ¥10, dial 503-2911. No money returned.

In Kyoto, insert ¥10, dial 361-2911. No money returned.

For French language, in Tokyo only, dial 503-2926. To reach this number from outside Tokyo, add area code 03 before number.

Japan Travel Phone service is available 7 days a week, 9 A.M. to 5 P.M.

---

like. Standard rate to the U.S., station-to-station, is ¥1,890 ($11.45), for 3 minutes and ¥630 ($3.82) for each additional minute. Canada is the same rate, and for Britain it's ¥2,250 ($13.64) and ¥750 ($4.55). After you have an outside line, dial 001 for access, then country code (U.S. is 1, for example), then the number.

Telegrams cost ¥826 ($5) for 7 words, ¥118 (72¢) for each additional word, ¥1,298 ($7.87) for a letter telegram of 22 words. Same for Canada, and ¥1,344 ($8.15) for the 7 basic words to Britain, ¥192 ($1.16) each additional word. Britain does not have letter telegrams. You can send telegrams at your hotel, a post office, or offices of KDD (Kokusai Denwa Denshin) International.

Telex is also operated by KDD and most hotels have the equipment.

Airmail postage from Japan to the U.S. and Canada is ¥150 (91¢) up to 10 grams, ¥90 (55¢) each additional 10 grams, and ¥100 (61¢) for postcards. To all of Europe it's ¥170 ($1.03), ¥110 (67¢), and ¥110 respectively. You can also use Telefax in Japan, as many hotels have it, so if you have the equipment back home, you can communicate quite easily. There is a philately counter in the Central Post Office, Marunouchi, Tokyo (opposite Tokyo Station), where you can purchase all sorts of beautiful Japanese stamps. Some English spoken.

BUSINESS HOURS

Here is the official rundown:

	Weekdays	Saturdays	Sundays & holidays
Banks	9 A.M.–3 P.M.	9 A.M.–noon[1]	Closed
Post offices	9 A.M.–5 P.M.	9 A.M.–12:30 P.M.	Closed
Department stores	10 A.M.–6 P.M.[2]	10 A.M.–6:30 P.M.	10 A.M.–6:30 P.M.
Other stores	10 A.M.–8 P.M.	10 A.M.–8 P.M.	10 A.M.–8 P.M.
Restaurants	Lunchtime and dinnertime 7 days a week[3]		
Private companies	9 A.M.–5 P.M.	9 A.M.–noon[4]	Closed
Government offices	9 A.M.–5 P.M.	9 A.M.–noon	Closed
Most museums	10 A.M.–5 P.M.[5]	10 A.M.–5 P.M.	10 A.M.–5 P.M.

[1] Closed on 2nd Saturdays.
[2] Closed once a week on weekday, varies.
[3] Some close once a week, frequently on Sundays. Most lunch hours are noon to 2 P.M., dinner from 6 to 8 P.M.
[4] Some closed on Saturdays.
[5] Closed once a week on weekday, varies, very frequently Mondays.

You should also note that many restaurants close early, the last order being around 8:30 P.M., and that public transportation stops around midnight, resuming about 5:30 A.M. From January 1 to January 3, practically everything is closed, except for restaurants in hotels. During Golden Week, April 29 to May 5, when there are three national holidays, tourist-related facilities, including restaurants, are open, but the downtown areas of cities grow very quiet.

MAKING FRIENDS WITH THE JAPANESE

If you belong to any societies with connections to Japan, use the links when you get here. Your own social or business associations may have some contacts, or even your old alma mater. Many such organizations exist more for foreign residents in Japan, of course, but you can take advantage of them in some cases. At the very least, religious services might provide a key (see suggestions below).

As to casual contact with the people, be advised that

the Japanese, though shy, are only that way because of language barriers. They are very curious, especially the children. (I have seen female teenagers run up to a hairy-chested American man and run their fingers through his Brillo-like mat, then dash away, giggling and screaming.) It's easy to initiate conversations with them in simple English, best done when you have a legitimate question to ask, as the Japanese delight in helping out. If you're seated opposite someone on a train or boat, all you have to do is to practice your few words of Japanese, or even ask, "Excuse me, do you speak English?" The reply, especially from younger people, is likely to be, "A little," and you're on your way. There is practically no antiforeign feeling, as is so often found in certain parts of the world.

Try some of the following, or equivalents special to your case:

- America-Japan Society, 370 Marunouchi Building, 2-4-1 Marunouchi, Chiyoda-ku, Tokyo, tel. 03-201-0780
- Canada-Japan Society, Tsutsumi Flats, 2-17-3 Nagata-cho, Chiyoda-ku, Tokyo, tel. 03-581-0925
- Japan-American Cultural Society, 1-10-3 Kudan Kita, Chiyoda-ku, Tokyo, tel. 03-239-7231
- Japan British Society, Tokyo Building, 2-7-3 Marunouchi, Chiyoda-ku, Tokyo, tel. 03-211-8027
- Harvard Business School Club of Japan, c/o Mr. G. Watanabe, Fertilizer Div., Mitsui & Co., 1-2-1 Otemachi, Chiyoda-ku, Tokyo, tel. 03-285-5405
- Kiwanis Club of Tokyo, Sankei Building (7th floor), 1-7-2 Otemachi, Chiyoda-ku, Tokyo, tel. 03-242-0637
- Lions Club of Tokyo, Honyaesu Building, 1-5-1 Hatchobori, Chuo-ku, Tokyo, tel. 03-552-1761
- Mensa Japan, 7-12-28 Roppongi, Minato-ku, Tokyo, tel. 03-408-3366
- Rotary Club, Osaka, c/o Royal Hotel, 5-3-68 Nakanoshima, Kita-ku, Osaka, tel. 06-441-7930
- Rotary Club, Tokyo, Marunouchi Building, 2-4-1 Marunouchi, Chiyoda-ku, Tokyo, tel. 03-201-3888
- Catholic Bishops Conference of Japan, 10-1 Rokuban-cho, Chiyoda-ku, Tokyo, tel. 03-262-3691
- Jewish Community of Japan, 3-8-8 Hiroo, Shibuya-ku, Tokyo, tel. 03-400-2559
- National Christian Council in Japan, 2-3-18 Nishi Waseda, Shinjuku-ku, Tokyo, tel. 03-203-0372

INSIDERS' TIPS

The Home Visit Program, operated through the Japan National Tourist Organization, allows you to get a glimpse of life in Japan through short visits with families. They are typically middle-class or upper-middle, with the difference that someone in the family speaks good English. Several cities participate in this scheme. There is no charge, but if you have some inexpensive personal memento or wish to bring a flower or small box of sweets or fruits, as you might do at home, it would be a nice gesture. Don't worry if you forget; nobody expects this kind of thing.

Kagoshima: tel. 0992-24-1111
Kobe: tel. 078-232-1010
Kurashiki: tel. 0864-24-3593
Kyoto: tel. 075-752-0215
Nagoya: tel. 052-961-1111
Osaka: tel. 06-261-3948 or 345-2189
Otsu: tel. 0775-23-1234
Sapporo: tel. 011-211-3341
Tokyo: tel. 03-502-1461
Yokohama: tel. 045-681-0007

STUDYING IN JAPAN

Learning Japanese. Although there are several important institutions teaching the language to long-term residents, there are many smaller organizations eager to help you learn a little in a shorter time. In Kyoto, try the YMCA Japanese School, Sanjo Yanagi-no-banba, Nakagyo-ku, Kyoto 604, tel. 075-2311-4388. In Osaka, the Kumon Institute of Education, Kumon Kyoiku Kaikan, 5-6-6 Nishi Nakajima, Yodogawa-ku, Osaka, tel. 06-304-7005. In Tokyo, try one of the following: ISS-JLIS, No. 2 Sogo Building, 1-6 Kojimachi, Chiyoda-ku, Tokyo 102, tel. 03-265-7103; or Edo Language & Culture Center, ICA, 1-26-30 Higashi, Shibuya-ku, Tokyo 150, tel. 03-486-7745.

Ikebana (flower-arranging lessons). Can be taken in Tokyo at the Ohara School, 5-7-17 Minami Aoyama, Minato-ku, Tokyo 107, tel. 03-499-1200, ext. 216/217 (International Division). Classes weekdays only, 10 A.M. to noon, beginners' and advanced courses, and those for teachers and assistant teachers, ranging from ¥1,200 ($7.27) to ¥1,800 ($10.91) per hour. You pay extra for the flowers, of course, and there is no entrance fee.

Zen in English. In Kyoto, there are at least five places to practice meditation or to learn about it:

Kenninji Temple, Shijo-sagaru, Yamato-Oji-dori, Higashiyama-ku, tel. 075-561-0190, has a 1-hour talk on Buddhism and an hour of meditation on the 2nd Sunday of each month, beginning at 8 A.M. Costs ¥300 ($1.82).

Shokokuji Temple, Karasuma Higashi-iru, Imadegawa, Kamigyo-ku, tel. 075-23100301, has the same kind of program on 2nd and 4th Saturdays, starting at 9 A.M. Costs ¥100 (61¢).

Seitaian Temple, tel. 075-491-2579, also has programs on the 1st and 4th Saturdays, with an American Buddhist priest.

Sosenji Zazenkai, Sosenji Temple, Takakura Gojo-sagaru, Shimogyo-ku, tel. 075-351-4270 or 6823, has English lecture on 1st and 3rd Mondays of the month at 6 P.M., followed by *zazen* until 9 P.M.

Zenjoji Temple, in the town of same name outside Kyoto, conducts a 5-day session beginning at 4 A.M. on the Friday before the 2nd Sunday of each month and ending at 5 P.M. on the following Tuesday. (No sessions in February or August.) You are asked to note (this is a test, so be alert) that if the Monday following the 2nd Sunday is the 3rd Monday of the month, the session is from Wednesday to Sunday. You should donate ¥1,000 ($6.06) per day to cover food and bedding costs, but you can donate less if you don't stay overnight. You are busy from 4 A.M. to 9 P.M. on 4 of the days, and inexperienced Zen practitioners are asked to attend the evening session at Sosenji referred to earlier. On the 2nd and 4th Saturdays, there is an evening sitting at the temple, too. Address: Zenjoji, Ujitawara-cho, Tsuzuki-gun, Kyoto Prefecture 610-02, tel. 0774-88-4103.

Tea ceremony demonstrations. These are given at many hotels, such as the Imperial in Tokyo, where you should inquire about time and cost. Also you can visit, in Kyoto, the Ura Senke Center, which has its own tea ceremony research group, at Horikawa Teranouchi-agaru, Kamikyo-ku, Kyoto 602, tel. 075-431-6474.

Crafts. Traditional crafts are the theme of the Kyoto Municipal Museum of Traditional Industry, which has demonstrations and sales. Located just north of Yasaka Jinja Shrine. Closed Mondays and 1 week at New Year's. Watch weaving, doll dressing, pattern cutting, *yuzen* dyeing, etc. 9-2 Seishoji-cho, Okazaki, Sakyo-ku, Kyoto, tel. 075-761-3421.

Woodblock printmaking is demonstrated, and instruction given, at the Gabo Gallery, 27 Miyashiki-cho, Hirano, Kita-ku, Kyoto, tel. 075-464-1655. Open every day from 10 A.M. to 6 P.M. except during O Bon (Festival of the Dead) in mid-August and at New Year's holiday. In 2½ hours, you can learn to make your own woodblock print and send copies of it home as postcards. Only ¥1,000 ($6.06), phone first, come anytime between 1:30 and 3:30 P.M. on the 1st and 3rd Wednesday of each month.

Fabric dying is demonstrated at the Kodai Yuzen Gallery, Takatsuji, Horikawa-nishi, Kyoto 600, tel. 075-811-8101, small admission charge. Apply for class one week in advance; only ten persons per class. Choose from hand-painting or stencil dyeing. There is also a tea ceremony room, where that can be demonstrated to you. Another place, this one demonstrating indigo dyeing, is Aizenkobo, Nakasuji Omiya-nishi, Kamigyo-ku, Kyoto 602, tel. 075-

---

PERILS & PITFALLS

During your travels in Japan, especially if you're there in spring or fall, you may encounter the dreaded Japanese School Trip. In an admirable boost to domestic tourism, the lower and middle schools give organized trips around the country. The kids come in swarms, wearing their uniforms often as not, but certainly wearing identically colored caps so their teachers can sort them out. Predominant colors are yellow, red, green, and orange for easy visibility. They will all cry out hello as you pass by, and that is innocent enough. But heaven help you if some of the children are autograph collectors. They will have learned "Sign, preeze," and will thrust an autograph book and pencil at you. The first will be followed by many more. They're not after your name, but your country, and after you sign, they'll say, "Country, preeze," and you scribble some more. They are like railway train spotters, bird watchers, or other collectors. They don't even want you at all, just your "country." Make them happy—write down Tanzania, Antarctica, or, for a thrill, Russia.

441-0355. Open daily 9 A.M. to 5 P.M. This is an old Kyoto tradition, and the indigo color is particularly attractive.

The Nishijin Textile Center not only will show you how to make a beautiful *kimono,* but loan you one at no charge to wear around for the day. (Warning: They are not easy to wear, so learn how at the center first.) Weaving demonstration, dyeing. If you join the *kimono*-fitting class, you get a 10 percent discount on any goods you buy. Currently offering the course only from December to March. Apply by mail in advance (3 weeks at least) to Nishijin Textile Center, Imadegawa Minami-iru, Horikawa, Kamigyo-ku, Kyoto 602. Enclose a return envelope, addressed to yourself. Give your name, address, day class requested, age, sex, height, and yes or no on whether you want to participate in fitting class. (Otherwise, you're just borrowing the *kimono* at no charge.) If you don't have your own *tabi* (split socks), give your foot size. It will cost ¥1,300 ($7.88) to buy them.

Other studies. If you take the time and trouble to look at local English-language publications in Japan, you can find all sorts of things to study in addition to the ones already mentioned. In the *Kansai Time Out,* for example, published in the Osaka-Kyoto-Kobe area, the following courses were advertised in just one issue: calligraphy, *oshie* (fabric pictures), *kabuki* dancing, flower arranging, flamenco guitar, and *prajna shiatsu* (massage).

SPORTS IN JAPAN

The Japanese are mad for baseball and *sumo,* about equally. If you want to watch the big fat men try to roll each other off the mud-packed ring, be in Tokyo during the three tournaments held there annually (for 14 days from 2nd Sunday of January, May, and September), or in Osaka, Nagoya, or Fukuoka, when it is those cities' turn (for 14 days each from 2nd Sunday in March, July, and November). Although activities start at noon, the best fights are from 4 to 6 P.M. If you can, get *masu* seats (box seats) for about ¥4,000 ($24.24) per person. Also for good seating in balcony, be sure to ask for *shomen* (north) or *mukojomen* (south) seats for best views.

You can see the wrestlers in the stadium restaurant or

adjoining *chaya* (teahouses), but for a real look, visit one of the *heya* (stables) around 8 A.M. for a practice session. Try the Kasugano Heya, 1-7-11 Ryogoku, Sumida-ku, tel. 03-631-1871, or the Kokonoe Heya, 1-16-1 Kamezawa, Sumida-ku, tel. 03-621-1800. Good idea to phone ahead, in Japanese, to find out who is practicing on which day.

You can watch the martial arts performed in many places, and I list a few in Tokyo:

Judo: Kodokan, 1-16-30 Kasuga, Bunkyo-ku, tel. 03-811-7151. You can watch or have lessons.

Karate: Inquire at the World Union of Karate Organizations, Sempaku Shinkokai Building, 1-15-16 Toranomon, Minato-ku, tel. 03-503-6637.

Aikido: International Aikido Federation, 102 Wakamatsu-cho, Shinjuku-ku, tel. 03-203-9236.

There are soccer matches, boxing, Western-style wrestling, swim meets, you name it, all listed in the English-language daily newspapers for venues throughout the country.

The country has excellent skiing facilities, a lot of golfing (but crowded), horseback riding, hiking, and mountain climbing. About the only thing you can't do easily is to rent a boat, as Japan sensibly requires a license before letting anyone operate a powered craft.

TRAVELING WITH CHILDREN

The old saw may still be true that there are two types of travel, first-class and with children. But the Japanese adore children, being fond of those with blond, brown, or red hair, or well-behaved kids with black hair. The Japanese spoil their children up until the time for "examination hell," around the end of high school, when they have to get into good universities or condemn themselves to being "failures" forever. You can park children with hotel-recommended baby-sitters. If that fails, in Tokyo, try Tokyo Domestic Service Center, tel. 03-584-4769, preferably the day before you need someone. Fee about ¥4,000 ($24.24) first 3 hours, ¥1,000 ($6.06) per hour after that.

Before going to Japan, your youngster might want to find a pen pal. Do so through Japan Pen Pal Society, PO Box 6, Tamagawa, Tokyo, or when you get there, phone

03-702-0456. This is for children over 10, and, of course, for adults, too.

If you're in big trouble, try the Toyoko Baby Diaper Service, tel. 03-720-8162. It will provide up to 70 changes per week, for 4 weeks, for about ¥8,000 ($48.48), delivered twice a week. There is a nursery for children 2½ to 4½ at St. Albans (Episcopal) Church, 3-6-25 Shiba Koen, Minato-ku, Tokyo, tel. 03-431-8534. Twice or thrice weekly, depending on age of child.

In addition to keeping the children busy with sports or sightseeing or even studying, you could take them to a *yuenchi* (amusement park), or have a Japanese friend or guide do that for you. Among the biggest is Korakuen, at 1-3 Koraku, Bunkyo-ku, Tokyo, tel. 03-811-2111. It is also the most centrally located. Ferris wheel, ghost house, roller coaster, carousel, go-carts, etc. Open 10 A.M. to 7 P.M. daily, closes earlier in winter, later in summer. Crowds mostly in afternoon, so try mornings to avoid them.

PERILS & PITFALLS

One out of every 500 Americans going abroad, the State Department said at a briefing not too long ago, gets into trouble and requires some form of assistance from the U.S. Embassy. (The officials sounded really put out about it, too.) They die, get arrested, become ill, run out of money, have a passport stolen, or otherwise find reason to impose upon the local embassy to help them. Having lived abroad nearly 20 years (in several countries), I can tell you that the help you get will be pretty slim. The staff say they are overworked, and they can't give you money if you're broke, or call off the cops if you're busted, or even recommend a doctor if you're sick. They will get you a new passport (for a fee, of course), and cable home to your relatives for money, and will make liaison with local authorities for the necessary paperwork if you die. If your folks back home prod them, they might visit you in jail if they are told you might not be treated right. And if in the extreme circumstance they do lend you money, they mark your passport, and it is taken away from you when you get home, returnable only when you pay the government back. There have been many instances of kindness toward citizens, but there are, the State Department says, too many Americans traveling abroad and bothering them. (British and Canadian travelers report better assistance, on the whole, than this.)

READING MATTER IN ENGLISH

Reading matter in English is available on an almost unbelievable scale, with six daily newspapers, many magazines, and whole stores full of books explaining everything Japanese to English-language readers. The four major Japanese national papers *(Asahi, Mainichi, Yomiuri, Nihon Keizai)* publish in English for reasons of prestige, not profit, but there is also the *Japan Times*, the most comprehensive of all, and the *International Shipping & Trade News*. You can also get the *International Herald Tribune* and the Asian Edition of the *Wall Street Journal* on the day of publication. There are Japan editions (in English) of *Newsweek* and *Time*, and excellent local products like the *Tour Companion*, distributed free at hotels and the Tourist Information Centers, and the *Tokyo Journal*, ¥200 ($1.21) at some bookstores, hotel newsstands, etc. Major book publishers in English here include Tuttle and Kodansha International. One of the best, and biggest, hotel bookshops (with plenty of English-language titles) is in the Hotel Okura basement, Tokyo. Another good one is in the Miyako Hotel, Osaka.

LEAVING JAPAN

GETTING TO THE AIRPORT

The same services that brought you in will take you back. To avoid disappointment, reserve the airport bus as soon as you can at your hotel's front desk. (Or make other arrangements if you wish to use the train, taxi, or chauffeured car to the terminal.) Remember to keep enough Japanese yen to pay your ¥2,000 ($12.12) departure tax if you leave via Narita Airport. The regular shops at Narita are extensive, occupying the central part of the terminal and on several floors, along with dozens of restaurants. The shops' prices are about the same as you would find in town, so no problem. There is even a fairly inexpensive supermarket in the basement where you can buy a snack of yogurt, a sandwich, or whatever. There is a small duty-free shop, for the usual liquor, tobacco, perfume, etc., even some audiovisual equipment, inside the customs area as you depart, but there are no bargains here, so I don't recommend it.

Remember to exchange your Japanese yen (except for that vital ¥2,000 departure tax at Narita) before going through immigration's passport control, as there is no exchange facility inside. You may take out up to ¥5,000,000 ($30,303) in Japanese currency if you wish (!) and any amount of foreign currency. This is where you may be asked to show your tax-free purchases, so keep them and the papers relating to them in your hand luggage and ready for inspection if required.

Departure Tax

From Tokyo's Narita Airport, there is a Passenger Service Facility Charge, a euphemism for departure tax, to help pay for this expensive new place: ¥2,000 ($12.12), which you must remember to have ready, in cash only, as you enter the immigration area. It's ¥1,000 ($6.06) for children 2 to 12; free for under 2. Transit passengers continuing their travel by the same or first connecting flight on the same day are not taxed. There is no departure tax from Japan's other international airports (Osaka, Fukuoka, Naha, etc.).

CUSTOMS ON RETURNING HOME

American customs. If you are an American citizen, you may make an oral declaration in most cases, and the limit without duty is $400 (retail value), provided you haven't used that limit up in the past 30 days, and that you have been out of the U.S. longer than 48 hours. After the first $400 exemption, you pay duty of only 10 percent on the next $1,000 worth of goods. You may pool your family's exemptions if traveling together, but those under 19 can't have exemptions for liquor or perfume. You are allowed only 1 bottle of spirits, 1 bottle of wine duty-free, but the duty isn't high if you bring in more. Importing fresh fruit, plants, meats, soil, etc., is forbidden, as are the usual no-nos, such as drugs, guns, pornography, etc. Remember that you may mail home small packages valued up to $25 without paying duty, though this cannot include alcohol, tobacco, or perfume. Antiques (defined as being over 100 years old) and other works of art are generally exempt from duty, too.

British customs. You're allowed to bring in the items on the non-EEC list, meaning 200 cigarettes or equivalent, 1 liter of strong spirits, 2 liters of still wine, 50 grams of perfume, and .25 liter of toilet water, plus other gifts up to the value of £10.

Canadian customs. You may bring in duty-free a maximum of 200 cigarettes or equivalent and 40 ounces of liquor, with a total exemption of $150. You may mail home unsolicited gifts of up to $15 each.

TOKYO

Tokyo wears a mask to fend off inquiring foreigners. It has done its job well. A highly polished visage, cunningly crafted, its half-closed eyes spell mystery, its chin determination. The forehead bulges with wisdom, the cheeks with prosperity. The mouth, flaunting seductive lips, remains firmly closed. There is no clue as to its age, or, for that matter, its sex.

This is the face the Japanese want us to see when in Tokyo. (There are other, simpler, masks for places like Kyoto, Nara, Hiroshima, or Osaka.) It is the disguise of Japan, Inc., a visage which says, "You *gaijin* (outsiders) will never, ever, understand me." It does not say, but thinks, with not a trace of irony, "And I like it that way." This is the face of all Japan, so far as the media of the world would have it, making of this nation a land of successful schizophrenics, working like beavers to build the economy, yet possessed of deep spiritual attitudes handed down from ancient times, cultural skills which will never die, and a group ethic combining Puritanism and Zen. It is, in fact, the collective countenance of a myth, of a super-race that doesn't exist.

This is not a book on How to Understand the Japanese, of which type there are plenty, but a guide. What this means to a visitor, as it meant to me, a former longtime resident, is that we must look beneath the surface of Tokyo, or any other place in Japan, to lift the mask.

This official mask, of a Tokyo with gleaming skyscrapers, efficient public transportation, and dramatic ancient theatrical presentations, is real, but it is only the first of many layers of faces, just as real, and easier to read.

There are, at least, five Tokyo masks, and I'll reveal them for visitors in the order of interest. They are:

1. Establishment Tokyo
2. Old-Fashioned Tokyo

3. Boomtown Tokyo
4. Foreign Tokyo
5. Expense-Account Tokyo

In short, there are several cities here, not just one. Japanese and foreign writers for at least a century have described Tokyo as a collection of villages linked together (so is London), and everyone is impressed with the amazing vitality of the place (as everyone is with New York). Many have been impressed by the fey serendipity of Tokyo, the juxtaposition of gray lumps of concrete and glass with an exquisite little temple, its tile roof nestling amid azalea bushes. (But juxtaposition has no monopoly in Tokyo, as any visitor to Philadelphia can attest.)

The trap most visitors fall into is just going along for the ride. If they're on a tour, they do as they're told, and that's the end of it. Exhausted after a day of bouncing around the capital in a bus, and suffering from museum feet, they flop in their hotel rooms in the evening and don't emerge until the next roll call by the tour guide. Conversely, independent travelers may not have enough time to spend, and try to rush off wildly in all directions, without a plan. Yes, you need a plan. Sorry, I know it's a vacation, but you need a plan to see Tokyo, unless you just want serendipity to whisk you where it will. (I love to do that, but then, I know I am coming back. If this may be the only time you'll ever be in Tokyo, you have to plan.)

Tokyo is multicentered, with about 12 main areas to contend with. Most important to the foreign visitors are (1) the Ginza, sometimes called the Fifth Avenue of Tokyo; (2) Asakusa, old-fashioned Tokyo; and (3) the Akasaka-Roppongi area, where hotels and nightlife are predominant. West of these areas are the Imperial Palace and two important transportation centers, Shinjuku and Shibuya. To the north is Ueno, where trains leave for Tohoku and Hokkaido. To the south is Shinagawa, where you catch trains for the beaches south of Yokohama. Most of what you want to see will be in these few areas.

Treat Tokyo as several cities, and decide, perhaps, to see one or two of them. Or parts of all. If you're here for 2 weeks, you can see everything, or at least enough to understand all five Tokyos. And, as some cities can be seen chronologically (Rome, for instance), or even geographically (Venice is a good example), Tokyo is best seen mask by mask. (You should remember, too, that 50 percent of Tokyo was simply obliterated in the firebombings of World War II. That took care of what little was left after the Great Earthquake of 1926. And the Japanese habit of building with wood ensures that there are very few ancient structures in the city.)

HOW TO GET AROUND

If you are rich, hire a car and driver (English-speaking) through your hotel. If you're super-rich, hire car, driver, and guide in the same manner, or through Japan Travel Bureau, tel. 03-276-7803, or other reputable agent.

If you're not rich, consider a taxi for the day, but write down the itinerary and have the hotel front desk translate it into Japanese for you and arrange for the taxi. Do not let the hotel get a *haiya* (hired car) for you, as that will be a lot more expensive.

Don't consider a rental car, especially in Tokyo; see page 68 for the reasons.

Subways

I suggest the subway wherever possible, then occasional taxis when the subway isn't practical. Subway maps are available, free, everywhere (hotels, shops, department stores, even the subway ticket booths) and in English. To buy a ticket, there are three techniques: (1) In the ticket-machine area, try to find the window with a human being selling tickets, put down a 500-yen coin or note ($3.03), and utter your destination. (2) More complicated, find the overhead illuminated chart showing the subway grid, with names of stations and the fares to those stations written together. Most such charts are, of course, in Japanese, but there are a few in "English," or romanized characters. Find your destination, note the price, go to machine, and insert the coins. (3) Trickier, buy a minimum fare from a machine—currently ¥140 (85¢)—and board your train. At the end of the trip (see below), when you turn in your ticket, pause, and if the ticket-taker says something, you know you have to pay more. There will be a fare-adjustment window nearby; that is where you have to go. You may, if you wish, ask the taker "OK?"—now a Japanese phrase—and he will probably say, "OK." If he says anything else, you probably will have to cough up more money.

INSIDERS' TIPS

There is a 1-day pass on seven of Tokyo's ten subway lines, including the ones that serve most tourist destinations, namely, the Ginza, Chiyoda, Hibiya, Yurakucho, Hanzo-mon, Tozai, and Marunouchi lines. Only ¥600 ($3.64), it allows you to ride anywhere all day, and can be purchased from 7:40 A.M. to 8 P.M. at any major subway ticket office. Just ask for "*ichi-nichi pass, kudasai*" and hand over ¥600. A monthly pass costs ¥13,700 ($83.03), and should be bought the day before you wish to use it. A 3-month pass is ¥39,050 ($236.67), a 6-month (watch out, you've over-stayed your visa!) is ¥73,980 ($448.36). Buy at major stations, such as Akasaka Mitsuke, Ginza, or Shimbashi. Again, only on seven lines listed.

As you will have noted, you must keep your ticket until the end of the trip and hand it in. This applies to all forms of public transportation in Japan, except air.

Taxis

Always have with you the name and address, in Japanese, as well as telephone number, of your hotel. The hotel's matchbook or card is just the thing for this. If you think your destination might be obscure, get your hotel to write it down in Japanese, preferably with a phone number. As there are very few named streets in Japan, less-than-famous destinations are often hard to find. (Japanese houses and buildings are arranged first by ward, then precinct, then "block," and finally by number. Until recently, buildings were numbered according to when they were erected, not by geography.) This is why so many advertisements in Japan carry a small map showing the shop's location.

Buses

With the exception of the airport bus, you can forget about these, unless you read Japanese, or perhaps speak it. (In some smaller towns, bus transport is possible, as I'll explain later.)

Trains

The Japan National Railway has two lines in Tokyo which may be a great help to travelers. The first, the Yamanote Line, circles the main portion of the city, and the second, the Chuo (Central) Line, cuts across the circle from Tokyo Station to Shinjuku and farther to the west. If you have a Japan Rail Pass, you can ride these free. The trains are just as good as the subway trains, and like them should be avoided during rush hours if possible (7 to 9 A.M. and 5 to 7 P.M.), Monday through Friday. To buy tickets on the JNR lines, follow the same suggestions as for subways (above).

Private railway lines go from four or five major terminals and seven minor ones out to the suburbs, or to places like Nikko, Yokohama, and Hakone. There is practically no use of *romaji* (romanized Japanese), so you'll need help trying to use any of these lines: Keihin Railway from Shinagawa to Yokohama and beyond, Keisei Railway from Ueno to Narita Airport, Keio Teito from Shinjuku westward, Tokyu from Shibuya to Yokohama, Odakyu from Shinjuku to Hakone and Kamakura, Seibu from Ikebukuro or Shinjuku westward, and Tobu from Asakusa to Nikko and other northern points.

TOKYO IN A HURRY ITINERARIES

If you have only 1 day: Imperial Palace, Ginza, Asakusa Kannon Temple, Asakusa Shrine, Ueno Park, Tokyo National Museum, Takashimaya Department Store, dinner in Akasaka or Roppongi

If you have a 2nd day: Meiji Shrine, Omote Sando shopping area, kabuki theater

If you have a 3rd day: Akihabara Electronic Center, Tokyo Metropolitan Art Museum, National Museum of Modern Art, Nishi Shinjuku, Kabuki-cho nightlife area

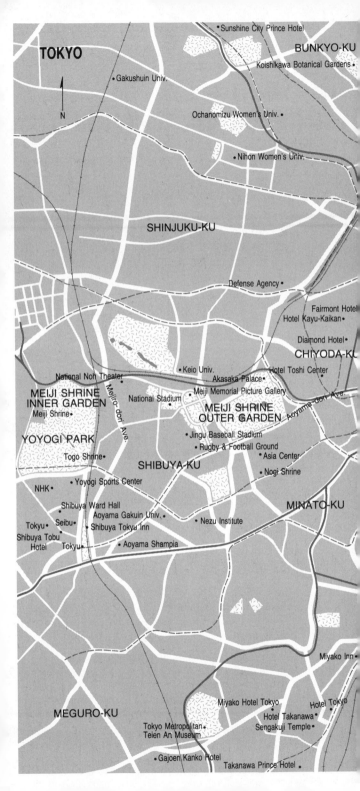

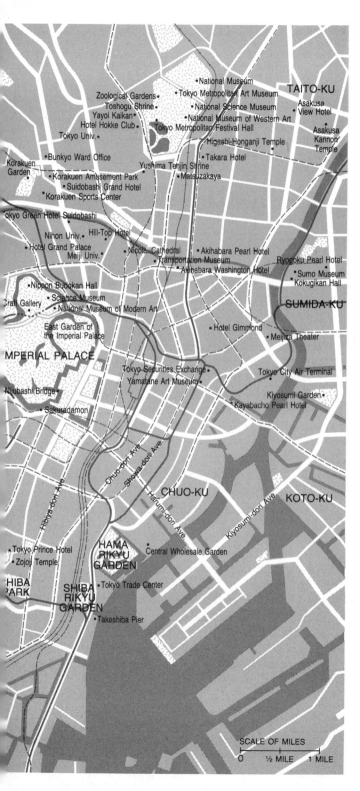

TOKYO IN A HURRY

You have to see Establishment Tokyo, one of the five masks the capital wears, if you have only 1 day. You can't go home and say you didn't see the Ginza, for instance. My advice is to take a half-day tour in the morning (they also function in the afternoon) from JTB-Hato Bus or Gray Line. These can be arranged through your hotel or you can telephone JTB at 03-276-7777, or Hato Bus at 03-435-6081. The JTB-Hato Bus arrangement offers two different morning tours and two in the afternoon, each costing ¥4,500 ($27.27). The Beautiful Morning Tour includes Tokyo Tower, Keio University, a tea ceremony at bonsai-decorated Happoen Garden, the Ginza, the Imperial Palace East Garden, and a demonstration of flower arranging and cultured-pearl growing. The Highlight Morning Tour does the pearl and flower bit, but also visits the Imperial Palace Plaza and World Trade Center Building and drives through the Kanda, Akihabara, and Ueno areas to Asakusa Kannon Temple with its old-fashioned shopping center, then takes you on a cruise down the Sumida River and ends at the Ginza. Each of these tours is accomplished in only 4½ hours. The all-day tours, interestingly enough, get about the same amount of sightseeing covered, but include lunch at Chinzanso, a rambling old villa once owned by Baron Fujita. The Gray Line Morning Tour, also costing ¥4,500 ($27.27), covers Tokyo Tower, Imperial Palace Plaza, the Asakusa Kannon Temple, and the Ginza. The afternoon tour is not very interesting.

Should you decide to spend the day on your own, or if you wish to combine some sightseeing with a half-day bus tour, consider the following highlights:

Get yourself to the Imperial Palace ♛ ♛ for starters. The best views of this immense target in the middle of Tokyo are between Sakurada-mon (*mon* = gate) at its southern extremity and the Palace Hotel at its eastern extremity. (Nearest subway stations: Sakurada-mon, Hibiya, and Nijubashi-mae; *mae* = in front of.) After you've looked at the guard towers (all you can see) and the famous double bridge, over which the public (including you) enters the palace to see the emperor on January 1 and April 29 (his birthday), walk eastward to the Ginza.

Where the palace moat meets the front line of Japan,

Inc., the line of buildings stretching south to north from near the Imperial Hotel to the Palace Hotel, you'll find the former headquarters ♛ of General Douglas MacArthur, the only Yankee shogun. It's the low, dark building just north of the police box here. From the Dai Ichi Seimei (Number One Insurance) company building, the general ruled Japan after World War II, and it was here that the emperor came to call, fearful and proud, to acknowledge MacArthur's supremacy and offer to take upon himself the blame for all the war crimes committed from 1936 to 1945. This is one of the few prewar buildings still standing in the Marunouchi district, headquarters of Mitsubishi, Mitsui, and the other giant trading firms that run the country.

Continue eastward and you'll be in the heart of the Ginza. Here familiar names leap out at you: Sony, National, Canon, McDonald's. This is still the heart of commercial Japan, and though other areas have bigger crowds and higher turnovers, the Ginza is still tops in prestige. On Sundays, the entire Ginza-dori (Ginza Street) ♛ ♛ ♛ is blocked off for pedestrian use between Nihonbashi and Shimbashi (*bashi* = bridge). In addition to the showrooms for famous products and the always-crowded department stores, go behind the main streets and look at the small shops, selling elegant ceramics, imported clothing, or Japanese gourmet food, like cakes and biscuits.

It should be midmorning now, and time to see Old-Fashioned Tokyo. Get on the subway, Ginza Line, at the Ginza Station (underneath the tall, round San-Ai Building), or at Kyobashi Station (underneath the Meidiya Food Store), or Nihonbashi (underneath Takashimaya Department Store), if you've walked that far north. Get off at the end of the line, Asakusa Station. Walk 2 blocks west (away from the river), and you'll see a wonderful 1958 copy of an old Japanese temple gate, with a huge red lantern. This is the Kaminari-mon (Thunder Gate) ♛ ♛ ♛ of Asakusa Kannon Temple. Kinryuzan Sensoji (its proper name, "Gold Dragon Mountain Asakusa Temple") is a collection of buildings, centered on the Main Hall, but you don't come here for the architecture (see below) or the antiquity. You come here to get a sense of old Tokyo, old Japan, with the crowds of farmers and school kids, gawkers and hustlers, buyers and sellers that make up this large compound.

Behind Thunder Gate stretches Nakamise-dori ♛ ♛ ♛, the street of shops, a wonderful collection of everything from food to toys, hammers to crackers, *kimono* to masks (more than five, you can bet!). If you don't know what else to buy, try some *sembei* (rice crackers), which come in hundreds of varieties, especially if they are being baked on the spot. Other popular shops are for seaweed alone, for *tenugui* (hand towels), *Ginkado* (fans and other accessories for the dance), and *Matsuzakaya* (hair ornaments). Behind the Nakamise are residences, shops, little factories-in-the-home, and several fascinating restaurants (see listings). After seeing the temple, it's a good idea to have lunch in this area.

The Main Hall ♛ of the temple is new (1958), ugly as only ferroconcrete can make a building, but nonetheless a moving experience. Here you'll see many worshipers approach the huge incense burner in front of the Main Hall, brushing clouds of the smoke toward them. It is thought to be helpful in cases of sickness, especially trachoma. The hall's predecessor was built by Tokugawa Ieyasu in the 16th century, though there has been a temple here for 900 years before that. During the great air raids of March 1945, fear of the American B-29s and the ensuing fire storms drove thousands of Japanese into the temple compound, which had survived the earthquake and subsequent fire of 1923. Their lucky temple was not so lucky this time; the Main Hall burned to the ground, and many perished on the spot. (Others, in their thousands, drowned in the nearby Sumida River.) High up under the eaves, inside, are some interesting paintings, which had been removed during the war and stored for protection.

INSIDERS' TIPS

There is a Tourist Information Center (a rare English-speaking-staffed one) in Asakusa, just opposite the *koban* (police box) at Kaminari-mon (Thunder Gate).

Asakusa Shrine ♛, north of the temple, and a Shinto place of worship, survived both earthquake and air raids, dating back to 1649. If you have time, visit here for a short lesson in the difference between Shinto architecture and symbolism and those of Buddhism, evinced by the temple you saw earlier.

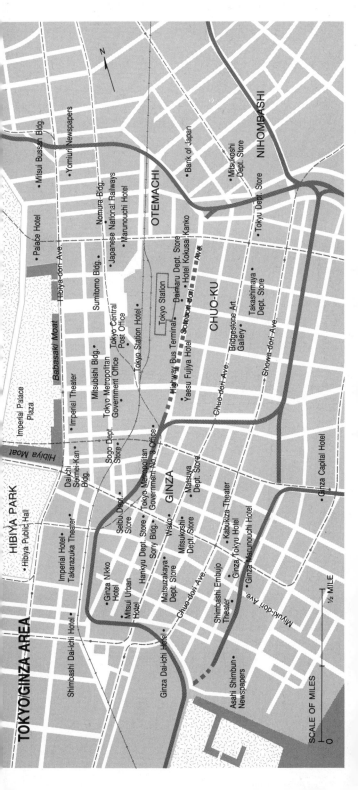

TOKYO/GINZA AREA

HIBIYA PARK

Hibiya Public Hall

Imperial Palace Plaza

Hibiya Moat

Babasaki Moat

Palace Hotel

Mitsui Bussan Bldg.

Yomiuri Newspapers

Bank of Japan

NIHOMBASHI

Mitsukoshi Dept. Store

Tokyu Dept. Store

Nomura Bldg.

Japanese National Railways

Marunouchi Hotel

OTEMACHI

Sumitomo Bldg.

Tokyo Central Post Office

Tokyo Station

Daimaru Dept. Store

Hotel Kokusai Kanko

Tokyo Station Hotel

Highway Bus Terminal

Sotobori-dori Ave.

CHUO-KU

Bridgestone Art Gallery

Takashimaya Dept. Store

Showa-dori Ave.

Imperial Theater

Mitsubishi Bldg.

Tokyo Metropolitan Government Office

Yaesu Fujiya Hotel

Chuo-dori Ave.

Daiichi Seimei-Kan Bldg.

Sogo Dept. Store

Tokyo Metropolitan Government No. 3 Office

GINZA

Matsuya Dept. Store

Ginza Capital Hotel

Imperial Hotel

Takarazuka Theater

Seibu Dept. Store

Hankyu Dept. Store

Sony Bldg.

Wako

Mitsukoshi Dept. Store

Kabukiza Theater

Ginza Tokyu Hotel

Ginza Marunouchi Hotel

Shimbashi Dai-ichi Hotel

Ginza Nikko Hotel

Mitsui Urban Hotel

Matsuzakaya Dept. Store

Chuo-dori Ave.

Shimbashi Embujo Theater

Miyuki-dori Ave.

Ginza Dai-ichi Hotel

Asahi Shimbun Newspapers

SCALE OF MILES

0   ½ MILE

N

After lunch, if you're feeling ambitious, get yourself over to Ueno Park, preferably by taxi, otherwise by subway (same line, Ginza, back to Ueno Station). Come up for air, and strike out into the park, passing a statue of Saigo Takamori, a hero of the Meiji Restoration (late 19th century).

On your left is Kiyomizu Kannon-do Temple ₩ (1631), a branch of the more famous edifice in Kyoto. Farther north are four museums, and if you are ambitious and have time, you should visit at least one of them, the Tokyo National Museum ₩ ₩ ₩ ₩, at the far end.

Containing the largest, and best, collection of Japanese art anywhere, the Tokyo Kokuritsu Hakubutsukan (its Japanese name) consists of three large buildings and, nearby, two halls of Kan Eiji Temple. The most important of the three is the Hon Kan (Main Building), erected in 1937 and designed by the same man who built General MacArthur's headquarters in Marunouchi, the Dai Ichi Insurance Company. The museum is no improvement. There are, throughout the three buildings, 84 items which have been designated National Treasures, and 520 called Important Cultural Properties. (A person, by the way, can be designated a Living National Treasure, and there are several of them, all artists or craftsmen, and most of them in their 70s or 80s, or even older.) The displays change frequently, and labeling in English is inadequate, as is the terrible lighting, but go, nonetheless. Sculpture, lacquer-ware, swords, ceramics, it's all here.

Except for archaeology, which you'll find in the smaller building on the left as you enter, the Hyokeikan ₩ ₩ ₩ (1909). Look here for the *haniwa* (tomb figures) and roof tiles. English-language explanations are good, as is the lighting.

On the right as you enter the compound is the Toyo Kan (Asia Building) ₩ ₩, built in 1968 and devoted to non-Japanese Asian art. It is the most attractive of the three buildings, but has no Japanese objects.

If you stay too long at the museum, you may as well return to your hotel and rest up for dinner. If you've given the place a quick look and it's only about 4 P.M., take the same subway line back down to the Nihonbashi or Ginza areas to look at a department store, especially if you want to do some little bit of shopping anyhow. If you're really

---

INSIDERS' TIPS

If you're at the Tokyo National Museum on a Thursday, you're lucky, as the Treasure House of Horyuji Homotsukan (Horyuji Temple) 👑 👑 👑 is open only on that day, and only if it's not raining, or hot and humid, in which cases it is still closed. Horyuji Temple, near Nara, gave several hundred of its exhibits to the museum back in 1878. Most of the items date back to the 7th century, and in this treasure house (1964), behind the Hyokeikan, there are wonderful scrolls, masks, daggers, etc.

---

tired, you can even take a private railway line from the National Museum (entrance behind the Horyuji Treasure House) down to Asakusa Station of the Ueno Keisei-Ueno Line. It's underground, like the subway, but as it is the end of the line, you have to come up and go down again for the regular subway, Ginza Line, across the street.

For the Takashimaya Department Store 👑 👑, which I think is the best in the Ginza, get off at Nihonbashi Station, just underneath the store. In the basement, should the entrance off the subway be open, you'll find the food section, filled with things you've never seen before. (If you don't like Japanese food, you may wish you never had seen them.) Pickles and their odor set the theme, followed closely by soy sauce, which is used, it seems, in everything, from rice crackers to seaweed. A little comparison shopping will show you that in this relatively expensive food store, meat is priced as high as the sky, and food generally is not cheap. Note especially the prices of imported items, whether they be oranges or whiskey, and of the luscious luxury fruit, such as Japanese melons, strawberries, apples, and *nashi* (the apple-shaped pear, tasting like a pear, but mouth-wateringly crisp and crunchy). Here also is the antiques and secondhand section, where very rarely you can find a relative bargain. Only high-quality goods are accepted here, many coming from Japanese families, longtime customers. This is, after all, the department store that is a purveyor to the Imperial Household. (Unlike the case in Britain, holders of warrants to supply the sovereign with goods are not permitted to use this fact in their advertising.)

Higher up, you can safely ignore the usual things department stores sell throughout the world and head for the *kimono* section, the ceramics section, or, for late news on the electronic front, the audiovisual department. There are restaurants in the store, displays of art, and departments for weddings, from *kimono* to gifts.

Should Takashimaya be closed (as it is on Wednesdays), head for Mitsukoshi♛, 6 blocks north on the Ginza (nearest subway station, on same Ginza Line, Mitsukoshi-mae; closed Mondays).

Around 5 or 6 P.M. you might want to rest a bit, but around 7, arrange for dinner outside the hotel, perhaps in Akasaka or Roppongi, where you can savor yet a third Tokyo mask, that of Expense-Account Tokyo (Akasaka) or Foreign Tokyo (Roppongi).

TOKYO ON THE 2ND DAY

If you have 2 days for seeing Tokyo, you'll have the opportunity to look at the last of the five cities making up this metropolis, Boomtown Tokyo. Start off your second day, however, with a peaceful morning visit to Meiji Jingu (Meiji Shrine) ♛ ♛ ♛, on the western edge of the city's center. (Nearest subway station, Meiji Jingu-mae on the Chiyoda-Line; nearest JNR station, Harajuku on Yamanote Line.)

Built to honor the emperor who brought Japan into the modern world, Meiji Shrine was completed in 1920, destroyed by air raids in 1945, rebuilt in 1958. A haven of peace and quiet (except on festival days), Meiji Shrine is best approached through the main entrance (near Harajuku JNR Station), under two gigantic *torii* gates (the symbols of a Shinto shrine) and down a broad avenue of trees. En route, you may wish to visit the famous iris garden (open March through October), especially in May or June, when the iris are in full bloom.

The Honden (Main Hall) is absolutely beautiful, despite its youth, as it was made in the traditional manner, using traditional materials, and in a style unchanged for nearly 2,000 years. Note the worshipers washing their hands and mouths at the entrance, a symbolic act of great importance, since Shintoism's main enemy is not sin, but uncleanliness in any form. (The Judeo-Christian concept of sin had to have a new word invented for it when Christian missionaries tried to explain things to the pragmatic Japanese.) You may also see the faithful (or hopeful) watching a purification ceremony in the outer courtyard or worship hall, paid for by anyone who wants such a ceremony. In addition to the beating of a drum, the waving of a sacred *sakaki* wand, festooned with white paper strips, will clear the air of any evil spirits.

The Treasure House of Meiji Shrine is of interest only if you have plenty of time to spare. Its main feature is the carriage Emperor Meiji once used.

After this bit of serenity, plunge yourself into ultramodern Tokyo, an aspect of that fifth mask, representing the Boomtown ambience. As Japan has grown to be the second-richest country in the world (in terms of GNP), her citizens have tended to save a lot of their money (around 20 percent on average), and to spend the rest on clothing, electronic equipment, vacation trips, and gourmet food. (They don't spend it on buying houses, as land is so scarce.) The result is conspicuous consumption, not by a few plutocrats, but by masses of middle-income Japanese, especially the young.

You can see part of this craze for the fashionable, gimmicky, or just plain crazy on Omote-Sando, one of several streets in this neighborhood specializing in the latest in everything. Leading eastward from JNR Harajuku Station's south exit, this street has world-famous boutiques (Hanae Mori's main shop, for example) and souvenir shops left over from the days of GI Joe (Oriental Bazaar). There's an Italian restaurant (named French Quarter; don't ask), but more fun is the Café de Rope, a terraced place where you can sit and watch the people. At the other end of the street is the Key West Club, where you can do the same thing.

If it's Sunday, save Omote-Sando for later. When you emerge from Meiji Shrine, you'll face a crowd of young kids break-dancing, doing the bobby-sox hop, and otherwise strutting their stuff, always in groups, at the entrance of Yoyogi Park, adjoining the shrine. The few Japanese punks show up here on Sundays in a kind of established thumb-your-nose session, shocking their elders (who come in droves to watch) and causing foreign observers to wonder if this is, after all, the beginning of the end for Japan, too. (It isn't; most of the kids change their clothing before going back home and show up at school, factory, or office the next day looking as brushed, tailored, and manicured as every other student, factory worker, or *sarariman*— "salaryman.")

About now, you should be thinking of an early lunch. I suggest you try Akasaka or Roppongi, whichever one you didn't go to last night for dinner (see listings). If you want to eat in this area, try the aforementioned French Quarter, just around the corner from Kiddy Land, or Ryu no Ko, a cheap and good Chinese place on Meiji-dori Street, one block north of the Omote-Sando crossing.

After lunch, I think you might easily visit one or two antique shops, not to buy so much as to get an idea of the range of Japanese artistry. You might want to do this back at or near your hotel, as the main event of the day is yet to come, and you will probably want to change clothes or just rest.

This main event is the Kabukiza ♛ ♛ ♛ ♛ ♛, the *kabuki* theater, which, in one evening, will infuse enough Japanese culture, theater, and, perhaps, history to last a lifetime, if you don't want more. Visiting Tokyo without seeing the *kabuki* is almost as bad as seeing London without the theater or Paris without the opera. Tickets can be had through your hotel, or by going to the theater in advance, or by phoning 03-541-3131 in English for reservations. There are two performances daily, 11 A.M. and 4:30 P.M. Closed in August and for the last 5 days of each month. Tickets range from ¥1,500 ($9.09) to ¥11,000 ($66.67) at time of writing. The performances last about 4 to 5 hours, divided into two or three plays or scenes from different plays. A combination of drama, opera, dancing, and orchestral virtuosity, *kabuki* is *the* traditional art form of Japan. If you don't want to pay for an entire session, you can purchase a restricted ticket, about ¥1,000 ($6.06), for the 4th floor, but you can't see the most important part of the theater, the *hanamichi* ("flower walk"), along which the most important actors make their entrances and exits.

You will already know that all the parts are played by men, a feature of *kabuki* since the mid-17th century. The plays were originated by women, some of whom were probably prostitutes, in Kyoto in 1596. The authorities were upset by the fact that women played the men's roles, and vice versa, so the managers tried the novel idea of

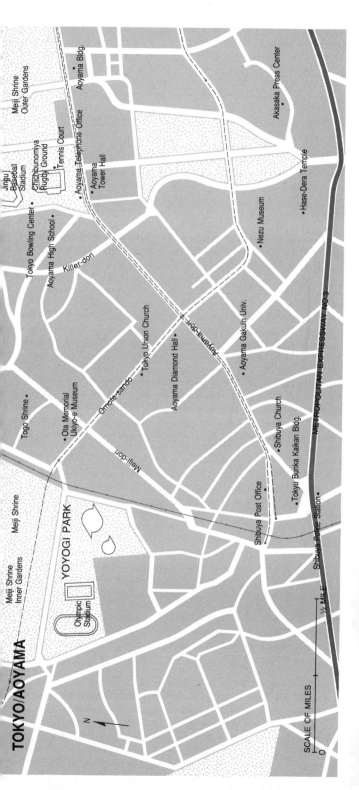

having each sex play its own role, but the authorities finally forbade women altogether. There is always an orchestra of drums and *samisen* (a kind of banjo), and one or more chanters who describe what is going on. *Kuromaku*, stagehands clad from head to toe in black, including masks, move props around and are not supposed to be seen by the audience. They also help actors with onstage costume changes and the like. For at least 250 years, the Kabukiza has had a revolving stage, which allows fairly quick changes of scene. If you come for nothing else, you will enjoy the scenery and the gorgeous costumes. The Kabukiza is a private enterprise, owned by Shochiku Company, which also makes movies.

Although no librettos with English translations are available, there is simultaneous interpreting (see below), and several excellent books on *kabuki* are available in the better hotel newsstands or bookshops.

If you plan to buy tickets at the theater yourself, be advised that advance tickets are sold on the far right, then, reading right to left, tickets for the 1st and 2nd floors, then a booth for 3rd-floor tickets, and to the far left, tickets for the 4th floor. An Earphone Guide, through which you can enjoy the *kabuki* in English, can be rented for about ¥600 ($3.64) plus deposit of ¥1,000 ($6.06). There is also an English-language program. You may wish to eat dinner at the Kabukiza, and I recommend it, especially if you are with friends. Go to the restaurant of your choice (there are three—Western, Japanese, and a *sushi* bar) and place your order before the theater if possible, so you won't have to wait. The traditional restaurant serves a fine meal of broiled eel, done in soy sauce on a bed of rice, in a nice lacquered box, with a couple of side dishes, for less than ¥2,000 ($12.12).

The Kabukiza is on Harumi-dori Street, east of the main Ginza 4-chome intersection, and just above the Higashi Ginza Station of the Hibiya and Toei Asakusa subway lines. The building you see today, by the way, was erected in 1925, in the traditional Momoyama style of architecture dating from the 16th century.

Should the Kabukiza be closed, ask about performances at the Kokuritsu Gekijo (National Theater) ♨ ♨, at your hotel, or phone 03-265-7411, or the third possibility, Shimbashi Embujo ♨, tel. 03-541-2211. Tickets at the National range from ¥1,000 to ¥6,300 ($6.06 to $38.18) at press time, half the Kabukiza price.

At the Kabukiza, you'll see the Japanese in their second-most-formal wear (the ultimate is a wedding or funeral), and this is often a place for *mi-ai*, the planned encounters between families with marriageable children, who are then given the chance to look one another over, without any commitment. Plenty of souvenirs are available, and you would be wise, if interested in the theater, to look for *The Kabuki Handbook* or one of the other good explanations of this form of entertainment.

A 3RD DAY IN TOKYO

Having seen all five faces of Tokyo during your first 2 days, you can now slow down the pace somewhat. It's hard to put the new, dynamic Japan of Sony and Hitachi and Nissan out of mind, so I suggest giving in to the impulse, and a trip in the morning to Akihabara ♛ ♛, the electronic heaven for shoppers. (Nearest subway stations: Akihabara on the Hibiya Line, Iwamoto-cho on the Toei Shinjuku Line. Nearest JNR station: Akihabara on Yamanote and Sobu lines.)

In the forest of buildings housing electronic equipment, there are only a few catering to foreigners in English and/or providing the tax-free forms which help you save on your purchases. Laox, with eight stores in the area, has a tax-free floor (the 7th) in its main store just west of JNR Akihabara Station, tel. 03-255-9041. Yamagiwa and Hirose also have tax-free corners. They all take major credit cards, and you need your passport to get tax-free privileges.

Before shopping here, you will have checked out the price of the items you are interested in, especially with discount stores back home. Then compare with the prices here. Make sure the equipment you are buying is calibrated to U.S. conditions and standards, and that the instruction booklet is in English. Don't settle for "It's in the carton." Laox will deliver to major hotels, and all the places will pack for carrying home, or will arrange for mailing and delivery themselves, if you give them enough time.

After a couple of hours of the electronic jungle, lunch may sound good, and in Kanda, look for a traditional eating place, featuring noodles, *dombori*, or *tonkatsu*. In addition to restaurants in our listing, you could experiment on your own and search. If you could read Japanese, it would be easy. But if you can't, just look for simple little places with glass display cases outside. There you'll find the reproductions in realistic wax of dishes that are noodles, or pork cutlets on rice, or whatever else may be featured within. The prices will also be written there, and if you're lucky, in Arabic numerals instead of the Chinese figures (which are now traditionally Japanese). In any case, the meal will be cheap, under ¥1,000 ($6.06), not counting drinks.

In the afternoon, it's museum time, so I hope you're wearing comfortable shoes. Though there are one or two more important museums, two in Ueno Park deserve your attention because of their quality, and also because they are close to hand; the others are not.

The first of these is the Tokyo-to Bijutsukan (Tokyo Metropolitan Art Museum) ♛ ♛, in the same Ueno Park as the Tokyo National Museum you saw on the first day. Get yourself to Ueno Station by subway again (Ginza Line) or by JNR on the Yamanote Line. The museum is halfway through the park, on the left, or west, across a little pond from the National Museum of Western Art (great, but you didn't come to Japan to see Rodin, did you?) and the National Science Museum.

The Tokyo Metropolitan has its own collection of Japanese modern art, in itself worthy of a trip, but, even more important, it rents out the galleries to private Japanese art groups. Here you might see anything from photographs to Nihonga paintings (basically ink and watercolors) or sculpture, whatever the sponsoring group is presenting. All of it will be the latest work of Japanese artists or craftsmen. The building, completed in 1975, was designed by the same man who built Tokyo Metropolitan Festival Hall, the performing-arts edifice across the park, south of the National Museum of Western Art.

When finished with the Metropolitan, take a taxi, if possible, because you're going to the Imperial Palace, to the National Museum of Modern Art ♛ ♛, to be precise. If you can't find a taxi, take the Ginza Line subway again, and change at Nihonbashi for the Tozai Line, going west toward Mitaka. Get off at the 2nd stop, Takebashi. The MOMA of Japan is located in the northern part of the Imperial Palace grounds, between a busy road and an expressway. Once you're inside, and the roar of traffic no longer bothers you, look for works by such famous artists as Yokoyama Taikan and Umehara Ryuzaburo.

You'll be suffering from museum feet about now, so I suggest a return to your hotel and some rest. About 7 P.M., head for Shinjuku and dinner. This will give you a chance to see that fifth face of Tokyo, Boomtown, close up, maybe too close for some readers. All roads lead to Shinjuku, it seems, looking at the transportation map, but you can get there by subway (Marunouchi and Toei Shinjuku lines) or by JNR (Chuo and Yamanote lines), as well as by private railway lines from the suburbs, or by taxi.

Nishi Shinjuku (West Shinjuku) is not your ultimate destination, perhaps, on this occasion, but it is where the meaning of Boomtown becomes most apparent. Here are Japan's first true skyscrapers, ranging up to 56 stories in height. Before modern architecture had, we fervently hope, solved the problem of high-rises toppling in earthquakes, the Japanese built low, rarely rising above 8 or 9 floors. Here, on land that was until a few years ago a sewage-treatment plant, you now find a Hilton Hotel at 38 floors, a Sumitomo Building at 52 floors, and a Mitsui Building at 55 floors. The most attractive of the structures is the Yasuda Insurance Building, 43 floors high, with walls sloped to resemble those of a Japanese castle. It has a nice little museum devoted to the works of Togo Seiji on its 42nd floor, open only in daytime, Monday to Friday.

You might very well want to have dinner in one of the many restaurants in these new buildings. I recommend, if you like Chinese food, the excellent branch of the Okura Hotel's To-Kah-Lin ♛ ♛ ♛, on the top floor of the Nomura Building, with nice views of Shinjuku.

If you want to get down among the masses, go over to the east side of Shinjuku Station and plunge into Kabuki-cho, the gaudy nightlife center of Tokyo. It's all jazz coffee shops, sing-along bars, *hotto pantsu* (hot-pants) and no-pants bars, Turkish baths (with masseuses), and hundreds of cheap little eating places. Here is where the lower-salaried wage earner comes to blow off steam, get drunk, cop a feel, touch the waitresses, or join up with someone for an "instant honeymoon," easily celebrated in any of a hundred or more cheap hotels in the district. There are a few legitimate restaurants, too, such as the giant Tokyo Dai Hanten ♨ ♨, a Chinese establishment featuring several types of cuisine on 7 floors. On Yasukuni-dori Street, behind Isetan Department Store.

Better yet, drop in at one of the cheap, and clean, little spots featuring a Japanese specialty. Again, look for samples in the display cases outside the windows. If you spot a *tonkatsu* place, ask for your pork cutlet in just that way— "*Tonkatsu, kudasai,*" holding up as many fingers as portions you require. *Yakitori,* chicken bits on a stick, is ordered in the same manner. If you see other things on top of rice, you're looking at *donbori.* A shrimp *donbori* is "*Ebi don, kudasai,*" and a chicken-egg combination is "*Oyako don, kudasai.*" (*Oyako* means, literally, parent and child, which seems to fit here.) *Sushi* gets more complicated (see our Menu Translator at end of the book), but if you are daring, you could order "*Mori awase, kudasai,*" in which case you'll get a sampling of several items. If you like the hand-rolled *sushi,* wrapped in seaweed, ask for "*Maki zushi, kudasai,*" or the loosely wrapped (again, in seaweed) rolls, "*Temaki, kudasai.*" In the latter two cases, you'll have to know what kind of *sushi* to order, so remember *maguro* (tuna), *anago* (eel), *kyuri* (cucumber), *takuan* (pickles), or my favorite, *kampyo* (dried gourd shavings, not as bad as it sounds). Beer goes best with most Japanese foods, *sake* if you're courageous.

After dinner, if you want to explore the nightlife of Shinjuku, you're strictly on your own. The most expensive-looking places, and the most quiet, can be the most dangerous to your pocketbook. (You never have to worry about physical danger, robbery, violence, rape, or even harassment, anywhere in Japan, Shinjuku included. And this applies to single women as well as men, though my foreign female friends tell me they just don't feel comfortable surrounded by mobs of carousing people, nearly all of whom are men. Certainly two or more females have no reason even to feel uncomfortable, and a male escort of any race wards off even covetous glances.)

Beware, though, of bars with touts outside, or the

aforementioned high-class places. The latter are for expense-account Japanese, a privileged race in their own country, men (99.9 percent of the time) who can spend more in an evening than they earn in a month, all on the company. You just can't afford this kind of place, and they are boring, to boot. If you're looking for companionship, it won't be here among the non-English-speaking hostesses. You'd probably wind up listening to the former branch manager for Nanika & Company in New York, crying on your shoulder for the good old days at the Waldorf-Astoria.

Look, instead, for places with windows, where you can see what's going on inside, or else just step inside for a quick once-over. The younger the crowd, the less likely it is to be a clip joint. If classical music is playing, you're in a coffee house, which may also serve drinks. Jazz is featured at other coffee houses, and in bars, of course. Loud, amateur singing is the sign of a *karaoke* bar, where the customers take turns singing, trying to keep up with a recorded-tape musical background, the bartender providing booklets with the words for that purpose. Some of the microphones are rigged to an applause meter, the "best" singer being determined by the other customers in the bar. These customers, by the way, will usually be men, and the women are hostesses.

A final word or two on Shinjuku nightlife. If you don't want to experiment as described above, hie thee to Roppongi, where several clubs encourage the presence of foreigners, women in particular. There you will meet other foreigners and some Japanese who might speak English. Certainly the hostesses and bartenders will, even if only a little. Finally, there is an area in Shinjuku with many gay bars and bathhouses, the AIDS menace not having hit Japan too hard as yet. It is the 20-block-square area just east of the Isetan Department Store, behind the Scala-za Theater and above the Shinjuku San-chome subway station of the Marunouchi Line. There are said to be over 200 such bars here. You'll never be in any physical danger in this (or any other) part of Tokyo, but the adventurous should note that the after-midnight nightlife can be very expensive, especially when renting a room for an "instant honeymoon" (the Japanese use the English words).

TOKYO WITH PLENTY OF TIME

Should you have more time, you will want to see many more aspects of this fascinating city's five faces. The following itinerary should keep you busy, with time to rest, dine well, and enjoy nightlife, for about 7 more days. I've organized the remainder of this chapter for walking, with an occasional taxi, subway, or other mode of transport as indicated.

You've heard about the famous Tokyo Fish Market♥♥, but you don't want to stay up all night in order to be up early? Well, you could take this tour the very first day after arriving, when you're bound to be awake at 3 A.M. anyhow, thanks to jet lag. Or you could go to bed at 9 P.M. and get up at 4 A.M. In any case, you'll have to get up early if you want to see the auctions, which begin at 5 A.M. and end at 6. If you don't care about the auctions, you can get to the market as late as 8 A.M. and still have about 90 minutes of activity to watch. It's fascinating to see, as the bidders, not the auctioneers, do the yelling. It's a bit like the floor of the stock exchange in any country, except here it's just fish they're screaming about, not bread, bullets, cosmetics, or futures. You'd be wise to wear old slacks and rubbers, or boots, as it's wet and wild in there. Also watch out for the madly careening trucks and carts. You'll be amazed at the cleanliness of it all, and at the neighboring market for fruit and vegetables, a sight of beauty after the gutsy world of dead and dying fish. Go by taxi, telling the driver *"Chuo Oroshi-uri Shijo"*—"Central Wholesale Market."

The Gray Line runs a regular Fish Market Tour on Monday, Wednesday, and Friday, Japanese breakfast included, for ¥4,900 ($29.70). Pickups at major hotels from 4:30 to 5:10 A.M. (the Imperial is one of the last, as it's not too far from the market). You'll have coffee on the bus, and the company lends you waterproof boots at no extra charge. After visiting the 56-acre market, you'll visit some small shops outside and have breakfast there. The Japanese breakfast will consist of *sashimi, miso* soup, pickled vegetables, a fried egg roll, and rice. (Western-style breakfast available if ordered when booking the tour.) Around 9 A.M., you'll be returned to your hotel. Gray Line, 03-433-5745 or 436-6881.

If you're on your own, you should note that the auction bidders are wholesalers. Restaurant owners and shop-keepers come in around 9 A.M. to the wholesaler's offices to buy their fish.

After the fish market, and breakfast perhaps, you might wish to look in on Tsukiji Temple Honganji ♛, one of the strangest-looking buildings in Tokyo. Built in 1935 to replace an earlier edifice destroyed by the Great Earthquake of 1923, it is made of stone in a quasi-Indian manner, very much unlike traditional Japanese Buddhist temples. It certainly is vastly inferior to its mother temple, Nishi Honganji, in Kyoto. Nonetheless, it is worth visiting, especially if you are not going to Kyoto, as it is one of the largest Buddhist houses of worship in Japan (and definitely the largest one made of stone). There are also occasional classes in Buddhism in the English language, about which you can inquire at the temple, or more easily at the Tourist Information Center of JNTO in Yuraku-cho. The temple is a kind of patron of fishermen, who still perform a dance in honor of the sect, at the Obon festival in mid-July. There are no scheduled times for services on a weekly basis, as is the case in all Buddhist temples in Japan.

It's an easy walk back to the Ginza, passing the venerable-looking Kabukiza (it dates from 1889, 1925, or 1950, depending on which guidebook you read; the diversity of dates is best explained by the *Official Guide to Japan,* which says it was "reconstructed in 1950"). On the left (south) side of Harumi-dori Street, just before you reach the important intersection with Chuo-dori, known as the Ginza Street to foreigners, is the Nihonshu (Japanese *sake*) Center. You can go in and taste some samples, although I doubt you'll be able to try them all, as there are said to be 6,000 different brews on file, or on the computer no doubt. Open daily except Thursdays, until 6 P.M.

From the corner of Chuo and Harumi streets, a walk north along the main street, Chuo-dori, can be instructive and fun, too, if you didn't do it your first day out. The first thing you'll see, on the right, just after the Mitsukoshi Department Store (a branch of the main store farther up the street), is McDonald's, in the prime real estate spot in Japan. If I tell you it tastes different from the ones back home, you'll want to try it just to see if I am right, so

I won't tell you that, but urge you to move right along. Next door, heaven on earth for toy mavens and lovers of crazy gadgets, is Kintaro, a narrow (but 3-floored) shop crammed with singing birds and monkeys, fire-spitting Godzillas, peace-keeping robots, whatever. Buy one for the kid, even if the kid is you.

Keeping on the east side of the street (you're coming back down the other side, later), you'll spot Matsuya, a second-rate department store, something on the order of Gimbels, the late great store in New York. Farther yet is Tsumugiya, famous for its beautiful (and incredibly expensive) hand-spun silk material, primarily used these days for Japan's mortgage-bearing *kimono*.

This is as good a point as any to turn around and return down the west side (right side again, after you turn around), aiming first for Kagami Crystal. Connoisseurs know that Japanese crystal is stunning, and this shop has been producing it since 1939, in almost sculptured forms. Purveyors to the Imperial Household, also, who just may be able to afford the prices. A short distance south is Mikimoto, Japan's most famous pearl dealer, and this is the main store. Having started the whole thing, Mikimoto deserves its worldwide fame. Marvelous displays of all its designs, and I've never heard a complaint about the quality of its wares. Back at the 4-chome corner is Wako, the ultraexpensive department store. The clock atop the building is a favorite landmark ("Meet me under the Wako clock") just as was the Biltmore's clock in New York or, back in Tokyo, the statue of Hachiko, a Faithful Dog, at Shibuya Station. Owned by Seiko watches, the store also distributes things like Steuben glass and Lalique crystal.

Across the street is the San-Ai Dream Center, an ugly round building plastered with advertising. Don't go inside, unless you like being part of a Japanese girl teenager's most extravagant dreams, as it's all boutiques and noise.

Turn right (west) here—again you're on Harumi-dori— and head for the Imperial Palace, beyond the overhead JNR railway tracks, beyond the moat. One of the first shops you'll notice on your left is maybe one you'll want to browse through, as it's Jena, one of Japan's oldest, best, and biggest foreign-language bookshops. Most of the material is in English, and you'll find here local guidebooks, everything you ever wanted to know about the

Japanese "economic miracle," and current (fairly so) magazines from back home. Sukiya Camera, with a tax-free counter, is practically next door. Farther along is Tenshodo, a mecca for model-train fans. At the next major intersection, Sotobori-dori, on your left is the Sony Building, where you can look over the latest electronic gimmick, and buy (tax-free, if you remembered to bring along your passport).

On the southwest corner here is the Hankyu Department Store, a branch of the Osaka establishment, but it has little to recommend it to short-term foreign visitors.

Tourist Information Center. Down beyond the tracks, after you pass the *yakitori* booths and emerge, is one place you should on no account miss in Tokyo, and that is the Tourist Information Center of the Japan National Tourist Organization. English-language brochures and maps, assistance with accommodations, advice on where you can study Buddhism in English, all these, and perhaps the answer to the riddle of life, are available here, free of charge. It is Japan's first face in diplomacy, dealing with the ordinary people of many countries who have come here and are, at least to some extent, bewildered. They do a magnificent job, by the way, and your key to success is to inquire, not demand.

Opposite the TIC is a new (1984) department store, the Hanshin, a branch of yet another Osaka transportation-and-department-store empire. There is little of value to the tourist here, but if you enjoy looking for trends and/or people-watching, this is definitely the place.

Turn left at the next street, before the airline building (several lines have their offices on the ground floor), and head for the Imperial Hotel. (Forget the Imperial Palace—you've already played the palace, on your first day in town.) You're now in theaterland, with three legitimate stages in this short block, plus a couple of cinemas.

At the end of this short street is the Imperial Hotel, listed elsewhere. Its newest building, the Imperial Towers (1983), contains a fascinating mix of ultraexpensive shops, often with Italian and French names which have yet to make their mark in America or England. They are said to be branches of shops in the parent country, however.

Back out the Imperial's doors, and right to the Imperial Palace moat, where once again, you can take a look at General MacArthur's old roosting place, the Dai Ichi

Mutual Insurance Company. To its north a few feet is the Idemitsu Museum of Arts ♛ ♛, on the 9th floor of the Teikoku (Imperial) Theater. The Chinese collection here is especially impressive, but even more so is the magnificent view of the Imperial Palace and surroundings. The Teikoku Theater, by the way, is famous for its big-stage productions, like *Fiddler on the Roof*, or, more notoriously, the first production of *Gone with the Wind* ever onstage. (It lasted for years, by the way.)

The business district marches northward, as you will if you want to visit the Imperial Palace's East Garden, open to the public only since 1969. En route, you might want a cold drink at the coffee shop of the Palace Hotel, just opposite the garden's Otemon Gate. Famed author Mishima Yukio, who killed himself by *hara-kiri* (*seppuku* in polite Japanese) because he thought Japan was growing soft and lazy, used to frequent the bar of this hotel.

The East Garden ♛ ♛, where the Imperial Guard was billeted in former days, is not ablaze with color. It is an uninspired mixture of formal Western and ditto Japanese, but the visit is worthwhile for the views of the towers of the castle, especially. When you enter, you are given a token or ticket, which you must return upon leaving, no fooling, for obvious security reasons. Open daily except Mondays and Fridays, 9 A.M. to 3 P.M. May be closed for state reasons without advance notice.

Just north of the garden are the National Museum of Modern Art, previously described, and the Science Museum ♛ ♛ (not to be confused with the National Science Museum, in Ueno Park). This science museum is filled with the latest in gadgets, not concerning itself very much with the past. The one in Ueno Park is firmly anchored in history, however. Nearby is the Crafts Gallery ♛ of the Museum of Modern Art (closed Mondays), in the former home of the palace guards (19th-century). Contemporary works, of course.

From Kitanomaru Park, where the museums are located, it's a short walk, again northward, to the Nippon Budokan Hall, constructed for the 1964 Olympics in Tokyo. Shaped like the Yumedono Hall of Horyuji Temple near Nara, the Budokan (Martial Arts Hall, literally) is used for all sorts of public events, from rock concerts to college commencements. It's an interesting, and successful, example of applying modern craftsmanship and design to traditional architecture.

Across the street from the Budokan, and one long block to the left (west), is Yasukuni Jinja Shrine ♛ ♛, the Valhalla of fallen warriors in past wars. Before Japan's defeat, before the emperor renounced his divinity, before MacArthur ordered the disestablishment of religion, Yasukuni Jinja was the Arlington Cemetery, the Tomb of the Unknowns, to Japan. Here the emperor and his ancestors used to come to pray, to report, and to meditate. Nowadays, not even a prime minister can make an official visit to the place, lest antiwar sentiment again be excited. You can go, if you wish, but it is a grimly solemn place, stark and severe, with aging relatives of the deceased paying respect. The usual nonchalance of Shintoism is nowhere visible at Yasukuni Shrine. The Treasure House, behind the shrine's main hall, contains war-related items, from blood-soaked flags to swords, rifles, and so forth.

In case you missed it during your earlier walks along the Ginza, you might now want to visit the Bridgestone Museum of Art ♛ ♛, on Chuo-dori Street midway between the Nihonbashi and Kyobashi subway stations. Although it is mostly Western art, it includes Japanese artists' interpretations in the Western manner, i.e., with oils. Yōga, as Western paintings are known here, include Picasso, but you will want to look for the better-known Japanese artists, such as Foujita. Closed Mondays, small admission charge.

On Eita-dori Street, east of Showa-dori, is the Yamatane Museum of Art ♛ ♛, which specializes in Japanese painting, Nihonga (not Yōga), from the Meiji Period to today. It is located on the 9th floor of the Yamatane Shoken Building, directly over the Kayaba-cho Station of the Tozai and Hibiya subway lines. This securities company has dedicated 2 floors of its main office building in the heart of Kabuto-cho, Tokyo's Wall Street, because of its public-spirited attitude. The gallery was designed by the famous architect Taniguchi Yoshiro. If you're looking for a name artist in this style of wonderfully subtle, usually pastel watercolors and ink, look for Yokoyama Taikan. Closed Mondays, small admission charge.

Take a taxi now, or pop downstairs into the Kayabacho Subway Station, where you take the Hibiya Line to Akihabara, the electronics center of Tokyo. Although you may have come here on an earlier visit (see above), if you are interested in audiovisual equipment of any kind, or other electric/electronic devices, you'll want more time. In addition to Laox, Yamagiwa, and Hirose, mentioned in my 3rd-day itinerary, there are another 900 or so shops. Most are situated along Chuo-dori Street, running north and south parallel to the JNR's Yamanote Line. If you want to work your way up the street one way, you can escape the area from the Suehiro-cho Subway Station on the Ginza Line.

Bargaining is common in these shops; in the rest of Japan, except in antique shops, it is considered uncouth. Regulars say they are accustomed to at least a 20 percent discount, and often work it up higher. Some boast of 50 percent, but I think that not likely unless the customer knows a lot about the item and can converse easily with the salesmen. (Some speak "a leetle" English.) Offer one-third or one-half, and then compromise. In Laox, they have been known to serve free soft drinks if they see you're a serious browser, and it is probably most famous among audio fans. Yamagiwa is known primarily for ultramodern lighting units. Other good audiovisual outlets include Rajio (Radio) Kaikan, Sato Musen, and Rocket, all on Chuo-dori. From mid-June to mid-July and from early December through mid-January, Electronics Fair means cheaper prices.

Just south of the main Yamagiwa store, across the Kanda River and under the elevated JNR tracks, you'll find on Chuo-dori the Kotsu Hakubutsu Kan (Transportation Museum) ♨. It's easy to recognize, as the front end of two trains (one steam, one ultramodern) stick out from the front. Models of many JNR trains and other displays make this great fun. Open daily except Mondays, small admission.

You might be feeling hungry about now, and you could visit a restaurant that is also beautiful and historic, Yabu Soba (see listings). Exit the museum, take first street right, then first left.

NORTHERN TOKYO

Another day, perhaps, another district of Tokyo. This time, the center of Old-Fashioned Tokyo, Asakusa (pron. Ah-SOX-ah), where you may already have visited the famous old temple at the heart of the area. You may wish to go back again, especially to look more closely at the shops along the Nakamise street behind the big red lantern at Kaminari-mon (Thunder Gate). If you're lucky you might be here on a festival day (there are about 13 of them each year). If you're here around cocktail time, you may want to visit Japan's first Western-style bar, the Kamiya, above the subway station at Asakusa.

Rather far to the north of Asakusa Temple and Shrine is the old red-light district, Yoshiwara, officially licensed for houses of prostitution until March 31, 1958, when a new law forbade legal whoring. There is precious little to see here today, but you may be part of a tour group that visits the Matsubaya♛ ♛, one of the more elegant of the "green houses," as they were called, for *sukiyaki* dinner and a performance of dancing by *geisha*. (You may, of course, dine here individually, without joining a group.)

More pertinent to modern living is a trip west of the Thunder Gate to Kappa-bashi, the center of kitchenware and everything related to cooking. It's a good 10-minute walk, along Asakusa-dori to where it intersects with Kappa-bashi. Turn right, another 5-minute walk, and you'll see a 4-story building with a 40-foot-tall head of a chef on top, white toque and all. You'll find over 50 shops here, selling everything from bamboo *sushi* rollers to complete chef's uniforms. Most foreigners love to buy the plastic or wax models of food, the kind seen in inexpensive restaurants' display cases. You can buy an imitation steak, *sushi*, curry and rice, whatever. Among the more popular items is a dish of spaghetti, several strands rising into the air and wrapping themselves around a miraculously suspended fork. The models are not cheap, but make for a good joke back home.

A good 15-minute walk westward from Kappa-bashi (or take a cab) is Ueno Station, our next destination. If you like museums, Ueno is for you. In addition to the Tokyo National Museum and the Metropolitan Museum of Art, already visited, there are three more. Fanciers of European and American art will want to see the Kokuritsu Seiyo Bijutsukan (National Museum of Western Art) ♛ ♛, halfway through the park on the right-hand (east) side. Built in two sections (1959 and 1979), the first designed by Le Corbusier, the museum contains works by Cézanne, Degas, Manet, and Monet, but also works dating back to the Renaissance. There are about 50 Rodin sculptures in the courtyard!

When leaving, note the stupendous Metropolitan Festival Hall, looking vaguely like a ship. It was designed in 1961 by Maekawa Kunio, who also did the 1979 building of the Western Art Museum.

North of the Western Art Museum is the Kokuritsu Kagaku Hakubutsukan (National Science Museum) ♛ ♛, housing the usual things you'll find in these anywhere in the world. (Examples include whales, trains, and steam engines.)

Back behind the Tokyo National Museum itself is Kan'eiji ♛, the remains of what once was the most important Buddhist house of worship in the capital. During the Meiji Restoration, heavy fighting between loyalists of the shogun and the troops of the emperor took place on the vast acreage of the temple, and most of the buildings were destroyed. After the battle, the temple's property was turned into Ueno Park. Today the only original structure remaining is the pagoda. The present Kan'eiji Temple is a building moved here from outside Tokyo.

If you can't get to Nikko, you can be content with second-best at the Toshogu Shrine ♛ here in Ueno Park. Also dedicated to Tokugawa Ieyasu (the hero of television's *Shogun*), it was built in 1651, and is done in the same elaborate, wildly colorful manner that the one in Nikko is. Interior paintings by Kano Tan'yu and an avenue of stone lanterns are among the other highlights of this beautiful shrine, sadly sited next to the zoo and a short-distance monorail. Open daily, small admission.

Just outside the park's main (south) entrance, on the western side of Chuo-dori Street, is the Shita-machi Fuzoku Shiryokan (Shita-machi Museum) ♛ ♛. Shita-machi (lit. Downtown) is the name of Old-Fashioned Tokyo, centering in Ueno, Asakusa, and down to Tsukiji, east of the Ginza. Much of it was destroyed by the Great Earthquake of 1923 and the air raids of 1945. Here, however, you can see reconstructed rooms, life-size human figures, toys, utensils, and the like, nicely displayed in a manageable amount of space. Open daily except Mondays, small admission.

SOUTH-CENTRAL TOKYO

Geographically and spiritually the opposite of Shita-machi, Downtown Tokyo, are the outposts of Expense-Account Tokyo, the Akasaka area, and Foreign Tokyo, centering around Roppongi. These and neighboring districts all the way to Tokyo Bay constitute what many consider to be the heart of the modern capital.

Certainly the area includes the most important buildings of Establishment Tokyo, too, ranging from the National Diet Building itself down to IBM Headquarters.

You may as well start at the epicenter of Japanese politics, the Kokkai Gijido (National Diet Building) ♛, easily reached by subway on three lines (Kokkai Gijido stations on either the Marunouchi or Chiyoda lines, Nagata-cho Station on the Yurakucho Line). Erected only in 1936, this is a very un-Japanese-looking building, bearing some passing resemblance to many United States state capitols and set imposingly on a hall looking eastward toward Tokyo Bay. As you face the building from its east side, the right wing holds the House of Councillors (formerly the House of Peers), the left the House of Representatives. The councillors resemble United States senators and are elected on a nationwide basis. The representatives are very much like their American counterparts, and are elected in proportional representation voting from limited constituencies, where they must have a residence. To gain admission, you must show your passport at the reception desk, west side entrance. Entrance may be forbidden for security reasons. You really won't miss much if you can't get in, as the chambers are quite undistinguished. There is a Parliamentary Museum north of the Diet for those really interested in politics.

Of prime interest in this part of the city is Hie Jinja (Hie Shrine) ♛ ♛, down the hill from the Diet's west central entrance, past the Capitol Tokyu Hotel, then up a flight of steps. If you have skipped the Diet Building, you could start out right here the easy way by taking a taxi to the hotel, then walking up a gentle slope from the hotel entrance to Hie Shrine. Even better, and cheaper, take the Chiyoda subway line to Kokkai Gijido-mae (*mae* = in front of) Station, then walk out its western exit and there, on the right about 100 yards away, is the basement entrance, also banqueting entrance, of the Capitol Tokyu Hotel. Go in there, ride up the elevators, perhaps have a cold drink in the bar or coffee shop, and then walk up to the shrine. The Capitol Tokyu, formerly the Tokyo Hilton, is one of the city's best hotels and is nicely designed, with a pretty garden off the main lobby.

Hie Shrine, also known as Sanno-sama to the locals, is the second of Tokyo's Big Two Shinto neighborhood places of worship (the other being Kanda Jinja). Its grand festival is held on June 15 of every even-numbered year, and features many palanquins carried through the streets of Ginza and Kyobashi by very tipsy gentlemen.

The shrine is of typical Shinto styling, and was constructed only in 1967, after being destroyed in the 1945 air raids, the original dating to 1657. If you're lucky, you might see a priest blessing a new automobile at the top of the main stairs. For a substantial donation by the proud owner, the priest does a typically Japanese thorough job, waving his *sasaki* branch wand over front and back, trunk and hood open, inside and out, doors open too. The accepted way of calling attention to your presence is to ring the shrine's bell, clap your hands two or three times, and keeping them in the prayer position, bow your head and make your request. You then should throw some money into the large donation box nearby. If you do this solemnly, you won't upset anyone, but smiling or making a joke of it won't win you any friends among the other visitors to the shrine. (Protocol at Buddhist temples is quite different, and can involve lighting candles or incense, depending on the place, time, etc. You'd best be advised by Japanese friends if you want to pray at a Buddhist place of worship and are afraid of making a gaffe.) Hie Shrine is open daily except Friday, small admission. You can buy good-luck medallions, tablets ensuring traffic safety, or other forms of blessings on the way out.

The Akasaka district is fascinating by day, frenetic by night. Assuming you are here sightseeing during daylight

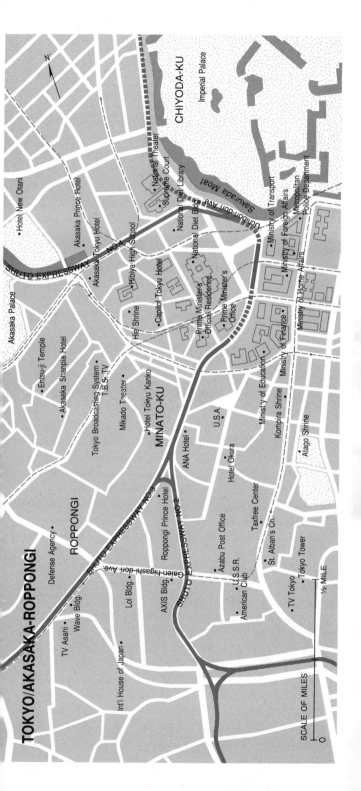

hours, you can still get some idea of its appeal to expense-account biggies by looking carefully along the quiet little streets leading south from the Mitsuke intersection and parallel to Sotobori-dori Avenue. Here, frequently on the even more narrow side streets running east and west, you'll find discreet *ryotei*, higher-class traditional restaurants which cater usually only to guests who have been introduced by other guests. These are the *ryotei* where, newspapers sniff, Japanese politicians conduct the real business of government, while being coddled by *geisha*, toadied to by lobbyists, and flattered by the *mama-san*. Here, too, in wilder moments, high-ranking guests doff their jackets and play bumps-a-daisy with the *geisha*, or sing a song of their school days, or play baby, letting the *geisha* feed them, morsel by morsel. And why not? It's probably not taxpayers' money, at least directly. The lobbyists are paying, or even the politicians themselves, recipients as they are of huge war chests from the various industrial and financial divisions of Japan, Inc. An evening out in this kind of place is likely to run $600 or more per person.

If you can't tell which are the *ryotei*, look for buildings that look like residences, which bear no name or only a small sign, and, if a door is open, which look just like the entrances to the most expensive *ryokan* (inns). The presence of big black automobiles outside should also provide a clue.

Farther down the central street of Akasaka's entertainment area, again parallel to Sotoboro-dori, beyond the big Mikado Cabaret, to the left just past the police box, is the Geisha Exchange. No sign, but a row of old-fashioned rickshaws gives it away. Here the *geisha* sit, waiting for their calls to the *ryotei*. Many are booked well in advance, others are summoned at the last minute. All sit, perfectly groomed and made up, keeping the white powder on their faces dry until the telephone rings.

In olden times, the *geisha* often were attached to a particular *ryotei*, but in order to preserve their image as entertainers, not prostitutes, the exchange was conceived as a kind of dormitory, where the girls could also live. These days the girls live in their own apartments and come to work in the evening like any cabaret hostess, making the exchange their base. They will, indeed, be hauled to the *ryotei* by an old rickshaw, one of the very few remaining in all of Japan. There are a few remnants of other *geisha* quarters in Tokyo, but nearly all will be gone by the end of this decade.

For details of suggested night spots in Akasaka, see pages 172–173.

To the east of Akasaka, toward the Ginza, you'll find the huge American Embassy, virtually a fortress nowadays, and two of Tokyo's best hotels, the Okura and the ANA Tokyo.

At the Okura, up the hill and across the street from the American Embassy, you should take a look at the hotel's museum♛, just in front of the entrance. It is, in fact, specifically designed as a museum, in the Chinese style (1928), but resembles a large house's treasure house, similar to those you'll see on large estates and in places like Kurashiki, in western Japan. Some sculpture, scrolls, and screens. Closed Mondays, small admission.

Japan Tax-Free Center. Going out the back door of the Okura, so to speak, and down the hill toward Kamiya-cho, south of the hotel, you'll find the Japan Tax-Free Center, operated by the Amita Damascene Company. It's a 6-story building, some 200 yards south of Kamiya-cho Subway Station on the Hibiya Line toward Tokyo Tower. A good sampling of many items, from pearls to toys. Open daily at 5-8-6 Toranomon, Minato-ku, tel. 03-432-4351.

Another 200 yards or so south of the center is an amazing building, the Reiyukai Shakaden, center of a relatively new Japanese religious cult. Built in 1975, it was designed by architect Iwasaki Kenichi. The crescent and golden ball on top are ominously reminiscent of the decorations on a *samurai*'s helmet.

Across the street, behind a barricade of police, is the Soviet Embassy. It is of interest only because of its position, sitting squarely in front of the posh American Club, down the side street to the embassy's east. Expense-Account Tokyo, of whatever nationality, makes use of the American Club, especially popular among families for its summertime swimming pool.

A few hundred yards to the east of the embassy is Tokyo Tower♛, a monstrosity, like the Eiffel in Paris, which everyone criticized to the highest heavens when it was built, but which everyone now accepts, hardly noticing it. It is 333 meters tall (about 1,000 feet), and you can go up to a platform 250 meters off the ground for a view. The shops at the base are almost prize-winningly tacky. Lovers of history and ethics will be interested to know that a lot of important persons' graves had to be moved to make way for this tower, the golf driving range, and a nearby hotel when Zojoji Temple sold off the land to developers.

Zojoji Temple ♛, again to the east (of the tower this time) a few hundred yards, is blessed with two magnificent gates, one old, one new. The Sanmon (Triple Gate) ♛ ♛, to the east of the temple itself, dates from 1622. Less magnificent, and standing even farther east, is the Daimon (Great Gate) ♛, a modern copy of the original. To the left and right of the Sanmon are four more gates, divided north and south of the Sanmon, that are also interesting, and old (not to say poorly maintained). The Main Hall of the temple, constructed only in 1974, is not very interesting, but there are the graves of at least six shoguns north of this, behind a wrought-iron gate. They are all Tokugawas, as it was the great Ieyasu himself who created this temple, along with Kan'eiji, to mark the southern and northern limits of the capital in the days of his reign. They were also fortified camps, and travelers to and from the capital had to pass customs and immigration, so to speak, at these two temples. It's a bit of an unlucky temple, as it has been destroyed three times by fire between 1873 and 1945, twice by arsonists and once by American bombs.

East of Zojoji a good 15 minutes by walking is the Kyu Shiba Rikyu Teien (Shiba Detached Palace Garden) ♛ ♛, a lovely spot, but completely surrounded by industrial Tokyo. A classical Japanese garden, with hills representing mountains, ponds representing lakes and the sea, it is 300 years old, and as graceful as ever. Open daily, small admission.

A short walk north of Zojoji, past another of its gates, Onari-mon, is the Matsuoka Museum ♛, on Hibiya-dori Avenue. There is a good collection here of Chinese ceramics and Japanese paintings, especially Nihonga, on the top two floors of an office building. Look for Yokoyama Taikan's work, again. Closed Mondays, small admission.

The Roppongi area is headquarters of Foreign Tokyo, one of the city's five aspects. But it is also headquarters of Japan's Defense Agency, the Boei-cho, or at least a major part of it. The agency's land occupies a large tract between the Roppongi crossing and Aoyama, and visitors are not permitted. Until a few years ago, it was an American camp, and you can believe the troops were unhappy to vacate this choice land just next to a sparkling nightlife area.

Roppongi (Six Trees) itself has little to attract foreign visitors by day, unless you're a shopper, in which case you'll love it. (See page 170.) And there are many fine restaurants here. (See page 151.) The essence of Roppongi, however, is best seen at night, when it becomes a playground for foreigner and Japanese alike. As Shinjuku attracts students and lower-range workers, including clerks and machine operators, Roppongi draws the yuppies of Japan. Here you're apt to meet the internationally minded citizens of Japan, including those who may even be toying with the idea of opting out of the rat race. You can learn a lot if you meet some of the English-speaking men and women who congregate here.

One particular attraction for visitors is a tiny, almost pint-sized shrine tucked away in a courtyard just east of the Axis Building on Gaien-Higashi-dori Avenue (south side). This is dedicated to travelers, particularly those who go by air. You can say a little prayer here, perhaps, then have a cold drink in the same courtyard, a pretty place sheltered from the passing traffic.

An important art gallery, the Nezu Bijutsukan (Nezu Institute of Fine Arts) 🌑 🌑 🌑, is much farther west in this area, at 6-5 Minami Aoyama. It is, quite simply, one of the leading art institutions in Tokyo, though a private one. Nice display of bronzes, changing displays of the large collection (only small amount on show at a time), including screens by Ogata Korin and ceramics by Kenzan. Closed Mondays and all of August, small admission.

WESTERN AND SOUTHERN TOKYO

The Shinjuku area, all that Boomtown Tokyo could hope to be, glitters by night, but works hard in daylight. Only a few touristic highlights draw visitors here, but it is easy to get to the place. Shinjuku's central shrine is Hanazono 🌑. To reach it by taxi is simple—just tell the driver, *"Hanazono Jinja, kudasai."* By subway, take the Marunouchi Line to the Shinjuku San-chome Station, and come up either exit. Go down the side of the huge Isetan Department Store (either side), and cross broad Yasukuni-dori Avenue. Continue on another 250 yards, and you'll be at either the front or back entrance of the shrine.

Dedicated to the fox god, Inari, it is painted a brilliant red. Flower Garden Shrine (the literal translation) is supposed to serve farmers and merchants, but it is most famous for its Tori no Ichi Fair (Cock Fair), in November, when believers buy decorated rakes, to draw in good fortune.

From Sendagaya Station, it's a 3-minute walk eastward, past the Metropolitan Gymnasium and an enclosed swimming pool, to Meiji Shrine Outer Garden. (Don't confuse this with the Inner Garden, more than a mile to the west, which surrounds Meiji Shrine itself.) In the Meiji Jingu Gaien (Outer Garden) are the National Stadium (built for the 1964 Tokyo Olympics), the Jingu Stadium, a baseball ground, and the Prince Chichibu Rugby Stadium. There are also tennis courts, a pool, and a skating rink. The park was intended to have as its center the Meiji Jingu Homotsuden (Meiji Shrine Memorial Picture Gallery) ♛, and you can still visit it. Here you'll see memorabilia of the Emperor Meiji, with many undistinguished paintings, and various artifacts. Also destroyed during World War II bombings, and reconstructed. In June, look for the lovely iris garden here (not so gorgeous as the one at the shrine itself, however).

A side trip may be in order here for fans of the Japanese sword. A couple of miles west of Sendagaya Station, best reached by taxi, is the Token Hakubutsukan (Sword Museum) ♛, at 4-25-10 Yoyogi. About 25 swords at a time are on display, and the gallery is open daily except Mondays, with a small admission charge.

From the vicinity of the Olympic Stadium (National Stadium) in the Outer Garden, take a leisurely walk through the residential and business area of Sendagaya, heading southwest toward Harajuku Station of the JNR. Your ultimate destination is the Togo Shrine, but en route you'll pass dozens of boutiques, many of them on Killer-dori Street, so named because the up-to-the-minute fashions on display here will knock you dead. On Killer Street itself is Yamamoto Kansai's boutique. Other shops

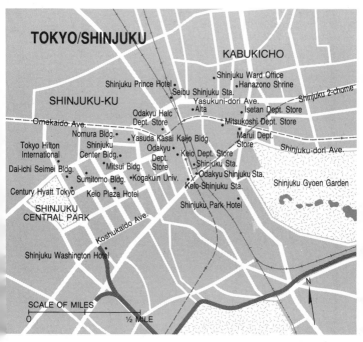

to watch for in your walk between here and Harajuku Station include Comme Ça du Mode, Barbiche, Boutique Nicole, and Palais France.

Just east of Harajuku Station about 2 blocks is Togo Jinja Shrine ♨, dedicated to the memory of the great admiral who defeated the Russian fleet in the battle of Tsushima Straits in 1905. This was the first victory over a European power by an Asian nation, and was the beginning of the Japanese quest for an empire that resulted in World War II. Togo was a great inspiration for a young American naval attaché in Tokyo some years later, taking under his wing young Chester Nimitz. Today, if you visit Nimitz's hometown of Fredericksburg, Texas, you'll find an exact replica of Admiral Togo's home in the Peace Garden behind the Nimitz Memorial (itself a building that resembles a battleship!). Togo Shrine is not in any way outstanding, but is a good example of the Shinto shrine, and as a focal point for the militarists, is still of interest today.

South 2 blocks from the shrine and behind the Harajuku LaForet Building is the Ota Bijutsu Kinenkan (Ota Memorial Museum of Art) ♨ ♨, a gallery of fine *ukiyoe* woodblock prints. There is a small teahouse here, too. Closed Mondays and the last 3 to 6 days of each month, small admission.

Lovers of folk arts will want to visit the Nippon Mingei Kan (Japan Folk Crafts Museum) ♛ ♛ ♛, a short taxi ride from Shibuya Station, or reachable from the station on the Inokashira Line (private railway, 2 stops only). It's the home of a lately departed collector and includes furniture, pottery, textiles, and all sorts of artifacts by anonymous craftsmen around the country. In November you can also expect to find a large collection of folk craft for sale here. It is a beautiful building, an old farmhouse moved here before the war from the north of Japan. If you're looking for names, there are a few. The world-renowned potter Kawai Kanjiro is one. Open daily except Monday, small admission. Exact address: 4-3-3 Komaba, Meguro-ku, tel. 03-467-4527.

Southern Tokyo

Another excellent museum is Hatakeyama Kinenkan ♛ ♛, south of Shibuya Station and not far from Meguro Station. It is situated just behind Hannya'en, one of the city's most elegant restaurants, and is itself the former residence of Mr. Hatakeyama. You might want to combine dinner here (no lunch served), if you're rolling in money, with a visit to the museum. (It would have to be an early dinner, as the gallery closes at 5 P.M.) Beautiful collection, especially of ceramics. Big names: Kenzan for ceramics, Ogata Korin for paintings. Exact address: 2-20-12 Shiroganedai, Minato-ku, tel. 03-447-5787. Closed Mondays, also last 2 weeks of March, ditto September. If you didn't come here by taxi, you might have tried the Takanawadai Station of the Toei Asakusa subway line. It's a 5-minute walk from there.

The only other spot of real touristic interest in southern Tokyo is Sengakuji Temple ♛ ♛, burial place of the Forty-seven Ronin, or masterless *samurai*. These hapless gentlemen are the heroes of Japan's most famous play, performed both on the *kabuki* stage and in the *bunraku* puppet theater. The author, Chikamatsu, often called Japan's Shakespeare, wrote his play for the puppet theater, but it had been adapted for every other form of dramatic interpretation, including movies, television, musicals, the all-girl Takarazuka, vaudeville, and mime. The gory tale is based on fact.

In a nutshell, the *ronin* conspired to avenge the death of their master, the Lord of Ako, caused by an insult from a corrupt court official of Edo (Tokyo) Castle. They achieved their surprise attack on the official by lulling him into a sense of false security, through their conspicuous drunkenness and debauchery. (You can see how all this makes for lip-smacking theater.) They knew they would have to pay for their deed with their lives, and after they had carried the official's severed head through the streets to lay it upon the tomb of their master at Sengakuji, they were, as expected, condemned to death. As *samurai*, they were allowed to commit *hara-kiri* (*seppuku* is the correct word), just as their master. Again, the essential Japanese trait of loyalty and single-minded devotion, not to say doggedness, was celebrated by their deeds and subsequent fame.

You can see all the graves, over which incense has burned constantly since 1702, inside the main gate of the temple, on the left, up the stairs. Sengakuji is best reached by taxi, a short ride from the Hatakeyama Museum, or by subway, the Sengakuji Station of the Toei-Asakusa Line, one stop from Takanawadai.

EXCURSIONS FROM TOKYO (KAMAKURA, YOKOHAMA, NARITA)

The most popular day excursions from the capital are to Kamakura, Nikko, and Lake Hakone. In my opinion, the last two deserve at least an overnight stay, so I'll get to them later in the book, in the northern Japan and central Japan chapters respectively. In addition to Kamakura, though, I can recommend a trip to Yokohama and even one to Narita, under certain circumstances.

Kamakura

This pleasant little town about 1 hour on the train south of Tokyo was once the capital of Japan, and it retains the kind of grand temples one associates with imperial power. The authority wasn't that of the emperors, however, but of the *bakufu* (military shogunate), established by Minamoto Yoritomo in 1192 and lasting until 1868. The actual period of Kamakura governance ended in 1333, when an exiled emperor managed to make a comeback and restored nominal rule from Kyoto.

The easiest way to reach Kamakura is on the JNR Yokosuka Line from Tokyo, Shimbashi, or Shinagawa stations, service running every 10 or 15 minutes. Yokosuka Line trains are painted blue with white stripes.

From Kamakura Station, there is frequent bus service to most of the popular sights, or you can, of course, take a taxi. The bus stations are marked clearly, and you'll be using those from platforms 3, 5, 6, 7, or 9 at the east exit of the JNR Kamakura Station.

The undisputed highlight of Kamakura is the Dai Butsu (Great Buddha) 🏯 🏯 🏯 🏯 of Kotokuin Temple. I recommend you go here by taxi, a few minutes' drive. The second-largest bronze image of Buddha in Japan (the largest is at Todaiji in Nara), this serene statue is 37½ feet high and sits quietly overlooking its viewers, a hint of a smile on its face. As a work of art, it is far superior to its big brother in Nara. You can walk inside the statue through a door in the back. Believed to have been cast in 1252, the 93-ton image was originally enclosed in a hall, which was finally swept away by a tidal wave in 1495. This particular position of meditation, with legs crossed and thumbs touching, represents affirmation of faith. Kotokuin Temple itself is pleasant, but of little note.

From the Dai Butsu, walk back toward the ocean to Yuigahama-dori Street, and turn right, into Hasedera Temple 🏯 🏯, dedicated to the Eleven-Headed Goddess Kwannon (goddess of mercy). Standing nearly 30 feet in height, this is the largest wooden religious image in Japan and was said to have been carved in 721 from half of a huge camphor tree. (A duplicate, in the Hase Temple in Nara, is alleged to come from the other half of the same tree.) The beach here is one of Japan's most popular, and can be fun if you are with friends or like large, boisterous crowds.

Go back out the gate, turn right, and walk toward the

ocean until you come to the Hase Station of the little Enoden Railway Line, a kind of Toonerville Trolley compared to the big trains. Board this and ride back to Kamakura Station. If the time is right, you might have lunch about now, perhaps near the station.

After lunch, strike out on foot to the Tsurugaoka Hachimangu Shrine ♛ ♛ ♛ ♛, about 10 minutes away. This is really more important a destination than the Great Buddha, and even more dramatic. You cross first an incredibly steep arched bridge, or walk around it, and then come upon the main buildings of the shrine. The brilliant red-and-white patterns of the shrine make for excellent photography, and you should also be impressed by the swords and other artifacts hanging around. Many of them have been designated National Treasures. The shrine was built in 1063 on another spot and moved here in 1191 by Yoritomo. At its spring and autumn festivals (see page 175), *yabusame* (archery from horseback) is practiced here. In front of the main hall are two ponds, one for the Heike (Red Lotuses) and one for the Genji (White Lotuses), the two warring factions in Japanese history akin to the English Wars of the Roses, Lancaster versus York. Between ponds and the main hall are a Noh stage (right) and Wakamiya Shrine (left).

Also on the shrine grounds are two museums, the Kokuho Kan (National Museum) ♛, which is filled with old relics of interest, and the Kanagawa-ken Kenritsu Kindai Bijutsukan (Prefectural Museum of Modern Art), boasting a fairly decent collection, but of less interest to foreign visitors, perhaps. The former museum, erected in 1928, is patterned after the Shosoin in Nara and has a particularly good collection of articles relating to Zen, plus some nice woodblock prints.

Another 10-minute walk northwest, beyond the Hachimangu Shrine and the Museum of Modern Art annex, is Kenchoji Temple ♛ ♛, the oldest Zen training grounds in Japan. (Occasionally has space for serious foreign students.) Kenchoji is the best of the "Five Great Zen Temples of Kamakura," as classified by the Japanese. (The other four are Engakuji, Jochiji, Jomyoji, and Jufukuji.) A contemplative mood strikes one here, and it is further intensified in the splendid Zen garden behind the main hall.

You are now higher up along the slopes of the hills partly surrounding Kamakura in a semicircular pattern. Note the wonderfully scented cedar trees, and their great height. Although it was founded in 1253, the buildings were destroyed several times by fire, and what you see today are mostly mid-17th century. The setting is as important here as are the buildings and bells, one of which, inevitably, is a National Treasure.

Another 10-minute walk to the north takes you over the pass between the hills, and on your left is Tokeiji Temple♛. As divorce was not permitted in Japan until after World War II, it was almost impossible for a woman engaged in a disastrous marriage to get out of it. Suicide was often the only way. But Tokeiji offered one of the rare forms of escape, for if a distraught woman could make her way here, she was thereafter sheltered by the temple, and most of the time became a nun. The temple was founded in 1285 for the purpose of providing such a refuge.

Finally, the third-most-important tourist destination in Kamakura, Engakuji Temple♛ ♛, can be reached with only a 5-minute walk, again to the north. Just before Kita Kamakura (North Kamakura) Station, it is a complex of buildings nestled in a cedar grove. Founded in 1282 by the Hojo family, regents to the shoguns, Engakuji has seen its old buildings destroyed by fire and earthquake (including that of 1923). The oldest remaining structure, the Shariden (Hall of Holy Relics), dating from 1285, is said to contain a tooth of Buddha, and is open only January 1 to 3 each year. The big bronze bell, cast in 1301, is the largest in Kamakura and has been designated a National Treasure.

At this point, it is easy to return to Tokyo. Simply board the Yokosuka Line again, this time at Kita (North) Kamakura Station, just across the street from Engakuji.

INSIDERS' TIPS

Free guide service is offered in Kamakura by members of the Kanagawa Student Guide Federation, on Saturdays and Sundays. Depart from Kamakura Station at 10 A.M. You should make reservations through the JNTO Tourist Information Center in Tokyo, tel. 03-502-1461.

Yokohama

The only reasons to come to Yokohama are if you have business or want to see Chinatown. If it's the latter, you have to eat here, so I would recommend you come down for a little tour of the city, then lunch, and return back to Tokyo in time for evening activities. Getting to Yokohama is easy. Simply take the JNR Tokaido Line regular trains or those of the Yokosuka Line (as for Kamakura). Traveling time is only 30 minutes, and the trains run every 15 minutes. You could be lucky enough to find a connection to Kannai Station when you arrive in Yokohama, and that is closer to Chinatown, but then again, it's easier just to take a taxi. Tell the driver, *"Hikawa-maru,"* and he'll take you right to this old tub, now anchored firmly to the pier in Yamashita Koen Park. In summer, it's a floating beer garden. In winter, there's little point in going aboard. From the ship, walk north (away from the ugly Marine Tower), past the Star and New Grand Hotels. If you hate Chinese food, you might want to have lunch at the New Grand, in its excellent 5th-floor restaurant (see page 149). Passing the Sokka Gakkai building on the left, you should note that they are always interested in converts. In America, the cult is known as Nichiren Shoshu of America, and this branch of Buddhism has many adherents. Next is the Hotel Yokohama, where you should turn left to find Chinatown.

The main entrance to Chinatown ♛ ♛ is about 2 blocks from the sea, behind the Satellite Hotel and Holiday Inn. (The latter has a good Chinese restaurant ♛ ♛ if you want a more dignified lunch than you are liable to get in the independent places down the street.)

Turn into Chinatown and walk along its main street, which is filled, cheek by jowl, with restaurants, at least 50 of them. Among the better known are Heichinrou ♛ ♛ ♛, Kaihokaku ♛ ♛, and Tung Fat ♛ ♛. If you don't find what you want at one restaurant, go to another. English is spoken in all, thanks to Yokohama's status as a port, the continued presence of American military personnel in the vicinity, and the fact that many of the Chinese started out in Hong Kong before coming to Japan. You may as well get used to the fact that they consider the Japanese bigger spenders than foreigners these days, so guess who gets better treatment?

If you have time to spare, there are two sights in Yokohama worthy of interest. The first is Sankei-en Garden ♛ ♛, a long ride south of Chinatown by taxi. It is indeed a lovely classical garden, but not worth a trip from, say, Tokyo to see. If you have business in Yokohama and are staying for some time, it is a truly pleasant retreat. If you're here in flower time, it's especially nice. (Plum blossoms in February, cherry in April, wisteria in May, iris in June, chrysanthemum in November.)

Another spot of great interest to students of religion and history is Sojiji Temple ♛ ♛, to the north of the town's center, near Tsurumi Station on the JNR Keihin Tohoku Line. Although it was founded in 1321 in northern Japan, the buildings you see date from 1911, when the temple was moved here. It is one of the two greatest Buddhist training centers in Japan, and you may see an applicant lying on the temple steps, waiting to be summoned in. (He may have been there for several days, maybe only a few hours.) Although the main hall (1964) is of concrete, the rest of the buildings are of wood, and very typical of Japanese Buddhist styling. Note the huge imperial chrysanthemum on the main gate, symbol of imperial favor for the temple.

Also of interest is the British Commonwealth War Cemetery, west of town, where more than 2,000 war dead lie. Address: Kariba-cho, Hodogaya-ku.

Narita

Few visitors to Japan think of Narita as anything other than the name of the new international airport, but I have a surprise for you—the town itself is quite nice, and worth a trip. You might want to combine a visit here with your trip to the airport, or from it, for that matter. In either case, you can have you luggage sent ahead to your hotel (or to the airport if departing) by ABC Baggage Service System, tel. 03-284-2525, or arrange through your hotel front desk. For normal-sized bags, the charge is only ¥2,000 ($12.12) for the first bag, ¥1,000 ($6.06) for each additional bag.

So, sans luggage, you are free to visit Narita. The most interesting spot here is Narita-san Shinshoji Temple ♛ ♛ ♛, a huge place of immense dignity. As it is also dedicated to transportation safety, it is a good spot for a prayer for the road, so to speak. You can buy amulets here, akin to St. Christopher medals, to hang on your automobile, airplane, boat, or skateboard. Long before Narita Airport was a twinkle in the eye of a former transport minister, Narita-san did a brisk business of blessing automobiles. Founded in 939, the temple wasn't moved to its present site until 1705. The Main Hall is quite new, but nonetheless imposing.

Down in the town, at the foot of the temple steps, a winding road leads to the JNR Narita Station, passing *ryokan*, restaurants, and little shops. It's a pleasant place, and if, for example, you've only seen big cities during your Japanese stay, this is a welcome contrast.

You get to Narita town in almost the same fashion as you do the airport, with the exception that the airport buses do not stop in the town in either direction. So you're best off taking either JNR from Tokyo Station or the private Keisei Railway from Ueno. Get off in the town stations, which are next to each other, and walk 10 minutes to the temple. Between the town and airport, take the Keisei rail line (JNR doesn't yet operate all the way to the airfield), or the JNR connecting bus, between station and air terminal. You can also take taxis, of course. If you're planning to drive by cab to Narita from the airport, note that there are separate lines for Narita cabs and Tokyo cabs, for the obvious reason that a Tokyo driver doesn't want a Narita-bound passenger.

Many travelers en route to Southeast Asian destinations from Europe (over the pole) or North America take a break at Narita, staying overnight at one of the fine hotels near the airport. They, too, might welcome a 2-hour visit to the town.

INSIDERS' INFORMATION FOR TOKYO AND VICINITY

HOTELS

Note: Nearly all Tokyo hotels have cable television, on which Channel 2 is the English-language station, broadcasting locally originated programs from JCTV and also picking up many of the programs of Cable News

Network, live by satellite from the United States. Arranged alphabetically within crown rating categories.

Imperial ♛ ♛ ♛ ♛ (Teikoku in Japanese)
1-1 Uchisaiwaicho 1-chome, Chiyoda-ku, Tokyo 100, tel. 03-504-1111
Two persons in twin, $145–155
Most famous, best sited for tourists. New tower better than main building. Biggest lobby in country, favored by local rich. Marvelous collection of restaurants, shops, services. Splendid service, 1,125 big rooms, every amenity.

Okura ♛ ♛ ♛ ♛ ♛
2-10-4 Toranomon, Minato-ku, Tokyo 105, tel. 03-582-0111
Two persons in twin, $140–200
Favorite of business and diplomatic travelers, with fantastic service. Opposite U.S. Embassy. Outstanding restaurants, 2 fine shopping arcades, 910 big rooms, but those in Main Building more convenient than South Wing. Best facilities for business people in Executive Service Salon.

Akasaka Prince ♛ ♛ ♛ ♛
1 Kioi-cho, Chiyoda-ku, Tokyo 102, tel. 03-234-1111
Two persons in twin, $135 up
Splendid, gleaming architectural triumph, excellently sited near Akasaka transport crossroads and entertainment center, 760 big rooms, each with corner views of city center, 8 excellent restaurants, excellent service, but no shops. Club floor. Westin Hotels. The lobby is a sea of white marble.

ANA Tokyo ♛ ♛ ♛ ♛ (Zen Niku Tokyo in Japanese)
12-23 Akasaka 1-chome, Minato-ku, Tokyo 107, tel. 03-505-1111
Two persons in twin, $135
Opened in June 1986, will compete with Tokyo's best. Grand lobby, 900 largish rooms (304 square feet for twin), fine array of restaurants, including top-floor *teppanyaki* with best views in town.

Capitol Tokyu ♛ ♛ ♛ ♛
2-10-3 Nagata-cho, Chiyoda-ku, Tokyo 100, tel. 03-581-4511
Two persons in twin, $160
Formerly the Hilton, ideally sited for government visitors

near Diet Building, Hie Shrine. Outstanding Keyaki Grill, other restaurants, pool, 480 biggish rooms. Tok*yu*, chain, not to be confused with Tok*yo*, the city. Tok*yu* means "Express."

Fukudaya Ryokan ♛ ♛ ♛ ♛

6-12 Kioi-cho, Chiyoda-ku, Tokyo 102, tel. 03-261-8577

Two persons in room, $265, breakfast and dinner included

Elegant Japanese-style inn, only 11 rooms (some with bath), lovely garden. Behind Sophia University, near New Otani, opposite Akasaka Palace.

Hilton International ♛ ♛ ♛ ♛

6-2 Nishi Shinjuku 6-chome, Shinjuku-ku, Tokyo 160, tel. 03-344-5111

Two persons in twin, $135

Opened 1984 out of center, but worth the detour. Three executive floors, 842 good-sized rooms, Business Service Center, sauna, gym, pool, tennis. Several fine restaurants (outstanding Chinese).

Keio Plaza Inter-Continental ♛ ♛ ♛ ♛

2-1 Nishi Shinjuku 2-chome, Shinjuku-ku, Tokyo 160, tel. 03-344-0111

Two persons in twin, $115

Tokyo's second-biggest, a city in itself, 1,482 rooms, 19 restaurants, 10 cocktail lounges, shops, Executive Service Center. South Tower newer than Main Tower.

New Otani ♛ ♛ ♛ ♛

4-1, Kioi-cho, Chiyoda-ku, Tokyo 102, tel. 03-265-1111

Two persons in twin, $140 up

Asia's biggest, with 2,047 rooms in two towers. Huge shopping arcade, including gourmet food mart. Branch of Tour d'Argent of Paris and 12 other restaurants. Ten-acre 400-year-old garden, chapel, women-only floor, nonsmoking floor, teahouse.

Century Hyatt ♛ ♛ ♛

2-7-2 Nishi Shinjuku, Shinjuku-ku, Tokyo 160, tel. 03-349-0111

Two persons in twin, $110 up

Nice hotel, despite lobby looking like Mussolini's tomb (had he designed one). A fair walk from public transport, but has own bus, next door to Hilton. Good choice of restaurants, 762 largish rooms, several shops. Try Raymond Olivier's restaurant, Chenonceaux.

Miyako ♛ ♛ ♛
1-1-50 Shiroganedai, Minato-ku, Tokyo 108, tel. 03-447-3111
Two persons in twin, $110
Would be 4 crowns but for distant location. Quiet area, several free buses daily to nearby rail stations and Ginza, 488 good-sized rooms, lovely garden, nice restaurants.

Pacific Meridien ♛ ♛ ♛
3-13-3 Takanawa, Minato-ku, Tokyo 108, tel. 03-445-6711
Two persons in twin, $100 up
Near Shinagawa Station, allied with French chain, 954 average-sized rooms (ask for one facing Tokyo Bay). Very good French restaurant, 2 good Chinese.

Palace ♛ ♛ ♛
1-1-1 Marunouchi, Chiyoda-ku, Tokyo 100, tel. 03-211-5211
Two persons in twin, $115 up
Fine service, excellent French restaurant and 4 others, 404 good-sized rooms, as close to Imperial Palace as possible. Excellent business location.

Tokyo Prince ♛ ♛ ♛
3-3-1 Shiba Koen, Minato-ku, Tokyo 105, tel. 03-432-1111
Two persons in twin, $110 up
Seven restaurants, 484 average-sized rooms, pool, shopping arcade, 4 bars and lounges. Ask for Tokyo Tower—side rooms.

Akasaka Tokyu ♛ ♛
2-14-3 Nagata-cho, Chiyoda-ku, Tokyo 100, tel. 03-580-2311
Two persons in twin, $120 up
Convenient location at Akasaka crossing, 566 smallish rooms, several restaurants, many shops.

Asakusa View ♛ ♛
3-17 Nishi Asakusa, Taito-ku, Tokyo 111, tel. 03-842-2111
Two persons in twin, $110 up
New (1985) and near Asakusa Kannon Temple, old "downtown" area of Tokyo, 342 smallish rooms, 3 restaurants. Trains to Nikko and northern Japan, express to airport.

Gajoen Kanko ♛ ♛
1-8-1 Shimo Meguro, Meguro-ku, Tokyo 153, tel. 03-491-0111
Two persons in twin, $75
Looks run-down, but lovingly serviced, 82 large rooms,

rambling wreck of prewar decor, almost Art Nouveau.

Ginza Tokyu♛♛
5-15-9 Ginza, Chuo-ku, Tokyo 104, tel. 03-541-2411
Two persons in twin, $120 up
Excellent location near Kabukiza Theater, 4 restaurants, 447 average-sized rooms.

Grand Palace♛♛
1-1-1 Iidabashi, Chiyoda-ku, Tokyo 102, tel. 03-246-1111
Two persons in twin, $105–130
Good location near Kanda book district, Imperial Palace Garden, 500 bigger-than-average rooms, 4 restaurants.

Hilltop♛♛ (Yamano-ue in Japanese)
1-1 Kanda Surugadai, Chiyoda-ku, Tokyo 101, tel. 03-293-2311
Two persons in twin, $85 up
Only 75 rooms, good-sized, in artists' and writers' retreat near universities, 2 restaurants, outdoor beer garden in summer.

Kayu Kaikan♛♛
8-1 Sanbancho, Chiyoda-ku, Tokyo 102, tel. 03-230-1111
Two persons in twin, $75–90
Operated by 5-crown Okura, at half the price, at convenient and quiet location along "Embassy Row" of Tokyo, 2 restaurants, fantastic service, but not to room. 60 rooms.

Keiunso Shinkan Ryokan♛♛
Yoyogi 2-chome, Shibuya-ku, Tokyo, tel. 03-370-0333
Two persons in room, $55 (room only)
Fairly quiet location, 13 rooms, good business-residential district.

Mikawaya Bekkan Ryokan♛♛
1-31-11 Asakusa, Taito-ku, Tokyo 111, tel. 03-843-2345
Two persons in twin, $50 (room only)
Member Japanese Inn Group, 12 rooms, near Asakusa Kannon Shrine, public bath only.

Mitsui Urban Ginza♛♛
8-6-15 Ginza, Chuo-ku, Tokyo 104, tel. 03-572-4131
Two persons in twin, $75
Business hotel, nice location, better than most in this category, 263 small rooms, 3 restaurants.

Miyako Inn♛♛
3-7-8 Mita, Minato-ku, Tokyo 108, tel. 03-454-3111
Two persons in twin, $70–100
Convenient location near Hamamatsu-cho Station (mono-

rail, etc.), 403 smallish rooms, 3 restaurants.

President ♛ ♛

2-2-3 Minami Aoyama, Minato-ku, Tokyo 107, tel. 03-497-0111

Two persons in twin, $70 up

Excellent location near Aoyama shopping streets, 212 fair-sized rooms, 2 restaurants.

Roppongi Prince ♛ ♛

3-2-7 Roppongi, Minato-ku, Tokyo 106, tel. 03-587-1111

Two persons in twin, $95–110

Sexy hotel, colorful, designed around 9-story atrium with fishtank pool in middle, 237 fairly small rooms, 6 restaurants. Room decor a trendy whore's dream. Opened 1984, next door to IBM.

Seifuso Ryokan ♛ ♛

1-12-15 Fujimi, Chiyoda-ku, Tokyo 102, tel. 03-263-0681

Two persons in room, $110 (room only)

Lovely Japanese inn, charming garden, in heart of Tokyo, 16 rooms, half (new wing) with bath. Old-wing rooms smaller, cheaper by up to half.

Shin Komatsu Ryokan ♛ ♛

1-9-13 Tsukiji, Chuo-ku, Tokyo 104, tel. 03-541-2225

Two persons in room, $80, breakfast and dinner included

Nicely sited near Tsukiji attractions (temple, fish market), 13 rooms, most with bath.

Sunshine City Prince ♛ ♛

1-5 Higashi Ikebukuro 3-chome, Toshima-ku, Tokyo 170, tel. 03-988-1111

Two persons in twin, $85–105

Designed for business travelers, with 1,166 smallish rooms in big tourist complex in out-of-the-way Ikebukuro (a second-class shopping and transport center), 6 restaurants. Next door to aquarium, planetarium, shopping mart.

Takanawa ♛ ♛

2-1-17 Takanawa, Minato-ku, Tokyo 108, tel. 03-443-9251

Two persons in twin, $70–85

Slightly frayed, old-fashioned, 217 smallish rooms, pool, garden. Near Shinagawa Station.

Takanawa Prince ♛ ♛

3-13-1 Takanawa, Minato-ku, Tokyo 108, tel. 03-447-1111

Two persons in twin, $105–135

Would have one more crown if not located near distant Shinagawa Station; 418 middle-sized rooms, 2 pools, garden, 7 restaurants, the works. Next door is New Takanawa Prince, same address, tel. 03-442-1111, 1,000 smallish rooms, 4 restaurants, pool, few shops, JAL office. Rooms $10–20 more than older hotel. Lobby is a sea of marble, otherwise could be airplane hangar.

Yaesu Fujiya ♕ ♕
2-9-1 Yaesu, Chuo-ku, Tokyo 104, tel. 03-273-2111
Two persons in twin, $70–110
Charming yet ultramodern business-oriented hotel on busy side (Yaesu) of Tokyo Station, 3 restaurants, 377 moderately sized rooms. Convenient to Ginza shopping. Branch of famous Hakone Fujiya at Miyanoshita.

Akasaka Shampia ♕
7-6-13 Akasaka, Minato-ku, Tokyo 107, tel. 03-586-0811
Two persons in twin, $65 up
Excellent location, 250 small rooms designed for business travelers.

Akihabara Washington ♕
1-8-3 Kanda, Chiyoda-ku, Tokyo 101, tel. 03-255-3311
Two persons in twin, $65
Three restaurants, 312 small rooms, especially nice Sanjusan Gendo, Japanese-style with *tatami* mats, *kotatsu* well to hang your feet in. Electronic shopping heaven all around.

Asia Center ♕
8-10-32 Akasaka, Minato-ku, Tokyo 107, tel. 03-402-6111
Two persons in twin, $40 up
Almost a hostel, but there are 180 rooms, some with bath. Many Southeast Asian visitors. Restaurant so-so.

Atagoyama Tokyu Inn ♕
1-6-6 Atago, Minato-ku, Tokyo 105, tel. 03-431-0109
Two persons in twin, $65
Good location for business travelers, advantages of mighty Tokyu chain. 200 rooms.

Daiei ♕
1-15-8 Koishikawa, Bunkyo-ku, Tokyo 112, tel. 03-813-6271
Two persons in twin, $50–55
Standard business-type hotel in north-central part of town, 80 small rooms.

Dai Ichi Inn Ikebukuro ♕
1-42-8 Higashi Ikebukuro, Toshima-ku, Tokyo 170, tel. 03-986-1221

Two persons in twin, $65

Near station, 140 smallish rooms in chain operation, 2 restaurants, sauna.

Dai Ichi Inn Omori♛

1-8-8 Omori-cho, Ota-ku, Tokyo 143, tel. 03-768-3111

Two persons in twin, $60

Charming garden, 104 smallish rooms, 2 restaurants. Next to motorboat racecourse and harbor.

Diamond♛

25 Ichibancho, Chiyoda-ku, Tokyo 102, tel. 03-263-2211

Two persons in twin, $70–120

Behind British Embassy, quiet neighborhood, 159 rooms, pleasant restaurant.

Fairmont♛

2-1-17 Kudan Minami, Chiyoda-ku, Tokyo 102, tel. 03-262-1151

Two persons in twin, $80–110

In quiet embassy area near Imperial Palace, 235 smallish rooms, 2 restaurants.

Ginza Capital♛

3-1-5 Tsukiji, Chuo-ku, Tokyo 104, tel. 03-543-8211

Two persons in twin, $65 up

Business-oriented establishment, better than most, 528 small rooms, convenient location.

Ginza Dai Ichi♛

8-13-1 Ginza, Chuo-ku, Tokyo 104, tel. 03-542-5311

Two persons in twin, $90

Great location for theater, entertainment, shopping, 800 smallish rooms, 4 restaurants, shopping arcade.

Ginza Marunouchi♛

4-1-12 Tsukiji, Chuo-ku, Tokyo 104, tel. 03-543-5431

Two persons in twin, $85

Fairly good location between Ginza and Tsukiji, 225 smallish rooms.

Ginza Nikko♛

8-4-21 Ginza, Chuo-ku, Tokyo 104, tel. 03-571-4911

Two persons in twin, $90–110

Japan Air Lines hotel in busy shopping area, 112 small rooms, 2 restaurants.

Green Awaji-cho♛

2-6 Kanda Awaji-cho, Chiyoda-ku, Tokyo 101, tel. 03-255-4161

Two persons in twin, $35–55

Good location for book district, universities, 207 small rooms.

Harajuku Trim ♨

6-28-6 Jingumae, Shibuya-ku, Tokyo 150, tel. 03-498-2101

Two persons in twin, $65

Atop an office building, attached to health club, which you can use. 120 tiny rooms.

Hillport ♨

23-19 Sakuragaoka-cho, Shibuya-ku, Tokyo 150, tel. 03-462-5171

Two persons in twin, $60

Small hotel, 45 small rooms, nice modern decor. Walkable from Shibuya Station.

Hokke Club ♨

2-1-48 Ikenohata, Taito-ku, Tokyo 110, tel. 03-822-3111

Two persons in twin, $45

Not far from Ueno Park/Station, 309 small rooms, half of them Japanese.

Holiday Inn ♨

1-13-7 Hatchobori, Chuo-ku, Tokyo 104, tel. 03-553-6161

Two persons in twin, $94–103

Near City Air Terminal, 119 average-sized rooms, pool on roof.

Ibis ♨

7-14-4 Roppongi, Minato-ku, Tokyo 106, tel. 03-403-4411

Two persons in twin, $70

Atop shopping arcade near Roppongi crossing, 200 smallish rooms, 8 floors.

Inabaso Ryokan ♨

5-6-13 Shinjuku, Shinjuku-ku, Tokyo 160, tel. 03-341-9581

Two persons in room, $40–45 (room only)

Western-style toilet, refrigerator, TV, A/C, 13 adequate rooms, all with bath.

Kayabacho Pearl ♨

1-2-5 Hinkawa, Chuo-ku, Tokyo 104, tel. 03-553-2211

Two persons in twin, $45–80

Business persons' hotel, 270 tiny rooms, east of downtown, good for Harumi fairgrounds.

Meguro Gajoen Ryokan ♨

1-8-1 Shino Meguro, Meguro-ku, Tokyo 153, tel. 03-491-0074

Two persons in room, $145, 2 meals, tax, service included

Small, fadingly elegant, Meiji Period in style. Next door to Gajoen Kanko Hotel. 30 rooms.

Mikawaya Bekkan Ryokan ♛
1-31-11 Asakusa, Taito-ku, Tokyo 111, tel. 03-843-2345
Two persons in room, $50 (room only)
Just off Nakamise shopping street leading to Asakusa Kannon Temple, 12 rooms.

Metropolitan ♛
1-6-1 Nishi Ikebukuro, Toshima-ku, Tokyo 171, tel. 03-980-1111
Two persons in twin, $85–120
Huge Japan National Railway hotel 3 minutes from Ikebukuro station, 818 tiny rooms.

Namiju Ryokan ♛
2-24-4 Asakusa, Taito-ku, Tokyo 111, tel. 03-841-9126
Two persons in room, $40–48 (room only)
Short walk from Asakusa Kannon Temple, 8 rooms, public bath.

New Meguro ♛
1-3-18 Chuo-cho, Meguro-ku, Tokyo 152
Two persons in twin, $55–70
Quiet residential area, 32 rooms, 1 Japanese room.

Okayasu Ryokan ♛
1-7-11 Shibaura, Minato-ku, Tokyo 105, tel. 03-452-5091
Two persons in room, $35 (room only)
Modest establishment in odd but fairly quiet location, 14 rooms.

Okubo House Ryokan ♛
1-11-32 Hyakunincho, Shinjuku-ku, Tokyo 160, tel. 03-361-2348
Two persons in room, $40 (room only)
Near Shin-Okubo Station of JNR, quiet, 28 rooms, half of them Japanese.

Sansuiro Ryokan ♛
2-9-5 Higashi Gotanda, Shinagawa-ku, Tokyo 141, tel. 03-441-7475
Two persons in room, $38–40 (room only)
Five minutes from Gotanda Station, 9 rooms, tea ceremony on Sundays.

Satoh ♛
1-4-4 Hongo, Bunkyo-ku, Tokyo 113, tel. 03-815-1133
Two persons in twin, $45

Small hotel (small facilities), 74 small rooms, most Western-style.

Sawanoya Ryokan ♨

2-3-11 Yanaka, Taito-ku, Tokyo 110, tel. 03-822-2251

Two persons in room, $45 (room only)

Quiet neighborhood north of Ueno Park, station, zoo, 12 rooms. Old-time Tokyo.

Shiba Park Hotel ♨

1-5-10 Shibakoen, Minato-ku, Tokyo 105, tel. 03-433-4141.

Two persons in twin, $80–150

Quiet location, convenient, 400 rooms, evincing fading glory days, but good service à la Imperial Hotel. Good Chinese, Japanese restaurants.

Shibuya Tokyu Inn ♨

1-24-10 Shibuya, Shibuya-ku, Tokyo 150, tel. 03-498-0109

Two persons in twin, $65

Opposite Shibuya Station, 225 rooms, nice *sushi* bar, coffee house.

Shimbashi Dai-ichi ♨

1-2-6 Shimbashi, Minato-ku, Tokyo 105, tel. 03-501-4411

Two persons in twin, $75–105

Small rooms in this prewar spot (older building), equally small in new building, 1,106 rooms, 7 of them Japanese-style.

Shinagawa Prince ♨

4-10-30 Takanawa, Minato-ku, Tokyo 108, tel. 03-440-1111

Single rooms only, at $40, but extra bed $12

Adjoining huge year-round sports center, with ice skating, bowling, tennis, pool, gym, also supermarket, 1,016 rooms.

Shinjuku Prince ♨

1-30-1 Kabukicho, Shinjuku-ku, Tokyo 160, tel. 03-205-1111

Two persons in twin, $75–110

Opposite Shinjuku Station, world's busiest, and in nightlife quarter, 571 rooms, at least 6 restaurants, plus shops and bars.

Shinjuku Washington ♨

3-2-9 Nishi Shinjuku, Shinjuku-ku, Tokyo 160, tel. 03-343-3111/3

Two persons in twin, $65–80

Ten-minute walk to station, 1,300 tiny rooms, automatic check-in (if you want it), several restaurants, shops. Annex around corner has another 340 rooms. Owned by Fujita tourist conglomerate.

Suigetsu Hotel Ryokan ₩

3-3-21 Ikenohata, Taito-ku, Tokyo 110, tel. 03-822-4611

Two persons in room, $40–45 (room only)

Quiet neighborhood behind Ueno Zoo, 70 Japanese-style rooms, no private baths. Associated Ohgaiso Hotel next door has 80 Western-style rooms, with bath, prices slightly higher.

Sunroute Ikebukuro ₩

1-39-4 Higashi Ikebukuro, Toshima-ku, Tokyo 170, tel. 03-980-1911

Two persons in twin, $68 up

Two minutes from Ikebukuro Station, 144 rooms, 2 restaurants, modest but pleasant.

Sunroute Shibuya ₩

1-11 Nampeidai-cho, Shibuya-ku, Tokyo 150, tel. 03-464-6411

Two persons in twin, $65

Quiet neighborhood behind hotel, busy expressway in front, close to Shibuya Station, 180 rooms.

Sunroute Tokyo ₩

2-3-1 Yoyogi, Shibuya-ku, Tokyo 151, tel. 03-375-3211

Two persons in twin, $90–100

Despite address, very close to Shinjuku Station (2-minute walk), 544 small rooms, cuisines of China, Japan, and Europe, shops, etc.

Takanawa Tobu ₩

4-7-6 Takanawa, Minato-ku, Tokyo 108, tel. 03-447-0111

Two persons in twin, $68

Good service and convenient location, 201 undistinguished rooms.

Takara ₩

2-16-5 Higashi Ueno, Taito-ku, Tokyo 110, tel. 03-831-0101

Two persons in twin, $70–110

Ultramodern ambience, 140 rooms, indoor pool, gymnasium, 5 minutes to Ueno Station.

Tokiwa Ryokan Shinkan ♛
7-27-9 Shinjuku, Shinjuku-ku, Tokyo 160, tel. 03-202-4321
Two persons in room, $165, 2 meals, tax, service charge included
About 10 minutes from Shinjuku Station by car, 50 rooms, most with bath.

Tokyo ♛
2-17-18 Takanawa, Minato-ku, Tokyo 108, tel. 03-447-5771
Two persons in twin, $70–120
Quiet ambience, exterior castlelike, 46 rooms, mostly Western-style.

Tokyo Kanko ♛
4-10-8 Takanawa, Minato-ku, Tokyo 108, tel. 03-443-1211
Two persons in twin, $55–80
Not far from Shinagawa Station, 154 rooms, one-third of them Japanese.

Tokyo Marunouchi ♛
1-6-3 Marunouchi, Chiyoda-ku, Tokyo 100, tel. 03-215-2151
Two persons in twin, $100–130
Excellent location in heart of business district, 210 rooms, good restaurant.

Tokyo Station ♛
1-9-1 Marunouchi, Chiyoda-ku, Tokyo 100, tel. 03-231-2511
Two persons in twin, $80–90
Marunouchi side of station, 62 awful rooms, but soundproofed. Listed here only because of its location.

Tokyu Kanko ♛
2-21-6 Akasaka, Minato-ku, Tokyo 107, tel. 03-582-0451
Two persons in twin, $70–75
Part of Tokyu travel conglomerate's chain, great location, 48 small rooms.

Urashima ♛
2-5-23 Harumi, Chuo-ku, Tokyo 104, tel. 03-533-3111
Two persons in twin, $50–55
Business-style hotel, as Japanese say, 996 tiny rooms, outdoor pool.

Yaesu Ryumeikan Ryokan ♛
1-3-11 Yaesu, Chuo-ku, Tokyo 103, tel. 03-271-0971

Two persons in room, $140, 2 meals, tax, service charge included

Quiet inn in busy area, 60 rooms, business traveler–oriented.

Yashima Ryokan♛

1-15-5 Kyakunin-cho, Shinjuku-ku, Tokyo 160, tel. 03-364-2534

Two persons in room, $40 (room only)

Five minutes from Okubo Station, 13 rooms, some Japanese-style, some with bath.

Tokyo Airport Hotels

NEW TOKYO INTERNATIONAL AIRPORT, NARITA

Narita Prince♛ ♛ ♛

560 Tokko, Narita City, Chiba 286-01, tel. 0476-33-1111

Two persons in twin, $106

Five minutes by car from terminal, 321 rooms, pool, sauna, shop, tennis, 3 restaurants. Near Holiday Inn.

Narita View♛ ♛ ♛

700 Kosuge, Narita City, Chiba 286-01, tel. 0476-32-1111

Two persons in twin, $85–130

Ten minutes by car from terminal, 504 rooms, indoor and outdoor pools, tennis, gym.

INSIDERS' TIPS

Guests at the Hotel Okura can use the Health Club from 10 A.M. to 9 P.M., and if you forgot your clothes, you can buy a training jumper for ¥5,500 and shoes for about the same price. The poolside restaurant of the club has a diet menu ranging from a salad at 27 calories (it's seaweed) to sautéed scallops with basil at 240 calories. There are also four suggested jogging courses which take you as far as the Imperial Palace and the Diet Building.

Holiday Inn♛ ♛

320-1 Tokko, Narita City, Chiba 286-01, tel. 0476-32-1234

Two persons in twin, $75–100

Closest to airport by hair's breadth, 254 rooms, 7 of them Japanese-style, sauna, pool, tennis, golf, cycling, gym.

Nikko♛ ♛

500 Tokko, Narita City, Chiba 286-01, tel. 0476-32-0032

Two persons in twin, $65–110
Affiliated with Japan Air Lines, 523 smallish rooms, pool.
Near Holiday Inn.

HANEDA AIRPORT

Haneda Tokyu ♛ ♛
2-8-6 Haneda Kuko, Ota-ku, Tokyo 144, tel. 03-747-0311
Two persons in twin, $105–175
For busy business traveler, 307 rooms on small side, pool
in summer.

Disneyland

Sunroute Plaza ♛ ♛ ♛
1-6 Maihama, Urayasu City, Chiba 272-01, tel. 0473-54-7711
Two persons in twin, $90–110
Not inspected, as opened late 1986, but plans should make
it 3 crowns, 506 average-sized rooms, plus family suites
and 4-bedded rooms. Extra beds available for kids. Outdoor pool, 4 restaurants, beer garden. Next door to Disney-
land, 45 minutes downtown or Narita Airport.

Yokohama

Yokohama ♛ ♛ ♛ ♛
6-1 Yamashita-cho, Naka-ku, Yokohama, Kanagawa-ken
231, tel. 045-662-1321
Two persons in twin, $100
Attractively designed, very new hotel right on waterfront,
overlooking harbor at Yamashita Park, near Chinatown
too, 170 good-sized rooms, 3 restaurants, friendly top-floor
bar.

New Grand ♛ ♛ ♛
10 Yamashita-cho, Naka-ku, Yokohama, Kanagawa-ken
231, tel. 045-681-1841
Two persons in twin, $100
The older establishment hotel, with messy, shop-filled
entrance, but boasting 195 largish rooms and excellent
top-floor Star Light Grill, good food supplemented by nice

views of harbor. Also coffee shop, pool.

Holiday Inn ♛ ♛

77 Yamashita-cho, Naka-ku, Yokohama, Kanagawa-ken 231, tel. 045-681-3311

Two persons in twin, $95

Right at entrance of Chinatown, and featuring its own very good Chinese Chungking restaurant (plus 3 other kinds), 125 average-sized rooms, rooftop pool, sauna, beauty shop.

Tokyu ♛ ♛

1-1-12 Minami Saiwai, Nishi-ku, Yokohama, Kanagawa-ken 220, tel. 045-311-1682

Two persons in twin, $100

Next door and attached to Yokohama Station (serving 3 different rail lines), for the busy traveler, not near touristic Yokohama, 3 restaurants, 219 average-sized rooms.

Satellite ♛

76 Yamashita-cho, Naka-ku, Yokohama, Kanagawa-ken 231, tel. 045-641-8571

Two persons in twin, $70

Behind the Holiday Inn, 2 blocks from harbor, 105 small rooms, nice restaurant, the Portside.

Star ♛

11 Yamashita-cho, Naka-ku, Yokohama, Kanagawa-ken 231, tel. 045-651-3111

Two persons in twin, $65

About 150 small rooms (ask for one overlooking harbor), 2 restaurants, kind of "pink modern" decor.

INSIDERS' TIPS

The Prince Hotel chain, one of Japan's best, invites foreigners in Japan to an annual Cherry Blossom Viewing Festival at its Takanawa Prince Hotel each spring (usually early April). In the gardens, glowing with blossoms, the chain sets up several *yatai* (temporary food stalls), which serve such things as *sushi, yakitori,* and *tempura* under the trees. On entering, each guest is given coupons worth ¥1,000 ($6.06) to "spend" at these stalls as whimsy demands. You can observe an open-air tea ceremony, *mochi* rice pounding, and the battledore and shuttlecock game, among other arts and crafts that are demonstrated. Held from noon to 3 P.M. Phone 03-442-1111, ext. 5524 or 5527, if it's around that time of year, for details.

RESTAURANTS

Note: Arranged alphabetically within crown rating categories.

Apecius ♛ ♛ ♛ ♛ ♛

1-9-4 Yuraku-cho, Chiyoda-ku, tel. 03-214-1361

Average dinner, $60

Japan's best French restaurant, with elegant surroundings and cuisine not yet Japanized by the chef and management. Classic cuisine, with only traces of the *nouvelle* which customers still expect.

Fukudaya ♛ ♛ ♛ ♛ ♛

6 Kioi-cho, Chiyoda-ku, tel. 03-261-8577

Average dinner, $200 (no credit cards)

Classic Japanese *kaiseki* cuisine, in magnificent surroundings, exquisitely served, excruciatingly beautiful. An experience of a lifetime. To enjoy fully, go with Japanese-speaking friend to avoid any awkward moments. Ten courses, from tiny eggplants to *tempura*. Reserve well ahead.

Hannyaen ♛ ♛ ♛ ♛ ♛

2-20-10 Shiroganedai, Minato-ku, tel. 03-441-1256

Average dinner, $110

Traditional *kaiseki* cuisine, one fixed course daily, in very old house surrounded by gorgeous garden. Take Japanese-speaking friend for help in communications. Freshest of fresh, from fish to vegetables.

Jisaku ♛ ♛ ♛ ♛ ♛

14-19 Akashi-cho, Chuo-ku, tel. 03-541-2391

Average dinner, $55

Lovely old rambling house on banks of Sumida (but best views on inner gardens), with classic dishes (not *kaiseki*) like *mizutaki, shabu shabu, sukiyaki,* and *tempura*. Walkable from the Ginza. Some English spoken.

Arisugawa ♛ ♛ ♛ ♛

2-1-20 Moto Azabu, Minato-ku, tel. 03-442-4177

Average dinner, $45

In basement of Arisugawa National Court Building, near park of same name. Not fancy, but outstanding cooking, especially fish of the season. Reserve well ahead.

Fukuzushi ♛ ♛ ♛ ♛

5-7-8 Roppongi, Minato-ku, tel. 03-402-4116

Average dinner, $90

Best *sushi* in town if atmosphere counts and you like elegant surroundings. Traditional atmosphere, yet high-class. Try to sit at the counter, unless you're in a big party.

Hanamura ♛ ♛ ♛ ♛

6-6-5 Akasaka, Minato-ku, tel. 03-585-4570

Average dinner, $45

Great *tempura* restaurant, with tables for small parties, *zashiki* seating (on floor) for groups of 5 up. Purely traditional atmosphere, service.

Houmasa ♛ ♛ ♛ ♛

3-1-21 Moto Azabu, Minato-ku, tel. 03-479-2880

Average dinner, $60

Kaiseki cuisine in a tiny restaurant (seats less than 20) with perfect blending of excellent food and subtly understated ambience. No theater, no drama, just beautifully prepared fish, game, and vegetables from short menu.

Inagiku ♛ ♛ ♛ ♛

2-9-8 Nihonbashi Kayaba-cho, Chuo-ku, tel. 03-669-5501

Average dinner, $80

A longtime favorite of foreign visitors, but marvelous nonetheless. *Tempura* served in classic style, but with Western touches, such as drinks beforehand in waiting room, coffee afterward likewise, linen napkins, semi-European decor.

Kuremutsu ♛ ♛ ♛ ♛

1-34-2 Asakusa, Taito-ku, tel. 03-842-0906

Average dinner, $40

Kaiseki cuisine, plus other traditional Japanese specialties (grilled chicken, fish) in lovely old farmhouse transplanted from Gifu prefecture. Just off Nakamise (main shopping lane) leading to Asakusa Kannon Temple. *Kabuki* actors allegedly frequent the place.

Maxim's de Paris ♛ ♛ ♛ ♛

5-3-1 Ginza, Chuo-ku, tel. 03-572-3621

Average dinner, $100

Yes, a branch of *the* Maxim's, and in the 3rd basement of the Ginza Sony Building yet! Walk in via the elevator, or drive down a cobblestone street in the garage and arrive in style. On smaller scale than original, but outstanding food, not at all Japanized.

Shiruyoshi ♛ ♛ ♛ ♛

6-2-12 Akasaka, Minato-ku, tel. 03-583-0333

Average dinner, $45–85

Deluxe Western-style setting for traditional *kaiseki* cuisine or *tempura*, the latter costing about half the former. Imaginative *kaiseki* dishes, traditional *tempura*, in this branch of Osaka establishment. Very much "in" with local big shots.

Tatsumiya 🏮 🏮 🏮 🏮
1-33-5 Asakusa, Taito-ku, tel. 03-842-7373
Average dinner, $20
Affordable *kaiseki* cuisine, up to 7 courses, nicely done, attractively presented, in an antique-crammed old house where half the fun is looking at the objects from old farmhouses etc. surrounding you. (Some are for sale, too.) Owned by brother of Kuremutsu owner (see above).

Tenmo 🏮 🏮 🏮 🏮
4-15 Nihonbashi, Chuo-ku, tel. 03-241-7035
Average dinner, $35
Delicious *tempura*, light and fresh, and a treat for those sitting at the counter, watching the chef do his thing. Close to Japan's banking center.

Tour d'Argent 🏮 🏮 🏮 🏮
4-1 Kioicho, Chiyoda-ku, tel. 03-239-3111 or 265-1111
Average dinner, $110
The only branch of the Paris original, and serving a limited, but excellent, choice of courses. Naturally, the pressed duck (flown in from France) is what everyone wants, along with a good Burgundy and a rich dessert ("Parisian chocolate cake" is on the menu). The view is not Notre Dame, but a lovely Japanese garden.

Tsujitome 🏮 🏮 🏮 🏮
7-3 Ginza, Chuo-ku, tel. 03-573-5226
Average dinner, $120
Kaiseki cooking at its best, though ambience is not traditional old house, but modern basement (of Nihon Keikinzoku Building). Owner is a prolific cookbook writer.

A Tantot 🏮 🏮 🏮
5-17-1 Roppongi, Minato-ku, tel. 03-586-4431
Average dinner, $30–45
Axis Building, 3rd floor. Excellent French cuisine, splendid summer setting on terrace, refined modern otherwise. Special prices Monday evening. Slightly Japanized menu, nothing to worry about. A fun restaurant.

Brasserie Bernard 🏮 🏮 🏮
7-14-3 Roppongi, Minato-ku, tel. 03-405-7877
Average dinner, $20–30

Kajimaya Building, 7th floor. Fine French cooking, relaxed atmosphere, a favorite of French residents. Try grilled sausages.

Chez Figaro ♨ ♨ ♨
4-4-1 Nishi Azabu, Minato-ku, tel. 03-400-8718
Average dinner, $35
Owner-chef Iribe, trained at Lassère and La Pyramide, has one of Tokyo's longest-running success stories here. Traditional French cuisine, not Japanized, no hint of the *nouvelle*, for which many of its guests are grateful (including lots of French Embassy staff). Try duck or any pâté.

Chinya ♨ ♨ ♨
1-3-4 Asakusa, Taito-ku, tel. 03-841-0010
Average dinner, $15–45
Sukiyaki specialists, but other fixed-course meals, from cheap to expensive, all featuring specially selected beef, which melts like butter in the mouth. Traditional old house, near Kaminarimon Gate of Asakusa Kannon Temple.

Daikonya ♨ ♨ ♨
9-8 Sarugakucho. Shibuya-ku, tel. 03-496-6664
Average dinner, $40
Basement, Daikanyama Village Building. *Kaiseki* cuisine in modern surroundings. Traditional dishes, up to 8 per meal, from succulent baby shrimp to artfully designed snow peas. Menu changes monthly.

Edogin ♨ ♨ ♨
4-5-1 Tsukiji, Chuo-ku, tel. 03-543-4401
Average dinner, $28
Wonderfully old-fashioned *sushi* shop down in the fish market district, with generous servings and fresher than fresh. Belly up and shout out your order when the counterman looks at you.

Etchikatsu ♨ ♨ ♨
2-31-23 Yushima, Bunkyo-ku, tel. 03-811-5293
Average dinner, $30–40
Luxurious surroundings for *sukiyaki* in one of Tokyo's oldest establishments. Tables, yes, but also *zashiki* sitting on the floor if you reserve well ahead. Mill-on-the-pond bucolic atmosphere, good beef.

Goemon ♨ ♨ ♨
1-1-26 Komagome, Bunkyo-ku, tel. 03-811-2015
Average dinner, $20 up

Tofu, Japanese soft bean curd, done dozens of ways. Set course is best way to go, affording surprise and delicious delight. Garden breezes in summer, but ask for garden room any time of year.

Imari ♛ ♛ ♛

7-19-1 Roppongi, Minato-ku, tel. 03-479-0046
Average dinner, $60

The rage these days, French-style (accent the "style") food served on Japanese dishes, this time classic Imariyaki pottery, and in tiny Japanese-style portions. The result: duck pâté that looks like *kaiseki* cuisine, but is really French-inspired, to name just one example. Delightful.

Jiro ♛ ♛ ♛

4-2-15 Ginza Nishi, Chuo-ku, tel. 03-535-3600
Average dinner, $40

Sushi with a lot of theater, in decor and chef's exercises (try the counter in any *sushi* shop, of course). One of Tokyo's busiest intersections.

Kandagawa Honten ♛ ♛ ♛

2-5-11 Soto Kanda, Chiyoda-ku, tel. 03-251-5031
Average dinner, $25

Kabayaki, the classic Japanese eel dish, is the specialty here. Old-fashioned Western-style ambience, thoughtful service. Slightly out-of-the-way.

Kyubei ♛ ♛ ♛

8-5-23 Ginza, Chuo-ku, tel. 03-572-3704
Average dinner, $80

Home base for one of Japan's best *sushi* franchise operations (dare we say "chain"?), and considered *the* best *sushi* shop in Japan by some. Prime Ginza location.

L'Orangerie ♛ ♛ ♛

3-6-1 Kita Aoyama, Minato-ku, tel. 03-407-7461
Average dinner, $45

Hanae Mori Building, 5th floor. Branch of original in Paris (on Ile de la Cité). Delicious cuisine, pretentious surroundings, like parent. Favorite of nouveau-slightly-riche.

Mikawa ♛ ♛ ♛

3-4-7 Kayaba-cho, Chuo-ku, tel. 03-664-9843
Average dinner, $30

Tempura for the purist, without fanfare, in tiny shop, hard to find in out-of-way section of town (near Holiday Inn).

Minokichi ♛ ♛ ♛

5-5 Roppongi, Minato-ku, tel. 03-404-0767

Average dinner, $25

Basement, Roi Building. Branch of famous Kyoto establishment, with *kaiseki* cuisine (minus the fuss and feathers), *sukiyaki*, *shabu shabu*, etc.

Sasanoyuki ♔ ♔ ♔

2-15-10 Negishi, Taito-ku, tel. 03-873-1145

Average dinner, $12–15

Tofu is king here, and you can choose from 3 set meals (up to 8 dishes). Soybean curd has been the staple of Japanese vegetarian diet for centuries, and ranges from delicious to more delicious. Behind Ueno Park.

Sunaba ♔ ♔ ♔

4-5-4 Muromachi Nihonbashi, Chuo-ku, tel. 03-241-4038

Average dinner, $15

The best noodle restaurant in town, and open over 400 years! Noodles, yes, but Japanese *soba* can be prepared many delicious ways. *Soba* (buckwheat noodles) the specialty here, with *tempura soba* a favorite.

Takamura ♔ ♔ ♔

3-4-27 Roppongi, Minato-ku, tel. 03-585-6600

Average dinner, $55 up

Kaiseki cuisine, classical as possible, with garden views and *irori* (open hearth) in each room, in bustling, trendy Roppongi. Splendid presentations, outstanding taste.

Ten Ichi ♔ ♔ ♔

6-6-5 Ginza, Chuo-ku, tel. 03-571-1949

Average dinner, $30–35

Perhaps Tokyo's most famous *tempura* restaurant, with branches all around town. This is home base, and quite elegant. Tables or *zashiki* rooms. Cheaper *tendon* (*tempura* on rice) at lunch only.

Uozen ♔ ♔ ♔

1-2-10 Yanaka, Taito-ku, tel. 03-821-4351

Average dinner, $35–55

Elegant fish is the feature of this *kaiseki* restaurant, out-of-the-way but worthwhile with a Japanese-speaking friend. Very refined ambience, almost out of this (modern) world.

Yamazaki ♔ ♔ ♔

2-14-13 Akasaka, Minato-ku, tel. 03-583-2059

Average dinner, $80

Kaiseki cuisine, Kyoto-style, at high prices except for counter at lunchtime. Subdued elegance, decorous service, splendidly cooked and arranged dishes.

Yoshino ♛ ♛ ♛

3-10-10 Shinjuku, Shinjuku-ku, tel. 03-341-8788

Average dinner, $25

Nabe ryori (stewpot cooking) is the feature here, with *shabu shabu* (lamb beef, chicken, shrimp, you name it). Sit at counter or in *zashiki (tatami)* rooms. On edge of red-light and gay-bar district east of Isetan Department Store.

Yotaro ♛ ♛ ♛

4-11-4 Roppongi, Minato-ku, tel. 03-405-5866

Average dinner, $40

Tempura and *taimeshi* are the specialties here, the latter being the succulent *tai* (sea bream) with rice, unlike any other rice and fish dish you've ever had. Also have deadly *fugu* (blowfish) in winter. Branch of famous Osaka shop.

Zakuro ♛ ♛ ♛

5-3-3 Akasaka, Minato-ku, tel. 03-582-6841

Average dinner, $35–75

Basement of TBS television studio.

Shabu shabu (boiled meat and vegetables) prepared at your table, with lots of different sauces to dip the meat in. Lower prices at the table, higher if you want to sit on the floor in *zashiki* rooms.

Akimoto ♛ ♛

3-4 Kojimachi, Chiyoda-ku, tel. 03-262-6762

Average dinner, $45

Marvelous old building in center of city near palace, with eel the specialty. If you like it grilled and served on rice, ask for *unaju,* otherwise, *kabayaki,* without the bed of rice.

Bon ♛ ♛

1-2-11 Ryusen, Taito-ku, tel. 03-872-0375

Average dinner, $30–40

Shojin ryori (vegetarian cuisine), something like *kaiseki* but less elaborate. Japanese-style sitting, several *tofu* dishes in your set-course meal (3 prices).

Botan ♛ ♛

1-15 Kanda Sudacho, Chiyoda-ku, tel. 03-251-0577

Average dinner, $18

One item on the menu only—*torinabe,* chicken stewed in an old iron pot (over charcoal) while you watch. Sit on the floor, warm your hands by charcoal *hibachi* (brazier). Four generations of owners, hundreds of broods of chickens from same farm, no change in decor the 30 years I've been there.

Daikokuya ♛ ♛
1-38-10 Asakusa, Taito-ku, tel. 03-844-1111
Average dinner, $8
Tempura, but cheaply priced in form of *ten don (tempura donbori),* shrimp over rice. No frills, old-fashioned working-class ambience. Just great! Opposite Asakusa Kannon Temple entrance.

Hayashi ♛ ♛
1-12 Nihonbashi Muromachi, Chuo-ku, tel. 03-241-5367
Average dinner, $75
Tempura fit for a shogun, with scarcely any oil used. Elegant ambience, service of highest standards.

Hokkaien ♛ ♛
2-12-1 Nishi Azabu, Minato-ku, tel. 03-407-8507
Average dinner, $25
One of Tokyo's best Chinese restaurants, Peking-style this time.

Inakaya ♛ ♛
7-8-4 Roppongi, Minato-ku, tel. 03-405-9866
Average dinner, $40–50
Robata yaki (country-style grilled cooking) is an experience you shouldn't miss, unless you hate noise. Shouting is the rule here, as cooks grill your orders on open fires in front of you, shouting the menu, shouting when it's ready, shouting when you leave and arrive. All good fun, smoky and cozy.

Kogetsu ♛ ♛
5-50-9 Jingumae, Shibuya-ku, tel. 03-407-3033
Average dinner, $45
Kyoto cooking, almost *kaiseki,* but informal ambience. Elegantly simple.

Kyoaji ♛ ♛
3-3-5 Shinbashi, Minato-ku, tel. 03-591-3344
Average dinner, $70
Kyoto-style cuisine again, but with single menu daily. Restrained ambience.

L'Ecrin ♛ ♛
4-5-5 Ginza, Chuo-ku, tel. 03-561-9706
Average dinner, $85
Basement of Mikimoto Building. Considered by many Japanese to be one of country's finest French restaurants. Setting decidedly opulent.

Liu Yuan ♕ ♕
1-3-1 Shiba Koen, Minato-ku, tel. 03-432-6231
Average dinner, $35
One of best Chinese restaurants, with Peking and other cuisines. Large building specializing in banquets, but individuals also welcome. Why not try Peking duck?

Matsukan ♕ ♕
3-4-12 Azabu Juban, Minato-ku, tel. 03-455-4923
Average dinner, $30
Splendid *sushi* bar and restaurant in semiresidential area.

Nakasei ♕ ♕
1-39-13 Asakusa, Taito-ku, tel. 03-841-7401
Average dinner, $15–40
Wonderful ambience, excellent *tempura*. Higher-priced *zashiki* rooms or lower-priced tables. Near Asakusa Kannon Temple. Bargain: *tempura teishoku (table d'hôte)* set menu.

Nodaiwa ♕ ♕
1-5-4 Higashi Azabu, Minato-ku, tel. 03-583-7852
Average dinner, $24
Eel, natural instead of farmed, so they say, in old building with choice of tables or *zashiki* rooms. Dates back to Edo Period.

Queen Alice ♕ ♕
3-17-34 Nishi Azabu, Minato-ku, tel. 03-405-9039
Average dinner, $50
Tastefully designed French restaurant, with excellent cooking, in an old house with a pretty garden. Menu is whatever the chef feels like on the day.

Rakutei ♕ ♕
6-8-1 Akasaka, Minato-ku, tel. 03-585-3743
Average dinner, $30
Tiny little *tempura* place, with *nama ebi* (baby shrimp) a specialty.

Serina ♕ ♕
3-12-2 Roppongi, Minato-ku, tel. 03-403-6211
Average dinner, $40–50
Sukiyaki and *shabu shabu,* each prepared at your table, are favorites here, but also look into *ishiyaki* (steak on hot rocks).

Sasamaki Kenuki Zushi ♕ ♕
2-12 Kanda Ogawacho, Chiyoda-ku, tel. 03-291-2570

Average dinner, $25
For nearly 300 years, serving *sushi* in old style, wrapped in bamboo leaf after marinating in vinegar.

Tamura 𝖂 𝖂
2-12-11 Tsukiji, Chuo-ku, tel. 03-541-1611
Average dinner, $30–115
Kaiseki cuisine on several levels, at tables downstairs, on *zashiki* mats upstairs, and priced accordingly. Traditional elegance upstairs, pleasant service down.

Toriden 𝖂 𝖂
4-31-4 Jingumae, Shibuya-ku, tel. 03-405-9898
Average dinner, $15
Yakitori, the great Japanese snack of grilled chicken (over charcoal) on a stick, with soy-sauce basting. Trendy crowd here.

Tsuruhachi 𝖂 𝖂
2-4 Kanda Jimbocho, Chiyoda-ku, tel. 03-262-0665
Average dinner, $30
Sushi without frills or tears, either. Bookish district, intellectual crowd.

Yabusoba 𝖂 𝖂
2-10 Awajicho, Chiyoda-ku, tel. 03-251-0287
Average dinner, $12
Just the best *soba* (buckwheat noodles) in town. Splendid old house. Ask for *zaru soba* (cold) in summer. Beware of imitations, of which there are many.

Yakko 𝖂 𝖂
1-10-2 Asakusa, Taito-ku, tel. 03-841-9886
Average dinner, $15
Eel, in 200-year-old restaurant, smoky and inviting. Near Honganji Temple.

Yonekyu 𝖂 𝖂
2-17-10 Asakusa, Taito-ku, tel. 03-841-6416
Average dinner, $35
Gyunabe (meat stew, similar to *sukiyaki*) in old Edo-style house, with old Edo manners.

Aux Six Arbres 𝖂
7-13-10 Roppongi, Minato-ku, tel. 03-479-2888
Average dinner, $40
Fine French dining in restaurant with French name meaning Roppongi (Six Trees). Stylish decor, too. For dessert, white cheese and black-currant soufflé.

Bentenyama Miyako ♛
2-1-16 Asakusa, Taito-ku, tel. 03-844-0034
Average dinner, $45
Old-fashioned *sushi,* in Edomae (Tokyo) style. Try about 10 different kinds.

Bodaiju ♛
4-13-14 Shiba, Minato-ku, tel. 03-456-3257
Average dinner, $18 up
Bukkyo Dendo Center Building, 2nd floor. Vegetarian cuisine, Chinese-style. Lunch as cheap as $4.

Bistrot de la Cité ♛
4-2-10 Nishi Azabu, Minato-ku, tel. 03-406-5475
Average dinner, $38
Relaxed and charming bistro atmosphere. Try *crêpes oursin,* for instance.

Chisen ♛
4-12-5 Roppongi, Minato-ku, tel. 03-403-7677
Average dinner, $23
One of only two *kushi-age* entries. Deep-fried skewered fish, meat, vegetables (breaded). Set menu. Choice of rice or noodles at end.

Futaba ♛
2-8-11 Ueno, Taito-ku, tel. 03-831-6483
Average dinner, $12
Tonkatsu (deep-fried, breaded pork cutlet) is famous here, and this is one of two best places for it in Tokyo. Near Ueno Park.

Gonin Byakusho ♛
3-10-3 Roppongi, Minato-ku, tel. 03-470-1675
Average dinner, $18 up
Another place for *robata yaki* (country-style grilled cooking), like Inakaya, above, but not as noisy. Determinedly rustic atmosphere (name means "five peasants").

Hantei ♛
2-12-15 Nezu, Bunkyo-ku, tel. 03-823-7661
Average dinner, $20
Kushi-age again (see Chisen, above), slightly out-of-the-way but all the more "unspoiled." Ask for *zashiki* rooms in old warehouse.

Hasejin ♛
3-3-15 Azabudai, Minato-ku, tel. 03-582-7811
Average dinner, $20–30

Beef is the thing here, with *sukiyaki, shabu shabu,* some *kaiseki*-style beef dishes.

Honke Ponta ♛
3-23-2 Ueno, Taito-ku, tel. 03-831-2351
Average dinner, $9
Tonkatsu (deep-fried, breaded pork cutlet) in oldest such restaurant in town.

Ile de France ♛
3-11-5 Roppongi, Minato-ku, tel. 03-404-0384
Average dinner, $40
Excellent French cuisine with French chef, in heart of Roppongi. Try *cassoulet.*

Isehiro ♛
1-5-4 Kyobashi, Chuo-ku, tel. 03-281-5864
Average dinner, $8
Yakitori (chicken on a stick) by itself, on rice, whatever. Smoky and fun.

Ishikawa ♛
1-6-10 Shibuya, Shibuya-ku, tel. 03-406-4488
Average dinner, $45
Basement, Q Mansion. *Nabemono* (casserole) dishes, with handmade stone pots. Alternatively, barbecue.

Kakiden ♛
3-37-11 Shinjuku, Shinjuku-ku, tel. 03-352-5121
Average dinner, $35
Kaiseki food in untraditional, ultramodern (and very chic) surroundings, all butter-soft leather and lacquer. What the bored and rich Japanese like.

Kawakin ♛
3-15-10 Nishi Asakusa, Taito-ku, tel. 03-844-1017
Average dinner, $15–40
Tonkatsu (pork cutlet) again, this time with curry, and extra-large cutlets.

Kizushi ♛
6-17-2 Hongo, Bunkyo-ku, tel. 03-811-5934
Average dinner, $28
Sushi up near Tokyo University, and accordingly low-keyed.

La Colomba ♛
2-1-33 Kudan Minami, Chiyoda-ku, tel. 03-230-1933
Average dinner, $35
One of our two listed Italian restaurants, Northern in tone. Game, veal.

La Granata ♛
5-3-3 Akasaka, Minato-ku, tel. 03-582-3241
Average dinner, $25
Basement of TBS television studio. Southern Italian generally, bistro atmosphere. Many local Italian residents dine here.

Mamiana ♛
3-5-6 Azabudai, Minato-ku, tel. 03-583-0545
Average dinner, $8
Old house, nice garden, middle of Roppongi, yet cheap and good *soba*.

Miyako ♛
2-1-16 Asakusa, Taito-ku, tel. 03-844-0034
Average dinner, $10
Old-fashioned *sushi* in 100-year-old shop, and inexpensive.

Munakata ♛
3-1-17 Nihonbashi, Chuo-ku, tel. 03-281-3288
Average dinner, $18
Kaiseki cuisine plus *shabu shabu* and other traditional items.

Nagasaka Sarashina ♛
1-8-7 Azabu Juban, Minato-ku, tel. 03-585-1676
Average dinner, $9
Soba (buckwheat noodles) in several varieties, including *macha* (green tea).

Okajoki ♛
5-59-3 Nakano, Nakano-ku, tel. 03-388-3753
Average dinner, $25
Near Nakano Station, a bit out of the way, but good *robata yaki* ambience.

Omatsuya ♛
5-14-18 Ginza, Chuo-ku, tel. 03-571-7053
Average dinner, $18
Ginza 1-N Building, 2nd floor. Game and fish in rustic (authentic) setting.

Rogairo ♛
3-17-7 Roppongi, Minato-ku, tel. 03-586-3931
Average dinner, $45
Excellent Chinese, Shanghai-style, with fish the best taste bet.

Santomo ♛
6-14-1 Ueno, Taito-ku, tel. 03-831-3898
Average dinner, $40

Fugu (blowfish), the occasionally deadly dish, and other fresh fish.

Tamahide♛
1-17-10 Ningyo-cho, Nihonbashi, Chuo-ku, tel. 03-668-7651
Average dinner, $24
Chicken in all varieties. For cheap lunch, *oyako don* (on bowl of rice).

Tambaya
3-2 Kojimachi, Chiyoda-ku, tel. 03-261-2633
Average dinner, $12
Unagi (eel) in 300-year-old establishment, but housed in modern surroundings.

Tokaien♛
1-6-3 Kabukicho, Chinjuku-ku, tel. 03-200-2924
Average dinner, $12–45
Korean food, 8 floors, from "Viking" (smorgasbord buffet) to "Royal" set menu, priced accordingly.

Toricho♛
7-8-2 Roppongi, Minato-ku, tel. 03-401-1827
Average dinner, $20
Yakitori (skewered chicken), in fairly elegant surroundings. Sit at counter.

Kamakura

Hachinoki Honten♛ ♛ ♛ ♛
Tel. 0467-22-8719
Average dinner, $40
Traditional *shojin ryori* (vegetarian) cuisine in exquisite surroundings, delicious servings. A dining experience, best with Japanese-speaking friend.

Kamakura Maruyama-Tei♛ ♛ ♛ ♛
Tel. 0467-24-2452
Average dinner, $25
French cuisine since 1980, and very good. Limited menu, painstaking attention to details. Very close to station. Try the fish with wild mushrooms.

Okadatei♛ ♛ ♛
Tel. 0467-24-9630
Average dinner, $50

Kyoto-style *kaiseki* (classic) cuisine in traditional surroundings, opposite Kenchoji Temple.
Oebi♛♛
Tel. 0467-22-0405
Average dinner, $15
Seafood restaurant on Yuigahama Beach.
Lamp Post♛
Tel. 0467-23-3857
Average dinner, $8
Western-style food, in front of Kamakura Station (east exit).

Narita

Buffalo♛♛
Tomisato Interchange, near airport, tel. 0476-93-4302
Average dinner, $20
Steak grilled on American-made charcoal.
Victoria Station♛
Funabashi City, near airport, tel. 0474-34-0510
Average dinner, $15
Maybe you came all the way to Japan to visit this branch of an American operation. Then again, maybe you didn't. The same in every way, except for better service.

Yokohama

Heichinrou♛♛♛
149 Yamashita-cho, Naka-ku, tel. 045-681-3001
Average dinner, $15
Best Chinese restaurant in town, and that's saying a lot. Basically Cantonese, but it has everything.
Kani Ichi♛♛♛
6-100-4 Chojamachi, Naka-ku, tel. 045-261-1133
Average dinner, $35
Seafood is king here, including the crab flown in daily. Also *tempura*.
Ten Ichi♛♛♛
Yokohama Station Building, 6th floor, tel. 045-311-1281
Average dinner, $40

Branch of the famous Tokyo establishment, *tempura* the specialty. Marvelous old-fashioned decor in modern building.

Ten Shichi ♨ ♨ ♨
1-4 Sumiyoshi-cho, Naka-ku, tel. 045-681-3376
Average dinner, $30
Also *tempura*, name suspiciously like Ten Ichi. Just as good, but cheaper.

Kani Doraku ♨ ♨
2-84 Isezaki-cho, Naka-ku, tel. 045-252-5511
Average dinner, $20
Crab is specialty here (look at the sign!), some in *sukiyaki*, *sushi*, or *tempura* form, among others.

Araiya ♨
2-17 Akebono-cho, Naka-ku, tel. 045-251-5001
Average dinner, $25
Sukiyaki basically, but other dishes beloved by foreigners, such as beef stew.

BEST SHOPPING

Antiques. In addition to the places mentioned in the text, such as the Tokyo Komingu Kottokan in Kanda and the flea markets (see below), Odawara Shoten, in the Imperial Hotel Arcade, is outstanding, and pricey. Tel. 03-591-0052. (*Kottohin* = antiques.)

Arcades. Of many, International Arcade is one of the best, 30 shops with kimono, pearls, electrical goods, toys, dolls, you name it. Next to rail tracks between Imperial Hotel and Yuraku-cho. 2-1-1 Yuraku-cho, Chiyoda-ku, tel. 03-591-9826. Open daily.

Art. Also an antiques store, but many paintings and scrolls. Prices tend to be cheaper up here in Asakusa, so try Miyamoto Shoten, 1-8-5 Kaminari-mon, Taito-ku, tel. 03-844-5417. Closed 3rd Wednesday of month.

Bamboo. Iwai Tsuzuraten, 2-10-1 Ningyo-cho, Nihon-bashi, Chuo-ku, tel. 03-668-6058. Mostly baskets, tiny to huge. (*Take*, pron. tah-kay = bamboo.)

Books. Sanseido Shoten, 1-1 Kanda Jimbo-cho, Chiyoda-ku, tel. 03-293-3312. Biggest bookstore in Japan, lots of English-language books in special section. Closed Tuesdays. Also Jena Seiko, see page 112.

Cameras. Yodobashi Camera, 3-26-8 Shinjuku, Shinjuku-ku, tel. 03-346-1010. Open daily. Across street from station's east exit.

Ceramics and porcelain. Roppongi Tsukamoto, 4-1-19 Roppongi, Minato-ku, tel. 03-403-3747. Across street from ANA Tokyo Hotel. Also: Bizenyaki-den, 3-11-14 Akasaka, Minato-ku, tel. 03-582-6994. On Tamachi-dori Street in the Akasaka entertainment quarter. (*Toki* = ceramics, *setamono* = porcelain.)

Cloisonné. Ando, 5-6-2 Ginza, Chuo-ku, tel. 03-572-2261. (*Shippo* = cloisonné.)

Coins. Ginza Coin, 5-1 Ginza, Chuo-ku, tel. 03-573-1960.

Combs. Traditional boxwood combs at Jusanya, 2-12-21 Ueno, Taito-ku, tel. 03-831-3238. Just south of Ueno Park and Shitamachi Museum. (*Kushi* = comb.)

Damascene. Japan Tax-Free Center, 5-8-6 Toranomon, Minato-ku, tel. 03-432-4351. Amita Jewelry in the center. Open daily. (*Kane* = damascene.)

Dolls. International Arcade; see Arcades and Japan Tax-Free Center listings above, or Department Stores section below.

Electronics. Akihabara, of course (explained in detail page 105), where LAOX is probably the best of many excellent shops. 1-2-9 Soto Kanda, Chiyoda-ku, tel. 03-253-7111. Open daily. Also Nishi Ginza Electric Center, next to International Arcade at Yurakucho. Much smaller than Akihabara, but good location, tel. 03-503-4481.

Fans. Arai Bunsen-do, 1-20-2 Asakusa, Taito-ku, tel. 03-841-0088. On Nakamise shopping street, leading up to Asakusa Kannon Temple. Open daily.

Flea markets. Everything from antiques to carpentry tools and clothing, not to mention food. (1) Harajuku, before JNR Station, 1st and 4th Sundays. (2) Ikebukuro, in front of JNR Station, 3rd Saturday, 3rd Sunday. (3) Nogi Jinja Shrine, near Nogizaka Subway Station, Chiyoda Line, 2nd Sunday, canceled if rain. (4) Roppongi, next to subway entrance, 4th Thursday, 4th Friday. The Nogi Shrine action starts at dawn, most others a little later, and all continue until about 4 P.M. or the business dies down. (*Ichi*=market. Forget the flea, an idea not up to scratch in Japan.)

Flower-arranging equipment. Dai Ichi Engei, 1-1-4

Shibuya, Shibuya-ku, tel. 03-409-6671. Closed Thursdays. (*Ikebana*=flower arranging.)

Folk arts and crafts. Japan Traditional Craft Center, 3-1-1 Minami Aoyama, Minato-ku, tel. 03-403-2460. A little of everything, buying encouraged. Closed Thursdays. (*Mingei hin* = folk art.)

Go boards. Maruhachi Goban-ten, 3-5-7 Ginza, Chuo-ku, tel. 03-561-0574. Also books in English on how to play the game.

Hair ornaments. Yonoya Kushiho, 1-37-10 Asakusa, Taito-ku, tel. 03-844-1755. Just off Nakamise-dori shopping street. Closed Thursdays.

Kimono. Hayashi Kimono, International Arcade, 2-1-1 Yuraku-cho, Chiyoda-ku, tel. 03-591-9826. Used ones. Also department stores for new ones, more expensive.

Lacquerware. Takemura Shikki-ten, 4-10-8 Moto Asakusa, Taito-ku, tel. 03-841-4362. Craftsmen work from here, too. Closed Sundays, holidays. (*Shiki* = lacquerware.)

Lanterns (paper). 2-6 Kasacho, Kanda-tacho, Chiyoda-ku, tel. 03-256-7007. Closed Sundays and holidays.

Men's clothing. Barbiche, 3-1-28 Jingumae, Shibuya-ku, tel. 03-404-8757. Open daily.

Obi **cords.** Domyo, 2-11-1 Ueno, Taito-ku, tel. 03-831-3773. Open daily.

Paper. Isetatsu, 2-18-9 Yanaka, Taito-ku, tel. 03-823-1453. Open daily. Just south of Shinobazu Pond. Also: Washi Kobo, 1-8-10 Nishi Azabu, Minato-ku, tel. 03-405-1841. Between Roppongi and Azabu. Closed Sundays and holidays. (*Kami* = paper.)

Pearls. Mikimoto, 4-chome Ginza, Chuo-ku, tel. 03-535-4611. Six other branches, two of them in Tokyo. (*Shinju* = pearl.)

Samisen. Bachi-ei, 2-10-11 Ningyo-cho, Nihonbashi, Chuo-ku, tel. 03-666-7263. Closed Sundays and holidays.

Silk. Kyoto Silk, International Arcade, 2-1-1 Yuraku-cho, Chiyoda-ku, tel. 03-501-5789. (*Kinu* = silk.)

Stamps. Okada Stamp, International Arcade, 2-1-1 Yuraku-cho, Chiyoda-ku, tel. 03-501-1788. Also Central Post Office, in front of Tokyo Station, Marunouchi side. (*Kitte* = stamp.)

Swords. Japan Sword, 3-8-1 Toranomon, Minato-ku, tel. 03-434-4321. On Sakurada-dori. (*Katana* = sword.)

Tansu. Japanese traditional chests at Edo Antiques, 2-21-12 Akasaka, Minato-ku, tel. 03-584-5280. Store will ship for you. Opposite ANA Hotel Tokyo. Closed Sundays.

Tax-free items. Japan Tax-Free Center, 4-8-6 Toranomon, Minato-ku, tel. 03-432-4351. Eight floors of shopping, plus inexpensive restaurant, restrooms. Open daily.

Textiles. Nuno, 5-17-1 Roppongi, Minato-ku, tel. 03-582-7997. Modern, but based on traditional. Closed Mondays. (*Orimono* = textiles.)

Towels. Traditional Japanese *tenugui* (hand towels) at Fujiya, 2-2-15 Asakusa, Taito-ku, tel. 03-841-2283. Closed Thursdays. Fujiya can make one with your name or whatever.

Toys. Hakuhinkan Toy Park, 8-8-11 Ginza, Chuo-ku, tel. 03-571-8008. Japan's biggest toy store, with English information posted on each floor. Open daily. On Chuo-dori Street, south end of Ginza. (*Omocha* = toy.)

Umbrellas. Traditional Japanese-style at Nishijima Shoten, 1-30-1 Asakusa, Taito-ku, tel. 03-841-8560. On Nakamise-dori shopping street. Closed 4th Tuesday. (*Kasa* = umbrella.)

Watches. Nippon-do, 5-7-5 Ginza, Chuo-ku, tel. 03-571-5511. (*Tokei* = watch.)

Women's clothing. Kawakubo Rei (Boutique Comme de Garçons), 5-3-10 Minami Aoyama, Minato-ku, tel. 03-499-4370. Closed Mondays. Also: Yamamoto Kansai (Boutique Kansai), 3-28-7 Jingumae, Shibuya-ku, tel. 03-478-1958. Open daily. Also: Hanae Mori, 2-6-1 Kita Aoyama, Minato-ku, tel. 03-406-1021. Open daily. Also: Issei Miyake Boutique, 5-3-10 Minami Aoyama, Minato-ku, tel. 03-499-6476. Open daily. Same building as Kawakubo Rei.

Woodblock prints. S. Watanabe, 8-6-19 Ginza, Chuo-ku, tel. 03-571-4684. On street between Imperial Hotel and Ginza.

Shopping Areas and Streets

These are as I described in the text earlier, but in terms of geography, the trendy young people like to shop near Harajuku Station, on Omote Sando, and on Killer-dori Street, and their satellite streets. The establishment goes to the Ginza and to the conservative department stores. (The very rich get their clothes in London, Paris, Milan, and New York, of course.) The middle-class Japanese shop in department stores at any of the terminals (Shinjuku, Shibuya, etc.), and young people love Shibuya and its stores, not quite so exotic as Harajuku. Asakusa is for bargain hunters and lovers of the traditional, Roppongi and Aoyama for Japanese yuppies. Our best advice, if you don't find what you want from our lists, from local magazines and newspapers, and from all the tourist handouts you'll be papered with: Just wander in any of the areas mentioned.

Department Stores

These are vital to the Japanese way of life, so are scattered everywhere throughout the city. When they are owned by a transportation company (Seibu, Tokyu), the railway terminals are right in the store. Subway stops are named for them, and the entrances are sometimes right there when you get off the trains. They all have restaurants, most have English-speaking assistance (usually at an information desk near one of the entrances). Nearly all accept the major credit cards.

I list them in the order, I think, of their importance to a foreign visitor:

- Takashimaya, 2-5 Nihonbashi-dori, Chuo-ku, tel. 03-211-4111. Closed Wednesdays.
- Mitsukoshi, 1-7-4 Nihonbashi Muromachi, Chuo-ku, tel. 03-241-3311. Closed Mondays. (Has a smaller branch

---

INSIDERS' TIPS

If you're serious about buying electronic equipment at Akihabara, you'll want to get a copy of Japan Travel Bureau's *Akihabara Jiyu Jizai (Akihabara at Your Fingertips)*, issued in 1986 for first time, and probably available for 1987, the publishers say. It costs ¥780 ($4.73) and is bilingual, with photos and brief analysis of about 450 shops, with maps on how to find them. Also suggests restaurants and coffee shops in areas. Ask at JTB or bigger bookshops around town.

farther down Chuo-dori Street, near main Ginza crossing of 4-chome, which is not as good.)

- Isetan, 3-8 Shinjuku, Shinjuku-ku, tel. 03-352-1111. Closed Wednesdays.
- Seibu, 1-28-1 Minami Ikebukuro, Toshima-ku, tel. 03-342-1111. Closed Thursdays.
- Sogo, 1-13 Yuraku-cho, Chiyoda-ku, tel. 03-215-6711. Closed Thursdays.
- Daimaru, Tokyo Station Bldg., Yaseu-guchi, Chuo-ku, tel. 03-212-8011. Closed Wednesdays.
- Tokyu, 1-9-2 Nihonbashi-dori, Chuo-ku, tel. 03-211-0511. Closed Thursdays. Tied with preceding in importance.
- Matsuzakaya, 6-10-1 Ginza, Chuo-ku, tel. 03-572-1111. Closed Wednesdays.
- Seibu Yuraku-cho, 2-5-1 Yurakucho, Chiyoda-ku, tel. 03-286-5482. New, but has aggressive Foreign Customer Liaison Office, discounts, free parking.
- Hankyu, 5-2-1 Ginza, Chuo-ku, tel. 03-573-2231. Closed Thursday.
- Matsuya, 3-6-1 Ginza, Chuo-ku, tel. 03-567-1211. Closed Thursdays. Tied with preceding in importance.
- Keio, 1-1-4 Nishi Shinjuku, Shinjuku-ku, tel. 03-342-2111. Closed Thursdays.
- Odakyu, 1-13 Nishi Shinjuku, Shinjuku-ku, tel. 03-342-1111. Closed Thursdays. Tied with preceding in importance.
- Wako, 4-5-11 Ginza, Chuo-ku, tel. 03-562-2111. Closed Sundays.

Best Shopping in Yokohama

Yokohama is famous for its arcades, which have everything. Most convenient to foreign visitors is Motomachi Shopping Center, Naka-ku. Larger, however, is Isezaki-cho Shopping Arcade.

NIGHTLIFE

- Kabuki-za, 4-12 Ginza, Chuo-ku, tel. 03-541-3131. See pages 102–104 for details.

PERILS & PITFALLS

Don't go into any bar or nightclub where the hawker calls you in—you will be ripped off. Similarly, don't go into any quiet little place with a discreet sign and no prices or advertising posted outside. On entering, if the place looks elegant, the girls are superbly dressed, and the customers seem surprised by a foreigner's face, turn and run. Even if you're allowed in, you will have to pay sky-high expense-account prices. Unlike the other guests, you won't be able to put everything on the company tab, no questions asked.

- Kokuritsu Gekijo (National Theater), 4-1 Hayabusa-cho, Chiyoda-ku, tel. 03-265-7411. For *gagaku* and *bugaku*, also *kabuki* and Noh. See pages 104–105 for details.
- Kanze Noh Gekijo, 1-16-4 Shoto, Shibuya-ku, tel. 03-469-5241. Tickets from ¥2,500 to ¥10,000 ($15.15 to $60.61).
- Tokyo Takarazuka Gekijo, 1-1-13 Yurakucho, Chiyoda-ku, tel. 03-591-1711. Tickets from ¥1,500 ($9.09) up.
- Suehiro-tei, 3-6-12 Shinjuku, Shinjuku-ku, tel. 03-351-2974. *Rakugo* and music-hall-style acts. Tickets from ¥1,800 ($10.91) up.
- Ginza Kyukyodo Ticket Service, tel. 03-571-0401. Or ask your hotel front desk or concierge. For anything from concerts and dance to baseball games.
- Mikado Nightclub, 2-14-6 Akasaka, Minato-ku, tel. 03-583-1101. Seating for 1,700, plus 800 hostesses with beepers, world's largest indoor waterfall (so they say), big show at 8:30 and 10 P.M. nightly except Sunday and holidays. Cover and service charge about ¥4,000 ($24.24), drinks from about ¥1,000 ($6.06). Hostess charge is ¥3,500 ($21.21) per hour plus *her* service

INSIDERS' TIPS

The Japan Folkloric Art Dance Troupe can be seen about 12 times a year in Tokyo, at the Yubin Chokin Hall. Tickets are from about ¥1,500 ($9.09) to ¥2,000 ($12.12) and may be booked in advance by writing to the International Artists Center, 5-4-28 Akasaka, Minato-ku, Tokyo 107, or phone 03-582-9172. There are said to be more than 3,000 regional folk dances around the country, and this group performs many of them, in Japan and on overseas tours.

charge of another ¥1,000 ($6.06) or so.

- Cordon Bleu Nightclub, 6-6-4 Akasaka, Minato-ku, tel. 03-582-7800 or 478-3000. Flat fee of ¥15,000 ($90.91) gets you dinner (with beer or whiskey), including service and cover charges, but there is that 10 percent tax. Topless revue.

- Sunshine Theater, Sunshine City, Ikebukuro, tel. 03-987-5281, puts on all-girl dance revues from time to time. Prices about ¥2,000 ($12.12) to ¥3,000 ($18.18).

- El Cupid, 3-10-9 Roppongi, Minato-ku, tel. 03-405-6339. Drinks from ¥1,000, English-speaking (it says here) hostesses from ¥3,000 ($18.18) per hour unless you choose, which is about double the price. Cover charge ¥1,500 ($9.09), but only ¥500 ($3.03) if you sit at bar or hang around the piano. Closed Sundays, holidays.

- Byblos, 3-8 Akasaka, Minato-ku, tel. 03-584-4484. One of two most famous discotheques in Tokyo. Several floors of happiness, admission ¥3,000 ($18.18) for men, ¥2,000 ($12.12) for women, 2 drinks included. After that, ¥500 ($3.03) up.

- Mugen, 3-8-17 Akasaka, Minato-ku, tel. 03-584-4481, next door to Byblos, has same price policy.

TOKYO TELEPHONE NUMBERS

Japan Travel Phone, Tokyo	03-503-2911
JNTO Tourist Information Center, Tokyo	03-502-1461
JNTO Tourist Information Center, Narita	0476-32-8711
Tokyo English Life Line (advice, support)	03-264-4347
American Embassy, Tokyo	03-583-7141
Australian Embassy, Tokyo	03-453-0251
Canadian Embassy, Tokyo	03-408-2101
British Embassy, Tokyo	03-265-5511
Theater and other tickets, Play Guide, Tokyo	03-561-8821

- Sarani Six Tuxedo Rental, 3-3-12 Azabu-dai, Minato-ku, tel. 03-587-0648. Closed Sunday, Monday, holidays.
- Chaps Country & Western Club, 3-14-8 Roppongi, Minato-ku, tel. 03-479-2136. Features American singers. Closed Sunday.
- The Last 20 Cents, 3-8-20 Roppongi, Minato-ku, tel. 03-405-7965. Features live rock and roll ("1950 style"), costing ¥2,500 ($15.15) for men, ¥1,800 ($10.91) for women, 3 drinks included.
- Hard Rock Cafe, 4-5-1 Roppongi, Minato-ku, tel. 03-408-7018. Can't be missed if you get near, as it has a 25-foot King Kong clinging to its side (a towering 3-story building). Loud music, moderately priced drinks (¥500 or $3.03 up).

INSIDERS' TIPS

Offbeat? A "new mood cabaret" is Banana Power, 3-13-6 Roppongi, tel. 03-402-9306, where the end of each show, featuring local comedians, features pie-throwing orgies, and for real embarrassment of the largely male Japanese audience, a British male stripper. Watch also for performances by the *buto* (modern dance) superstar Furukawa Anzu, or for the Heavy Metal of Japan, Loudness. Billed as the Japanese Blues Brothers are the Bubblegum Brothers, who can be seen from time to time. For these performers and others, look in the monthly *Tokyo Journal* (English-language).

Experimental theater, music, anything, can be seen at La Mama, in the basement of the Primera Dogenzaka, itself behind the Cabaret Empire in Shibuya, tel. 03-464-0801. In the basement of the Yamate Kyokai (Yamate Church) on Koen Dori in Shibuya is Jean Jean, tel. 03-462-0641, another small theater for jazz, solo dance performances, and the like.

Live jazz can be appreciated at two Roppongi locations: Birdland, Roppongi Square Building, basement, tel. 03-478-3456, from 9 P.M. Also Ink Stick, Casa Grande Miwa Building, basement, tel. 03-410-0429. You'll find country and western live at Aspen Glow, Gogenzaka GM Building, 6th floor, Shibuya, tel. 03-496-9709.

FESTIVALS

Note: See also national holidays listings, pages 21–22.

January 6	Dezomeshiki (Fireman's Parade)♛. Stunts on ladders, etc. Harumi, Chuo-dori.
Mid-January	Sumo tournament♛ ♛ for 15 days. Kuramae Kokugikan Sumo Hall.
April 1–25	Azuma Odori♛ ♛, Shimbashi Embujo Theater. *Geisha* dances.
April	*Gagaku* court dances at Imperial Palace♛ ♛ ♛, 3 days, change yearly. Watch newspapers or ask Tourist Information Center.
May 12–15	Kanda Matsuri♛ ♛ ♛. One of Tokyo's biggest, held in odd-numbered years only.
Mid-May	Summer Sumo Tournament♛ ♛, 15 days.
May	3rd Saturday and Sunday, Asakusa Jinja Shrine's Sanja Matsuri Festival♛ ♛. Over 100 *mikoshi* shrines in parade on Saturday.
June 10–16	Sanno Matsuri of Hie Jinja Shrine♛ ♛ ♛, even-numbered years only. Along with Kanda Matsuri (see above), Tokyo's biggest festival. June 15 is big parade.
Mid-September	Autumn Sumo Tournament♛ ♛, 15 days.
September 14–16	Tsurugaoka Hachimangu Shrine Festival♛ ♛, Kamakura. Parade of *mikoshi* (portable shrines) on 15th, *yabusame* (horseback archery) on 16th, a very photogenic event.
October	*Gagaku* dances at Imperial Palace♛ ♛ ♛; see April.
November	Tori no Ichi (Cock Fair)♛ at many shrines, especially Otori Jinja, Asakusa. You buy a rake to pull in money for future years. Also fun at Shinjuku's Hanazono Shrine, behind Isetan Department Store. Watch newspapers or ask TIC for exact dates, which change yearly.

CENTRAL JAPAN

Lake Hakone and Mt. Fuji are traditional side trips from Tokyo, but I think you'd have more fun visiting them as part of a longer expedition, tying them in with a look at the Japan which wears its own face, not a succession of masks. After a while in the capital, you need a break, and the cooler, cleaner air of the Fuji Five Lakes or Hakone area will refresh you considerably.

HAKONE AND MT. FUJI

Getting to Hakone is easy, but there are several choices. Apart from a hired car, prohibitively expensive, you can take a direct bus from Shinjuku Bus Terminal (west side of Shinjuku Station), taking 2 hours 10 minutes to Ashikono (Lake Hakone), costing ¥1,600 ($9.70). The same company (Odakyu) runs a Romance Car train from the Odakyu Shinjuku Station to Hakone Yumoto, taking 1½ hours, costing about ¥1,250 ($7.58), reservations required, phone 03-342-1651 in Japanese. Finally, there is the JNR from Tokyo Station to Odawara Station, where you have to change to a local train, the Hakone Tozan Line for Hakone Yumoto. From there to Lake Hakone is a 45-minute bus ride. Between Tokyo and Odawara, you can even take the Shinkansen (Bullet Train) every 20 minutes, taking only 45 minutes for the journey. The regular train on the Tokaido Line takes 90 minutes, but costs less than half, ¥1,500 vs. ¥3,500 ($9.09 vs. $21.21). You can also take buses from Odawara Station to various points throughout the Hakone area.

The Japanese come to this area to get away from the pressure of Tokyo living. You too can come here for golf or hiking, but you may wish to reserve that for home, so I'll

176

concentrate here on scenic, historic, and cultural points that you'll probably like.

Fuji-san (Mt. Fuji) ♛ ♛ ♛, never Fujiyama to the Japanese, can be seen best in winter, so consider yourself lucky if you spot it any other time. You can climb it in July and August, starting in any of six different spots. The easiest is the Fujinomiya Trail, starting at the JNR station of that name, because you take the bus to the 5th station, then climb for about 3 miles (5 hours, perhaps) to the summit. Some people like to climb all night, so that they can be at the top before sunrise, to make the experience even more holy. (It is a sacred mountain, after all.) Efforts to build a monorail up to the top failed because of conservationists' protests, even though the developers planned to put the train in a trench all the way up.

If you go, take heavy boots and sweaters (it gets cold at 12,393 feet, even in August). Be sure to buy a climbing stick and have it branded at each stop, or you won't have any proof for folks back home. It takes only 2 hours to come down, by the way, digging in your heels and taking giant steps on the Sunabashiri (Sand-Sliding) Trail to Gotemba Station.

Ashinoko (Lake Hakone) ♛ ♛ is the heart of Hakone, and tends to be rather touristy. Ignore that, take a cruise on one of the boats plying back and forth along its shores, and marvel at the vulgarity of some of the craft. One looks like a cross between Nelson's flagship and a Mississippi River gambling palace, but what the hell. From Hakone Yumoto, if you came that route, get up to Ashinoko, then cruise across the lake, and, if you are not afraid of heights, take the Hakone Ropeway ♛ ♛ ♛ all the way from Togendai to the top of Sounzan, a distance of 2½ miles. You'll get a marvelous view of the whole area, rising as high as 2,000 feet, passing over many of the hot springs bubbling up, including some sulfurous ones of muddy yellow color, and then, from Sounzan, descend eastward on a funicular railway firmly anchored to mother earth. From Gora, the Hakone Tozan Tetsudo takes you back down the valley to Hakone Yumoto or even to Odawara, completing your circular trip.

En route, if you have the time, you should see at least two things, the Hakone Barrier ♛ and the Hakone Open

Air Museum♛ ♛ ♛. The barrier, Hakone Seikisho-ato, was erected by the Tokugawa shogunate in 1618 and remained in operation until the modernization of the country began with the abolition of the shoguns in 1868. Straddling the Tokaido, famous in woodblock print and literature, it prevented guns from getting into Tokyo and women from getting out. (The shogunate required outlying feudal lords to keep their womenfolk in Tokyo as hostages. Guns, then as now, were strictly controlled in Japan, no private ownership being allowed.) What you see today at the barrier is a reconstruction of a guardhouse, and just between it and the town of Hakone-machi is a mile-long stretch of the old Sugi Namiki (Tokaido Road) itself, narrow and peaceful beneath twin rows of stately cedars. If you're ambitious, walk back to the town to board your boat for a lake tour.

The Chokoku-no-mori Bijutsukan (Hakone Open Air Art Museum; lit. Statues-in-the-Woods Art Museum) is up near the station of the same name on the Hakone Tozan Railway between Gora and Kowakien. Perhaps, after your ropeway and cable-car trip to Gora, you'd like to see this gem of a museum. The huge outdoor park features sculptures by Rodin and Moore, to mention only two, and an indoor Picasso Gallery. Open daily, small admission.

There are many hotels here (see listings), and several good restaurants.

To get to Mt. Fuji without passing through the Hakone area, there are four routes. (1) Most direct is the Chuo Kosoku Express Bus from Shinjuku Station (west side) directly to the 5th Station on Mt. Fuji, taking 2½ hours, operating from mid-April to early November on Sundays and holidays, but every day from mid-July to end of August, ¥2,100 ($12.73). Make reservations at 03-374-2221 in Japanese or through travel agents. (2) On JNR from Shinjuku Station, express train to Kawaguchi-ko, 2 hours 10 minutes, mid-July to end of August, plus Sundays and holidays, ¥2,750 ($16.67). From Kawaguchi-ko, you take a Fuji Kyuko Bus from mid-April to early November, 1 hour, ¥1,350 ($8.18), right up to the 5th station. (3) Coming from the southeast, get yourself to Gotemba, where the same company's bus takes you up in 45 minutes, from early July to end of August, ¥860 ($5.21). (4) If you are coming from the south, there is a new route from Mishima.

Same company, taking 2 hours, early July to end of August, ¥2,100 ($12.73).

You don't have to head for the summit. You may just enjoy staying in a nice resort hotel down on the shores of one of the Fuji Five Lakes (see hotel listings). In any case, if you don't climb, there isn't anything to do except rest, or engage in sports of one kind or another.

ATAMI AND IZU

Atami, south of Tokyo on Sagami Bay, is a typical hot-springs-resort town. Which is to say, pretty awful, but with a few marvelous exceptions. The best hotels are expensive and small, the biggest hotels are noisy and vulgar. Unless you're a hot-springs freak, I'd suggest passing through. If you insist on sampling the waters, spend your spare time in the Bijutsukan (Kyusei Art Museum) ♛, not the awful castle, a concrete-and-neon nightmare. Paintings, screens, and bronzes, including some famous names like Utamaro, Hiroshige, etc., adorn the museum.

The Izu Peninsula, much of which lies to the south of Atami, is a kind of rustic hideaway for wealthy Japanese. There are some splendid villas hidden away in the hills, plus good hunting (wild boar, for example). Two of Japan's great golf courses can be found at Kawana, just 15 miles south of Atami, and the beaches are practically deserted. The trouble is, you didn't come to Japan to get away from everything, you came here to experience something new. If you're in Japan on business and need a break after working hard, though, ask your travel agent to fix you up with something here. Perhaps you'll suggest the town of Shimoda, where America had its first consulate (1856–57). You can visit Townsend Harris's residence in Gyokusenji Temple ♛ ♛, just east of town at the harbor, and look at the monument where he raised the first foreign flag to fly on Japanese soil. From his diary, these words are engraved on the stone: "Grave reflections. Ominous of change. Undoubted beginning of the end. Query, if for the real good of Japan?" In May there is an annual festival named for the Kurofune Matsuri (Black Ships) which brought Commodore Perry and, later, Harris to these shores.

NAGOYA

Nagoya used to call itself the Detroit of Japan, until the American city began to be a less enticing role model, and now enthusiasts say it is the industrial ceramics capital. It still makes cars, notably in neighboring Toyota, but its history of producing ceramics now promises to be even as important. Artisans still manufacture Noritake and other china here, but innovators have begun to develop automobile engines made of ceramics, which are said to be tougher than those made of steel. There are also many other forms in which ceramics may be used, and investors may wish to take note. (Noritake china can be shopped for at 5-2 Yuheicho, Higashi-ku, tel. 052-961-6831.)

Nagoya itself is a fairly unattractive city, its newer buildings tending toward the utilitarian instead of the fanciful. Most of the city was destroyed in World War II, so practically everything is new. Among the highlights:

Nagoya Castle♛ ♛, a 1959 reconstruction of the 1610 original, was headquarters of the Tokugawa shoguns, who lived in a mansion inside the castle for 250 years. Note the gold dolphins on the castle's roof, unique to donjons like this. Closed Monday, small admission.

The third-most-important shrine in Japan, Atsuta Jinja♛ ♛, in the southern part of the city, is the repository of one of the Imperial Regalia. Here is kept the Kusanagi-no-Tsurugi, or grass-cutting sword. (The sacred mirror is at Ise Shrine, the sacred jewels in Tokyo's Imperial Palace.) The town's two other major shrines, Toshogu and Aichi, were both destroyed in World War II and rebuilt.

Far more interesting is Tagata Jinja Shrine♛ ♛, in nearby Komaki City, center of fertility cultism in Japan. Two shrines, one male and one female, are crammed with representations of the two sexes' genitals. On March 15 each year, the Tagata Jinja Matsuri♛ ♛ ♛ festival sees parades through the streets of the larger totems, out for their annual airing. (The two parades, male and female, used to meet, but the local PTA, with postwar powers it didn't have before, soon put a stop to that.) You'll find most worshipers, including lots of grandmothers, praying for offspring at the male shrine. There is a certain tree in the garden under which, it is said, a child conceived will be sure to be healthy, wealthy, and wise, or something like

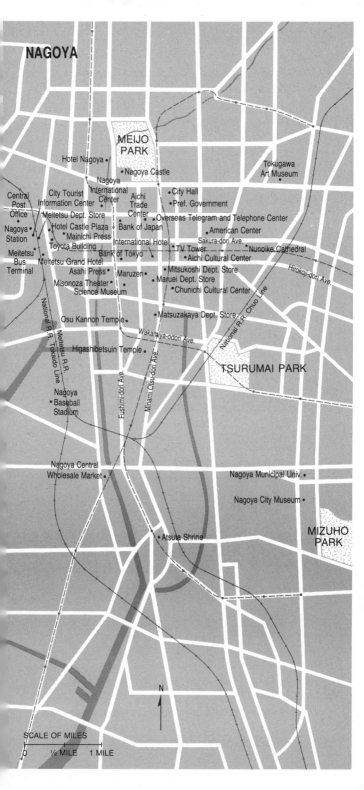

NAGOYA

MEIJO PARK

Hotel Nagoya •
• Nagoya Castle
Tokugawa Art Museum •

Nagoya International Center

Central Post Office
City Tourist Information Center
Aichi Trade Center
• City Hall
• Pref. Government

Nagoya Station
Meitetsu Dept. Store
Hotel Castle Plaza
• Mainichi Press
Bank of Japan
• Overseas Telegram and Telephone Center

Toyota Building
International Hotel
• American Center

Meitetsu Bus Terminal
Meitetsu Grand Hotel
Bank of Tokyo
• T.V. Tower
Sakura-dori Ave.
Nunoike Cathedral •

Asahi Press •
Maruzen
• Aichi Cultural Center
Hirokoji-dori Ave.

Misonoza Theater •
Science Museum
• Mitsukoshi Dept. Store
Maruei Dept. Store

Osu Kannon Temple •
• Chunichi Cultural Center

• Matsuzakaya Dept. Store

Wakamiya-odori Ave.

Higashibetsuin Temple •

TSURUMAI PARK

Nagoya Baseball Stadium

Nagoya Central Wholesale Market •

Nagoya Municipal Univ. •

Nagoya City Museum •

MIZUHO PARK

• Atsuta Shrine

National R.R. Tokaido Line
Meitetsu R.R. Tokaido Line
Fushimi-dori Ave.
Minami Otsu-dori Ave.
National R.R. Chuo Line

N

SCALE OF MILES
0   ½ MILE   1 MILE

that. A lot of the phalluses in the temple are gifts from parents who believe their successful children are a result of the tree's influence. (Take Meitetsu Ihuyama line to Tagata Jinja-mae Station, 30 minutes.)

Back in town, you might wish to see the Bijutsukan (Tokugawa Art Museum)♨♨, which contains several thousand items relating to past glories. Ieyasu's armor, Noh masks, and the *Tale of Genji* scrolls, the last a National Treasure, are among the highlights.

The underground arcades near Nagoya Station and in the Sakae area are good examples of their genre. In the former, there are three cinemas, a telegraph office, department stores, and restaurants, to mention only a few of the facilities present. Nagoya is famous for its *nishimen*, flat, white noodles, and you could do worse than try them here (or on the station platforms upstairs, for that matter).

You can see the city by taxi with Meitetsu Kotsu, tel. 052-331-2221, with English-language tape-recorded information. Costs ¥10,000 for three hours, for carload.

There are four subway lines, and English-language maps are available at hotels. The Nagoya International Center, on the Sakuradori Street and Egawa-sen Street corner, says it will answer questions from 9 A.M. to 8:30 P.M., tel. 052-581-5678.

INUYAMA

An excursion from Nagoya to Inuyama and Gifu should be fun. Inuyama, just 23 minutes from Shin Nagoya Station on the Meitetsu Inuyama Line, has Japan's only privately owned castle♨, and one of the four such edifices to be listed as a National Treasure. A nearby teahouse, the Jyo-an♨, is also a National Treasure. Both are situated on the Kiso River, known to the locals as the Japanese Rhine. You can shoot the Kiso rapids all year, about 8 miles in length, by phoning Meitetsu Nippon Rhine Center (in Japanese), 0574-26-2231.

Just outside Inuyama is Meiji Mura Museums (Meiji Village)♨♨♨, of interest to students of things Japanese. Nearly 60 buildings, including the front of Frank Lloyd Wright's old Imperial Hotel, are preserved here to honor the era in which Japan cartwheeled from feudalism to modern times. Old locomotives and Kyoto streetcars run in the village, too. Open daily, small admission.

At Inuyama you can also go cormorant fishing ♛ ♛ ♛, a nighttime activity in which fishermen send their pet cormorants diving for *ayu*, delicious little trout, in the Kiso River. June through September. At nearby Gifu, the same thing, from mid-May to mid-October.

If you love cars and want to see how the Japanese put them together so well, visit the Toyota Motor Corporation in Toyota City, weekdays except during company summer and winter vacations, tel. 0565-28-2121, ext. 1657. Takes about half an hour.

ISE

The most important Shinto shrines in Japan, and a most impressive sight, are the Ise Jingu Shrines ♛ ♛ ♛ ♛, in Ise, south of Nagoya. Getting there is simple if you take the private railway Kintetsu on its Ise-Shima Line. The train operates every 15 to 30 minutes and takes about 90 minutes. If you want to go by JNR because you have a Rail Pass, you have to change at Taki, and the trip takes about twice as long. The Kintetsu station in Nagoya is just a few hundred feet south of JNR's Nagoya Station and on its east side.

At Ise, you can walk (10 minutes) from the station to the Outer Shrine, where you should look for the Shoden (Main Hall). Note in particular its pristine new wood, polished beautifully, yet seeming almost virginally fresh. To the right is an enclosure where an exact replica will be built in 1993, when the building on the left is torn down. The Shinto religion, which despises dirt above all else, demands the Main Hall be replaced every 20 years, and so it has, allegedly, since before the birth of Jesus. At the Kaguraden, back toward the entrance, you may pay (a lot) to have sacred dances performed. If you're lucky, some wealthy pilgrim or a group may have organized such a ceremony, and you may, of course, look on.

The Naiku (Inner Shrine, as opposed to Gekku, outer shrine) is almost 4 miles away, so you'll want to take a taxi or bus, the latter a shuttle practically. The Inner Shrine is laid out in similar manner to the Outer (they're dedicated to different gods), and the protocol at both is about the same. The Japanese prefer to have hats and overcoats removed by anyone approaching the shrines. At the Outer Shrine, you may proceed as far as the second fence, marked by a white curtain; at the Inner Shrine, no farther than the first fence. The architectural style here, since it has been adhered to for 2,000 years, is as traditionally Japanese as you can get. If the clean, smooth lines of the shrine remind you of other places, a family home or even a *sushi* bar, it's no accident. The Japanese adore wood, and better if it's unpainted. Plain wood represents nature, virtue, cleanliness, all the good things a person is supposed to believe in. You will have noticed the Japanese visitors washing their hands and mouths at the Isuzu River at the entrance of the Inner Shrine. Inside this holy of holies, so to speak, is the Yata-no-Kagami (Sacred Mirror), one of the three sacred treasures constituting the regalia of the Imperial Family. Legend says the sun goddess, Amaterasu Omikami, sent the mirror down to earth with her grandson, with instructions to become a mortal and start populating the world.

TOBA

At nearby Toba (5 miles from the Inner Shrine) is the Mikimoto Pearl Island, where there is a new Pearl Museum ₩, a Mikimoto Memorial Hall, and a Women Divers' Museum, where divers demonstrate the collecting of oysters. They don't dive topless as they did at the turn of the century, but there are topless ladies in some of the nightclubs around the area, who often end up simulating dives in large fishtanks above the bar. I don't think it's worthwhile to visit Toba for the pearl farm. I do think it's worthwhile for the scenery, which is splendid, and even more so down around Kashikojima, a few more miles south. From the Shima Kanko Hotel there (see listings), there are gorgeous displays of the oyster beds stretching far out into the bay. Catch a sunset, especially if you can preserve it on film.

INSIDERS' INFORMATION FOR CENTRAL JAPAN

HOTELS
Atami

Taikanso Ryokan ♛ ♛ ♛ ♛
7-1 Hayashigaoka-cho, Atami, Shizuoka-ken 413, tel. 0557-81-8137
Two persons in room, $400, breakfast and dinner included
Former villa of famous painter, nice views of sea, 43 elegant rooms.

Torikyo Ryokan ♛ ♛ ♛ ♛
824 Izusan, Atami, Shizuoka-ken, tel. 0557-80-2211
Two persons in room, $400, breakfast and dinner included.
Famous thatched teahouse of Oishi, leader of the Forty-seven Ronin, beloved in Japanese history. Main house, 33 rooms, annex, 5 rooms. Nice sea views.

New Fujiya ♛ ♛
1-16 Ginza-cho, Atami, Shizuoka-ken 413, tel. 0557-81-0111
Two persons in twin, $85 (a few much cheaper)
Own hot springs, indoor pool, sauna, shops, 3 restaurants, 316 rooms, half of them Japanese-style.

Fuji Lakes

Mt. Fuji ♛ ♛ ♛ ♛
Yamanaka, Yamanakako-mura, Yamanashi-ken 401-05, tel. 05556-2-2111
Two persons in twin, $130
Bowling, pool, tennis, gold, riding, skating, boating, sailing, fishing, and bicycling facilities, 108 nice-sized rooms, mostly Western-style.

New Yamanakako ♛ ♛ ♛ ♛
Yamanaka, Yamanakako-mura, Yamanashi-ken 401-05, tel. 05556-2-2311
Two persons in twin, $80
Own hot springs, pool, tennis, golf, skating, boating, 66 smallish rooms, 6 of them Japanese-style.

Fuji View ♛ ♛ ♛
5-11 Katsuyama-mura, Minami-tsuru-gun, Yamanashi-ken 401-04, tel. 05558-3-2211

Two persons in twin, $60
Tennis, golf, boating, fishing, 66 rooms, a few of them
Japanese-style. Older hotel.

Hakone

Ryuguden Ryokan (Prince) ♛ ♛ ♛ ♛ ♛
144 Moto Hakone, Hakone-machi, Kanagawa-ken 250-05,
tel. 0460-3-7111
Two persons in room, $350, including breakfast and dinner
This villa, part of Prince Hotel, has 20 rooms, each of
which affords views of Lake Ashi (which foreigners call
Lake Hakone) and Mt. Fuji. The hotel itself has 96 rooms,
about $170 for two persons in a twin. Tennis, golf, skating,
fishing, boating.

Naraya Ryokan ♛ ♛ ♛ ♛
162 Miyanoshita, Hakone-machi, Sashigara-shimo-gun,
Kanagawa-ken 250-04, tel. 0460-2-2411
Two persons in room, $225, breakfast and dinner included
A lovely inn, very traditional and quietly elegant, 26
rooms, most with private bath. Fourteen generations have
run this place. Ask for main building, with 12 rooms,
unless you want to be in any of 7 other separate buildings.

Fujiya ♛ ♛ ♛
359 Miyanoshita, Hakone-machi, Kanagawa-ken 250-04,
tel. 0460-2-2211
Two persons in twin, $65
An old wreck of a building, but beautifully so (and now
undergoing renovation). One of Japan's oldest Western-
style hotels, and most historical, in same family for several
generations. Own hot springs, indoor and outdoor pools,
golf, skating. Interesting hillside gardens, former imperial
villa for *tatami*-style dining, 150 rooms.

Kanko ♛ ♛
Sengokubara, Hakone-machi, Kanagawa-ken 250-06, tel.
0460-4-8501
Two persons in twin, $105
An impressive, slightly older establishment with reputa-
tion for good service and food. Own hot springs, pool, golf,
skating, boating, fishing, 109 good-sized rooms.

Kowakien ♨

Ninotaira, Hakone-machi, Kanagawa-ken 250-04, tel. 0460-2-4111

Two persons in twin, $69

Big establishment filled with bus groups, but you might enjoy seeing the Japanese (and other foreigners) at play. This is where you can wear your *yukata* (summer *kimono*) without feeling embarrassed. Own hot springs, sauna, indoor and outdoor pools, golf, tennis, gym, cycling, skating, boating, fishing, 245 fair-sized rooms.

Izu Nagaoka Spa

Sanyoso Ryokan ♨ ♨ ♨ ♨ ♨

270 Domano-ue, Izu Nagaoka-machi, Tagata-gun, Shizuoka-ken, tel. 05594-8-0128

Two persons in room, $475, including breakfast and dinner

One of most beautiful of inns in Japan, this is a former Mitsubishi (i.e., Iwasaki) family villa. Relax in luxurious elegance of its 20 rooms.

Kashikojima

Shima Kanko ♨ ♨ ♨

731 Shimmei Ago-cho, Shima-gun, Mie-ken 517-05, tel. 05594-3-1211

Two persons in twin, $90

Nicely sited hotel on promontory overlooking oyster beds where cultured pearls are grown. Famous and pricey French-style restaurant, cookbook-writing chef. Pool, golf, boating, fishing, 200 largish rooms, excellent service.

Nagoya

Castle ♨ ♨ ♨ ♨

3-19 Hinokuchi-cho, Nishi-ku, Nagoya 451, tel. 052-521-2121

Two persons in twin, $120

Marvelous views of Nagoya Castle from this hotel, with

253 fair-sized rooms. Pool, 3 restaurants, barber shop, gift shop, nice setting.

Miyako ♛ ♛ ♛
4-9-10 Meieki, Nakamura-ku, Nagoya 450, tel. 052-571-3211
Two persons in twin, $100
Close to Nagoya Station, convenient for rail or business travelers, 400 smallish rooms, 3 restaurants.

Kanko ♛ ♛
1-19-30 Nishiki, Naka-ku, Nagoya 460, tel. 052-231-7711
Two persons in twin, $110
Traditional favorite of foreign visitors in past, 505 average-sized rooms, average everything else.

Dai-Ichi ♛
3-27-5 Meieki, Nakamura-ku, Nagoya 450, tel. 052-581-4411
Two persons in twin, $90
Ideal for business or rail travelers as near Nagoya Station, 314 small rooms, 2 restaurants.

International ♛
3-23-3 Nishiki, Naka-ku, Nagoya 460, tel. 052-961-3111
Two persons in twin, $90
Midway between station and central business area, 260 smallish rooms, 6 restaurants.

RESTAURANTS
Nagoya

Torikyu ♛ ♛ ♛
Tel. 052-541-2747
Average dinner, $24
Outstanding chicken dishes, including *yakitori*, skewered. Elegant surroundings.

Kanidoraku ♛
Tel. 052-583-0012
Average dinner, $20
One branch in Ciao building, one off underground arcade, Sakae subway station. Crab it is, signified by huge moving crab outside building.

Kishimen ♛
Tel. 052-951-3481
Average dinner, $4

The thick, flat, white noodles that are a specialty of Nagoya, available even on train platforms, is considered best here.

FESTIVALS

Note: See also national holidays listings, pages 21–22.

April 16–18	Nagoya: Toshogu Shrine Grand Festival ♛ ♛. Floats in a parade.
May 3–5	Hamamatsu: Giant kite battle in the skies ♛ ♛ ♛. Also evening parade of floats.
May 11– October 15	Gifu: Cormorant fishing nightly ♛ ♛ ♛.
June 5	Nagoya: Atsuta Jinja Matsuri ♛ ♛. Decorated boats, sports events.
November 3	Hakone: Daimyo Gyoretsu (Feudal Lords' Procession) ♛. Files along the old Tokaido Road.

KYOTO

There is nothing like Kyoto in any other country. Especially if you have traveled to nations where the biggest city is the political capital, the cultural capital, and the economic capital all rolled into one, Kyoto stands out. Although it is a "sister city" of Paris, it hasn't been the capital of Japan for more than 100 years. And yes, it's also a sister city of Boston, but the latter never was a capital. Comparisons are always difficult, frequently ludicrous, and occasionally odious, but if someone put a gun to my head and said, "Make one for Kyoto," I'd have to say Florence is the Italian Kyoto, to name the best example I can think of.

I lived in Tokyo for 8 years, but my heart was in Kyoto, whose gardens and temples I preferred to the cramped and confused capital. I contrived to spend as much time in Kyoto as possible, even though, I have to warn you, the people are more reserved (other Japanese say haughty) than elsewhere. The hotels are not as good, there isn't much to do at night, and English isn't spoken very much here, but it is still the most beautiful, most interesting, most everything place in Japan.

This is the place, or one of the places, where you could stay in a *ryokan,* though the good ones are very expensive. Perhaps even for just a night. You've come here to see temples, shrines, gardens, palaces, teahouses, pagodas, charming shops full of often-mysterious objects, and traditional Japanese cuisine. Bring good walking shoes, comfortable clothes, and as much money or plastic as you can manage. What you save on sensible accommodations you'll want to spend on shopping.

Kyoto and Nara were not bombed during World War II, thanks mostly to the intervention of Professor Langdon Warner, a fine-arts professor at Harvard. On hearing that the American government had included Kyoto on its list of primary targets for the atom bomb, he not only got Kyoto deleted from that list, but prevailed upon the armed forces to spare the city from "ordinary" bombing. He claimed, falsely as it turned out, that Kyoto had no war industries, and could therefore pose no hazard to the American war effort. When news of his death reached Japan in 1955, a most impressive memorial service was held for him at Nara's Todaiji Temple, the greatest of all Japanese temples in size.

Even so, many of the supposedly ancient buildings you see in Kyoto are not all that old, because fire, the curse of Japanese culture, carried many original structures away. Almost always, however, the good citizens of Kyoto rebuilt in exactly the same style as the former structure, and art objects and religious regalia were frequently saved from the burning buildings and put back into the new. So when you're admiring a particular place, if you worry about such things as exact dates and the age of something, read the fine print.

Kyoto was made for walking, but it is still a large city, of over 1,000,000 inhabitants, and stretching for some 18 miles north and south and 13 miles east and west. Protected on the east and north by fairly high mountains and on the west by lesser ones, Kyoto is in a kind of weather trap, holding smog as does Los Angeles or Mexico City. In no way is the air so dirty as either of those places, but the peculiar geography does mean that Kyoto is colder in winter than many of its nearby neighbors, and also hotter in summer.

There are two main tourist areas in Kyoto and two minor ones. The major areas are east and west of the Kamogawa River; the minor areas are the south, around Kyoto Station, and the north, above the old Imperial Palace. We'll take a good look at all the highlights, wherever they may be. Unlike Tokyo, Kyoto has no masks, only its aristocratic face, which it isn't afraid to show, at any time or any place.

HOW TO GET AROUND

Now let's talk about how to get around. There is only one subway in Kyoto, and it runs straight up the middle of the

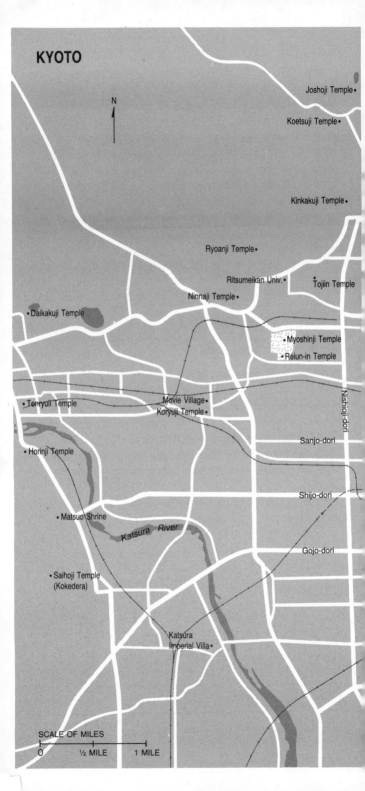

KYOTO

N

Joshoji Temple •

Koetsuji Temple •

Kinkakuji Temple •

Ryoanji Temple •

Ritsumeikan Univ. •

Tojiin Temple

Ninnaji Temple •

• Daikakuji Temple

Myoshinji Temple
Reiun-in Temple

• Tenryuji Temple

Movie Village •
Koryuji Temple •

Sanjo-dori

• Horinji Temple

Nishijo-dori

Shijo-dori

• Matsuo Shrine

Katsura River

Gojo-dori

• Saihoji Temple
(Kokedera)

Katsura
Imperial Villa •

SCALE OF MILES

0   ½ MILE   1 MILE

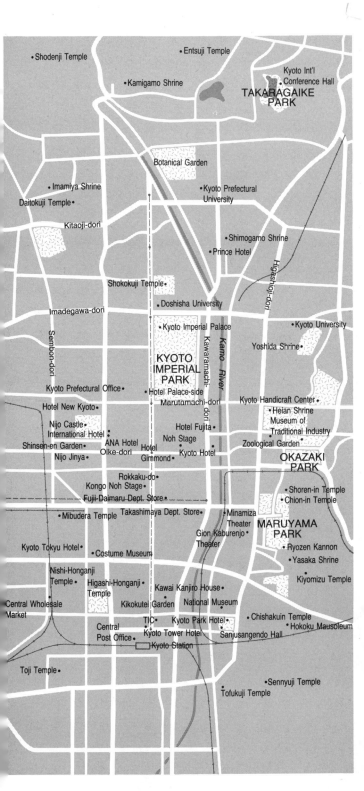

city, underneath Oike-dori Street, all of 7 stations plus Kyoto Station, the southern terminus. It's handy for going north to south, or vice versa, but for nothing else. There is only one price, ¥140 (85¢), and hold on to your ticket in order to get out of the station.

The taxi is really the only way to get around the city if you are here for only 1, 2, or 3 days. There is an excellent bus system, but learning how to use it and waiting for up to 20 minutes between buses will waste too much of your time. If, on the other hand, you're here for 4 days or more, and wish to economize, you might find my brief explanation of the bus system of interest. Taxis form lines at major hotels, and from smaller ones, ask the front desk to phone for one. They can also be hailed while cruising the streets. If a cab is available, it will have a small red light in the lower right-hand corner (as you face the car), and if a night surcharge is in effect, the light will be green. If the light is out, the cab is occupied. Fares are not high, starting at ¥470 ($2.85) for the first 2 kilometers, then an additional ¥80 (48¢) for each 370 meters. There may be a variance if you get a bigger cab, however. It all works out to about $1.90 for the first mile at time of writing. When using a cab, if you can't pronounce the Japanese name of the place given here, have your hotel write it down for you. And always carry a hotel card or matchbox so you can get back when you want to.

Buses

Since Kyoto is laid out on a grid, like Peking, after which it was modeled, the town is nowhere nearly as confusing as Tokyo. The buses have numbers on them, and I'll list appropriate numbers when I can, and when I think they're appropriate. There are two systems in Kyoto, the City Bus and the Kyoto Bus. The City (pronounced, unfortunately, shee-tea) is most useful for short distances. They are painted pale green. The Kyoto buses are better for longer runs, and are painted pale brown. The buses with one or two digits run either from Kyoto Station (JNR) or from Sanjo Keihan (a private railway station just across the river from the Kyoto Hotel, approximately). A bus with three digits is a loop bus, running around in circles, some small, some big. The signs at bus stops are, fortunately, in English as well as Japanese. The times are in the European fashion, using the 24-hour clock, so that 1 P.M. is 1300 and 6 P.M. is 1800. On the top plate of the bus-stop sign, you'll see a list of what buses stop here, and if there are many, a little map showing exact stopping points around you. Below is a schedule of when the bus is due. City Bus stops are shaped like a half-circle, Kyoto Bus stops a full circle. You have to know the numbers of the bus routes you're looking for, and they'll be in this text. Again, I feel it's worthwhile saving on something else to use taxis, unless you have plenty of time to burn.

JTB can also arrange private tours by car and guide, the minimum charge for 3 hours being ¥34,000 ($206.06) and another ¥1,000 ($6.06) for each additional person. Larger cars available, and four persons in a big car costs ¥39,000 ($236.36) for 3 hours, for example. They'll also sell you meal coupons, ¥3,600 ($21.82) or ¥5,000 ($30.30). Tel. 075-361-7241.

INSIDERS' TIPS

Kyoto has a ¥890 ($5.39) 1-day bus and subway pass which you should look into, in case you don't want to use taxis. Ask the Tourist Information Center in Kyoto how to get them, tel. 075-371-5649. At press time, they could be bought at the Kyoto City Visitor's Information Center, in front of Kyoto Station.

STANDARD PACKAGE TOURS

The three major companies visit exactly the same places, and two charge the same price. A third costs about $2 less. Here is what they show you, and it is a good representation of what Kyoto has to offer:

Morning tour. Pickups from hotels between 8:15 and 9 A.M.; tour lasts 3 or 3½ hours. Nijo-jo (Nijo Castle) is first on the list, and with good reason. Everything a Japanese castle should be, this was built by the first Tokugawa shogun, Ieyasu, who started it in 1602, when the land was at the southeast corner of the Imperial Palace. It is a glorious expanse of waiting rooms, landscaped gardens (said to have been designed by Japan's most famous gardener, Kobori Enshu, the Capability Brown of the Orient), and squeaky corridors (designed that way to warn of trespassers). You'll see, probably in too much of a hurry on the tour, up to 25 rooms, bare mostly except for wonderful painted sliding doors, nearly all from the Kano school, contemporary to the building of the castle. Of all the painters named Kano, the most famous were Tanyu and Sanraku. Note how the rooms get smaller, the corridors narrower, but the paintings better as you progress toward the shogun's private quarters. In order, you'll go through the Administration Office (Willow Room), the Retainer's Room (leopards and tigers on the doors), Greater Waiting Room, Imperial Messenger's Waiting Room (animals and bamboo), then the Reception Room (huge pine tree by Kano Tanyu). This was used for reception of feudal lords, but they didn't get to see the shogun here.

Next, another Anteroom (more pines), then the Grand Audience Chamber (peacocks and more pines). The shogun sat on the upper matted portion, lords on the lower. It was in this room that the Emperor Meiji proclaimed the abolition of the shogunate in 1868, leading to the modernization of Japan. This is the most elaborate of all the rooms. After, more waiting rooms (peonies in one, pines in another) and a Black Chamber, where favored lords were received by the shogun (heron and more pines).

The last part is the shogun's private quarters, only five rooms, named for and decorated with a sleeping sparrow in one case. You then come back along the other side of the buildings, passing a Spear Hall, ministers' offices, and more audience chambers and waiting rooms.

Next on the morning tour is the Old Imperial Palace, which really isn't very old by Japanese standards, the buildings dating back to 1855. Kyoto was the capital, of course, from 794 until 1868, and the original palace dates back that far, though the present location was established only in 1788. The originals of the buildings you see now were erected in 1790, destroyed by fire in 1854. They are exact duplicates, however.

On the tour, you'll be led in a group (no wandering, please) directly around to the Shishinden, or Ceremonial Hall, where the most important state functions took place. Some activities are still carried on here, such as the enthronement of the present emperor in 1926. The Cherry Tree of the Left and the Orange Tree of the Right grow in front of the hall, in which there is a dais, not a throne in the Western sense. Several stands are intended to hold the Imperial Regalia, sword, mirror, and beads, entirely analogous to Western royalty's sword, scepter, and crown. (The real regalia are scattered, however, in three places throughout Japan—Tokyo, Nagoya, and Ise.)

After seeing this, you'll be led to the garden, which is very attractive, featuring a lovely pond. The Kogosho (Minor Palace) facing the pond burned down as recently as 1954, so what you see is an exact replica dating from 1958. The last building you'll see is the Gogakumonjo, a hall used for monthly poetry parties.

Never open to the public at large are the buildings in which the Imperial Family actually resided, though you pass through the gate of one to exit the garden area. You have seen the ceremonial third of the grounds. Another third, called Otsune Goten, was devoted to living quarters of former emperors, and Emperor Meiji lived in these until he moved the capital to Tokyo in 1868. Another third, to the north, called Kogo Goten, was the home of the empress. Each of these had extensive gardens. They are pleasant enough, but don't feel too much sense of loss, as there are far more beautiful gardens, and buildings for that matter, which are available to you outside the palace walls.

The third spot on all the organized morning tours is Kinkakuji, the Temple of the Golden Pavilion, made famous to foreigners by Mishima Yukio's great novel of the same name, and even, perhaps by the movie made from that book. The book and film told the story of how this marvelous structure, erected in 1394, was destroyed by a crazed novitiate monk in 1950. Five years later, an exact replica was opened, and this is what you see today.

A shimmering, glittering fantasia, the Golden Pavilion was never liked by purists, who considered it garish. But it was very much to the Japanese taste, though it does offend the sensibilities of those who feel the *shibui* (astringent) feeling of Zen, with its understatement, is somehow more, or more truly, Japanese. The third shogun, Ashikaga Yoshimitsu, decreed in his will that the building, which he built as a villa for his retirement, be made a Buddhist temple, and so it is today, with the official name Rokuonji.

The last place in all the morning tours is the Kyoto Handicraft Center, the price you must pay for joining a tour. Unless you are really pressed for time, you may as well go in and see the demonstrations and browse among the souvenirs, many of very high artistic quality (but most are not). But if you feel you want to do your shopping later, take this time to leave the tour (be sure to tell your guide), and spend the minutes saved walking through the narrower streets of Kyoto.

Afternoon tour. None of the tours feature lunch, but two companies have afternoon tours, which you may join by being picked up at your hotel (between 1 and 2 P.M.) or by prearrangement, perhaps, at the last such hotel even if it isn't your own. The afternoon tours last 3 hours and go first to Heian Jingu Shrine. Built in 1895 to commemorate the 1,100th anniversary of Kyoto as a capital, it is a reproduction, on a very reduced scale, of the original palace, including the bright coloration. In a sense, Heian Shrine is a last gasp of the Shintoists, who feared loss of power when Emperor Meiji moved the capital to Tokyo. They couldn't know then that militarists would seize upon Shinto, add a twisted version of Confucian ethics, and transform emperor worship into a form of fascism a generation later.

Dedicated to the first and last Kyoto emperors, Kammu (794) and Komei (1866), this shrine is wildly popular with school groups and for weddings. The *torii* gate, by the way, was not part of the palace and is the traditional entrance to any Shinto shrine. There is nothing of interest inside the buildings.

INSIDERS' TIPS

Visitors to Kyoto should see the Kyoto Handicraft Center, just behind the Heian Jingu Shrine at Kumano Jinja Higashi, Sakyo-ku, Kyoto 606, tel. 075-761-5080. You can see arts and crafts being made here, six skills being represented (dollmaking, porcelain painting, woodblock-print making, silk weaving, handbag making, and silver and damascene jewelry making). There is also a coffee shop, and, of course, you can buy right on the spot. Open daily except 4 days at New Year's, 9:30 A.M. to 6 P.M. (closes half an hour earlier in winter).

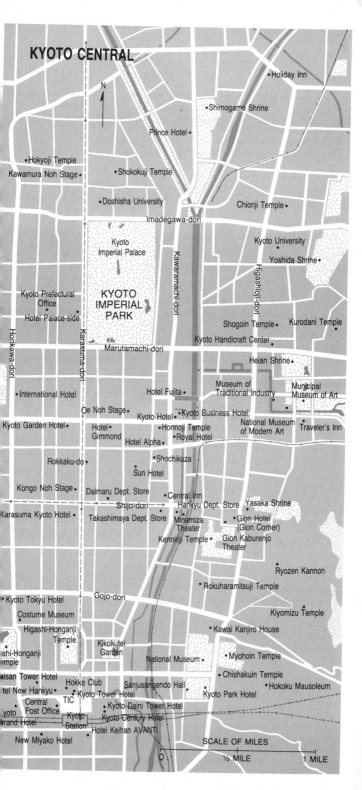

Next you will be taken to Sanjusangendo (Hall of 33 Bays), the unofficial name of Rengeoinji Temple. This long building, filled with elegant images of the Buddha, has been around since 1266, its original (1164) having been destroyed by fire. A National Treasure, it is named after the spaces between the pillars supporting the structure. The chief image, itself a National Treasure, is the Thousand-Handed Kwannon, carved in 1254 by an 82-year-old sculptor, Tankei. Another 28 National Treasures are statues of the Buddha's faithful followers, and to top off all this, there are an additional 1,000 smaller images of the big statue. You will probably be walked through at too quick a pace, but fast is better than not at all.

The third, and final, part of your itinerary takes you to majestic Kiyomizu-dera Temple, a huge complex of Buddhist temples hanging on the edge of Higashiyama (Eastern Mountain). The Hondo (Main Hall) is unlike most other Buddhist temples in the shaping of its huge cypress roof, curled up at each corner. The wide verandah jutting out over the valley was used for ceremonial dances, the wings of the Hon-do on either end being called *gakuya* (orchestra stands). To do something impetuous or to make a grand gesture in Japan is "to jump off the Kiyomizu-dera verandah," as an old saying has it. Erected in 1633, the temple dates back to 798. Because of fires again, most of those you see are from the later date.

The most important image in the Hondo is that of the Eleven-Headed Kwannon, goddess of mercy. It is so sacred that it is open to view (even by the monks) only once every 33 years (next is 1997). Look for the waterfall below the verandah. You may see some penitent standing under it, even in winter, hoping for purification.

Details of the morning and afternoon tours. You can arrange these through your hotel front desk or by phoning the following: Japan Travel Bureau, tel. 075-361-7241; Fujita Travel Service, tel. 075-222-0121; or Gray Line, associated here with Kintetsu, tel. 075-691-0903. The JTB and Fujita morning tours are ¥4,300 ($26.06), Gray Line ¥4,000 ($24.24). JTB tour lasts 3½ hours, the others 3 hours. The Gray Line has no afternoon tour of Kyoto. Fujita and JTB tours for the afternoon cost ¥4,300 ($26.06) and take 3 and 3½ hours respectively. You do get more time for your money with JTB, according to the schedules.

INSIDERS' TIPS

Visitors to Kyoto can have their luggage delivered to their hotels while they go about their sightseeing or shopping. If your train arrives at Kyoto Station between 8 A.M. and 1 P.M., you may go to the Daitetsu window at the West Karasuma exit of the station (that's the main entrance, not the Shinkansen Bullet Train side). Leave your luggage there, pay ¥400 ($2.42) per bag, and tell the attendant the name of your hotel. It will be at your hotel by 5 P.M. The bags should weigh less than 30 kilos (66 pounds) and measure under 3 meters (9.9 feet) in length.

Conversely, on leaving Kyoto, if your train leaves between 1 and 8 P.M., have it picked up at your hotel by 10 A.M. (arrange through front desk) and you can claim it at the station before your train departs.

Either way, you have extra time for sightseeing in Kyoto, without having to worry about your luggage.

KYOTO IN A HURRY

If you're unlucky enough to have only 1 day, you could see (very quickly) seven major palaces, temples, and shrines on the combined morning and afternoon tours of JTB or Fujita Travel. You won't have more than half an hour at each place, and on every morning tour you have to visit the Kyoto Handicrafts Center. This is a worthy place, but it, and the tours, are organized to encourage you to buy. This may not be what you want to do if there's only a day to see this marvelous old capital. So you might want my own tour, which visits the four best, or at least most representative of the best, places in town. You'll have more time at each place, and you'll enjoy it more, I think, and be able to absorb more.

Instead of joining a tour, you could see just four things during your Kyoto stay, and they constitute a better picture than that presented by the commercial operations. As you are not part of a group, you'll have more time in each place, and I've arranged the itinerary to avoid those times when the foreign groups, at least, are not there. (I have no control over Japanese groups, needless to say, and especially school groups, who swarm like bees to honey, and

KYOTO IN A HURRY ITINERARIES

If you have only 1 day: Kiyomizudera Temple, Ginkakuji Temple of the Silver Pavilion, Kyoto Imperial Palace, Nijojo Castle

If you have a 2nd day: Sanjusangendo Hall, Kiyomizudera Temple, Kyoto Imperial Palace, Daitokuji Temple

If you have a 3rd day: Katsura Rikyu Detached Villa, Kitano Jinja Shrine, Kinkakuji Temple of the Golden Pavilion, Ryoanji Temple

they may be anywhere, anytime.)

In the morning, assuming you're possessed of a full morning, you have to make an important decision very early. You must decide if you want to see the Imperial Palace in the morning (10 A.M.) or afternoon (2 P.M.), as these are the times for the English-language tours. In either case, you must be at the palace no later than 20 minutes earlier, with your passport. (No tours Saturday afternoons or on Sundays, admission free.) The best time to go is afternoon, as the package tours go in the morning usually. The afternoon trip, however, means you must have an early lunch.

Assuming you follow my advice, then, get yourself over to Kiyomizudera Temple ♛ ♛ ♛ ♛ as your first stop of the day. If you don't go by cab, get there on the buses numbered 18, 202, 206, or 207, getting off at Gojozaka and walking up the hill. I've mentioned the Main Hall already, but in addition, be sure to walk around the far edge of it, past some trees with their prayer slips tied to the branches, to the Okuno-in (Innermost Temple) above the waterfall. From here is the best view of the Hondo (Main Hall) and a great photographing point. For instant purification, pick up the small ladle behind this building and pour water over the small statue of Nurete Kwannon (Wet Kwannon) there. Showing the tolerance of religions toward each other in Japan, there is a nice little Shinto shrine, Jishu Gongen, behind the Main Hall. Take a look at the ship paintings hanging under the eaves of the Main Hall, dating from 1634. Back toward the entrance is the Tamura-do, the Founder's Hall (named for Tamuramaro, who founded the temple here after having a semimystical experience when he killed a stag on this site). It dates

from the 11th century, and was originally the Shishinden
(Ceremonial Hall) of the Imperial Palace in Nagaoka,
where the capital was situated between 784 and 794. It is
in the same style as the Ceremonial Hall at Kyoto Imperial
Palace, which you will see in the afternoon.

You can't stay here forever, so down the hill you go,
walking this time, all the way to the bottom, where you
should be able to find a taxi on Higashi-oji-dori Street.

You want to go north, to Ginkakuji Temple ♛ ♛ ♛ ♛,
the Temple of the Silver Pavilion. If you don't have to wait
too long (see schedule on bus-stop sign), take the 18, 202,
or 206 bus to Higashiyama Sanjo, where you transfer to a
5 or a 203 directly for Ginkakuji-michi (Street of the Silver
Pavilion).

The Temple of the Silver Pavilion is a splendid example
of delicate Japanese sensitivity in architecture, landscaping, and furnishings. The eighth shogun, Ashikaga Yoshimasa, taking a cue from his grandfather, Yoshimitsu, decided to build a villa for his retirement. Just as the old man
had built the Kinkakuji (Golden Pavilion), Yoshimasa
would erect a Silver counterpart. Picking the opposite side
of town, he finished Ginkakuji in 1483, and moved in.
About a dozen structures compose the villa; the pavilion is
at the center. It was never coated with silver, Yoshimasa
being happy with other plans, particular with the tea
ceremony, of which he was perhaps the greatest of pa-
trons. Other buildings here he had constructed for the sole
purpose of moongazing, poem composing, incense sniffing,
flower viewing, etc. In the northeast corner of the Togudo
(East Request Hall) is a 4½-mat room, said to be the
oldest tearoom in Japan. The hall itself dates from 1486,
one of the two original buildings remaining. It is a National
Treasure. The pavilion itself is the purest form of the
Japanese quest for simplicity, yet the elegance of the lines
makes it a thing of beauty in any eye.

As was the case with his grandfather, Yoshimasa willed
his villa to Buddhist priests, who organized a temple here.
The official name of Kinkakuji is Jishoji Temple. The gardens are almost as important as the buildings, and were
said to have been designed by Soami. The *karesansui* (dry
garden) consists of large white sand shapes, one a cone,
the other a plateau, representing China's famous West
Lake and a mountain. The main garden is one of the

prettiest in Japan, with a tiny waterfall (called Moon-Washing Fountain), and islands in its pond resembling a turtle and a crane. In designing this garden, Soami was said to have been influenced greatly by the garden at Saihoji Temple, the so-called Moss Temple. Since it is hard to get into that temple (see later in this section), you should take special note of this garden design.

Now for that early lunch. In order to be at the Old Imperial Palace ♛ ♛ ♛ ♛ no later than 1:40 P.M., you should plan your time carefully, and allow an extra 15 minutes for slow traffic, etc. You don't want to risk a bus getting to the palace, but if you're only going to slurp a bowl of noodles (or the Western equivalent, grab a sandwich), you could take bus 203 to the Karasuma Imadegawa stop, just north of the palace. There are no particularly distinguished lunch places in either the Ginkakuji or palace areas, so try anything that looks interesting. If you want Western-style or just familiar surroundings, try the Palace-side Hotel, which is by the Karasuma Marutamachi subway station and not far from the Old Imperial Palace entrance.

Before 1:40 P.M., present yourself to the Old Imperial Household Agency office inside the palace (the cab can drive you this far, inside the central gate and to the left). The 2 P.M. tour, in English, will take you through the sights described earlier in this section. Since you're not allowed to go off on your own, you'll have to leave at the end of the tour. (You may stay behind at the souvenir shop, or to have a drink there, or to use the facilities, of course, but no more looking at the precious palace.) Now, get yourself to Nijo Castle by cab or by going over to Horikawa-dori Street and catching bus 9 to the castle stop.

Nijojo (Nijo Castle) ♛ ♛ ♛ ♛ ♛ was the seat of the Tokugawa shoguns for 265 years. Here is the most room to expand on the standard tour's offerings. Not only can you spend more time looking at all the paintings on the sliding doors and screens, and the carvings above the doors, and the metal door handles (Tokugawa crests in some cases replaced by imperial chrysanthemums), but you can try to spy out the (closed) secret chambers in each of the four buildings of the main palace. These were used for bodyguards, for stowing prisoners, or for concealing spies to listen in on happenings in the public rooms.

The garden of Nijojo is unique, for it had no trees at first, the shogun stating that he didn't want the falling leaves of autumn to remind him of the impermanence of life itself. It was thought to be designed by Kobori Enshu around 1626.

Go through the rooms of the Nino-maru Palace of the castle, looking for the works of Kano Tanyu and others of the Kano school. Note the weird-looking leopards and tigers (animals the artists had never seen), the gorgeous peonies, cherry blossoms, and bamboo. There are also wonderfully carved lintels, mostly showing flowers, but also the mythical phoenix, which is seen frequently. When you have finished with the palace, the highlight of the tour, go around to the right as you exit, and visit the garden. From there, mount the steps leading to the bridge across the inner moat to the site of the old castle itself. The main keep here was destroyed by fire in the 18th century, and the present building on the site, the Honmaru Palace, was moved here in 1893. It was the residence of Prince Katsura, and was on the grounds of the Old Imperial Palace. It is used occasionally for state functions, such as the banquet held here on the occasion of the enthronement of the present emperor in 1928. The inside, when open, is of little interest. A walk through the garden here is a pleasant experience. Go on past, down the steps and across another bridge, turn left, and work your way back to the entrance. On the left and right of this second bridge are rice storehouses.

After all this, you will be suffering from museum feet and will need a little rest, perhaps a good lie-down, as the British would say, a cold drink of some kind, and then dinner. If you don't taxi back to your hotel, you could try bus 9 north or south from in front of the castle, and transfer if necessary at the next stop.

KYOTO ON THE 2ND DAY

Instead of just adding on to your first day, I suggest a grand rearrangement of everything, starting off with a taxi ride to the Sanjusangendo Hall ₩ ₩ ₩ ₩. Buses 18, 206, and 208 stop right in front. Described earlier (see package tours, page 195), the building is filled with fascinating images of the Buddha in the form of Kwannon, goddess of mercy. (Buddha takes many shapes and forms, and both sexes, as the occasion demands.) Take plenty of time, for there are slight differences in the many images, and on a quiet day, this temple can have a splendid peace, all its own. I hope you won't be there when several busloads of school kids throng the hall. In January, should you be lucky enough, you might see a demonstration of *yabusame*, archery, in which contestants try to shoot their arrows at least as far as the length of the building.

From here it's an instructive, but uphill, walk to Kiyomizudera Temple. You can't take a cab all the way up, but at least partway, so try that. Buses 8 and 206 go to the bottom of the hill, if you want to ride cheaply. (The stop is called Gojozaka.)

On your own at Kiyomizu, follow the description given earlier, page 202. After lunch, head for the Old Imperial Palace (same description as above). From Kiyomizudera, should you not wish to take a cab, try bus 207 to Hijo Karasuma, and transfer there to the subway, getting off at Imadegawa, 3 stops north. The tour in the afternoon also is described earlier.

After the palace, head next for Daitokuji Temple, a marvelous complex north of here. If you don't take a taxi, take the subway 2 stops to the end of the line, Kitaoji, and walk west for several blocks.

Daitokuji (Temple of Great Virtue) ♛ ♛ ♛ ♛ is one of Japan's most important centers of Zen, the meditative form of Buddhism. Its gardens are among Kyoto's best, and its rambling array of temples extremely impressive. It has more than 20 subordinate temples right on the 27 acres of its grounds, not to mention branches around the country. Among the treasures, the best display of which is in October, that you should look for are a fine painting of Kwannon with a monkey and crane by Mokkei (a National Treasure) and the image of Kwannon carved by Gekko. Founded in 1324 by a monk who lived among beggars for 20 years to gain the proper humility, the temple burned to the ground twice, so that the present buildings date from 1468. The second gate, the Karamon (Chinese Gate), a National Treasure, was brought here from Hideyoshi's Fushimi Castle when it was torn down. If you enter by the East Gate, you'll turn right and pass through two huge gates. The first, Chokushi-mon (Imperial Messenger Gate), used to be at the Old Imperial Palace, and dates from 1590. The next, San-mon (Triple Gate), dates from 1523, but has an upper story added 65 years later by the master of the tea ceremony, Sen-no-Rikyu. (There is today, still, a Sen-no-Rikyu, operating the family business, that of teaching the tea ceremony. He is the pope of the tea ritual, and has thousands of faithful disciples.)

INSIDERS' TIPS

On October 10 each year, the paintings and scrolls of Daitokuji Temple, Kyoto, are hauled out of their boxes to be aired, usually laid out across the *tatami* mats and along the corridors of the temple's various buildings. Visitors are allowed to view them. Every Japanese painting and scroll has its own box, and families, for instance, usually change the most important scroll hanging in their houses at least once each season. The rest of the year, back in the box.

The Butsu Den (Buddha Hall) dates only from 1665, thanks to fire again, but has images dating back to at least 1540, and paintings (originally elsewhere) earlier than that. Next door, the Hatto (Lecture Hall) is considered more important. The building you see dates from 1636, making it as old as Harvard University. Most impressive is the Hojo (Superior's Quarters), again to the right, with its own walled garden. Also dating from 1636, it is a National Treasure, mostly because of the paintings of Kano Tanyu therein. The smaller garden, serene and dry, was designed (again!) by Kobori Enshu. It is an excellent example of a Zen garden, though the addition of nearby houses, trees, etc. has reduced the effect.

Behind the Hojo are two important temples, Shinju-an and Daisen-in. The former can be visited only with advance permission, so is not discussed here. It is, in fact, less important than Daisen-in, its neighbor. You can look here for paintings by Kano Motonobu, but what you really must see is the garden, designed by Kogaku Shuko in around 1492. Considered by many to be the single most beautiful garden in the country, for its purity of design, the east garden of Daisen-in is organized around a single rock. It is supposed to be a ship, the white gravel a river. Some scholars interpret the ship as representing a person or the soul, on the river of life, but make of it what you will.

If you have the opportunity, as it may be the end of the day, sit for a while and just empty your mind of extraneous thoughts. It will be easier to do it here than at the more famous Ryoanji Temple, with its white sand and islands of stone.

A 3RD DAY IN KYOTO

I'm cheating a bit here. Before you do anything on your 3rd day, you have to make arrangements even before you arrive in town. That is, if you want to see Katsura Rikyu (Katsura Detached Villa) ♛ ♛ ♛ ♛, the building and gardens of which probably had more influence on the West and its acceptance of Japanese taste than any other place. Back in the 1950s, *House Beautiful* magazine devoted two complete issues to the Japanese concept of *shibui*, astringent taste, using Katsura Villa as a model for its depictions not only of architecture and garden landscaping but of textiles, ceramics, painting, you name it. The issues were sell-outs, and the boom in things Japanese followed. Those funny little people who tried to defeat America in the war were suddenly human again, and artists at that.

Apply at least 5 days in advance for a permit to visit Katsura Rikyu. Take any appointment you can get, and base the rest of your 3rd day around it. You can phone the Imperial Household Agency, tel. 075-211-1211, and pick up the permit the day before going. If you wish to write in advance, send a letter to the Imperial Household Agency, 3 Kyoto Gyoen, Kamigyo-ku, Kyoto. Include your name, address when in Japan, nationality, passport number, and dates requested. Tours of the Katsura Rikyu are at 10 A.M. and 2 P.M.; tours of Kyoto Imperial Palace at the same hours; tours of Shugakuin are at 9, 10, and 11 A.M. and at 1:30 and 3 P.M. Go to the agency (inside the Old Palace gate) in person and, after showing your passport, pick up the written permit. Do this at least a day before your planned visit. You could, of course, make this request when you present yourself at the palace for the earlier tour there. Sometimes the answer is "All full up, sorry."

Built in 1620, the villa and its garden were designed together, the brothers of Kobori Enshu being involved with the landscaping. The story goes that when Kobori was requested by Toyotomi Hideyoshi, the great shogun, to build this villa for a brother of the Emperor Goyozei, the gardener replied that he would, if Hideyoshi would promise never to question the cost, never to order him to hurry up, and never come to see the project until it was finished. (Hideyoshi died before it was finished, in any case.)

The villa, now owned by the Imperial Household, is a supreme example of understated elegance. Every part of the garden is designed so that you cannot say one view is better than another, or that there is a "wrong" side of any part of the vista. The house itself, Shokintei, is simple, yet possessed of small details that make the difference between rusticity and refinement. Note the tearoom here. The Hall for Imperial Visits seems to dominate the pond, but it was in fact added after the other buildings on the occasion of a visit from an ex-emperor. Gepparo, on a hill near the Visits Hall, has a verandah of bamboo, a ceiling of reeds. This kind of simplicity was almost necessitated by aesthetic reaction to the flamboyance of the brief-lived period of extravagance and conspicuous consumption when Hideyoshi was shogun, the Azuchi Momoyama Period (1573–98).

To get to Katsura, you'll have to take a taxi, as there is no direct bus service from the center of the city. Have the

---

INSIDERS' TIPS

Plan ahead for Kyoto perks. If you really want to see the Katsura Detached Villa or the Shugakuin Detached Villa in Kyoto, phone in Tokyo to the Imperial Household Agency, 03-213-1111, ext. 485, and ask for a permit. The sooner you reserve (5 days minimum in advance) the better your chances, as there are a limited number of permits. (Katsura is much more popular than Shugakuin.) You may also phone directly to Kyoto's office of the same agency (called Kunaisho in Japanese). In either case, you must pick up the permit at least a day before the appointed day. In Kyoto, you pick it up at the Old Imperial Palace (see text). In Tokyo, you get it at the Kunaisho, which happens to be inside the Imperial Palace too. Go to the Sakashitamon Gate of the palace (with your passport), fill out a form and get your ID badge, then walk to the agency and pick up your permit. (In Kyoto, no badge is required to visit the agency to get your permit.)

taxi wait, as cabs are practically impossible to find at Katsura Rikyu.

For the rest of your 3rd day, I recommend three spots, the first of which is Kitano Jinja Shrine, up in the northwest quarter of Kyoto. If you're coming here from Katsura Imperial Villa, you'll need a cab, at least as far as Nishi-oji Shichi-jo, where you can get a 205 bus. This stops at Kitano Hakubai-cho, just a few yards from the shrine. The 203 bus also goes here.

Kitano Jinja Shrine ♛ ♛ ♛ is famous for many things, among them Toyotomi Hideyoshi's decision to have a tea party here, inviting everyone in Kyoto. He was a little sick of what he thought were the pretensions and fussiness of the tea ceremony, and yes, he did go through with it, in November 1587. The buildings you see today were constructed by his son, Hideyori, in 1607, replacing originals from 947.

The marvelous cypress-shingled roofs of the buildings rise above a sea of plum trees, especially beautiful when in bloom in February or March. The Main Hall and the Oratory are both National Treasures. This shrine is dedicated to Sugawara Michizane, patron saint of scholars, whose favorite tree was the plum. Just before university and other school entrance examinations, usually in the early spring, you'll see many students here, lighting candles and writing good-luck plaques for the attention of the gods. The *ema* (plaques) are hung from trees. On the 25th of every month, there is a marvelous flea market in the compound and along the eastern edge of the shrine. You'll find everything from antiques to *yakimochi* (baked rice cakes). Starts early in the morning, peters out in late afternoon.

Lunchtime again, and up in this neighborhood, I strongly recommend you try an "ordinary" restaurant, not one primped up for foreign tourists. A nice place, featuring wonderful *soba* (noodle) dishes, is Gontaro, down the street toward Kinkakuji, your next destination anyhow.

A 15-minute walk southwest from Kitano Shrine is Kinkakuji Temple (Temple of the Golden Pavilion) ♛ ♛ ♛ ♛, which I described at some length earlier, page 197. I noted at the time that you wouldn't have much time here, and certainly there would not have been an occasion to visit even the Main Hall of the temple, which is splendid by itself. There is a fine grouping of statues here, especially the one of Kwannon. (For some reason, the goddess of mercy always seems to attract the attention of the best artists.) In the courtyard here is a wonderful old pine tree, bent to resemble a sailing ship. For a little relaxation, I recommend highly a walk along the paths up and around the pond. Allow yourself to get lost, and try to forget your worries, whatever they may be. Taking oneself too seriously is what caused the teenage monk who torched this place back in 1950 to go off the deep end.

Your final destination on this 3rd day is another 10-minute walk, again to the southwest. Ryoanji Temple (Dragon Peace Temple) 👑 👑 👑 👑 is probably Kyoto's most famous, because of its so-called Zen rock garden. Because it is so popular, there are now recordings (in Japanese only, thank God) telling the crowds how to behave, where to walk, how long to meditate, and so forth. This goes on only when there are large groups present, so if you go at the end of the day and if you're lucky, there won't be many people around and it might be relatively quiet.

Established in 1473 by the Hosokawa family, many of whose members are entombed here, Ryoanji burned to the ground in 1790, and the buildings you see now date from the reconstruction that followed. The rock garden was created in 1500 by Soami, who fashioned this white expanse of sand and 15 stones in such a manner that scholars have debated ever since what it all "means." Measuring about 100 by 50 feet, the expanse keeps everyone guessing, which is not the purpose of meditation at all. My favorite "explanation," which is hoary with age, is that the stones represent a mother tiger and her cubs crossing a river. At any rate, the accepted protocol suggests that you sit down on the verandah and try to empty your mind, noise permitting, while gazing at the sand and rocks. The fact that the garden was once without a wall and that you could look beyond the stones to trees and a distant view of mountains makes all the talk about "meaning" a little meaningless, the addition of a wall changing every aspect of the garden completely.

Behind you, the Hojo (Superior's Quarters) has some nice paintings on the screens, with dragons, naturally, predominating. Nicest of all is the small moss garden alongside the Hojo, but there are more than 100 acres here, and you could even climb up the hill behind the Hojo to see the tombs of seven emperors (9th to 12th centuries), none of them famous these days. After that, you might wish to wander down the hill past the rock garden to the big Kyoyo-chi (Mirror-Shape Pond), with its islands and a bridge leading to a small Shinto shrine to Benten, one of the Fukurokujin (Seven Gods of Luck). She is the patroness of arts, literature, music, and eloquence. She plays the *biwa*, a kind of mandolin, and hangs around with a sea serpent.

KYOTO WITH PLENTY OF TIME

If you have more than 3 days, you may wish to visit some of the following sightseeing destinations. Before striking out, however, consider a day or half-day spent with no schedule at all, just wandering through the narrow streets of the more interesting quarters and looking. Perhaps this can be combined with casual shopping. Among the areas I think best for this are the following, in order of preference: (1) The Gion area, just east of the Kamogawa River, and between Sanjo-dori Street and Gojo-dori Street. On the east, the border is Higashiyama-dori. This is a mixture of shops, temples, and houses, with the entertainment world. (2) The Kawara-machi area, just west of the river, and also between Sanjo and Gojo Streets, with Kawara-machi-dori as its western flank. This is a very narrow area, completely devoted to restaurants, private clubs, and bars. Especially charming at night. (3) The Kawara-machi Shopping Arcades, west of Kawara-machi-dori, between Oike-dori Street and Shijo-dori Street. Of special interest are the covered streets, Shinkyogoku-dori and Teramachi-dori (the latter means Temple District Street). In among all the souvenirs and junk, you'll see little shops selling funeral plaques, incense, silken purses, tortoiseshell hair ornaments, marvelous dolls, antiques, pickles, Japanese sweets, handmade paper, you name it. You'll also see, every so often, a tiny shrine or temple tucked in behind the frontage it has sold to keep going. Not to mention the more powerful religious establishments, of which there are still plenty.

Serious travelers, of course, will want to see some more

of the places that make Kyoto unique. For the sake of helping you find them on the map, I have organized a description of the remaining Kyoto highlights in a route that takes us in a counterclockwise fashion from the rail station out and back again.

A short distance north of Kyoto Station (main entrance, not the Shinkansen side) and past the superefficient and friendly Tourist Information Center (operated by the Japan National Tourist Organization), then a long block west, is Nishi Honganji ♔ ♔ ♔, one of the best examples of Buddhist architecture in Japan. The huge buildings, with their soaring tiled roofs, look almost like helmeted palaces. This is the headquarters of the Honganji school of the Jodo-Shinshu sect of Buddhism. St. Shinran, its founder, was the man who led Japanese Buddhists along a new path, stating that salvation could be attained by faith alone, especially when invoking the name of Buddha with the now-famous formula Namu Amida Butsu. He also married a former prime minister's daughter, thus ending the supremacy of the celibate priesthood (some of them were never very celibate anyway), and began to eat meat, a radical idea in the 12th century.

The Hondo (Main Hall) and Daishi-do (Founder's Hall) are both registered as Important Cultural Properties. The Hondo you see was reconstructed in 1760 after a fire. The interior is richly decorated and contains paintings by artists of the Kano School. The Daishi-do was built in 1636, and contains an image of Shinran, who carved it himself when he was 71 years old. It was a gift to his daughter, a nun. After his death, his ashes were mixed with lacquer and the image varnished with the stuff. Of greater interest to art lovers, though, are the Daisho-in Hall and the Karamon Gate, both National Treasures, and both brought here when Hideyoshi's Fushimi Castle was dismantled in 1632. The gate is gorgeous, boasting carvings by Hidari Jingoro, whose work you will also see at Nikko. This period in the 17th century, corresponding to the Elizabethan period and slightly later, was one of Japan's most productive in the arts.

Two more buildings in this compound are National Treasures. The Kuroshoin is so, mostly because of paintings on its sliding doors by Kano Eitoku. The Hiunkaku Pavilion, at the southeast corner of the compound, contains Hideyoshi's private quarters. Every room is filled with gorgeous paintings by the best members of the Kano school—Tanyu, Eitoku, and Sanraku. (Bus 9, Nishi Honganji stop.)

You can visit the temple interiors only by getting permission at its office, on the left corner of the Main Hall as you face it when coming through the gate. Tours only, no individual wandering inside the buildings at least, and they are at 10 and 11 A.M., 1:30 and 2:30 P.M., daily except Saturday afternoons. The explanations will be in Japanese only.

Just across the street from Nishi Honganji (at its northernmost corner) is the Costume Museum♛, on the 5th floor of an office building (English sign outside). This is a superb display of clothes from early times to the Meiji Period (late 19th century). Closed Sundays, small admission.

Higashi Honganji♛ ♛ (Higashi = east, Nishi = west), a few blocks east and visible from the western temple, was created in 1602 by Ieyasu, the first Tokugawa shogun, fearful that the influence of Hideyoshi still lingered on and that the monks of Jodo Shinshu might undermine his authority. Accordingly, he gave a former abbot permission to start a new branch of the sect, then and now called the Otani School, and helped the monks build Higashi Honganji. Ieyasu had the standard vindictiveness of the era, pulling down Hideyoshi's beautiful castle at Fushimi and giving parts of it to various temples in Kyoto. All the buildings of Higashi Honganji have been destroyed by fire several times, but the current Hondo (Main Hall), Kyoto's largest wooden building, has stayed trouble-free since 1895. If you see a lot of thick ropes hanging about, note that they are made of human hair sent by women members of the sect at the time the Main Hall was rebuilt, and the ropes were used during construction. The Daishi-do (Founder's Hall) is also open to the public, but everything else requires application a day in advance. To tell the truth, I wouldn't bother unless you are a serious student of Jodo Shinshu. (Buses: all that go to Kyoto Station.)

THE EAST SIDE

Across the Kamogawa River and opposite the Sanjusangendo Hall is the Kyoto Kokuritsu Hakubutsukan
(Kyoto National Museum) ♕ ♕ ♕, one of the three or four
best museums in Japan. The collection changes frequently,
but in the more than 100 years it has been open, a goodly
number of fine Buddhist paintings and ceramics, especially, have been accumulated. Look particularly for
works by the Kano school again, and by Kenzan, the
master potter. Closed Mondays, small admission. (Buses:
18, 206, 208, Hakubutsukan stop.)

Chishaku-in Temple ♕, east of the museum about 200
yards, is a quiet and elegant place, though the buildings
are very recent, most of the old ones having been destroyed in a 1947 fire. What is best here is the lovely
garden, designed by Sen-no-Rikyu, the great tea ceremony
teacher, in the late 16th century. The pond is especially
impressive. (Buses: 18, 202, 206, 207, 208, Higashiyama
Shichi-jo stop.)

Up the street (north) and on the left, look for a sign
reading "Kawai Kanjiro's House" ♕ and follow the arrow.
Here is a pleasant house, left in the condition it was when
the owner, a famous potter, died in 1966. The house itself
is fascinating, the few works on display less so. Closed
Mondays, mid-August, and a week at New Year's.

A few hundred feet up the main Higashiyama-dori
Street again, you'll find two buildings, crammed with ceramics of all kinds, mostly modern dinnerware and the
like—Kyoto Tojiki Kaikan on the right, Kiyomizu-yaki
Pottery on the left.

Walk, cab it, or take the bus one stop now to Yasaka
Jinja Shrine ♕, up the street to the north. Located in
Maruyama Koen Park, Yasaka is busiest at New Year's,
when all of Kyoto comes here to celebrate the date change.

Walk through the park, behind the shrine, and a bit
northward, you'll find Chion-in Temple ♕ ♕, its huge
buildings dating back to 1633 (replacing earlier ones from
1234 and later). The temple is one of the largest in Japan,
and its Sanmon Gate certainly one of the most impressive.
This is the headquarters of the huge Jodo sect, parent to
the Jodo Shinshu sect we met at Higashi and Nishi Honganji temples earlier. The garden next to the Hojo (Super-

ior's Quarters) was designed by (all together, now) Kobori Enshu (d. 1647).

Just north of Chion-in is one of Kyoto's many lovely gardens, this one on the grounds of Shoren-in Temple 🏯, a former palace. The gardens were said to have been designed, at different times, by both Kobori Enshu and Soami (d. 1525). The buildings you see date only from 1895.

Now head for the hills. Your destination is Nanzenji Temple, and if you like the idea of a 20-minute walk, you'll pass through some of Kyoto's most interesting streets, featuring the famous old Yamanaka Fine Arts Company, the Miyako Hotel (where you turn left), past several of the city's most exclusive restaurants (Minokichi, Junsei, and Hyotei are the most important) and the Yachiyo Ryokan. You could also take a cab, but there is no direct bus route.

Nanzenji Temple 🏯🏯🏯 is often considered the most important Zen place of worship in Kyoto, and it is also one of the most attractive. At the Sanmon Gate, you might want to climb the narrow stairs for a view, which was inspiring enough when I tried it some years ago. Nowadays, I head straight for the Hojo (Superior's Quarters) and its garden. The suites of rooms here came from the Old Imperial Palace in 1611 and from Fushimi Castle in 1632. The earlier one is a National Treasure. Kano Tanyu painted the tigers in a bamboo grove found in the later set of rooms. I think the garden here at the Hojo is better than that of Ryoanji Temple. Another fine garden here is at a subordinate temple, way off in the southwest corner, Kon-chi-in. It was designed by Kobori Enshu in 1632. More pleasing than this second garden, though, is a walk through the temple grounds to another subsidiary temple, Nanzen-in. You pass under a rare structure for feudal times, an aqueduct, part of a stream flowing from faraway Lake Biwa.

When you come out of Nanzenji, turn right (north), pass Zenrinji Temple, and just before you reach Nyakyuoji Jinja Shrine, you'll spot a small creek. This is the southern end of the Philosopher's Walk 🏯🏯, a famous path of about 1 mile which will lead you toward the Ginkakuji (Silver Pavilion). Still a favorite of teachers and students from nearby Kyoto University, it is a quiet path, and very pleasant. Something philosophical might even spring to mind, but there are coffee shops along the way (one named

Bobby Soxer) to remind you of our "real" world. There are paths on either side of the stream, so take your pick.

About halfway along the Philosopher's Walk is Honen-in Temple ♛ ♛, one of my two favorite small Buddhist places of worship. I like it because the priest Honen, who founded it, was responsible for beginning the movement to make Buddhism a religion of the masses, not just of the court and its hangers-on. For 400 years, Honen's followers had no temple of their own, but Ieyasu, the first Tokugawa shogun, gave them parts of Hideyoshi's Fushimi Castle and helped them build a home in the early 17th century. The beauty of this place is the marvelous juxtaposition of buildings to garden, not for anything inside the (usually closed) Main Hall.

When you reach the end of the Philosopher's Walk, in front of the Silver Pavilion, I recommend you find a cab for the next leg of your journey, to Shisendo, again to the north. It isn't all that far, but you could keep the taxi waiting while you see the temple, then go on to your ultimate destination on the east side of Kyoto, Shugakuin Rikyu Detached Palace.

At Shisendo (Poets' Temple) ♛ ♛, you'll find a bijou of a temple, small and elegant, at once cozy and refined. Built in 1631 as a retreat by a poet, Ishikawa Jozan, it became a temple after his death (1672). In the Poets' Room are portraits of 36 Chinese poets. (Japanese students even today have to learn at least a smattering of Chinese poetry, just as Americans until recently had to study Latin.) Nice as the temple itself is, the garden is better. Surrounded by a thick grove of pines and maples, a white sand garden and its beautifully designed pond will bring a sense of ease to your soul, especially if you're tired of Big Everything, of which you've probably seen enough.

If you've had the taxi wait, fine, but otherwise, go down the hill to Shirakawa-dori Street and look for one. If you're *genki* (in good health), walk north (about 20 minutes) to Shugakuin. Buses 16, 17, and 18 run along here, but the stops are few and far between, though there is one at the bottom of the hill from Shugakuin.

Since it's an Imperial Villa, you need written permission to enter. This you can obtain from the same Imperial Household Agency office in the Old Imperial Palace where you got your on-the-spot permits for the palace, and where you went to get your Katsura Rikyu permits at least 24 hours in advance (see page 209). Because Shugakuin is less popular than Katsura, you can sometimes get a permit in the morning for a visit in the afternoon. Nonetheless, it is still advisable to get it at least the day before. (Again, there is always the chance that the villa is booked up, so do try well ahead of the time you intend to go.)

Shugakuin Rikyu (Scholarly Detached Palace) ♛ ♛ ♛ stands on the site of an abandoned temple, which gives it the name. Although several emperors resided here from the early 17th century, when the Tokugawa allowed a retiring ruler to build here, the buildings and gardens fell into neglect, and the grounds that you see today date from 1883, though they follow the old patterns strictly. There are three villas, each with its own garden and *chaya* (tea-house). Each is separated from the other by rice fields, and each has its own character. The objective here was to be as natural as possible, just the opposite of so many of Kyoto's gardens, so there are few carefully trained trees, rocks that look like something else, or scaled-down mountains, rivers, and oceans of sand.

In the Lower Villa, the single building (1824) is a reconstruction of the original (c. 1650), and each wing has its own purpose and corresponding name (Luck-bringing Moon View, for example). The garden was designed by the first emperor to live here, Go-Mizu-no-o. The Middle Villa contains, in addition to the residence, a temple which is still a nunnery, dating from 1680. Rinkyuji Temple, as it is called, is not open to the public. It is the building on the left as you enter. The garden here is centered around a wide, flattish pine tree more or less resembling an open umbrella. The best of the gardens is in the Upper Villa. You'll pass a splendid collection of hill-clinging shrubs and a massive hedge. The objective of your climb is a small house called the Rin-Untei, created to command a panoramic view. You are now at the top of the most beautiful garden in Kyoto. The porch here is called Senshi-dai (Poem-Washing Platform).

At the other end of the villa, on an island in the Yokyuryu-chi (Bathing Dragon Pond), is the Kyusui-tei, which has a cozy little tearoom. Feeding the pond are two waterfalls, Odai and Medaki (Male and Female Waterfalls).

Getting back from Shugakuin can be a chore, unless you've kept a taxi waiting or arranged for one to come back for you. If none of the above, walk down the hill again to Shirakawa-dori Street, where you'll find, if no cabs, the Shugakuin station of the Keifuku Eizan (Private) Railway Line. A train here will take you to Sanjo Keihan Station, and you can go even farther with changes there. Buses 16, 17, and 18 also run here.

WESTERN KYOTO

Many important sights here have been covered in the earlier sections on Package Tours or 1-, 2-, and 3-day itineraries. Although there are over 1,700 temples and shrines in Kyoto, not to mention museums and other things to see, I'd suggest a side trip out to Arashiyama, in the western suburbs, to see two of them, and perhaps a movie-making center.

The easiest way to get to Arashiyama is to take the Keifuku Arashiyama Railway from Shijo Omiya Station in Kyoto, running every 10 or 15 minutes, and taking 20 minutes.

From the Arashiyama Station, it's a 2-minute walk to the front gate of Tenryuji (Temple of the Heavenly Dragon) ♛ ♛, famous for its garden. Though it was founded in 1309, its present buildings date only from 1900. The garden, designed by Muso Kokushi, is centered on a pond which is in the shape of the Chinese character for "heart." The grounds are especially pretty in cherry-blossom time (late March or early April).

When you finish here, exit the temple and turn left, going up the street to Seiryoji Temple. Do not enter, but turn right, then a quick left, another right, and another left, and you are at Daikakuji Temple ♛ ♛, founded in 876. The present buildings date from the 16th century. Of interest here, besides the nice pond and garden, are paintings by several members of the Kano school and by Korin, ranging from the 15th to 18th century.

Back on the Keifuku Railway, if you would like to see a movie set, in frequent use by filmmakers, get off at Uzumasa, 6 stops from Arashiyama. Toei Eiga-mura (Movie Village) ♛ is just north of the station a few minutes' walk, behind Koryuji Temple, itself of great interest. At the village, you might see a film being made. Even if you don't, it's amusing to see this large open-air set, all false fronts and squeaky-clean, and there are also a museum of sorts and some indoor studios. The Daiei and Shochiku film companies have their Movie Villages to the west and south of this station, respectively.

Koryuji Temple ♛ ♛ is most famous for possessing the first work of art in Japan to be designated a National Treasure, the Miroku Bosatsu. This is located in the Reihokan (Treasure Museum), behind the Lecture Hall and the Taishido Hall. Prince Shotoku (d. 621) is said to have carved this statue, plus one of himself in the Taishido. The prince, who is credited with bringing (*imposing* is more exact, perhaps) much of Chinese culture to Japan, also carved a likeness of himself at an earlier age, and this can be found in the Hakkakudo, the building itself being a National Treasure. In the Lecture Hall are three more National Treasures, an image of Buddha and large wooden statues of two aspects of Kwannon, the goddess of mercy.

SOUTHERN KYOTO

Take the train back to Shijo Omiya Station, and, perhaps on another day, look at two destinations in southern Kyoto. Most fun, if it happens to be the 21st of the month, is Toji Temple (Eastern Temple) ♛, just southwest of Kyoto Station (on the back, or new, side). The highest pagoda in Japan (about 180 feet) is here, and though the temple dates back to 796, the pagoda itself is from 1644, and was rebuilt then by the third Tokugawa shogun, Iemitsu. The Rengemon Gate, like the pagoda, is a National Treasure, but dates back to 1191. The Main Hall and the Founder's Hall are also National Treasures, as are many of the works of art in the Azekura (Storehouse), mostly Buddhist paintings. (Bus 207 stops in front of Toji, at the Toji Tomon stop.)

The second target, although perhaps more in the line of shopping, is the Avanti Center, on this side of Kyoto Station, just a few minutes' walk east of Toji. A quick walk through the many floors of this under- and overground maze will bring you back to modern Japan with a vengeance. Make use of its underground passage (near the Hotel Keihan Kyoto) to get you back to the "right" side of Kyoto Station, from which there are three forms of public transport back to your hotel (subway, bus, or taxi).

MOSS TEMPLE AND NIJO JINYA

In addition to the three Imperial Household properties which require advance permission to enter, previously described, the Moss Temple 👑 👑 likes to make entrance a chore. You have to write to get permission, using a prepaid return postcard. This you can do only from within Japan, and you might have time to do it. Kokedera Temple, also known as the Moss Temple, is worth the effort if you like moss, serenity, the sound of a bamboo deer warning (water-propelled), and good things like that. Reconstructed in 1339 by the priest Muso Kokushi, the garden has 40 different kinds of moss, and its sometimes slippery stone path will lead you around past them all. When I last inquired about getting in, I was told I'd have to sit through a long lecture (in Japanese), "donate" about ¥3,000 ($18.18), and show up promptly at the time specified. If you're a real moss fan, it may be worth it, but I haven't been there since the monks adopted this persnickety policy. Take taxi; there is no bus.

Much easier to visit now is the Nijo Jinya (Nijo Encampment House) 👑, just south of Nijojo Castle. A fortified house, it is a wonderfully intricate maze of disappearing ladders, escape holes and spy holes, dead-end corridors, and the like. The art of the *ninja* is supposed to be associated with this form of defense, for the usually aggressive *ninja*, when not out crawling up walls or flying on ropes into other people's gardens, had to defend himself while at home, too. Look for the stairway leading nowhere, the bodyguard's chamber in the ceiling, and secret cupboards. Still privately owned, the Jinya is open only by appointment, daily at 10 and 11 A.M. and 2 and 3 P.M. Phone 841-0972, in Japanese. Your hotel or the JTB or the Tourist Information Center can do this for you, if necessary. Small admission. (Nearest bus: 9, stopping at Horikawa Oike.)

INSIDERS' INFORMATION FOR KYOTO

HOTELS

ANA Kyoto ♛ ♛ ♛ ♛ ♛
Nijojo-mae, Horikawa-dori, Nakagyo-ku, Kyoto 604, tel. 075-231-1155
Two persons in twin, $140
Opened only in June 1986, this should prove to be the city's best. ANA is All Nippon Airways, Japan's biggest. Shopping arcade, 4 restaurants, 302 fair-sized rooms, indoor pool, sauna, beer garden on roof, etc. Opposite Nijo Castle.

Hiiragiya Ryokan ♛ ♛ ♛ ♛ ♛
Fuyacho Aneyakoji-agaru, Nakagyo-ku, Kyoto 604, tel. 075-221-1136
Two persons in room, $485, breakfast and dinner included
If you can afford it, the experience of a lifetime (I've said that once more, in the restaurant listings). Traditional Japanese elegance in most *shibui* (restrained) manner, with exquisite service, delicious and refined *kaiseki* cuisine. Like living with the Imperial Family, almost. Lovely garden, 31 quiet, large rooms, 28 with private bath.

Kyoto ♛ ♛ ♛ ♛ ♛
Kawaramachi Oike, Nakagyo-ku, Kyoto 604, tel. 075-211-5111
Two persons in twin, $120
Given this high rating mostly because of its location, best for visitors intent on covering all of Kyoto from central spot. New building with smaller rooms hides old building with larger, but frayed, rooms. Total of 507. Several restaurants, shops. English-language TV.

Miyako ♛ ♛ ♛ ♛ ♛
Sanjodori Keage, Higashiyama-ku, Kyoto 605, tel. 075-771-7111
Two persons in twin, $180
The old queen of Kyoto hotels, where crowned and uncrowned heads of state have stayed, a rambling assembly of buildings (600 rooms) on the slopes of a mountain on eastern edge of town. Pool, sauna, several restaurants, but being No. 1 has made it less interested in staying sharp.

Tawaraya Ryokan ♛ ♛ ♛ ♛ ♛
Fuyacho Aneyakoji-agaru, Nakagyo-ku, Kyoto 604, tel. 075-211-5566

Two persons in room, $400, breakfast and dinner included
Here, too, have stayed crowned heads, who have left testimonials to the outstanding service and food. A little smaller than its sister *ryokan*, Hiiragiya (see above), just across the street, with only 19 rooms, 15 with private bath. Cozy, ultrarefined, quiet.

Century ♛ ♛ ♛ ♛
Higashino Toin-dori, Shimogyo-ku, Kyoto 600, tel. 075-351-0111
Two persons in twin, $95
That imposing address disguises fact that hotel is next door to Kyoto Station (the front side), but it is very quiet. 350 average-sized rooms, nice atrium lobby, several restaurants, great location for train travelers. Also indoor and outdoor pools. English-language TV.

Grand ♛ ♛ ♛ ♛
Higashi Horikawa Shiokoji, Shimogyo-ku, Kyoto 600, tel. 075-341-2311
Two persons in twin, $100
Just west of Kyoto Station, but on highway, requiring use of pedestrian bridges or going everywhere by taxi. Well equipped with 574 slightly larger than average rooms, indoor pool, sauna, several restaurants. English-language TV.

International ♛ ♛ ♛ ♛
284 Nijo Aburanokoji, Nakagyo-ku, Kyoto 604, tel. 075-222-1111
Two persons in twin, $95
Just opposite Nijo Castle, next to ANA, this is owned by Fujita Kanko, a big tourist bus operator. Lobby is a maze of shops. Nice garden, several good restaurants, 332 rooms that are bigger than average but not by much. English-language TV.

Sumiya Ryokan ♛ ♛ ♛ ♛
Fuyacho-dori Sanjo-sagaru, Nakagyo-ku, Kyoto 604, tel. 075-221-2188
Two persons in room, $450, breakfast and dinner included
Elegant and lovely, with gorgeous garden, this inn has 26 rooms, half with private bath. Known for outstanding cuisine.

Holiday Inn ♛ ♛ ♛
36 Nishi Hirakicho, Takano, Sakyo-ku, Kyoto 606, tel. 075-721-3131

Two persons in twin, $85

A little out of the way, but as a holiday center, everything is here—indoor and outdoor pools, bowling, tennis, mini-golf, skating, sauna. Three restaurants, including excellent Chinese. 200 rooms. Good for hiking around temples of eastern edge of city.

Keihan 🏨 🏨 🏨

31 Nishi Sanno-cho, Higashi-kujo, Minami-ku, Kyoto 601, tel. 075-661-0321

Two persons in twin, $90

New hotel on back side of Kyoto Station, 308 smallish rooms but elegant lobby and restaurants. Attached to splendid shopping complex, which stretches under the station. Convenient for rail travelers.

New Hankyu 🏨 🏨 🏨

Shiokoji Shinmachi, Shimogyo-ku, Kyoto 600, tel. 075-343-5300

Two persons in twin, $95

Just in front of Kyoto Station's main exit, with 319 fair-sized rooms, several restaurants, including excellent Japanese, Chinese ones. Outstanding service.

New Kyoto 🏨 🏨 🏨

Horikawa Maruta-machi, Kamigyo-ku, Kyoto 602, tel. 075-801-2111

Two persons in twin, $70

Owned by renowned Kyoto Hotel, in west-side location halfway between station and business center, walkable to several famous temples. Nice garden, 320 good-sized rooms, 3 fine restaurants, especially Japanese and Chinese.

New Miyako 🏨 🏨 🏨

Nishi Kujo-incho, Minami-ku, Kyoto 601, tel. 075-661-7111

Two persons in twin, $85

Branch of venerable Miyako, uptown, this is on back side of Kyoto Station, good for rail travelers, 714 small rooms, 3 restaurants. English-language TV.

Royal 🏨 🏨 🏨

Kawaramachi Sanjo, Nakagyo-ku, Kyoto 604, tel. 075-223-1234

Two persons in twin, $90

Excellent location on main shopping street, equal access to all corners of town. Several restaurants, including splendid Azay le Rideau, one of Japan's best French eating places, 395 average-sized rooms. English-language TV.

Tokyu ♛ ♛ ♛

600-1 Kakimoto-cho, Gojo-sagaru, Inokuma-dori, Shimogyo-ku, Kyoto 600, tel. 075-341-2411

Two persons in twin, $110

One of famous Toky*u* chain (don't confuse with Toky*o*; Tokyu = Eastern Express, Tokyo = Eastern Capital), with nice garden, 3 excellent restaurants, 443 average-sized rooms, super service, shopping arcade, outdoor pool. English-language TV.

Yachiyo Ryokan ♛ ♛ ♛

34 Nanzenji Fukuchi-cho, Sakyo-ku, Kyoto 601, tel. 075-771-4148

Two persons in room, $350, breakfast and dinner included

Comfortable and yet elegant, with lovely garden in neighborhood of famous Nanzenji Temple, close to Miyako Hotel and eastern edge of town, 25 rooms, 20 with private bath. Very quiet, and as at all other *ryokan*, doors close fairly early at night.

Chikiriya Ryokan ♛ ♛

Takoyakushi-dori, Tominokoji Nishi-iru, Nakgyo-ku, Kyoto 604, tel. 075-221-1281

Two persons in room, $220, breakfast and dinner included

A very typical inn, with small garden, refined ambience and food, 48 rooms, 33 with private bath.

Gimmond ♛ ♛

Takakura Oike-dori, Nakagyo-ku, Kyoto 604, tel. 075-331-4111

Two persons in twin, $80

Centrally located, 142 small rooms, with cozy little Japanese restaurant in basement.

Kaneiwaro Bekkan Ryokan ♛ ♛

Kiyamachi-dori, Matsubara-sagaru, Shimogyo-ku, Kyoto 600, tel. 075-351-5010

Two persons in room, $300, breakfast and dinner included

Secluded garden, very quiet, 23 traditional rooms, all with private bath.

Park ♛ ♛

644-2 Sanjusangendo Mawari-machi, Higashiyama-ku, Kyoto 605, tel. 075-525-3111

Two persons in twin, $115

On east side of town, near fringe of temples there, with

270 smallish rooms, 4 restaurants, lovely garden (once belonging to Emperor Go-Shirakawa, 12th century). English-language TV.

Seikoro Ryokan♛♛

Toiyamachi-dori, Gojo-sagaru, Higashiyama-ku, Kyoto 605, tel. 075-561-0771

Two persons in room, $335, breakfast and dinner included
Nestled aside the eastern hills, smack in middle of famous temple territory, with beautiful garden, subdued and elegant decor, 23 rooms, all with private bath.

Shokaro Ryokan♛♛

Shijo-sagaru, Kiyamachi, Shimogyo-ku, Kyoto 600, tel. 075-361-9271

Two persons in room, $160, breakfast and dinner included
Small inn, near entertainment district, but quiet, refined. Each of 24 rooms has private bath.

Tsuruki Ryokan♛♛

Kiyamachi Gojo-agaru, Shimogyo-ku, Kyoto 600, tel. 075-361-9261

Two persons in room, $95, breakfast and dinner included
Quiet inn near nightlife district, 16 rooms, all with private bath.

Hinomoto Ryokan♛

375 Kotake-cho, Matsubara-agaru, Kawaramachi-dori, Shimogyo-ku, Kyoto 600, tel. 075-351-4563

Two persons in room, $40, no meals provided
Just south of city center, in amusement and nightlife quarter. Spartan inn setting, more like living with Japanese family than staying in *ryokan*.

Matsubaya Ryokan♛

Nishi-iru, Higashi-touin, Kamijuzuyamachi-dori, Shimogyo-ku, Kyoto 600, tel. 075-351-4268

Two persons in room, $40, no meals included
Near Kyoto station, Higashi Honganji Temple. No ambience, just a room.

Rich♛

Kawaramachi-dori, Gojo-agaru, Shimogyo-ku, Kyoto 600, tel. 075-341-1131

Two persons in twin, $70
Modern branch of good-bargain chain, on busy street between station and main shopping center of town, 109 small rooms, 2 restaurants.

Sunflower ♛
51 Higashi Tenno-cho, Okazaki, Sakyo-ku, Kyoto 6060, tel. 075-761-9111
Two persons in twin, $75
On east side, north of Heian Shrine, good for visiting string of temples here, 77 rooms, a few Japanese-style, 3 restaurants, big wedding business.

RESTAURANTS

Hyotei ♛ ♛ ♛ ♛ ♛
35 Kusakawa-cho, Nanzenji, Sakyo-ku, tel. 075-771-4116
Average dinner, $170
The experience of a lifetime, and your party (minimum of two) will need your hotel's introduction just to get in. Sit in your own private and ancient teahouse in garden setting, and watch a dozen or so courses arrive, each more exquisite and delicious than the last. Perhaps Japan's best restaurant, *kaiseki* cuisine of highest order.

Ikkyu ♛ ♛ ♛ ♛
Monzen-cho, Murasakino, Daitokuji, Kita-ku, tel. 075-493-0019
Average dinner, $40
Shojin ryori, vegetarian food, in purest Kyoto style. Nearly 500 years of serving the same kind of food, delicately presented in traditional surroundings.

Junidanya ♛ ♛ ♛ ♛
Gion Hanamikoji, Higashiyama-ku, tel. 075-561-0213
Average dinner, $60
Shabu shabu or *mizutake,* the casserole dishes of chicken, fish, or beef mixed with vegetables and wonderful sauces, are highlights here. Marvelous artsy-crafty ambience, with folkcraft and modern woodblock prints all around. Also *sukiyaki* and steak.

Junsei ♛ ♛ ♛ ♛
60 Kusakawa-cho, Nanzenji, Sakyo-ku, tel. 075-761-2311
Average dinner, $40
Marvelous old restaurant in pretty garden, serving delicious all-*tofu* meals if you wish, or *sukiyaki, shabu shabu* should you prefer. Nice couple, Mr. and Mrs. Watabe, will look after you. Lunches are cheaper by far.

Minokichi ❦ ❦ ❦ ❦
65 Torii-cho, Awataguchi, Sakyo-ku, tel. 075-771-4185
Average dinner, $45
Traditional Kyoto cooking, *ryotei*-style, in big restaurant where you're in sight of other guests. Not as formal as *kaiseki* places mentioned previously, but up to 16 little dishes of food. Also has *shabu shabu, sukiyaki,* and other more popular dishes. Branches throughout the country.

Minoko ❦ ❦ ❦ ❦
480 Gion, Kioi-cho, Higashiyama-ku, tel. 075-561-1329.
Average dinner, $50
Kyoto cuisine at its best, with *kaiseki* cuisine and, at other extreme, *ochabako bento,* a beautiful lacquered lunchbox of food.

Takasebune ❦ ❦ ❦ ❦
Sendo-cho, Shijo-sagaru, Nishi Kiyamachidori, Shimogyo-ku, tel. 075-361-0694
Average dinner, $30
Excellent *tempura,* traditional surroundings, outstanding service.

Azay le Rideau ❦ ❦ ❦
In Royal Hotel basement, tel. 075-223-0009
Average dinner, $60
One of Japan's best French restaurants, named for Loire chateau. Cozy ambience, stellar presentations. Try salads with fish, nougat ice cream with *framboise,* for example.

Gion Honke Jubei ❦ ❦ ❦
Shinbashi-agaru, Nawatedori, Higashiyama-ku, tel. 075-561-2698
Average dinner, $35
Sushi is not what Kyoto is known for, but it is excellent here.

Iroha ❦ ❦ ❦
Pontocho-agaru, Shijodori, Nakagyo-ku, tel. 075-221-3334
Average dinner, $25
Sukiyaki and *shabu shabu,* both better in winter months because of heat they engender, are favorites here. Also *teppanyaki* and *mizutaki.*

Okutan ❦ ❦ ❦
Kitamon, Nanzenji Temple, tel. 075-771-8709
Average lunch, $15
Lunch only, tofu in many different ways, right at temple gate. Thatched roof, Buddhist-inspired humility in presen-

tation, ambience, and amount of food, but delicious beyond belief. Sit inside or out, meditate a little.

Tensei ♛ ♛ ♛

Shijo-agaru, Shinkyogoku-dori, Nakagyo-ku, tel. 075-221-2421

Average dinner, $33

Tempura, in an inspired setting, traditionally Japanese. Start with shrimp.

Adachi ♛ ♛

347 Gion Hanamikoji-dori, Higashiyama-ku, tel. 075-561-0097

Average dinner, $40

Steak, in mixture of Japanese and Western ambience. "Kobe beef," a misnomer, used.

Kaneyo ♛ ♛

Rokkaku Higashi iru, Shinkyogoku, Nakagyo-ku, tel. 075-221-0669

Average dinner, $20

Kabayaki (grilled eel) is specialty here, and other eel dishes. Some fish specialties, too.

Les Champs D'ors ♛ ♛

Shijo-agaru, Higashi-iru, Shinkyogoku, Nakagyo-ku, tel. 075-255-2277

Average dinner, $40

French cuisine, scarcely Japanized. Famous for its lobster and salads.

Lyon ♛ ♛

Kyoto Asahi Kaikan Building, 9th floor, tel. 075-223-2303

Average dinner, $55

Another excellent French restaurant, with laid-back ambience. Try cassis sherbet at end.

Matsuzushi ♛ ♛

Sanjo-sagaru, Kiyamachi, Nakagyo-ku, tel. 075-221-2946

Average dinner, $25

Excellent *sushi* in center of restaurant and nightlife district.

Oiwa ♛ ♛

Nijo-sagaru, Kiyamachi-dori, Nakagyo-ku, tel. 075-231-7667

Average dinner, $25

Kushikatsu, lots of tiny little tidbits on skewers. Quail eggs, chicken, ginkgo nuts, vegetables, delicate and somehow filling.

Owariya ♛ ♛

Nijo-sagaru, Kurumayacho-dori, Nakagyo-ku, tel. 075-231-3446

Average dinner, $10

Noodles are the game here, and slurping them is the national sport. Ask for *soba* (buckwheat variety) or *udon* (flat, white, more slippery).

Paul ♛ ♛

Shijo-agaru, Hanamikoji-dori, Higashiyama-ku, tel. 075-561-2556

Average dinner, $35

Steak again, by Chef Paul, in cozy surroundings.

Rourantei ♛ ♛

Futasujime Higashi-iru, Shijo-agaru, Kawaramachi-dori, Nakagyo-ku, tel. 075-221-7756

Average dinner, $35

Teppanyaki, the bits of steak, shrimp, etc., fried on a stone or iron plate before your very eyes.

Yamamoto ♛ ♛

Nijo-agaru, Shin Karasuma-dori, Nakagyo-ku, tel. 075-231-4495

Average dinner, $13

Tonkatsu, the classic fast food of the Japanese, fried and breaded pork cutlets on a bowl of rice. Mustard and thick, sweet soy sauce on the side.

Yasaka ♛ ♛

Nishi-iru, Yasaka-dori, Higashi-oji, Higashiyama-ku, tel. 075-551-1121

Average dinner, $35

Sukiyaki and *shabu shabu* are the ticket here, in famous old establishment.

Agatha ♛

Sanjo-agaru, Kiyamachi, Nakagyo-ku, tel. 075-223-2379

Average dinner, $9

Yakitori, mostly chicken bits grilled on a stick, washed down with beer.

Gion Umenoi ♛

Shijo-agaru, Yamato-uji, Higashiyama-ku, tel. 075-561-1004

Average dinner, $20

Kabayaki (grilled eel) and other dishes made deliciously nonslippery.

Gonbei ₩

Shijo-agaru, Kiri-dori, Higashiyama-ku, tel. 075-561-3350

Average dinner, $12

Set meal dinners, on a tray, about 6 items. Also *soba* and *udon*, the traditional noodle dishes, even cheaper.

Izumoya ₩

Shijo Ohashi Nishizume, Ponto-cho, Nakagyo-ku, tel. 075-211-2501

Average dinner, $18

More grilled eel, a special dish for summertime, say the Japanese, and full of energy. Try it on a bed of rice in lacquered box.

Kawamichiya ₩

Sanjo-agaru, Fuyamachi-dori, Nakagyo-ku, tel. 075-221-2525

Average dinner, $10

Noodles, from *somen* (thin) to *udon* (flat), cold or hot, even "Chinese-style."

La Nouvelle Fontaine ₩

Rokkaku-sagaru, Nakagyo-ku, tel. 075-255-2328

Average dinner, $69

French, with a vengeance. Famous for innovative uses of *foie gras*.

Mishima-Tei ₩

Sanjo Teramachi, Nakagyo-ku, tel. 075-221-0003

Average dinner, $30

Wonderful *sukiyaki* in a beautiful restaurant, made over from old butcher shop. Also a beautifully designed branch in basement of Kyoto Tokyu Hotel, tel. 075-341-2411.

Oedo ₩

Takakura Nishi-iru, Shijo-dori, Shimogyo-ku, tel. 075-221-2846

Average dinner, $10

Tonkatsu (fried port cutlet) served in several ways. No need for reservation.

Sugiharu ₩

Sanjo-sagaru, Yamato-oji-dori, Higashiyama-ku, tel. 075-541-0333

Average dinner, $11

Yakitori (grilled chicken bits) in cozy ambience, barlike surroundings.

Tagoto ♨
Shijo-agaru, Shinkyogoku, Nakagyo-ku, tel. 075-221-3024
Average dinner, $8
Noodles and more noodles, close to shopping center of Kyoto. Main branch of a popular shop.

Yamatomi ♨
Shijo-agaru, Ponto-cho, Nakagyo-ku, tel. 075-221-3268
Average dinner, $15
Kushikatsu, bits and pieces of elegant things on skewers, and *sake* go well together.

Yoshida ♨
Shijo-sagaru, Gion Hanamikoji-dori, Higashiyama-ku, tel. 075-525-2025
Average dinner, $40
Steak is worshiped here, and has been for a long time. Japanized, and delicious.

BEST SHOPPING

Antiques. All the shops on Shinmonzen-dori Street and Furumonzen-dori Street, plus the flea markets at Toji Temple (21st of each month) and Kitano Jinja Shrine (25th of each month). Look at the two shopping streets for everything first.

Combs. Traditional combs at Jusanya, Shijo-dori Street, 3 lanes west of Kawaramachi-dori.

Dolls. Kyoto dolls, many styles, Tanakaya, Shijo Yanagino Banba, Shimogyo-ku, tel. 075-221-1959.

Fans. Miyawaki Baisen-an, Tominokoji Nishi, Rokkaku-dori, Nakagyo-ku, tel. 075-221-0181.

Fine arts. Since 1895, Yokoyama, main shop at Nawate-dori, Higashiyama-ku, tel. 075-541-1321. Two branches in Kansai, four in Tokyo.

Folkcraft. Yamato Mingei-ten, Takoyakushi-agaru, Kawaramachi-dori, Nakagyo-ku, tel. 075-221-2641.

Incense. Shoyeido, Nijo-agaru, Karasuma-dori, Nakagyo-ku, tel. 075-231-2307.

Kimono. Kinko-do, 1-264 Kiyomizu, Higashiyama-ku, tel. 075-561-5427.

Lacquerware. Zohiko, Okazaki Koen Park, Sakyo-ku, tel. 075-761-0212.

Paper. Handmade paper and more at Kawabun, south

side of Shijo-dori Street, halfway between Minamiza Theater and Ichiriki Tea House (big black-and-orange mansion on corner).

Pottery. Tachikichi, Shijo Tomikoji-kado, Shimogyo-ku, tel. 075-211-3141.

Silk. Nishimura, Yamato-oji Higashi-iru, Furumonzen-dori, Higashiyama-ku, tel. 075-561-1312.

Umbrellas. Traditional ones at Tsujikura, on east side of Kawaramachi-dori, 1 lane north of Shijo-dori Street.

Woodblock prints. Red Lantern Shop, Shinmonzen-dori Street, Nakano-cho, Higashiyama-ku, tel. 075-561-6314.

Shopping streets. In addition to the ones mentioned above and in the text, try the little street between Kiyomizudera Temple and Kodaiji Temple if you're in that neighborhood. Downtown, or centrally located, the main streets are Kawaramachi-dori, between the Kyoto Hotel and Takashimaya Department Store; Shijo-dori, between Yasaka Jinja Shrine and Karasuma-dori; and the arcades running parallel to Kawaramachi-dori just west of it, between Oike-dori and Shijo-dori. Among all the junk, you can find some good things, especially on Teramachi-dori.

Department stores. The same kind of merchandise as in Tokyo, with small regional differences, mostly in food. I list in order of my preference:

- Takashimaya, Kawaramachi-kado, Shijo-dori, Shimogyo-ku, tel. 075-221-8811, closed Wednesdays
- Daimaru, Takakura Nishi, Shijo-dori, Shimogyo-ku, tel. 075-211-8111, closed Wednesdays
- Hankyu, Kawaramachi-kado, Shijo-dori, Shimogyo-ku, tel. 075-223-2288, closed Thursdays
- Tied for 4th place: Fuji Daimaru, Teramachi Shigosagaru, Shiogyo-ku, tel. 075-221-8181, closed Thursdays; and Kintetsu, Karsuma Shichijo-sagaru, Shimogyo-ku, tel. 075-361-1111, closed Thursdays

Ultramodern arts and crafts can be seen at the Kyoto Craft Center, on Shijo-dori Street between Yasaka Jinja Shrine and Ichiriki (the big private clublike teahouse, painted red and black, on south side). Open from 11 A.M. to 7 P.M. It's very modern, and if adaptations of traditional Japanese works (to the point of absurdity, many times) appeal to you, this is the place. Tel. 075-561-9660.

Kyoto Handicraft Center, behind Heian Jingu Shrine, is

a must, especially if you have only a short time here. See text for complete details.

NIGHTLIFE

Gion Corner, Yasaka Hall, Hanamikoji Shijo-sagaru, tel. 075-561-1119 or 752-0225. Demonstrations of traditional Japanese arts, including the tea ceremony, *koto* music, *ikebana* (flower arrangement), *gagaku*, *kyogen* (comic interludes from the Noh theater), Kyomai (dance by *geisha* apprentices), and *bunraku*, all for ¥2,000 ($12.12). Two shows daily at 7:40 and 8:40 P.M., March through November, except August 16.

Kamogawa Odori at Ponto-cho Kaburenjo Theater, tickets through hotel front desks and travel agents. *Geisha* dance and sing, from about October 15 to November 7 each year. Tickets ¥2,500 ($15.15), and with tea ceremony ¥3,000 ($18.18). Three or four shows daily from about noon to 5 P.M. Similar Miyaoko Odori from March 1 to April 15 at Kaburenjo Theater, but no tea ceremony.

Kanze Kaikan (Noh Theater), tel. 075-771-6114.

Bel Ami Nightclub, Sanjo Ohashi, tel. 075-771-6191. At ease with foreign guests. Cover about ¥2,000 ($12.12), hostess charge ¥2,500 ($15.15), drinks from ¥1,000 ($6.06).

KYOTO TELEPHONE NUMBERS	
Japan Travel Phone	075-361-2911
JNTO Tourist Information Center	075-371-5649

FESTIVALS FOR KYOTO AND NARA

Note: See also National Holidays list, pages 21–22.

January 14	Hadaka Odori (Naked Dance) ♛ at Kyoto's Hokaiji Temple, in which young men in loincloths push each other around to encourage a good harvest.
January 15	Wakakusayama Hill, Nara, set on fire to burn off the dead grass ♛, with religious ceremonies at Nara temples. Best view from Nara Park at 6 P.M.

January 15	*Toshiya* (archery contest) ♛ at Sanjusangen-do Hall, Kyoto.
February 25	Baikasai (Plum Blossom Festival) ♛ at Kyoto's Kitano Jinja Shrine, featuring an outdoor tea ceremony.
March 1–15	Omizutori (Water Drawing Festival) ♛ ♛ at Nara's Todaiji Temple. Services every evening, nights of 12th and 13th the best, with fire-catching first night, water-throwing the next.
March 13	Kasuga Matsuri Festival ♛ ♛, Nara's Kasuga Jinja Shrine. Ancient court music, dances.
April	For 5 days (dates change annually) Old Imperial Palace open to public.
April 1–May 15	Miyako Odori (Cherry Dances) ♛ ♛ at Kyoto's Kaburenjo Theater. English name is mistranslation, adopted because *geisha* use about a zillion cherry blossoms as decoration. If you buy the higher-priced tickets, you can attend a tea ceremony before the performance.
April 13	Jusan Mairi (13-year-old's Pilgrimage) ♛, for children of that age, at Kyoto's Horinji Temple. Best *kimono*, a photo treat.
April 15–May 24	Kamogawa Odori (Kamogawa Dances) ♛ ♛, similar to Miyako Odori. Kaburenjo Theater, Kyoto.
April 21–29	Mibu Kyogen (Mibu mime plays) ♛ ♛ at Kyoto's Mibudera Temple. Noh theater in the open air.
May 15	Aoi Matsuri (Hollyhock Festival) ♛ ♛ ♛ in Kyoto, with parade of costumed retainers and an Imperial Messenger. Goes from Old Imperial Palace to Shimokamo Jinja Shrine, then to Kamikamo Jinja Shrine. Great photography possibilities.
May, 3rd Sunday	Mifune Matsuri (Boat Festival) ♛, Arashiyama, Kyoto.
June 1–2	Outdoor Noh Theater ♛ ♛, Kyoto's Heian Jingu Shrine (Takigi Noh).
July 1–August 31	Cormorant fishing demonstrations ♛ ♛ ♛ in Arashiyama, Kyoto, at night.
July 16–24	Gion Matsuri (Gion Festival) ♛ ♛ ♛ ♛ ♛, Japan's most important festival. Giant floats hauled through Oikedori, Shijodori, Kawaramachidori streets on 17th from 9 A.M., other days associated events. Magnificent, crowded, and usually hot as hell.
October 10–November 6	Kamogawa Odori ♛ ♛ again (see April) in Kyoto.
October 22	Jidai Matsuri (Festival of the Ages) ♛, in

	Kyoto. A new festival, with several thousand people dressed in old costumes, parading.
October 22	Kurama no Hi Matsuri (Fire Festival)♛♛ in Kurama suburbs, evening.
October	For 5 days (changes annually) the public is admitted without formalities to the Old Imperial Palace, from 9 A.M. to 5 P.M. Same holds true for spring, usually April.
November	In late October or early November (dates change annually), the annual Tea Ceremony of Nijojo Castle♛♛ is held there. Reservations from early October, ¥1,800 ($10.91). Price includes souvenir of occasion. Masters of several different schools participate (one recent year had Ura Senke, Omote Senke, and Yabunouchi-ke schools.)
December 17	On Matsuri (On Festival)♛ at Nara's Kasuga Jinja Shrine. Colorful procession of volunteer actors.

PERILS & PITFALLS

In a dispute between the Kyoto city officials and leading Buddhist temples over taxing admission receipts, ten major places of worship closed for over a year, on strike, so to speak. In the spring of 1986, a truce was declared, and visitors are admitted by pass only. The pass is available at major hotels, shops near the temples, and even from taxi drivers, so it is not difficult to get. Just in case the boycott by the bonzes resumes, however, ask your hotel front desk if the temples are open before you set out. Note that two temples always remained open "for prayers," even if off limits during the strike to sightseers.

Ginkakuji (Silver Pavilion)
Kinkakuji (Golden Pavilion)
Kiyomizudera (Kiyomizu Temple)
Koryuji Temple
Nisonin Temple
Rengeji Temple
Sennyuji Temple (open for prayers)
Shorenin Temple
Tofukuji Temple (open for prayers)
Zuishinin Temple

NARA

Even older than Kyoto is Nara, the capital of Japan from 710 until 784, a period when many aspects of Chinese culture were being brought to Japan and adapted while being adopted. Most visitors come to this peaceful little city (pop. about 250,000) on a 1-day excursion from Kyoto, and this is valid, provided you confine your sightseeing to the Nara Park area. Among the better 1-day tours is that organized by JTB. Leaving Kyoto at 9 A.M. and returning at 5 P.M., the visit includes the Big Three of Nara (Todaiji Temple, Kasuga Taisha Shrine, and the Deer Park) and also Kofukuji Temple. Cost is ¥9,500 ($57.58), lunch included. A Nara afternoon tour is operated by JTB and by the Gray Line. Both of these visit only the Big Three. JTB charges ¥5,000 ($30.30). Gray Line ¥4,800 ($29.09). Each tour takes about 5 hours. Gray Line tel. 0742-691-0903.

NARA ON YOUR OWN

If you plan to come here from Kyoto, take the JNR Nara Line from Kyoto Station, operating every 30 minutes and taking 1 hour. There is a faster service (33 minutes), the limited express on the private Kintetsu Rail Line, but the difficulty of getting to its station at Toji (behind Kyoto Station) and the lack of English-language signs make this not worth the effort.

From either Nara station, get a cab, say "*Daibutsu den, kudasai,*" and go to the Hall of the Great Buddha ♛ ♛ ♛ ♛ ♛ at Todaiji Temple. Located at the north end of Nara Koen Park, this should bring your mind to attention, if anything will. The largest wooden building in the world, the Daibutsuden houses the world's largest bronze statue, that of Buddha himself, all 53 feet (height) of him. Cast in 749, the statue represents about 6 years of work. Great fires having consumed the building over its history, the head dates from 1692, right hand from 1180. The rest is, with some patches here and there, the original. The right hand is in the position of bestowing peace of mind, the left that of granting wishes. The statue, a National Treasure, was created by a Korean sculptor in the period when Japan was absorbing a great deal of culture from Korea and China.

The Daibutsuden, itself a National Treasure, is only two-thirds the size of the original, built in 752. (The current one dates from 1709, with renovation in 1914, and new roof in 1982.) After viewing the Great Buddha, you might be amused to look at the big pillar with a square hole at the bottom, to the right behind the image. Popular superstition has it that anyone able to slide through the hole will enter paradise. (Only anorexics need apply.)

Go back out, past the splendid bronze lantern (c. 780), another National Treasure, and turn right, where you'll find the Kaidan-in Hall. Look in here for the Four Heavenly Guardians, each about 5 feet tall, made of clay, and each a National Treasure (7th century).

Behind the Kaidan-in is the Shoso-in Treasure House 👑👑, a repository which is open only once a year, for drying out (late October and early November). Occasionally, items from the Shoso-in are on display at the Nara National Museum. Continue on around the Daibutsuden from this log cabin (756) to the east of the great hall, where you'll see two important buildings, Nigatsudo 👑 and Sangatsudo 👑 (Second and Third Month Temples). They are so named because of religious ceremonies held during those time periods. Sangatsudo is a National Treasure, and the oldest building in the Todaiji complex, dating from 733. Nigatsudo, though founded in 752, burned once, and the present building dates from 1667.

Between the Chumon (Middle Gate) and Nandaimon (Great Southern Gate) of Todaiji, you'll encounter plenty of souvenir and food stalls, and perhaps meet your first deer. Though tame, they can be rambunctious in the rutting season. Feed them if you like (special deer food available at the stalls).

Half a mile south and east of Todaiji is Kasuga Taisha Shrine 👑👑👑, the family shrine of the famous Fujiwara clan. Like Ise Jinja Shrine near Nagoya, this used to

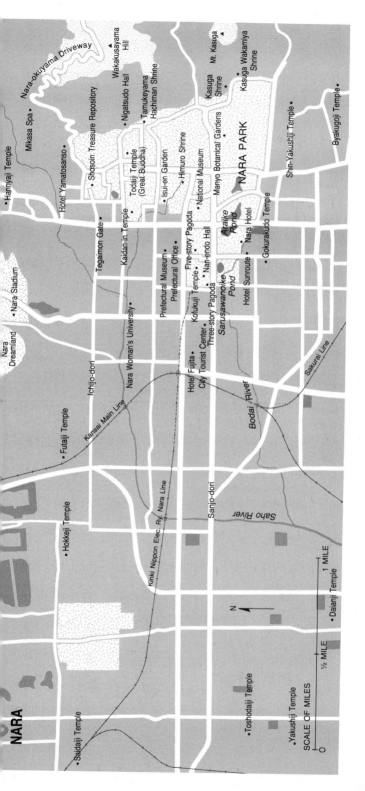

NARA

- Hannyaji Temple
- Mikasa Spa
- Nara-okuyama Driveway
- Wakakusayama Hill
- Mt. Kasuga
- Nigatsudo Hall
- Tamukeyama Hachiman Shrine
- Kasuga Wakamiya Shrine
- Shosoin Treasure Repository
- Kasuga Shrine
- Hotel Yamatosanso
- Todaiji Temple (Great Buddha)
- Isui-en Garden
- Himuro Shrine
- Tegaimon Gate
- Kaidan-in Temple
- National Museum
- Manyo Botanical Gardens
- NARA PARK
- Byakugoji Temple
- Shin-Yakushiji Temple
- Prefectural Museum
- Prefectural Office
- Five-story Pagoda
- Kofukuji Temple
- Nan-endo Hall
- Three-story Pagoda
- Araike Pond
- Nara Hotel
- Gokurakudo Temple
- Nara Woman's University
- Hotel Fujita
- City Tourist Center
- Sarusawanoike Pond
- Hotel Sunroute
- Nara Stadium
- Nara Dreamland
- Ichijo-dori
- Kansai Main Line
- Bodai River
- Sakurai Line
- Futaiji Temple
- Kinki Nippon Elec. Ry. Nara Line
- Sanjo-dori
- Saho River
- Hokkeji Temple
- Toshodaiji Temple
- Yakushiji Temple
- Daianji Temple
- Saidaiji Temple

N

SCALE OF MILES

0   ½ MILE   1 MILE

be reconstructed every 20 years in the interest of absolute purity, the Shinto religion despising, above anything else, uncleanliness. Founded in 768, it is one of Japan's most impressive shrines, situated on the side of a mountain (Wakakusayama) and nestled in groves of towering trees.

Behind the Chumon (Central Gate) of the shrine are four halls, last rebuilt in 1893, for about the 50th time since the temple was founded. If you can manage to be here in early February or mid-August when the 3,000 lanterns of Kasuga Shrine are lit, you'll experience something unique in today's hurried world. The combination of the red-and-white architecture, the somber lanterns, and the verdant forest make for an unforgettable experience. For a fee, fairly hefty and to be negotiated (in Japanese) with the shrine authorities, you can commission a ceremonial dance by the shrine's vestal virgins. Down in the parking lot of the shrine is the Treasure House, which has several nice items, including Noh masks.

Walk westward now from the shrine through the Deer Park to Kofukuji Temple ♛ ♛ (about 1 mile), where the 3-storied pagoda is considered one of the prettiest in Japan (National Treasure). Inside the concrete Treasure House of the complex are more than 20 statues that are National Treasures (look especially for the Twelve Divine Generals). Another pagoda, of 5 stories, also a National Treasure, is the second-highest in Japan, at about 165 feet. The present structure dates from 1426, fires having destroyed the original (730) and successors. Because the different parts of this temple are scattered over a large area, the dramatic effect of the whole is somewhat lessened.

You'll find several restaurants in this area, one of them the teahouse of Kofukuji itself (see listings). Just to the west is the central business district of Nara.

HORYUJI

Southwest of Nara on the way to Osaka is Horyuji ♛ ♛ ♛ ♛ ♛, which, if you could see nothing else, would make a trip to Japan worthwhile. Possibly the oldest wooden buildings in the world, and definitely the oldest extant temple in Japan, Horyuji dates from 607. The 45 buildings were constructed between that date and 1598, and 17 of them are National Treasures. The complex is divided into two groups, the To-in and Sai-in (East and West Temples), and the latter is the bigger of the two. The temple was founded by Prince Shotoku (Holy Virtue), the regent who brought so much of Chinese culture to Japan.

The entire grouping, though formidably large, impresses because of its subdued colors, mostly that of natural wood and earthen walls, and does not overwhelm the viewer, thanks to a generous use of space between the structures. With gentle landscaping, the entire effect becomes one of understated artistry, at once broad and sweeping, again precise and controlled.

You will enter through the Nandaimon (Great South Gate), rebuilt in 1438, then the Chumon (Central Gate), an original. Of the many buildings to see, concentrate on the exterior of the Gojunoto (Five-Storied Pagoda), a National Treasure and an original, and next to it, the Hondo (Main Hall), another National Treasure. Note inside the Sakya Trinity, a statue cast in 623, and another National Treasure. The three faces of this 3-foot-high statue are wonderfully serene. The wooden statues of the Four Heavenly Guardians and a bronze Yakushi Nyorai are all National Treasures.

Go next to the Daihozoden (Great Treasure House), two concrete buildings to the right, dating only to 1941, but housing a myriad of National Treasures. Look for the Tamamushino Zushi (Golden Beetle Miniature Shrine) and the Tachibanano Zushi (Lady Tachibana's Miniature Shrine) in the South Storehouse. In the North Storehouse, a 7-foot wooden Kudara Kwannon is beautifully done, as are the Yumetagai Kwannon and a Nine-Headed Kwannon. All are National Treasures.

Go now into the East Temple, where the centerpiece is the Yumedono (Hall of Dreams), where Shotoku Taishi used to meditate when he ran into trouble annotating the sutras. The Nyoirin Kwannon, a gold foil-covered wooden statue, is exhibited here only twice a year, mid-April to mid-May and mid-October to mid-November. Other statues, also National Treasures, are here on a permanent basis. Chuguji Temple, just north of the Yumedono, includes several National Treasures, among them the Tenjukoku

Mandala, and another exquisite statue of Nyoirin Kwannon (a.k.a. Miroku Bosatsu), this one attributed to Prince Shotoku.

Return to the West Temple, and if you have time, explore the principal temples of this area that you haven't seen yet. Look for the Kofuzo art repository and the Shoryoin (Sacred Spirit Hall), both National Treasures, between the storehouses and the Hondo. Behind the *pagoda* and Hondo is the Daikodo, a lecture hall. Inside is a splendid Yakushi Trinity statue. Both it and the hall are National Treasures, as are the hall's left and right neighbors: looking at the Daikodo, the Kyozo (Sutra Library) on the left, the Shoro (belfry) on the right.

If you want to know how the chief abbot and head priest live, look at the residences on the south side of the wide path leading from Todaimon Gate toward the exit. Beautifully manicured gardens behind formidably high walls surround small palaces, serenely shuttered from public view. (Bus service between Nara Station and Horyuji: 52 or 63, Horyuji stop.)

Back in Nara proper, if you have time, look at Toshodaiji Temple ♛ ♛, in the southwestern part of town. Dating back to 759, it has suffered few fires, so most of the buildings are original. There are several National Treasures here, the most beautiful of which is a 10-foot-high statue of Buddha, sitting on a pedestal and wearing a halo of 1,000 tiny Buddhas. (Bus to and from Nara Station: 63, stopping in front of Toshodaiji.)

By all means, go to the Nara National Museum ♛ ♛ ♛, housed in a modern and an old building in Nara Park, near Kofukuji Temple. When the ancient objects from Shoso-in are exhibited (annually, late October and early November), this is where you can see them. Regular exhibits include marvelous sculptures in the old building, and some scrumptious paintings in the new.

Festivals in the Nara area are listed on page 234.

Help? There is an English-language telephone service for tourists visiting Nara City. Tel. 0742-27-1313; in Japanese-language, 27-1212.

INSIDERS' INFORMATION FOR NARA

HOTELS

Royal ♛ ♛ ♛
254 Hokkeiji-cho, Nara 630, tel. 0742-34-1131
Two persons in twin, $100
Nara's newest (1985), with waterfall in lobby, natural hot spring pool, gym, saunas, 2 restaurants (Italian and Japanese), shops, 120 fair-sized rooms, some Japanese, some Western.

Fujita ♛ ♛
47-1 Shimo Sanjo-cho, Nara 631, tel. 0742-23-8111
Two persons in twin, $90
Quite new (1983) and centrally located, the Fujita has 120 fair-sized rooms, 3 restaurants, shops, and bars.

Nara ♛
1096 Takabatake-cho, Nara 630, tel. 0742-26-3300
Two persons in twin, $100
The old queen of Nara for visiting foreigners, with modern annex. Nice location on famous pond, 2 restaurants, 132 biggish rooms.

RESTAURANTS

To-no Chaya ♛ ♛ ♛
Tel. 0742-22-4348
Average dinner, $35
The teahouse of the Kofukuji pagoda, just down the street from it, toward the Nara National Museum (east). You can sit on benches in the garden and have an inexpensive *o-bento* (box lunch) for much less, but if you can afford it, I recommend going in, taking off the shoes, and resting while eating a leisurely *kaiseki* lunch of about 5 light courses.

Yanagi Chaya ♛ ♛ ♛
Tel. 0742-22-7560
Average dinner, $35
Farther down the street to the east, and similar in every way to To-no Chaya (above). Both are charming examples of old-fashioned Japan. In either, *chameshi kaiseki* is the *table d'hôte* menu. *Chameshi* is rice boiled in green tea, plus 5 other courses for full *kaiseki* meal.

OSAKA

Japan's commercial capital, Osaka is not on the itinerary of many leisure travelers, but it is visited by thousands of foreign business people every year. I can't in all honesty recommend Osaka as a destination unless you have business here, or unless you want a better class of hotel than Kyoto can provide, and want, perhaps, some nightlife. In that case, use Osaka as a base to explore Kyoto and Nara, as transport between those places and here is a matter of 40 to 60 minutes.

The Big Three touristic highlights of Osaka can be seen in a day, with time left over for shopping and, more important, the good eating the city provides.

GETTING AROUND

There are six subway lines, which you can use without much trouble should you prefer not to pay for taxis. Your hotel may have a map in English. The system works as it does in Tokyo (see page 89). Five of the lines are most important, and four of them run north and south under the main Osaka streets, reading from west to east, the lines bearing the street names as well, Yotsuhashi-suji Street, Mido-suji Street, Sakai-suji Street, and Tanimachi-suji Street. The fifth important line is the Chuo (Central) Line, running east to west, just south of the castle. Probably the two subways most useful to visitors will be the Midosuji (the Fifth Avenue of Osaka), which runs, among other places, straight north and south through the Shin Osaka Station (for Shinkansen trains), Umeda (next to old Osaka Station), Shinsaibashi, and Namba; and the Sennichimae Line, which runs east and west between Sakuragawa and the Kintetsu Department Store complex, among other places. Like the Tokyo subways, they close down about

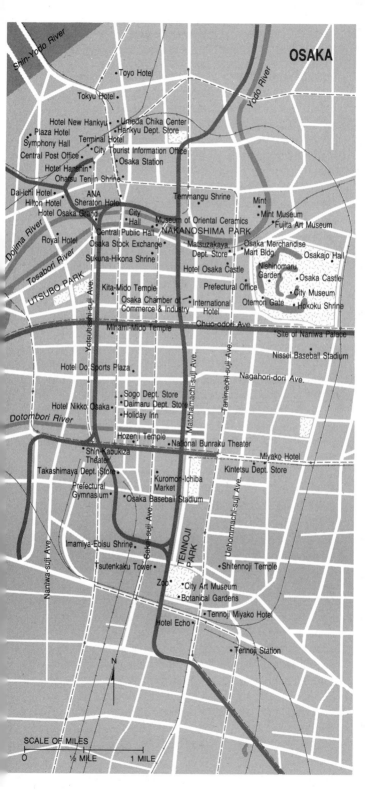

midnight, starting up again about 5 A.M.

Information Service System at the Royal and Nikko hotels has guided sightseeing of Osaka by taxi, at about ¥2,000 ($12.12) per half hour in a medium-sized cab. This applies only inside Osaka, not to Kyoto, etc. Rates do not include admission fee, toll charge, etc. Handling fee also about ¥2,000 ($2.12).

The course, unless you change it, is Fujita Art Museum, Osaka Castle, National Museum of Ethnology, Museum of Oriental Ceramics, Isshinji Temple, Sumiyoshi Taisha Shrine, and Shitennoji Temple.

Tenmangu Shrine 🏮 🏮, also called Tenma Tenjin by the locals, is Osaka's favorite, in many ways, and is the scene of one of the three greatest festivals in Japan, according to historians. (The others are the Gion Festival in Kyoto and the Festival of the Hie Shrine in Tokyo.) Though the buildings you see now were constructed only in 1901, they are a faithful copy of the originals, dating back to 949. The shrine itself is simple and straightforward, as Shinto imagines itself to be. (Nearest subway station: Minami Morimachi, on the Sakai-suji and Tanimachi-suji lines.)

From here, take a taxi or the Tanimachi-suji Line to Osaka Castle 🏮 🏮 (nearest subway stop: Tanimachi Yonchome; *yon* = 4). Though a newer version of an original, this may be the highlight of your touring day. The original castle, constructed in 1585 by the mighty Toyotomi Hideyoshi, lasted only 30 years, being destroyed by Tokugawa Ieyasu (of *Shogun* television fame) in his successful bid to keep the Toyotomi from making a comeback. Rebuilt by the Tokugawa later, it lasted until 1868, when this family burned it down before retreating, in the last days of the shogunate before the modernization of Japan. The present exact reproduction (on the exterior, that is) dates from 1931. There are many interesting exhibits here, and from the top floors you get a good view of the city.

Again, grab a cab or go back to the Tanimachi-suji subway line and go south to Tennoji, a goodly distance, to see Shitennoji Temple 🏮 🏮. Often called the Birthplace of Buddhism in Japan, this temple owes its creation to Prince Shotoku again, and dates from 593. The usual fires having occurred, plus air raids in World War II, some of the buildings are made of concrete and are less than 40 years old. A few, however, date back to 1623, and are conspicuous because they are made of wood. Even the concrete buildings (Main Hall and Lecture Hall, for example) are exact copies of the originals, so you can get a good understanding of Buddhist architecture despite their lack of antiquity. The Treasure House of Shitennoji is worth a visit, with portable shrines, Buddhist sculptures, and nice lacquerware.

There are other good museums in Osaka. The Fujita Bijutsukan (Fujita Art Museum) ♛ ♛ ♛ has nice collections of sculpture, ceramics, paintings, and lacquerware. 10-32 Amijima-cho, Miyakojima-ku, tel. 06-351-0582. Unfortunately it is closed quite often; open Tuesdays through Fridays in April, May, October, and November. It is a bit far away, but most of the other museums are even farther, so I don't include them here. The Toyo Togeikan (Museum of Oriental Ceramics) ♛ ♛ ♛ is a city-sponsored museum housing the Ataka Collection, which was donated by the Sumitomo group of companies. Fourteen of the 1,000 or more items are registered as National Treasures or Important Cultural Properties. 1-1 Nakanoshima, Kita-ku, tel. 06-223-0055. Closed Mondays, small admission. Nearest subway: Yodobashi Station on Mido-suji Line.

Finally, if you're lucky enough to be in Osaka in April, that is the month when the Osaka International Festival ♛ ♛ ♛ takes place. The greatest of the performing artists, worldwide, gather here that month. The 1986 program included the entire Vienna State Opera, Eric Leinsdorf conducting (*The Marriage of Figaro* was just one opera performed); the Vienna Philharmonic, Lorin Maazel conducting; Maurice Bejart directing a new ballet by May-uzumi Toshiro and featuring the Tokyo Ballet; the Prague Symphony; and traditional Festival Noh performances. Past performers have included the Boston and Cleveland orchestras, the Comédie Française, the Milan Opera, the Royal Ballet, the Juilliard String Quartet, Leonard Bernstein, Birgit Nilsson, Pinchas Zukerman, Claudio Arrau, Andrés Segovia, and the Munich Bach Choir, to mention only a few. Tel. 06-227-1063 for tickets, or write ahead from home to Osaka Festival, New Asahi Building, 2-3-18 Nakanoshima, Kita-ku, Osaka 530, Japan.

INSIDERS' INFORMATION FOR OSAKA

HOTELS

Hilton ♛ ♛ ♛ ♛ ♛
1-3 Umeda, Kita-ku, Osaka 530, tel. 06-747-7111
Two persons in twin, $136
Opened in September 1986, this is the city's newest and one of the two best. The location, just a block from Osaka's main rail station at Umeda, is enhanced by the lavish decor, 553 good-sized rooms, and extraordinary amenities. There are 6 restaurants, several lounges, bars, Sky Club.

Royal ♛ ♛ ♛ ♛ ♛
5-3-68 Nakanoshima, Kita-ku, Osaka 530, tel. 06-448-1121
Two persons in twin, $160
Still reigns as Osaka's best (unless Hilton topples it), and deservedly so. Its 1,459 rooms are bigger than average, and the service throughout the hotel is fantastic. Gym, indoor pool, sauna are complemented by big shopping area, and branches of some of Japan's most famous (and exclusive) restaurants. Well sited for vacationing travelers on island in mid-Osaka. English-language TV.

ANA Osaka ♛ ♛ ♛ ♛
1-30 Dojimahama, Kita-ku, Osaka 530, tel. 06-347-1112
Two persons in twin, $135
Quite new (1984), and for a while queen of the ANA chain of hotels, on river facing Nakanoshima (island in center of Osaka), 500 good-sized rooms, nice lobby, sauna and pool, 4 restaurants, shopping arcade, business travelers' service center.

Miyako ♛ ♛ ♛ ♛
6-1-55 Uehonmachi, Tennoji-ku, Osaka 543, tel. 06-773-1111
Two persons in twin, $130
Big, beautiful, and new (1985), but a little away from the center of the north-south axis that governs Osaka life. Big lobby up the escalator, many shops (including nice bookshop), 5 restaurants, baby-sitting service, beauty and barber shops, tea ceremony room, indoor pool, garden. 800 rooms. Attached to Kintetsu rail station (same owners) and near their department store, too.

New Otani 👑 👑 👑 👑
1-4 Shiromi, Higashi-ku, Osaka 540, tel. 06-941-1111
Two persons in twin, $152
Opened late in 1986, a beautifully sculpted building out in
Osaka 21, the new development east of the castle, where
local politicos feel they are recreating the city and develop-
ing a new life-style. (That in some sense means living
where you work, according to the plan.) Has 610 good-
sized rooms, 6 restaurants, nearly all other amenities.

Nikko 👑 👑 👑 👑
7 Nishino-cho, Daihoji-machi, Minami-ku, tel. 06-244-1111
Two persons in twin, $150
Japan Air Lines' flagship hotel, soaring up like a flying
wedge, with designer floor, no-smoking floor, huge lobbies,
fantastic service, 650 not-too-big rooms, English-language
TV, executive floors, 5 restaurants, nightclub, 2 floors of
underground shopping arcade and more restaurants, and
all this right on top of the Shinsaibashi Station of the
Mido-suji subway line. Great location for shoppers, with
Sogo and Daimaru department stores just across street.

Hanshin 👑 👑 👑
2-3-30 Umeda, Kita-ku, Osaka 530, tel. 06-344-1661
Two persons in twin, $100
Brand-new (1985) hotel developed by transit company
near Osaka Station, with dramatic lobby, 3 restaurants,
243 fair-sized rooms, sauna, English-language TV.

Plaza 👑 👑 👑
2-2-49 Oyodo Minami, Oyodo-ku, Osaka 531, tel. 06-453-
1111
Two persons in twin, $150
Once the darling of Osaka, now a little passé, and a
favorite of business travelers and local groupies who seem
to want to meet each other. Has 550 good-sized rooms,
several restaurants, pool, English-language TV.

Grand 👑 👑
2-3-18 Nakanoshima, Kita-ku, Osaka 530, tel. 06-202-
1212
Two persons in twin, $100
After several face-lifts, quietly elegant again, but a teensy
bit old-fashioned. Ideal location, 378 nice-sized rooms, 2
restaurants, English-language TV.

International ♛ ♛
58 Hashizume-cho, Uchihon-machi, Higashi-ku, Osaka
540, tel. 06-941-2661
Two persons in twin, $90
Over near the old exhibition halls, still a good business
travelers' haven. Wandering lobby, 394 smallish rooms, 2
restaurants, a few shops, English-language TV.

Tokyu ♛ ♛
7-20 Chaya-machi, Kita-ku, Osaka 530, tel. 06-373-2411
Two persons in twin, $85
Newish and known for good service, one of national chain
by same name, 340 fair-sized rooms, pool, 3 restaurants,
English-language TV.

Dai-Ichi ♛
1-9-20 Umeda, Kita-ku, Osaka 530, tel. 06-341-4411
Two persons in twin, $90
Good service, 478 rooms (small, as is customary with this
Tokyo-based chain), 3 restaurants, English-language TV.

Toyo ♛
3-16-19 Toyosaki, Oyodo-ku, Osaka 531, tel. 06-372-8181
Two persons in twin, $110
A very Japanese hotel, in northern part of town, with good
service, but average in every way. Quite a few of its 641
rooms are well below the average cost cited above. Has 4
restaurants, shops, bowling, sauna, English-language TV.

RESTAURANTS

Kitcho ♛ ♛ ♛ ♛ ♛
Basement, Royal Hotel, tel. 06-448-3168
Average dinner, $80
The stars are for the food, not the plain decor. Kitcho is
Japan's top private restaurant—the main Kitcho restaurant, that is—and you can't get the door open without an
invitation from an old customer. So here in the Royal Hotel
you can eat the same food at less than half the price, and
enjoy sitting at a table if you wish. About a dozen exquisite
kaiseki courses, the more enjoyable as people at the next
table scupper down the *sukiyaki*.

Tsuruya ♛ ♛ ♛ ♛
Basement, Royal Hotel, tel. 06-448-1121
Average dinner, $75

The same remarks made about Kitcho can apply to Tsuruya, whose main shop is as inaccessible as (almost) its Kyoto branch. Among some delights: prawn, Chinese lemon, devil's tongue, crab, egg, *sashimi*.

Bistrot Vingt Cinq ♛ ♛ ♛

25 Nishino-cho, Taihoji-cho, Minami-ku, tel. 06-245-6223
Average dinner, $50
One of Japan's best French restaurants, with tradition of big-shot clients. Try a *confit* of broccoli and *fois gras*, or *suzuki* (a local white fish) with vermouth and truffles, or for dessert, a lime mousse.

Kagazushi ♛ ♛ ♛

4-5-18 Nihonbashi, Naniwa-ku, tel. 06-632-3813
Average dinner, $45
Sushi in a town where they think they invented it. Superb, a little noisier than Tokyo *sushi* bars.

Kikuya ♛ ♛ ♛

1-9-5 Sonezaki Shinchi, Kita-ku, tel. 06-341-1716
Average dinner, $40
Tempura is the star here, in traditional surroundings, and with polite service.

Le Rendezvous ♛ ♛ ♛

Hotel Plaza, tel. 06-453-1111
Average dinner, $70
Superb French cuisine, French chef (M. Rimbeau). Innovative examples: parsley and snail cream soup, lobster soufflé.

Steak House Hama ♛ ♛ ♛

127 Doyama-cho, Kita-ku, tel. 06-312-7285
Average dinner, $35
Famous steak place, with different grades of meat, including the best, Wadakin beef.

Suehiro ♛ ♛ ♛

Sonezaki Shinchi 1-chome, Kita-ku, tel. 06-341-1638
Average dinner, $40
The birthplace of this chain, which has branches all over the country, featuring good steak at wide range of prices (from lower than $40 to higher).

Grill Moor ♛ ♛

Osaka Terminal Hotel, tel. 06-344-1235
Average dinner, $60
Another good French offering, rather Japanized in taste, but elegantly served. (Where do you think the French got

the idea of serving food so beautifully?) They do cute things with truffles and caviar here.

Ippo ♛ ♛
1-18 Edobori, Nishi-ku, tel. 06-443-9135
Average dinner, $40
Tempura is your choice here, amid spare but clean and light surroundings.

Kahala ♛ ♛
1-9-2 Sonezaki Shinchi, Kita-ku, tel. 06-345-6778
Average dinner, $25
Steak will draw you here, and for good reason, including price.

Mitsuya ♛ ♛
Doyama-cho, Kita-ku, tel. 06-312-9716
Average dinner, $30
Sukiyaki is first choice here, followed closely by *shabu shabu*. Nice decor.

Naemura ♛ ♛
2-11 Sonezaki, Kita-ku, tel. 06-312-3507
Average dinner, $24
Kushikatsu, things on sticks, are featured here. Try them with *sake*.

Rokuban ♛ ♛
39 Souemon-cho, Minami-ku, tel. 06-211-3456
Average dinner, $25
Teppanyaki without too many frills, hence a reasonable price.

Toritomo ♛ ♛
6-11 Doyama, Kita-ku, tel. 06-321-9007
Average dinner, $10
Yakitori (grilled chicken on skewers) is name of the game here. Good with beer.

Yoshino ♛ ♛
4-13 Awajimachi, Higashi-ku, tel. 06-231-7181
Average dinner, $40
Sushi is great here, and so is the atmosphere, very down-to-earth.

Bonchi ♛
1-10-7 Sotonbori, Minami-ku, tel. 06-211-5594
Average dinner, $8
Often considered the home of *tonkatsu*, the breaded, fried pork cutlet served usually on bowl of rice, or with raw cabbage salad. Yummy.

Imai ₩

1-7-22 Dotonbori, Minami-ku, tel. 06-211-0319
Average dinner, $8
Noodles of every kind, and don't bother making reservations in these cheaper places, as they usually don't accept them.

Osaka Joe's ₩

1-1-20 Sonezaki Shinchi, Kita-ku, tel. 06-344-1024
Average dinner, $35
1M Excellence Building, 2nd floor
Stone crab claws flown in from Florida, and folks from home glad to see you.

Ron ₩

1-10-2 Sonezaki Shinchi, Kita-ku, tel. 06-344-6664
Average dinner, $38
Steak is star here, and rightly so. Semi-quaint ambience and decor.

Torika ₩

1-40 Nihonbashi-suji, Minami-ku, tel. 06-211-1313
Average dinner, $12
Grilled chicken and other kinds of poultry will make you happy here.

BEST SHOPPING

The locals here claim they bargain all the time, and suggest you do so. This is definitely *not* the case in the rest of Japan, except for antiques.

Books. Asahiya Shoten, 2-12-6 Sonezaki, Kita-ku, tel. 06-313-1191.

Cameras. Camera Doi, 20 Okawa-cho, Higashi-ku, tel. 06-228-0103. Also six other branches.

Pearls. Okubo, Royal Hotel, 5-3-68 Nakanoshima, Kita-ku, tel. 06-443-3438.

The shops that might appeal to foreign visitors will be concentrated mostly in the Umeda (or Kita) area, just south of Osaka Station. Osaka hasn't much to offer in the way of traditional items, and you didn't come to Japan to buy the same thing Japan exports to us, unless it's cheaper here. With the understanding that you will have kept the prices of things back home firmly in mind, you may want to look for cameras and pearls here. If you're going to be in

Tokyo, it's best to save the audiovisual stuff for that city's Akihabara district.

Here are the Osaka department stores, in order as I rate them in interest to the foreign visitor:

- Daimaru, 1-118 Shinsaibashi-suji, Minami-ku, tel. 06-271-1231. Opposite Hotel Nikko. Branch in Umeda (tel. 06-343-1231) also very good. Main store closed Wednesdays, Umeda branch on Tuesdays.
- Takashimaya, 5-1-5 Nambam Minami-ku, tel. 06-631-1101. Near baseball stadium. Closed Wednesdays.
- Hankyu, 8-7 Kakuda-cho, Kita-ku, tel. 06-361-1381. Just east of Osaka Station. Closed Thursdays.
- Sogo, 1-38 Shinsaibashi-suji, Minami-ku, tel. 06-281-3111. Opposite Hotel Nikko. Closed Thursdays.
- Hanshin, 1-13-13 Umeda, Kita-ku, tel. 06-345-1201. Opposite Osaka Station. Closed Wednesdays.

NIGHTLIFE

- National Theater of Bunraku, tel. 06-212-2531.
- Shin Kabuki-za, tel. 06-631-2121.
- Cabaret Universe, Kawahara-machi, tel. 06-641-8731. Topless show, hostesses with charges from ¥3,000 ($18.18) per hour, cover of ¥2,500 ($15.15), drinks from ¥1,000 ($6.06) up.
- Club Arrow, Doyama-cho, tel. 06-315-8558, one of city's best known among foreigners. Hostesses, dancing, drinks, prices about same as for Cabaret Universe.

FESTIVALS

Note: See also National Holidays listings, pages 21–22.

January 9–11	Toka Ebisu Matsuri ♨ ♨ (*matsuri* = festival) at Inamiya Ebisu Jinja Shrine. Ebisu, the god of wealth, is honored in this allegedly money-mad town by carrying elegantly costumed ladies in palanquins through the streets. (Osakans are said to greet each other with the expression "Making money?" instead of "How are you?")
April 22	Shoryoe mass ♨ ♨, Shitennoji Temple. Court music and dances.

April–May	Osaka International Festival ♛ ♛ ♛. Performing arts. See page 247.
June 14	Otaue Matsuri (Rice Planting Festival) ♛ ♛ at Sumiyoshi Jinja Shrine. Virgins plant rice in temple paddies. Folk songs, dances.
July 9	Natsu Matsuri (Summer Festival) ♛ at Ikutama Jinja Shrine.
July 15	Minato Matsuri (Osaka Port Festival), a rather mundane affair.
July 24–25	Tenjin Matsuri ♛ ♛ ♛, one of Japan's biggest festivals. Evening of 25th best, with boats parading, fireworks.
July 30	Sumiyoshi Matsuri ♛ ♛ at shrine of same name. Young men carry palanquins across river and back, everyone gets drunk.
August 11–12	Takigi Noh dramas ♛ ♛ ♛, performed outdoors by torchlight at Ikutama Jinja Shrine.

WESTERN JAPAN AND SHIKOKU

Marvelous as they are, Kyoto and Tokyo are not a real picture of Japan. Monstrous Tokyo, dynamic and schizoid, gives us part of the scene, and Kyoto, with the face of a Buddha but the heart of a bookkeeper, gives only another. Just as Americans would decry a compounded picture of New York and Williamsburg, so must I urge you to get away from this well-worn tourist track and look elsewhere for another facet of this always intriguing country.

Western Japan is a good bet. The culture of Japan washed back and forth from Kyushu, where purists believe the race was born, to central Japan, where everything was crystallized, refined, and codified, around Kyoto and, currently, Tokyo. (The north of Japan, unhappily, was always a backwater, and some say still is.)

Shikoku, the smallest of the four major islands in the Japanese archipelago, is also a backwater, and glad of it. Still not connected by bridge to Honshu (the main island), though this will happen very soon, it delights in its peaceful existence, yet cries for an umbilical cord and the throngs of tourists who will come with it.

PACKAGE TOURS

These can be fun, and certainly cheaper if you're otherwise going first-class. JTB has a 2-day Sunrise Tour of the Inland Sea, departing Kyoto or Osaka on Sunday, Tuesday, and Thursday from March through November, costing ¥77,500 ($469.70). You visit Hiroshima, Miyajima, Omishima Island, Ikuchijima Island, and Fukuyama, and return to base. See text below for description of the destinations. JTB's 3-day Sunrise Tour is the same, but adds a day in Kurashiki and Okayama (see text). Cost is ¥111,000 ($672.73).

GETTING AROUND ON YOUR OWN

You could fly to Hiroshima, Matsue, Yamaguchi, or the four cities of Shikoku Island (Matsuyama, Takamatsu, Tokushima, Kochi), quickly, too (for example, 90 minutes to Hiroshima from Tokyo). If you're already in the Kansai area (Kyoto, Nara, Osaka), I recommend the train (only 2 hours 10 minutes on the Shinkansen from Kyoto to Hiroshima, for example). The journey by boat from Hiroshima to Matsuyama is also pleasant, and gives you an idea of the Inland Sea, particularly if you don't plan a cruise thereon. You can even take the boat all the way from Tokyo to Kochi, for example, but it's too boring even to contemplate (over 21 hours, all on the high seas).

KOBE

Still in the Kansai area, and closely linked to Osaka, Kobe is a kind of in-between city. Its present glory rooted in the prosperity that came with its status as open port to the Western world, Kobe now finds it must fight hard to keep abreast with Osaka and Yokohama. Kobe has built a huge man-made island, Port Island, which has been wildly successful, and is building another. The once-cramped city, stuck between mountains and coast, has simply decided to fill in the Inland Sea to suit its needs. The cleverly designed island hides its container shipping facilities behind trees, embankments, and hedges so carefully that you'd think you were in a suburb, until you get up high and get a panoramic glimpse.

I can't recommend Kobe as a touristic destination, but if you are here on business, with time to spare, you might wish to see the Shiritsu Hakubutsukan (Kobe City Museum) 👑👑, next door to the Oriental Hotel. There is a fine exhibition of *namban* (southern barbarian) art. All foreigners were called barbarians, and as they came from the south at first, the term *namban-jin* (*jin* = people) meant everyone, European, American, or whatnot. Lovely screens, amusing woodblock prints and drawings of the interaction between the cultures. Closed Mondays. A second good museum is the Hakutsuru Bijutsukan (Art Museum) 👑👑, up at 6-1-1 Yamate, Sumiyoshi, Higashi

Nada-ku, tel. 078-851-6001. Nice bronzes and ceramics, but collection changes frequently, so phone first. Closed Mondays, and June to mid-September, December to mid-March.

If you do nothing else here, though, do take the monorail ride from the JNR Sannomiya Station (2nd floor) to the new Port Island. The train makes a loop around the island and returns, in about 30 minutes. You might be wise to disembark at the Shimin Hiroba or Minami Koen stop and visit the marvelous Portopia Hotel, perhaps to have lunch or a cold drink there. The monorail here is called a Portliner, by the way. Much of the booming Japanese clothing industry is located on this new island.

Among temples and shrines, perhaps the most interesting is Ikuta Jinja Shrine♛, right in the middle of the nightlife district north of Sannomiya Station. This vermilion-painted shrine is said to have been founded in the 3rd century, but these buildings date from after World War II, thanks to the air raids.

OKAYAMA

Two places are next on your itinerary, a city and a town. Okayama, known primarily for its splendid Korakuen Park♛ ♛, is a good place to change trains for Kurashiki, your primary destination of the two. The park is considered by the Japanese to be one of the three most beautiful in the country, but this is an old classification that today bears no relation to reality. It's pretty, but not worth a trip in and of itself. One thing it has uniquely, a miniature working farm, so to speak, in the form of one rice paddy and a tiny tea-growing area. (This is evocative of the Imperial Palace in Tokyo, where the emperor ceremonially plants rice each spring and harvests it each fall, taking a few healthy swipes at the grain with a finely honed sickle.)

If you happen to be in Okayama the second Saturday in February, you shouldn't miss the Hadaka Matsuri (Naked Festival)♛ ♛ ♛ at nearby Saidaiji Temple (built 777). Thousands of young men, clad only in loincloths, jump from the rafters of the temple after two wands thrown by the priests. Bringing the wands to another shrine nearby means good luck for the town and the bearers. Many years ago, *Life* magazine made this scene famous, calling it "a vision of Dante's inferno."

KURASHIKI

Kurashiki is a lovely town, almost a museum town, attracting visitors with its splendid collections of art and handicrafts, its willow-lined streets and canals, its quiet calm. If you're here when there are no school trips, you'll feel some of the serenity of 18th-century Japan. Head first for the Mingeikan (Kurashiki Folk Art Museum) ♛ ♛ ♛ ♛, in a series of restored *kura* (warehouses) which once held grain. Nearly 5,000 objects, not all on display at once, of course. Next, the Ohara Bijutsukan (Ohara Art Museum) ♛ ♛, named for the industrialist who started the whole idea of Kurashiki as an art center when the town seemed to be dying a generation ago. You'll be amazed to find El Greco and Jackson Pollock here, and many chronologically in between. Mostly Western art, which is what Ohara collected. There is an annex, the Shinkan, next door, with more of the same. The Kurashiki Bitisukan (Kurashiki Art Museum) ♛ might appeal to you, with its collection of Middle Eastern and European bronzes and porcelain. Finally, look at the Kokokan (Archaeological Museum) ♛, if you're interested in the details. Don't come here on Monday, when all these are closed.

A new project in Kurashiki is Ivy Square, a renovated textile factory which now contains a hotel, restaurants, coffee shops, boutiques, and the other paraphernalia of tourism. Nicely done, with its own little museum. There are several antique shops in the area, and great photo opportunities everywhere. It's a little like a Japanese Williamsburg, but not yet so pretentious.

If you're here long enough, there are at least two more museums: Nihon Kyodo Gangu Kan (Japan Folkcraft Toy Museum) ♛ and the Kurabo Kinen Kan (Kurabo Memorial Hall), displaying the development of weaving in Japan.

HIROSHIMA

Hiroshima should be your chief destination in western Japan. The city is a natural center for the region, and from here you can take side trips to other important places. Its center completely destroyed on August 6, 1945, Hiroshima was said by the experts to be doomed; nothing would ever grow where the first atom bomb used in warfare was dropped. But within weeks, the grass was back, and the following spring, the flowers. A busy army and manufacturing center, Hiroshima was chosen for the first bombing because it had not been hit by earlier firebombing from the air, and because its geographical contours were considered a good test. The name itself means "broad islands," as the city is on a delta of the Ota River, its five tributaries dividing it into several islands between the mountains and the Inland Sea.

As a visitor, there are two places you can't miss—the atom bomb memorials and Miyajima Shrine. Get the difficult one over with, by visiting the Peace Memorial Park♛ ♛ ♛ ♛ first. Unless your hotel is within walking distance, take a taxi or streetcar (2 or 6, stopping at Genbaku Domu-mae). I recommend entering the area on Heiwa-dori (Peace Boulevard), and if you come by the streetcars mentioned above, you'll be at the opposite, or northern, end of the area. From Heiwa-dori, however, walk first to the Peace Memorial Museum, entrance on the left of the central building. It is unpleasant, but unless you see the damage that was done, you will have missed an educational opportunity not too easy to experience in these post-Chernobyl days. Then go down and walk toward the Memorial Cenotaph for Atom Bomb Victims, designed by Tange Kenzo. Shaped like the roof of tomb-figure houses found in ancient Japanese graves, the cenotaph houses a chest containing the names of those killed by the bomb (200,000 to date). Through the arch you can see the Flame of Peace and the Atomic Bomb Dome behind it.

The Flame of Peace is to burn, according to plan, until atomic weapons disappear from the face of the earth. Just behind it is a small tower containing the statue of a young girl. Representing all the children who died because of the bomb, it is always festooned with thousands of *origami* (folded paper) cranes. The girl whose story inspired the statue believed if she could make 1,000 of these birds, which are lucky in Japanese mythology, she would not die. Of course, she died of leukemia before finishing, but the story of her courage, made into movies, plays, and television productions, has inspired two generations of children by now. Farther to the left and north is a mound under which the remains of many of the victims were buried shortly after the bombing. Finally, you approach the Dome (the English word is used, pron. do-mu). This was the Industry Promotion Hall, and almost directly overhead, the bomb exploded. Its ruins have been left as they are, in the same manner as those of the Kaiser Church in West Berlin, as a reminder of the ravages of war. (The bombardier's target was the T-shaped Aoi Bridge, across the street from the Dome.) The bomb's code name, incidentally, was Little Boy. Its original name was Thin Man, for President Roosevelt, but the name was changed when the shape was. The bigger Nagasaki bomb was always called Fat Man, for Winston Churchill.

Again to the north, a short walk, is the rebuilt Hiroshima Castle♛, center of the Japanese Army headquarters the American B-29 bombardier hoped to obliterate (he was successful). The original dated from 1589, the current one from 1958. The exterior is more interesting than the inside.

Your next objective should be Miyajima Island, but if you have time, a visit to Shukkeien Garden♛♛ might refreshen your soul, perhaps soaking in morbid thoughts by now. A good 15-minute walk across town to the east from Hiroshima Castle, the park is, I think, one of Japan's most beautiful. It dates back to 1620, and between its little islands, ponds, bridges, and tree-lined surrounds, is a perfect example of the classical Japanese garden.

MIYAJIMA

Miyajima Island♛♛♛♛♛, a sacred island on which no births or deaths were allowed until recently, could be one of the highlights of your Japanese trip. Photogenic, attractive, and genuinely historic, it can make for a most memorable trip, especially if you can arrange to stay overnight.

You get there by taxi (expensive) or better yet by one of two railways, the JNR or the Hiroden (Hiroshima Electric). If you have a Japan Rail Pass, it makes sense to use JNR from Hiroshima (or Nishi Hiroshima) Station to Miyajima-guchi (*guchi* = entrance), operating every 15 to 30 minutes, taking about 30 minutes to get there. You could also take the Hiro-den, which runs from Koi Station, near Nishi Hiroshima Station of the JNR. Both lines end up a few hundred feet from the ferry or hydrofoil at Miyajima-guchi. There are constant trips between here and the island. (Rail Pass holders should be sure to take the JNR boat, which would be free.)

On arriving at the island, turn right and walk directly to the shrine. Itsukushima Jinja (Beautiful Island Shrine) is a National Treasure, and you can see why. At high tide, it floats on the sea, its vermilion-and-white buildings reflecting in the water. Surrounded by tree-covered hills, with a gorgeous Go-ju-no-to (Five-Storied Pagoda) towering from atop one of them, the scene says, "Now, this is Japan!" (This is what filmgoers around the world said back in the 1950s, when the first Japanese color movie, *Jigokumon* [*Gates of Hell*], filmed in Miyajima, stunned critics with its gorgeous costumes and scenery.) The large *torii* gate in front of the shrine is the largest in Japan, measuring 53 feet high. During the Tamatori Festival in July, priests in boats throw a colored ball into the water, and young people swim to catch it.

At the shrine, look to see if there is a white horse in the stall just to the left before you enter. It used to be a tradition to have one here. You will have noticed, before reaching the shrine, the presence of a lot of small deer, which are allowed to roam the island. (Dogs, therefore, are forbidden unless on a leash or carried in a container.) However cute, the deer can be pests, as they come up to you and demand food. Denied that, they get into the garbage cans.

Dating back to 811, the shrine is dedicated to the three lovely daughters of Susano-o, god of the moon and of the oceans. If you happen to be here when *bugaku* (court dances) are performed on the raised stage at the front of the shrine, you will feel very privileged indeed. These are among the most colorful, and visible, such performances anywhere in Japan. If you have a Japanese-speaking friend along, you can arrange for a performance yourself, though there is a hefty price connected with this. Also marvelous is the lighting of the many stone lanterns around the shrine, making the area a magic place at night. You can also commission the lighting of these.

While in the shrine, note the unpainted building just west of the Main Hall and stage. This is the oldest Noh stage in Japan, dating back to the Edo Period. At low tide, you'll see visitors digging around on the flats below the shrine. They're looking for clams, not treasure. When you leave the shrine at its western end, you might want to visit the Treasure House ♚ ♚, dead ahead and up a slight hill. A modern building, it contains over 100 items classified as National Treasures or Important Cultural Properties.

Another good time to visit Miyajima is for the Kangen-sai (Orchestral Festival) ♚ ♚ ♚, when barges carrying portable shrines and musicians cross the bay. This is in mid-June, lunar-style, so inquire ahead.

You could roam the entire island, which is quite big, but I doubt you'll have the time. Walk back through the shopping streets, not along the waterfront, and you'll see what the Japanese like to buy when playing tourist. The big spoons (for rice) and maple-leaf-shaped sweets are ubiquitous, but some other souvenirs could compete easily for the Best Worst-Taste Awards. You can return to Hiroshima port directly by hydrofoil if you wish.

HIROSHIMA AS SIDE TRIP CENTER

There are several side trips that can be organized from here: through part of the Inland Sea, to nearby Shikoku Island, to the Ura Nihon ("back side") of Japan, and to Yamaguchi, farther west.

The Inland Sea

Cruises on the Inland Sea ♚ ♚ ♚ can be therapeutic, unless you get on a large ship with a gang of school kids. If you ask for first-class tickets, you can avoid them in any case. The Seto Naikai (Inland Sea) Kisen (Steamship) Company operates half-day cruises from March through November, departing Hiroshima at 9 A.M. (They leave 30 minutes earlier from Miyajima, should you have spent the night there.) You then go east through dozens of verdant islands, stopping at Omishima Island to allow a visit to Oyamazumi Jinja Shrine ♛ ♛. This will interest admirers of Japanese armor, as victorious generals have donated their gear to this place since 1378, when it was built. The shrine, very impressive, is dedicated to the guardian of sailors and others who journey by sea. Eight of the many items on display are National Treasures. The boat waits for you, then takes you on to Setoda, the end of the line. Here there is a temple, Kosanji ♛, which contains replicas of many of the famous buildings of Japan. If you've seen the originals, you can only be amused, but if you haven't, well, why not get some idea here? The complex was built by a local businessman in 1946, in honor of his mother. It is sometimes called Nishi Nikko (West Nikko) because of its gorgeously colored gate, which resembles one in Nikko. The Yumedono of Horyuji and the Honden of Osaka's Shitennoji Temple are duplicated here, all in concrete, of course. Tour costs ¥6,200 ($37.58). Phone shipping line, 082-255-3344 in Hiroshima, 03-574-1311 in Tokyo.

From Setoda, you take a ferry (30 minutes) to Mihara, where you can catch a train back to Hiroshima or anywhere else. Ferry charge: ¥1,230 ($7.45).

Seto Lines also has day-long cruises (9 A.M. to 3 P.M.) from Hiroshima from March through November, on Friday, Saturday, Sunday, and Monday. Room for about 40–50 persons, costs ¥12,000 ($72.73), including lunch and beverage. You can get off at the old Naval Academy on Etajima Island and tour that, while the boat goes on, for an additional small charge. The boat cruises past Miyajima and Enoshima, and for those who stay on board, goes to Ondo-no-Seto, with its weird corkscrew bridge. You might also get a glimpse of the Kure Shipbuilding Works, until recently the largest in the world. For this and other Seto cruises, arrange through your hotel or phone 082-255-3344. For advance reservations, write to Seto Lines, 1-12-23 Ujina Kaigan, Minami-ku, Hiroshima 734.

The same line (Seto Naikai Kisen) has a sunset cruise toward Miyajima and back (no stopping) on the *Galaxy*, taking about 2½ hours and costing only ¥2,500 ($15.15). April through August, Friday, Saturday, and Sundays only. You can have dinner on board at an extra charge.

Shikoku Island

Although you could scoot over to Matsuyama for the day, I think there's no point in going unless you stay overnight, especially at Dogo Onsen (Dogo Hot Springs), a wonderfully old-fashioned spa. From Hiroshima Port at Ujina, a hydrofoil takes only 70 minutes to Matsuyama, the regular ferry 2 hours 40 minutes. You know the advantage of the hydrofoil; those of the ferry are its quieter nature, the ability to walk around on the decks and enjoy the scenery, the bar and food stalls, the slower pace.

In Matsuyama, which you reach from the separate port town, the main point of interest is Matsuyama Jo ♛ ♛, the castle, dating from 1602 and one of the best-preserved such edifices in the country. The Matsudaira feudal lords built this, and you can see in the museum in the dungeon here an impressive collection of armor, swords, and other paraphernalia. But what you really want is a good soaking in the hot springs of Dogo ♛ ♛, a suburb of Matsuyama (see hotel listings). You can get in the tub at your hotel, or go to one of the public baths (Shinrokaku is the biggest) and socialize. If you're here in cherry-blossom time (March) or leaf-turning time (November), you'll be especially blessed. (By no means go to Oku Dogo instead of Dogo. The former, another hot springs, is about 30 minutes out of town and in the middle of a garish amusement park.)

South of Matsuyama is Uwajima, which has a bull festival ♛ ♛ on October 28–29, but which is also known for its "sex shrine." At Dekoboko-dera Temple ♛ here, there is a museum housing about 2,000 exhibits of sex-related items from around the world. Most are folkloric in nature, but you'll have to use your imagination, as English-language explanations are practically nonexistent.

You could take a tour around the entire island, which would take several days. Devout Buddhist pilgrims do, in fact, just that, taking 60 days on foot (13 by bus), visiting all 88 important temples and shrines as an act of piety. The chief highlights, however, are few:

In Takamatsu, you should see Ritsurin Park ♛ ♛, considered the best on the entire island of Shikoku, and in my opinion as nice as Korakuen in Okayama, one of the Big Three of parks. (The other two are Koraku-en in Okayama and Kenroku-en in Kanazawa.) Created on command of the Matsudaira lords, it is loved for its natural pines and marvelously shaped rocks. In the park is a fine museum, the Sanuki Mingeikan (Sanuki Folk Art Museum) 🏯 🏯, with a very good collection. Closed Wednesdays. Another good museum in Takamatsu is the Seto Naikai Rekishi Minzoku Shinyokan (Inland Sea Historical Folklore Hall) 🏯, which, in addition to its interesting collection (including *haniwa* tomb figures), has a gorgeous view of the sea.

If it's August 15–18, get yourself down the coast to Tokushima, when the Awa Odori (Awa Dance) 🏯 🏯 🏯, usually known as the Fools' Festival, is held. You'll see the usually placid Japanese going crazy, dancing all night in organized fashion down the streets before a reviewing stand, then dancing in and out of bars and hotels in little groups, exhausting themselves in a kind of modified conga line. Visiting foreigners are sure to be invited to join, but to get in the spirit of things, you have to don a *yukata* (summer *kimono*) and learn the step (it's easy). Your hotel, should you be overnighting here, will provide you with a *yukata* and you can join the other guests to see if you can win a prize. (I did one year and still have my "Big Fool" award to show. It's not often you win an award for making an idiot of yourself.) Other than this, Tokushima has very little to offer foreign visitors. Even the castle is still in ruins.

Down on Shikoku's southern coast is Kochi, known for handmade paper (from nearby Tosagami), long-tailed (20 feet) roosters (at Oshino), and a 1748 castle (rebuilt in the pattern of the 1603 original). I can't recommend it as a destination, however, unless you have all the time in the world to spare.

Ura Nihon

Two places of interest might lure you to Ura Nihon, the Back of Japan, north of Hiroshima on the Sea of Japan. The most important of the two is Matsue, because of its proximity to Izumo Taisha Shrine, one of the two most sacred Shinto places of worship, the other being Ise Jinja Shrine, near Nagoya.

Izumo Taisha Shrine ♛ ♛ ♛ is Japan's oldest, its origins lost in antiquity, and you'll sense this as you visit. The oldest building extant is the Honden, dating from 1744, but the air of age hangs over the newer structures, dating from 1895. (Fires took away some buildings, others were replaced ritually as a matter of cleanliness.) The shrine is dedicated to the nephew of Amaterasu, the sun goddess, and it is here in October (lunar) that the gods gather, deserting the rest of Japan at that time. Especially if you're not planning to visit Ise, note here the architecture of the shrine, so typical of the very earliest Japanese styles.

Matsue itself is noted among foreigners and Japanese alike for its association with Lafcadio Hearn, one of the earliest Westerners to attempt explanations of things Japanese. Born of a Greek mother and English-Irish father, he lived and worked in New Orleans as a reporter, then made his way to Japan. Here he married, took citizenship, and began the writings for which he is most famous. (To become a naturalized Japanese, then as now, he had to take a Japanese name, so he became Koizumi Yakumo.) The house ♛ in which he lived has remained unchanged since he left town. It is next door to the castle ♛, dating from 1642.

If you can find the time to visit Hagi, you'll feel well rewarded for your effort. Considered one of the least-spoiled towns of Japan, it has nothing of touristic interest, except a large, sour grapefruit called the Watson pomelo. Few souvenir shops, no hordes of travelers, no school kids. Yet it is an attractive town, a fishing port of 50,000 souls, with an old pottery-making tradition. It has been written about extensively lately, so this may be the time to see it, before it does get too popular.

Yamaguchi

The last of the side trips from Hiroshima might be to Yamaguchi, beyond the Kintai Bashi (Iwakuni Bridge of Brocaded Sashes) ♛ ♛ about 50 miles. Yamaguchi was at the height of its power in the 16th century when St. Francis Xavier came here in his effort to Christianize the natives. Allowed to preach by a liberal *daimyo* (feudal lord), he stayed for a short while and met with some success. (Today, however, less than .005 percent of Japanese are Christians.) There is a cathedral named for St. Francis (1950), and Yasaka Jinja Shrine♔, of some interest, but little else to keep you here. On the other hand, if you're worn out, try a night at Yuda Onsen Spa♔ ♔, in the suburbs, where the waters are said to be good for rheumatism and skin disorders.

INSIDERS' INFORMATION FOR WESTERN JAPAN AND SHIKOKU

HOTELS
Hiroshima

ANA Hiroshima♔ ♔ ♔ ♔
7-20 Naka-machi, Naka-ku, Hiroshima 730, tel. 082-241-1111
Two persons in twin, $110
The city's best, right in heart of business district and neighboring Peace Park, site of Atomic Bomb Cenotaph and Museum. Health club (sauna, pool), shops, 4 restaurants, 431 comfortably sized rooms.

Grand♔ ♔ ♔
4-4 Kami Hatchobori, Naka-ku, Hiroshima 730, tel. 082-227-1313
Two persons in twin, $194
Sited halfway between station and city center, with good-sized rooms, several restaurants, 400 rooms.

Iwaso Ryokan♔ ♔ ♔
345 Miyajima-cho, Hiroshima-ken, 739-05, tel. 08294-4-2233
Two persons in room, $230, breakfast and dinner included
On Miyajima Island, an hour outside Hiroshima, and a place you must visit. Has 45 rooms in quiet and elegant style. Where else can you sleep over on a sacred island?

Kamefuku Ryokan♔ ♔
849 Miyajima-cho, Hiroshima-ken 739-05, tel. 08294-4-2111
Two persons in room, $100, breakfast and dinner included
Older inn, 72 rooms, 8 of them Western-style. Very close to shrine.

Kobe

Portopia ♛ ♛ ♛ ♛ ♛
6-10-1 Minatojima Nakamachi, Chuo-ku, Kobe 650, tel. 078-302-1111
Two persons in twin, $115
Ultramodern, yet elegantly designed, center of cunningly arranged man-made industrial island. So much greenery you don't notice the business buildings. Dramatic lobby, 533 largish rooms, several restaurants including Alain Chapel's French cuisinery, gym, English-language TV, indoor pool, sauna, tennis.

Oriental ♛ ♛ ♛
25 Kyomachi, Chuo-ku, Kobe 650, tel. 078-331-8111
Two persons in twin, $91
New building for Kobe's oldest hotel, with several restaurants, 190 average-sized rooms. All that cooking can make basement arcade smoky at times.

Rokkosan ♛ ♛
1034 Minami Rokko, Rokkosan-cho, Nada-ku, Kobe 657-01, tel. 078-891-0301
Two persons in twin, $66
Old hotel up on mountain behind city, with golf course, 75 biggish rooms.

Takayamaso Ryokan ♛ ♛
400-1 Arima-cho, Kita-ku, Kobe 651-14, tel. 078-904-0744
Two persons in room, $125, breakfast and dinner included
In Arima Hot Springs section of Kobe, with own big bath, bar, gameroom, 22 rooms, traditional styling.

New Port ♛
6-3-13 Hamabe-dori, Chuo-ku, Kobe 651, tel. 078-231-4171
Two persons in twin, $80
Cluttered lobby, 216 smallish rooms, some business travelers, some tour groups.

Toa Ryokan ♛
3-12-11 Kitanagasa-dori, Chuo-ku, Kobe 650, tel. 078-331-3590
Two persons in room, $58, breakfast included
Small inn right in heart of town, 12 rooms.

Kochi

Dai Ichi ♛ ♛ ♛
2-2-12 Kita Honmachi, Kochi 780, tel. 0888-83-1441
Two persons in twin, $65
In center of town, 118 smallish rooms.

Joseikan Ryokan ♛ ♛ ♛
2-5-34 Kami-machi, Kochi 780, tel. 0888-75-0111
Two persons in room, $100, breakfast and dinner included
Classically elegant inn, 54 rooms, lovely garden.

Kurashiki

Ishiyama Kadan Ryokan ♛ ♛ ♛
1-25-23 Chuo, Kurashiki, Okayama-ken 710, tel. 0864-22-2222
Two persons in room, $75, breakfast and dinner included
Old-fashioned interiors in its 68 rooms, not far from rail station.

Kokusai ♛ ♛
1-1-44 Chuo, Kurashiki, Okayama-ken 710, tel. 0864-22-5141
Two persons in twin, $75
Traditional, but fraying, establishment whose name means International, 80 rooms. Good location makes for second crown.

Matsue

Ichibata ♛ ♛ ♛
30 Chidori-cho, Matsue, Shimane-ken 690, tel. 0852-22-0188
Two persons in twin, $70
Best known for its own hot springs, a good place to relax and think about Lafcadio Hearn, whose early writings about Japan centered on this area. Has 138 rooms, about one-third of them Japanese-style.

Matsuyama

Funaya Ryokan ♛ ♛ ♛ ♛
1-33 Godo Yuno-machi, Matsuyama, Ehime-ken 790, tel. 0899-47-0278

Two persons in room, $180, breakfast and dinner included
Famous old Dogo Onsen, hot-springs spa, still typically
Japanese in style. Has 43 rooms, half with private bath.
Enjoy the large public bath, too.

ANA Matsuyama ♔ ♔ ♔
3-2-1 Ichibancho, Matsuyama, Ehime-ken 790, tel. 0899-
33-5511
Two persons in twin, $100
Bright, modern hotel in center of town, 4 restaurants,
shopping arcade, 246 average-sized rooms.

Juen Ryokan ♔ ♔ ♔
4-4 Dogo Sagidani-machi, Matsuyama, Ehime-ken 790, tel.
0899-41-0161
Two persons in room, $250, breakfast and dinner included
Modern-style inn at hot-springs resort, 76 rooms, nearly
all with private bath.

Okudogo Ryokan ♔ ♔
267 Sue-machi, Matsuyama, Ehime-ken 790-01, tel. 0899-
77-1111
Two persons in room, $150, breakfast and dinner included
Big and ugly, but lively, with 310 rooms, a third of them
Japanese-style, the balance Western (which is why they
call it a hotel). We suggest you stay *à la Japonais*, and try
the huge public bath.

Okayama

Kokusai ♔ ♔ ♔
4-1-16 Kadota Honmachi, Okayama 703, tel. 0862-73-
7311
Two persons in twin, $110
Best for business travelers, with outdoor pool, 194 fair-
sized rooms, 2 restaurants.

New Okayama ♔ ♔ ♔
1-1-25 Ekimae-cho, Okayama 700, tel. 0862-23-8211
Two persons in twin, $140
Best location for train travelers, in front of station, 82
nice-sized rooms, restaurant.

Grand ♔ ♔
2-10 Funabashi, Okayama 700, tel. 0862-33-7777
Two persons in twin, $60
Older hotel, average in every way including its 31 rooms.

Royal♛ ♛
2-4 Ezu-cho, Okayama 700, tel. 0862-54-1155
Two persons in twin, $65
Modern chain unit with 198 small rooms, but sauna and
bowling to divert your attention, 2 restaurants.

Takamatsu

Kawaroku Ryokan♛ ♛ ♛
1-2 Hyakken-cho, Takamatsu, Kagawa-ken 760, tel. 0878-
21-5666
Two persons in room, $150, breakfast and dinner included
Quiet little place right off main shopping street, 70 rooms,
all with private bath, most rooms Japanese-style. Ugly
exterior, charming interior, except for shops.

Keio Plaza♛ ♛ ♛
11-5 Chuo-ku, Takamatsu, Kagawa-ken 760, tel. 0878-34-
5511
Two persons in twin, $70
Best Western-style hotel in town, between business district and Ritsurin Gardens, 180 fair-sized rooms, 3 restaurants.

Rich♛ ♛
9-1 Furujin-machi, Takamatsu, Kagawa-ken 760, tel.
0878-22-3555
Two persons in twin, $70
Good location in center of town, on main drag, 126 fair-
sized rooms, 3 restaurants.

Washington♛ ♛
1-2-3 Kawara-machi, Takamatsu, Kagawa-ken 760, tel.
0878-22-7111
Two persons in twin, $50
In center of town, about 200 small rooms, 3 restaurants,
young clientele.

Grand♛
1-5-10 Kotobuki-cho, Takamatsu, Kagawa-ken 760, tel.
0878-51-5757
Two persons in twin, $65
Near the pier and station, very convenient for travelers
using boat or train, 136 rooms. Faded glory, but several
nice restaurants downstairs.

Tokushima

Park ♛ ♛
2-32-1 Tokushima-cho, Tokushima 770, tel. 0886-25-3311
In town center, 81 fair-sized rooms, restaurant, shop.

Tottori

New Otani ♛ ♛ ♛
2-153 Ima-machi, Tottori 680, tel. 0857-23-1111
Two persons in twin, $105
Branch of famous Tokyo biggie, with 143 good-sized rooms, 2 restaurants, shop.

Yamaguchi

New Tanaka ♛ ♛
2-6-24 Yuda Onsen, Yamaguchi 753, tel. 0839-23-1313
Two persons in twin, $100
In hot-springs-resort area of town, 198 smallish rooms, restaurant, souvenir shop, garden.

RESTAURANTS
Hiroshima

Kanawa ♛ ♛ ♛
Moored on river at Heiwa (Peace) Bridge, tel. 0822-241-7416
Average dinner, $50
Best oysters in Japan, and a whole meal of them if you wish, served 10 different ways. I'm not ordinarily an oyster fan, but I loved this.

New Suishin ♛ ♛
Tatemachi, tel. 0822-248-2985
Average dinner, $22
French-style, with *table d'hôte* menu or *à la carte*.

Tsukumo ♛ ♛
New Tokyo Building, 4th floor, Hatchobori
Average dinner, $12
Tempura, especially for lunch. Less crowded in evening.

Ten Ichi ♛ ♛
Sogo Department Store, 10th floor, Kamiya-cho, tel. 0822-225-2316
Average dinner, $30
Tempura in branch of famous Tokyo store.

Yagumo Chuo-dori ♛ ♛
Tel. 0822-244-1551
Average dinner, $25
Nabe (stew) dishes (seafood best) in pleasant surroundings.

Heidelberg ♛
Nakamachi, tel. 0822-246-8182
Average dinner, $18
German-style cuisine, rustic ambience.

Kurama ♛
New Yokyo Building, basement, Hatchobori
Average dinner, $15
Shabu shabu (beef stew *à la Japonais*).

Yamarai ♛
Naka-ku, tel. 0822-294-1200
Average dinner, $15
French-style cuisine here and in two branches.

Kobe

Alain Chapel ♛ ♛ ♛ ♛ ♛
Hotel Portopia, tel. 078-302-1111
Average dinner, $75
Outstanding French cuisine by the master chef, who commutes between here and his other restaurant in the homeland. Exquisite service, gorgeous decor, stunning views, one of two best French restaurants in Japan. For starters, how about a lobster salad like one you've never met before?

Jean Moulin ♛ ♛ ♛ ♛
3-1-1 Kitano-cho, Chuo-ku, tel. 078-242-4188
Average dinner, $40
Excellent French cooking, pleasant ambience. Mostly *nouvelle cuisine*, some classic dishes. Fine service. Look into asparagus or lobster soup. You could try "Kobe beef" with a Bordelais sauce, too.

Iroriya 👑 👑 👑
3-33 Kitano-cho, Chuo-ku, tel. 078-231-6777
Average dinner, $22
Country-style cooking in reconstructed old farmhouse.
Yummy dishes, including *kashiwa miso nabe*, chicken and
tofu (soybean curd) in *miso* (sweet bean) sauce.

Bistro Comme Chinois 👑 👑 👑
1-3-7 Motomachi-dori, Chuo-ku, tel. 078-391-3037
Average dinner, $35
If you've ever wondered about French cooking with a
Chinese accent, this is your chance to try it. Dessert, for
example, might be a jasmine-tea *baba au rhum*.

Le Chante Clair 👑 👑 👑
Terminal Hotel, tel. 078-232-1682
Average dinner, $45
Classic French dishes, with some difference, such as steak
with Calvados brandy, and for dessert, Opera Cake.

Akanoren 👑 👑
3 Sannomiya, tel. 078-391-2154
Average dinner, $30
Famous old (75 years) steak house, using "Kobe beef" (see
page 59). Decent wine list, too.

Aragawa 👑 👑
15-18-2 Nakayamate-dori, Chuo-ku, tel. 078-221-8547
Average dinner, $45
Another well-known steak place, beloved of foreign visitors, Japanese alike.

Kitano Club 👑 👑
1-5-7 Kitano-cho, Chuo-ku, tel. 078-231-4343
Average dinner, $50
A combination of nightclub, supper club, and French-style
restaurant, high on the hill overlooking Kobe, splendid
views, especially at night. Go for simple things, like steak.

La Table 👑 👑
3-3-8 Yamamoto-dori, Chuo=ku, tel. 078-241-3170
Average dinner, $40
Basement, Pearl Building. Traditionally French, but some
wild things like *"cassis baba rhum avec sauce anglais."*

Mitsuwa 👑 👑
1-1-3 Nakamachi-dori, Chuo-ku, tel. 078-341-0615
Average dinner, $30
Shabu shabu and *sukiyaki* the specialties.

Rengatei♛ ♛
5-5-5 Shimoyamate-dori, Chuo-ku, tel. 078-331-7168
Average dinner, $43
Wonderful steak, pleasing ambience on old Tor Road, haunt of foreign colony.

Ayakotei♛
3 Nakayamate-dori, Chuo-ku, tel. 078-221-8480
Average dinner, $15
Noodles are the specialty here, and you might ask for *sanuki udon*, yummy. Traditional decor, inside and out.

Benkei♛
24-7 Hanakuma-cho, Chuo-ku, tel. 078-341-3553
Average dinner, $25
Sukiyaki and *shabu shabu* are favorites here. Pleasant surroundings, too.

Koubekkan♛
2-9-2 Shimoyamate-dori, Chuo-ku, tel. 078-321-2955
Average dinner, $30
Teppanyaki, beef and shrimp (as you like) fried before your eyes, along with onions, soybean sprouts, other goodies.

Nakahama♛
12-2-3 Motomachi-dori, Chuo-ku, tel. 078-391-5375
Average dinner, $40
Shabu shabu and *sukiyaki* are what makes Nakahama famous. Traditional decor.

Sannomiya Steak♛
8-3-2 Sannomiya-cho, Chuo-ku, tel. 078-391-0150
Average dinner, $35
Teppanyaki is popular here, but you can also get steak.

Kumamoto

Tagosaku♛ ♛
Tel. 0963-53-4171
Average dinner, $20 up
Traditional rural cuisine, rustic surroundings. Raw horse-meat *"sashimi"* can be had here, too.

Wakaba♛
Tel. 0963-356-6060
Daiichi Ginnan Building, 5th floor
Average dinner, $15
Tempura and other full-course dinners.

Higokko ♛
Tel. 0963-322-6857
Average dinner, $13
Robata yaki, rustic-style food in smoky atmosphere. Fun, if you like it noisy.

Kurashiki

Kyutei ♛ ♛
Tel. 0864-22-5141
Average dinner, $15
Steak house beautifully sited on canal with weeping willows.

El Greco ♛
Tel. 0864-22-0297
Average dinner, $8
Lovely coffee house with limited menu of Western-style dishes.

Kamoi ♛
Tel. 0864-22-0606
Average dinner, $12
Sushi shop with coffee shop attached, opposite Ohara Museum.

Onishi ♛
Tel. 0864-22-8134
Average dinner, $7
Noodles, made on premises, hot in winter, cold in summer suggested.

Tsuta ♛ ♛
Tel. 0864-22-0011
Average dinner, $24
Traditional Japanese cuisine in wonderful Ivy Square, a renovated factory. Eight-course set meal suggested.

Takamatsu

Hamasaku ♛
Tel. 0878-21-6044
Average dinner, $13
Tempura is the thing here.

Tokushima

Saijo ♛
Tel. 0886-95-2775
Average dinner, $9
Local specialty, *udon* (thick white noodles), served in several different ways.

BEST SHOPPING
Kobe

Antiques. Harishin, 3-45 Motomachi-dori, Ikuta-ku, tel. 078-331-2516.

Lacquerware. Naniwaya Shikkiten, 4-74-1 Motomachi-dori, Ikuta-ku, tel. 078-341-6367.

Pearls. Tamakatsu, Sannomiya Chiagai, 1-1-1 Sannomiya-cho, Ikuta-ku, tel. 078-391-4325.

FESTIVALS

Note: See also National Holiday listings, pages 21–22.

February, 3rd Saturday	Okayama: Hadaka Matsuri (Naked Festival) ♛ ♛ ♛ at Saidaiji Temple. See page 258.
April 15–16	Kobe: Haru Matsuri (Spring Festival) ♛ of Ikuta Jinja Shrine.
May 24–26	Kobe: Nanko Festival ♛ of Minatogawa Jinja Shrine.
Mid–July	Miyajima: Kangensai Matsuri (Music Festival) ♛ ♛ ♛. See page 263.
August 6	Hiroshima: Heiwa Matsuri (Peace Festival) ♛ ♛ ♛ commemorates atomic bombing. Prayers, speeches, tolling of bells, and minute's silence.
August 15–18	Tokushima: Awa Odori (Awa Dance) ♛ ♛ ♛, usually known as Fools' Dance. See page 266.
October 14–15	Himeji: Kenka Matsuri (Fighting Festival) ♛ ♛ ♛ of Matsubara Jinja Shrine, one of Japan's most exciting. The young men who carry the portable shrines try to force each other out of the race.

KYUSHU

Though it's off the well-grooved tourist tracks, Kyushu shouldn't be. This is the birthplace of Japan, whether you're talking mythology or archaeology. The legend says the Emperor Jimmu set off from Miyazaki in 660 B.C. to the Nara area, on Honshu, where he founded the present imperial dynasty. There is a good amount of evidence to show that the conscious beginnings of the race we now know as Japanese did center here, in any case.

You should also go to Kyushu to keep warm, as it is the Florida of Japan. As pointed out earlier, the climate of Japan is similar to that of the United States East Coast, with Hokkaido having weather like Maine, Tokyo weather like Washington, D.C., and Kyushu that of the Sunshine State. You'll find a people less formal than those of Kyoto, less money-mad than those of Osaka, less status-conscious than the Tokyoites. If you could break the language barrier, you'd find they're even friendlier. To the utter amazement of people in Tokyo, they have no desire to move there, and are quite happy where they are, among the orange trees of Kyushu (which means Nine Provinces, literally).

GETTING TO KYUSHU

Getting to Kyushu isn't complicated. You have a choice of train, plane, or boat. You'd be crazy to take the bus, certifiable if you drove. There are direct or nonstop flights on Japan Air Lines, All Nippon Airways, and TDA (Toa Domestic Airlines). JAL flies 747s and DC-10s, ANA flies 747s and Tri-Stars, TDA flies the Air Bus. Flights operate between Tokyo and Osaka on the one hand, and, in Kyushu, Fukuoka, Kagoshima, Miyazaki, and Nagasaki. There are also flights from other spots outside Kyushu to these cities, and some internal services once you're here (for example, Nagasaki over to Kagoshima, by feeder lines such as NKA).

The Shinkansen (Bullet Train) operates straight through from Tokyo, via Kyoto, Osaka, and Hiroshima, to Fukuoka, which the JNR calls Hakata—they're twin cities. Takes 7 hours from Tokyo, 4 from Kyoto. Then JNR has lines running down to Beppu, Miyazaki, Kagoshima, Kumamoto, Nagasaki, and Sasebo, to mention only the most important ones.

By Boat

The Kansai Kisen Company operates from Osaka and Kobe to Beppu, the hot springs resort in Kyushu, taking 15 hours. There are three daily sailings round trip, but I recommend the nighttime departure from Osaka or Kobe, so that you can get up early to see the most beautiful part of the trip. The return trip covers this portion under cover of dark, so you should sail down, fly or train it back. Be sure to get the best cabins (Special A) for superior treatment. The food is all right.

PACKAGE TOURS

There are several package tours which I think are pretty good, so if you like the experience of traveling with a group, meeting people, and sharing the good times with the bad, you might look into the following JTB Sunrise Tours, starting in Kyoto, Osaka, or Fukuoka (your choice). They operate from March through November, every Tuesday, Thursday, and Saturday.

Five-day tour. Hakata free day, then travel to Beppu, where you visit a pottery kiln, and after lunch, see Monkey Mountain, the aquarium, and the boiling "hells."

- Day 3, drive the scenic Yamanami Highway and visit Mt. Aso, the world's largest active volcano crater (the last time anyone was killed was 1959). Concrete pillboxes will shelter you should it blow while you're there. Then down to Kumamoto to see its castle and spend the night.

- Day 4 takes you through the Amakusa Islands to Unzen Spa and finally to Nagasaki.
- Day 5, you'll see the Glover Mansion, Dejima, and Peace Park, all explained in the following text. Return to Hakata (Fukuoka), arriving there about mid-afternoon. Cost is ¥145,000 ($878.79), which includes 3 lunches.

Seven-day tour. First 4 days are similar to the 5-day tour, and on the 5th, you transfer at Hakata for a train to Hiroshima, where you spend the night.
- Day 6 you see the Peace Memorial Park and go to Miyajima.
- Day 7 you take a hydrofoil ride through the Inland Sea to Omishima Island (and its Oyamazumi Shrine), Ikuchi-jima Island (and its Kosanji Temple), then take the Shinkansen back to Osaka or Kyoto. Cost is ¥245,000 ($1,484.85), 4 lunches included.

ON YOUR OWN

I know it's not nice to knock a place for nothing, but I have to tell you that Fukuoka (or Hakata) isn't worth a visit unless one of the big festivals is taking place. The castle is a ruin, the best park is very ordinary, the temples and shrines are quite common. In February, there is the Tamaseseri Festival♛♛ of the Hakozakigu Shrine, in which two teams of young men fight for possession of a ball. It's typical of the so-called Naked Festivals of Japan, held in cold weather and with people clad only in loin-cloths. In July (1–15), the Hakata Yamagasa Festival♛♛ takes place at the Kushida Jinja Shrine. Beautifully deco-rated floats are carried around on young men's shoulders. On May 3 and 4, the Dontaku Festival♛♛ occurs. The chief attraction is a fancy-dress parade on both days, with costumes from all periods of Japanese history.

So, get off the Shinkansen here and hie thee to Nagasa-ki, Miyazaki, or Kagoshima, the Big Three of Kyushu tourism in my book. If you have time left, look at Kumamo-to, Unzen, Shimabara, and the Amakusa Islands.

NAGASAKI

Nagasaki is just what you might imagine from all the stories, a somewhat sleepy, semitropical town with a lot of memories, many of them foreign-born. The most vivid is a fiction, born of an opera that came from a play that was begotten as a story. From Pierre Loti's *Madame Chrysanthème* to David Belasco's scenario to Puccini's soaring notes took only a few years in the 19th century. But the memory lingers on, and the Japanese will show you "the house where Butterfly lived," though speaker and listener alike know it never happened. ("Well, it could have.")

The Glover Mansion ♛ ♛, commanding a fine view of the harbor, including the giant Mitsubishi Shipbuilding Yards across the way, is a romantic setting, and, in fact, has served as the basis for much opera scenery. Behind this house, once owned by a pretty stodgy British merchant, is a grouping of old Western-style buildings ♛ ♛ brought here from around the city. Don't be too alarmed by the height of the hill, as there's an outdoor escalator to take you up, then you walk down. It's a charming display, as is the Glover Mansion itself, and tells you a lot about the life of a foreigner here a century ago.

Although the Japanese adore the Butterfly legend, the average person is not sure of the details. I had an American friend who swanned around the city for several days, introducing himself to everyone as Lieutenant Benjamin Franklin Pinkerton of the U.S. Navy, serving on the battleship *Abraham Lincoln*, which he said was lying in the harbor, and nobody, from bar hostess to hotel clerk, made the connection. He even claimed to be interested in finding a *geisha* to become his wife, and no lights went on. Like most fables, the details are less important than the fact of the myth itself. (No. 5 streetcar from Nagasaki Station to Oura-tenshudo-shita stop.)

A second foreign-born memory, however, is only too real. It is the horror story of the atom bombing of Nagasaki on August 9, 1945, and the still-continuing aftermath. While Nagasaki lost fewer people than Hiroshima (75,000; Hiroshima lost 200,000), its tragedy was compounded by the failure of the American bomber to hit the target. Instead of dropping over the shipyards, as intended, the bomb exploded over the Urakami district and a Roman

Catholic church and school. Today you can visit the Peace Park♛♛♛, with a grotesque statue said to be the god of peace, and an International Cultural Hall, which has a museum and a nice garden. Nearby is the Urakami Catholic Church♛♛, rebuilt (1959) since the bombing, and visited by Pope John Paul II in 1981. This is, and was, the largest Catholic church in the Orient, and is quite impressive. (It is an odd coincidence that the atom bombs fell on the Japanese cities with the largest Christian populations, percentage-wise, Hiroshima being a Protestant center, Nagasaki a Catholic one.) (Streetcars 1 and 3 from in front of Nagasaki Station, the stop here being Matsuyama-machi.)

While you were up at the Glover Mansion, you couldn't help but notice the nearby Oura Tenshudo Catholic Church♛♛. Just above the Tokyu Hotel, it was built in 1864 to commemorate the 26 Martyrs of Nagasaki (see below). As the oldest Gothic structure, though wooden, in Japan, it is a National Treasure, and is utterly charming.

When you finish in this area, walk across the canal to the Tojinkan Hall♛, built by the Chinese community about 100 years ago. Dedicated to Confucius, it today has a lot of souvenir shops and a restaurant, which is best described as average. From here, walk northward and downhill on the Hollander Slope, which many foreign residents liked to stroll along in years past. (All foreigners were, until recently, called Oranda-jin, Hollanders, by the locals, as only the Dutch were allowed to retain a trading post here during the long period of Japanese isolation from the world, 1639-1859.)

Dejima Museum♛, between the business district and the harbor, is on the site of the actual island of Dejima, where the Dutch, and before them the Portuguese, were allowed to live and trade. (The Portuguese were expelled after the Tokugawa became worried that the missionaries, like St. Francis Xavier, were part of an advance team for invading armies. The Dutch, ever-thoughtful competitors of the Portuguese, and having no missionaries of their own to bother with, had pointed out to the Japanese that *conquistadores* frequently came with, or after, the converters.) The original Dutch residence still stands at this museum, a fascinating place if you're interested in the history of Japan's opening to the West. (Streetcar 5 from the Oura area to Irie-machi stop; Streetcar 1 from Nagasaki Station, Dejima stop.)

You're not far from Chinatown here, and you should indulge in a good Cantonese lunch or dinner, perhaps. Go out the museum door, turn left, and walk 3 or 4 blocks east to Chinatown.

The biggest of traditional sightseeing spots in Nagasaki is the Suwa Jinja Shrine♟♟, a most impressive shrine on a hillside near Nagasaki Park. Its Okunchi Festival♟♟♟♟, October 7–9, is a marvelous sight, with plenty of Chinese influence visible, though the shrine was inaugurated to stamp out Chinese and Christian influences in the city. The *torii* gate is the tallest bronze one in Japan.

The devout may wish to visit the site of the execution of the 26 Martyrs of Japan♟, canonized in 1862. The 26, 20 of them Japanese converts, were crucified by Toyotomi Hideyoshi on February 5, 1597, as they refused to denounce their religion after he had ordered it prohibited. Local legend says the bodies hung on their crosses for 80 days without decomposing, and miracles were said to have occurred in the vicinity. When Christianity was again tolerated, after 1859, the Kakure Kurishitan (secret Christians) were coaxed out of hiding and began to build churches, astonishing the priests who arrived to what they thought would be virgin missionary territory. The monument dates from 1962.

Unzen♟♟ is an old-fashioned hot-springs resort east of Nagasaki (2-hour bus trip), and I would recommend it if you have lots of aches, pains, and time. Near it is Shimabara, site of the last battle between Christians and the shogunate, where 30,000 rebellious peasants, including most of the Christians left in the country, died in 1637 defending the castle. It is now a museum♟, and after looking at it, you should go down to the beach, which is nearly deserted, except on weekends.

KAGOSHIMA AND IBUSUKI

Although the Japanese are fond of retracing historic steps in Kagoshima, I believe the main reason for coming here is to see Ibusuki Onsen (hot springs), just south of town. If you stop over in Kagoshima, however, you should look for the new Prefectural Museum♛, which has a very good ethnological and archaeological exhibit about the origins of the Japanese people. Students of religious history might wish to look at the monument to St. Francis Xavier, who landed here in 1549, and began his missionary work here after the feudal lord Shimazu granted him permission. For 2 years Xavier preached his way through Kyushu, going next to Yamaguchi and finally Kyoto, where he hoped to meet the shogun. In this he was disappointed, and within 2 years was on his way back to India, where he died a year later.

The volcano Sakurajima, on a peninsula of the same name (it used to be an island, hence *jima,* island), is still active, and emits showers of ashes from time to time (the latest big one in 1985). Because of it, Kagoshima calls itself the Naples of Japan.

Just south of town about 1 hour by train is Ibusuki Onsen, the most amusing of all Japan's hot-springs resorts. Here, in the huge Ibusuki Kanko (Tourist) Hotel, is the Fantasyland of public bathing♛ ♛ ♛. Fifty different pools are contained in the huge Junguru Buro (Jungle Bath), where (sorry!) men only can indulge in citrus baths, hormone baths, or whatever, under towering palm and banana trees. The women have a smaller section, itself boasting several baths, but apparently Japanese women prefer the private rooms, which are also available. Outside, both men and women together can enjoy a sand bath, where you lie down in your cotton *yukata* (summer *kimono*) and are buried for as long as you can stand it. The waters and sand are supposed to be good for rheumatism, neuralgia, digestive disorders, and "external injuries." The hotel also sports a huge Hawaiian Show, the equal of any vulgar display you've ever seen, and six restaurants, all pretty good. They don't miss a trick here. As a tour bus is leaving, a barely dressed woman and hotel photographer stand right by the door, ready for that last-minute shot with any visitor who hasn't yet had his hand around a "hula girl's" waist.

This is a good center for sporting activities, especially golf, riding, and hiking, and the English-speaking manager is always glad to see foreign visitors. If you want to stand out in the crowd, this is your opportunity.

MIYAZAKI

One of the most beautiful seacoasts in the world can be found along Kyushu's eastern shores, especially around, and south of, Miyazaki. I suggest a visit to this part of Japan for the scenery, Aoshima, the tomb figures of Miyazaki, and the golfing at the Sun Hotel Phoenix.

Get yourself to the city of Miyazaki first, then take a short excursion out to Aoshima (Blue Island) ♛ ♛, a small island connected to the mainland by bridge. It is as lush as the Garden of Eden must have been, and also sports an unusual layered rock formation, highly photogenic. (A 20-minute drive on the bus from Minami Miyazaki Station.)

In town, ask to see the Honbu Haniwa Plant ♛, which makes splendid reproductions of tomb figures from Japanese pre- or proto-history. You'll note a huge Happy Peasant figure welcoming visitors who come to the city by air. (15 Nakatuse-cho, Miyazaki, tel. 0985-23-6034.)

A pleasant city, Miyazaki has a splendid shrine, Miyazaki Jinja ♛ ♛, very similar to the Meiji Shrine in Tokyo in some ways, and dedicated to Emperor Jimmu, first of the present imperial line. Behind the shrine is a fine collection of four old farmhouses ♛ ♛ ♛, brought together here and lovingly restored. Although there is no English-language description, they make a fine target for photographers.

But I hope you came to Miyazaki to have a good time, because you can do so at the Sun Hotel Phoenix ♛ ♛ ♛ ♛, or its adjacent sister hotel. I don't usually plug hotels, and I'm not even a golfer, but this must be heaven for anyone enjoying a good day chasing the little white ball; 36 holes of golf on championship courses and every other kind of outdoor sport should keep you busy. The surroundings are attractive, the weather (except when it rains) and climate usually excellent.

BEPPU

Farther up the east coast of Kyushu is Beppu, said to be a world-famous hot-springs resort. I thought it fun when I first visited it, but then I was a student, and with a group of friends, sharing a cheap inn and our first trip together. Going back over the years, I find that the bubbling "hells" ♛ ♛ are still interesting, but the surrounding commercialization has made the town itself a tourist hell. (It's the kind of place where the city fathers have erected barriers against pedestrians, the better to let tour buses speed through, and you have to walk half a mile to cross the street.) The big, glittering hotels up on the mountain slopes (see listings) are fun, but the downtown area is shabby and nasty. I would recommend coming here only if you have either (a) a strong interest in natural hot springs, as some of them are quite pretty, or (b) a desire to soak in the hot springs, and unwind. Otherwise, forget it.

INSIDERS' INFORMATION FOR KYUSHU

HOTELS
Beppu

Shiragiku Ryokan ♛ ♛ ♛ ♛
16-35 Kamitano-yu, Beppu, Oita-ken 874, tel. 0977-21-2111
Two persons in room, $100, breakfast and dinner included
Big, modern building, 124 *tatami* rooms, but 16 Western-style. Own hot springs, lovely garden, pool, 2 restaurants.

Suginoi ♛ ♛ ♛ ♛
Kankaiji, Beppu, Oita-ken 874, tel. 0977-24-1141
Two persons in twin, $70
Huge place, 600 rooms, of which 10 percent are Japanese-style. Own hot springs, mammoth public baths with indoor jungle, several restaurants. Own amusement park, stage shows, pools, skating rink, bowling alley. You don't need to go out and see the rest of the town.

Onoya Ryokan ♛ ♛ ♛
284 Kannawa, Beppu, Oita-ken 874-01, tel. 0977-67-7711
Two persons in room, $105, breakfast and dinner included
Own hot springs, big public bath, entertainment, 83 rooms, 3 restaurants.

Oniyama Ryokan ♛ ♛
335-1 Oaza Kannawa, Beppu, Oita-ken 874-01, tel. 0977-66-1121
Two persons in room, $175, breakfast and dinner included
Smaller inn, 67 rooms, most with bath, up in hills overlooking town.

Tsurumien Grand Ryokan ♛ ♛

7-2141 Minami Tatsuishi, Beppu, Oita-ken 874, tel. 0977-22-6171

Two persons in room, $90, breakfast and dinner included

Modern on outside, classical Japanese inside, with 88 rooms, pool, big public bath.

Kamenoi ♛

5-17 Chuo-machi, Beppu, Oita-ken 874, tel. 0977-24-1141

Two persons in twin, $60

Older hotel in town center, a bit run-down, but with good food in 3 restaurants. Large public bath, 200 rooms.

Fukuoka (Hakata)

Nishitetsu Grand ♛ ♛ ♛ ♛

2-6-60 Daimyo, Chuo-ku, Fukuoka 810, tel. 092-771-7171

Two persons in twin, $95

Excellent location, 4 restaurants, indoor pool, shops are main reasons why this is tops in town. Has 308 rooms, a few of them Japanese.

ANA Hakata ♛ ♛ ♛

3-3-3 Hakata-ekimae, Hakata-ku, Fukuoka 812, tel. 092-471-1111

Two persons in twin, $95

Just around corner from JNR main station, with indoor and outdoor pools, sauna and gym, 3 fine restaurants, shops, 360 average-sized rooms.

New Otani ♛ ♛ ♛

1-1-2 Watanabe-dori, Chuo-ku, Fukuoka 810, tel. 092-714-1111

Two persons in twin, $120

Kyushu's largest hotel, 436 rooms, indoor pool, 4 restaurants, 2 shopping floors. Family buffet on weekends in top-floor restaurant is a bargain.

Clio Court ♛ ♛

5-3 Hakata-eki, Chuo-gai, Hakata-ku, Fukuoka 812, tel. 092-472-1111

Two persons in twin, $85

Very sleek and slick, on opposite side of Hakata JNR station, with several other new hotels. Too, too modern, with some rooms in "early American" decor looking like nothing New England ever saw, 7 restaurants, a fun place, 240 rooms.

Hakata Miyako🍷🍷
2-1-1 Hakata-eki Higashi, Hakata-ku, Fukuoka 812, tel.
092-441-3111
Two persons in twin, $75
Very modern, on back side of station, 3 restaurants, top-floor bar, beauty salon, shops, 269 fairly small but comfortable rooms.

Hakata Tokyu🍷🍷
1-16-1 Tenjin, Chuo-ku, Fukuoka 810, tel. 092-781-7111
Two persons in twin, $95
Riverside location, nice roof bar, excellent restaurant up there too, 3 others, 266 smallish rooms.

Centraza🍷
4-23 Chuo-gai, Hakata-ku, Fukuoka 812, tel. 092-461-0111
Two persons in twin, $78
Modern and spartan, with 200 small rooms, outdoor pool on roof. Other side of Hakata Station. Shopping center in basement, mostly for food items.

Rich Hakata🍷
3-27-15 Hakata-ekimae, Hakata-ku, Fukuoka 812, tel. 092-451-7811
Two persons in twin, $60
Convenient location, down the street on downtown side of station, 178 small rooms, nice top-floor bar, small restaurant.

Shiroyama🍷
5-3-4 Nakasu, Hakata-ku, Fukuoka 810, tel. 092-281-2211
Two persons in twin, $80
The old Nikkatsu Hotel, remodeled, with very good Chinese restaurant on top floor, 120 fair-sized rooms, sauna, several restaurants.

Station Plaza🍷
2-1-1 Hakata-ekimae, Hakata-ku, Fukuoka 812, tel. 092-431-1211
Two persons in twin, $69
Occupies 7 top floors of Asahi (Newspaper) Building, opposite Hakata Station, on the downtown side. Japanese restaurant on top floor with views, 2 others, 248 small rooms.

Ibusuki

Ibusuki Kanko ♛ ♛ ♛
3755 Junicho, Ibusuki, Kagoshima-ken 891-04, tel. 09932-2-2131
Two persons in twin, $85
A big place, with its own hot springs, and a "jungle bath" which features growing palm and date trees, as well as those bearing bananas and oranges. About 20 different pools in which to plunge (men and women segregated, unless you order a private pool for your own party). Get buried in the hot sand, if you like. Mammoth theater with corny floor show, "Hawaiian-style," in which audience participates. Many groups, but individuals have separate part of restaurant, etc., to avoid the noise if you so desire. Food is so-so, service great, 620 rooms, most of them Western-style. Bowling alley, pool, tennis, golf, beach, sailing, fishing, etc.

Kagoshima

Shiroyama Kanko ♛ ♛ ♛ ♛
41-1 Shinshoin-cho, Kagoshima 890, tel. 0992-24-2211
Two persons in twin, $65
High on a hill, for groups and honeymooners, but with fine restaurants, good service, 496 rooms, mostly Western-style. Gym, indoor pool, sauna, shops (oh, yes, shops almost obliterate the lobby).

Tokyu ♛ ♛ ♛
22-1 Shinmachi, Kamoike, Kagoshima 890, tel. 0992-57-2411
Two persons in twin, $76
Part of big chain effort, and very smartly done. Pool, 2 restaurants, 206 average-size rooms.

Kumamoto

New Sky ♛ ♛ ♛
2 Higashi Amidaji-machi, Kumamoto 860, tel. 096-354-2111
Two persons in twin, $95

Largest in town, with 358 rooms, most of them Western-style. Sauna, 3 restaurants.

Castle 𝖂 𝖂
4-2 Joto-machi, Kumamoto 860, tel. 096-326-3311
Two persons in twin, $80
Has 214 medium-sized rooms, 2 restaurants.

Maruko Ryokan 𝖂
11-10 Kamitoricho, Kumamoto 860, tel. 096-353-1241
Two persons in room, $86, including breakfast and dinner
50 rooms in modern building, but traditional style.

Miyazaki

Sun Hotel Phoenix 𝖂 𝖂 𝖂 𝖂
3083 Hamayama, Shioji, Miyazaki 880-01, tel. 0985-39-3131
Two persons in twin, $95
Luxurious property on sea, with 3 golf courses in front yard totaling 36 holes, 300 good-sized rooms, some Japanese-style, 3 restaurants, pool, bowling, tennis, mini-golf. Site of annual Dunlop Phoenix golf championships.

Seaside Hotel Phoenix 𝖂 𝖂 𝖂
3083 Hamayama, Shioji, Miyazaki 880-01, tel. 0985-39-1111
Two persons in twin, $80
Sister property to above, sharing sports facilities, 194 slightly smaller rooms, some Japanese-style, 2 restaurants.

Phoenix 𝖂 𝖂
2-1-1 Matsuyama, Miyazaki 880, tel. 0985-23-6111
Two persons in twin, $85
The downtown property of the Phoenix chain, with nice dining room, 117 rooms, a few of them Japanese-style.

Plaza 𝖂 𝖂
1-1 Kawahara-cho, Miyazaki 880, tel. 0985-27-1111
Two persons in twin, $65
Pool, restaurant, *sushi* bar, 173 smallish rooms.

Washington 𝖂 𝖂
1-1-3 Nishi Chuo-dori, Miyazaki 880, tel. 0985-28-9111
Two persons in twin, $50
Part of a splendid, money-saving chain, 210 small rooms, 3 restaurants including Sanjusan Gendo, Japanese-style.

Nagasaki

Shumeikan Ryokan ♛ ♛ ♛
3-11 Chikugo-machi, Nagasaki 850, tel. 0958-22-5121
Two persons in room, $285, breakfast and dinner included
Big Japanese-style inn, 106 rooms, mostly Japanese, usual
amenities of graceful living at floor level.

Tokyu ♛ ♛ ♛
1-18 Minami Yamate-machi, Nagasaki 850, tel. 0958-25-1501
Two persons in twin, $90
Celebrating Madama Butterfly, there is a Glover restaurant (for the house which stage sets are patterned after)
and a Pinkerton Bar. Good location just below Glover
Mansion and a collection of restored European houses of
the 1800s, 225 smallish rooms.

Grand ♛ ♛
5-3 Manzai-machi, Nagasaki 850, tel. 0958-23-1234
Two persons in twin, $80
Good location for business travelers, 126 fair-sized rooms.

Holiday Inn ♛ ♛
6-24 Doza-machi, Nagasaki 850, tel. 0958-28-1234
Two persons in twin, $70 (double rooms cheaper)
In business district, about 200 fair-sized rooms, 3 restaurants.

RESTAURANTS
(Street addresses not needed in small towns; hence, not
given here)

Beppu

Marukiyo ♛
Tel. 0979-22-4055
Average dinner, $15
Freshest of fish; best in town outside hotel dining rooms.

Fukuoka

Suigetsu ♛ ♛ ♛
Eki-mae, tel. 092-411-9501
Average dinner, $30
Nabe (stews) of fish, chicken, or meat are the specialties.

Amimoto♛ ♛
Kokutai-doro, tel. 092-271-2222
Average dinner, $22
Fish the specialty, including *sashimi*.

Shizuka♛ ♛
3-2 Tenjin, tel. 092-712-4500
Average dinner, $15 up
Fugu, sometimes-deadly blowfish, specialty here, plus other fish dishes.

Hakata-no-chaya♛
Nakasu, tel. 092-271-7294
Average dinner, $15
Seafood stews, such as *chankonabe*.

Rokumeikan♛
Nakasu
Average dinner, $17
Good Chinese food, mostly Cantonese.

Kagoshima

Satsuma Chaya♛ ♛
Tel. 0992-22-0500
Average dinner, $20
Upstairs for marvelous *satsuma-age* (deep-fried fish dumplings) and *kibinago sashimi* (tiny little raw fish).

Tanoura So♛ ♛
Tel. 0992-47-1567
Average dinner, $25
Traditional Japanese cuisine, but specializing in *mizutaki* (chicken stew).

Katsu♛
Tel. 0992-24-1037
Average dinner, $18
Kushi-age is specialty here (deep-fried everything).

Komurasaki♛
Tel. 0992-22-5707
Average dinner, $9
Noodles, with local version, *Satsuma ramen*.

Matsuki Shamon♛
Tel. 0992-24-4487
Average dinner, $8
Bargain basement traditional cuisine. Ask for *wappa meshi*, a steamed rice, chicken, and fish combination.

Miyazaki

Sato♛ ♛
Tel. 0985-27-1212
Average dinner, $20
Traditional Japanese dishes, including *sushi*.

Zushi♛
Tel. 0985-67-0122
Average dinner, $30
Sushi, as name indicates, and lobster served every which
way.

Nagasaki

Hamakatsu Bekkan♛ ♛ ♛
Tel. 0958-23-2193
Average dinner, $20
Nagasaki's most famous specialty, *shippoku ryori*, a mix-
ture of Chinese, Japanese, and other cuisines, looking like
a bastardized *kaiseki* set meal, is tradition carried on here.
Pork cutlets are cheaper.

Shikairo♛ ♛
Tel. 0958-24-4744
Average dinner, $14
Old and famous Chinese restaurant, much-touted, and sur-
prisingly good for such a big place. Ask for *champon*, a
noodle dish, if you want a local specialty, but all major
Chinese cuisines represented.

Kozanro♛
Tel. 0958-21-3735
Average dinner, $12
Chinese food, mostly Shanghai.

Yosso♛
Tel. 0958-21-0001
Average dinner, $18
For more than 100 years, has served traditional Japanese
cuisine, but home cooking, nothing fancy.

Fukudaya♛
Tel. 0958-22-0101
Average dinner, $15
Kabayaki (grilled eel) and other *unagi* (eel) dishes here.

BEST SHOPPING
Nagasaki

Tortoiseshell is big specialty, but you can't bring it back to United States, as the tortoise is an endangered species. Buy *castera* (sponge) cake instead, at any souvenir shop or hotel.

FESTIVALS

Note: See also National Holidays listings, pages 21–22.

January 3	Fukuoka: Tamaseseri (Ball Fighting Festival) ♛ ♛, Hakozaki Jingu Shrine (see page 281).
May 3 or 4	Fukuoka: Dontaku Procession ♛ ♛ (see page 281). Band of *shamoji* (rice-serving spoons) is one of many features.
June	Nagasaki: Early in month is the Peiron rowing race ♛ ♛ ♛, a Chinese import. Very colorful.
July 1–15	Fukuoka: Hakata Yamagasa Festival ♛ ♛ (see page 281). Early morning of 15th, the race of the 1-ton floats is most exciting part.
October 7–9	Nagasaki: Suwa Matsuri Festival ♛ ♛ ♛ ♛, one of Japan's biggest and best. Also called Okunchi (see page 284). Best seats at Kokaido at 5 P.M. on 7th, 8 A.M. on 8th. Obtain through your hotel or travel agent.
November 3–4	Karatsu, near Fukuoka: Okunchi Festival ♛ ♛ ♛, 14 huge floats parading down the streets. On 2nd day, floats carried to shore and back.
April 3–29	Nagasaki: Takoage (Kite-Flying Festival) ♛ ♛ ♛. Try to cut strings of other contestants' kites.

NORTHERN JAPAN

Nikko is what Japanese are really like, in their hearts, but they're ashamed to admit it. It's bright, wild and flashy, and many centuries of Confucian inhibition have tried to breed this out of the culture. Furthermore, the patrician sensibilities that led to Zen and its *shibui* (astringent) taste militated against admitting gorgeous colors to public buildings. In the same way that people have been led to believe that Bordeaux is somehow better than Burgundy in wines because the taste is less pronounced, Japanese and foreign observer alike have been told, repeatedly, that Katsura Rikyu and the Ise Shrines are somehow deeper portrayals of the Japanese ethos than, for instance, Nikko.

Most visitors to Japan take in Nikko on a day trip from Tokyo, allowing about 4 or 5 hours to see everything. This is certainly possible (see discussion of tours, below), but I recommend staying overnight and making this part of a tour of northern Japan. Aside from Nikko, few foreigners visit this area, regarded even by the Japanese as somehow not quite keeping up with the times. A little timid with foreigners, the people are nonetheless friendly, curious about you and your impressions. The scenery is splendid, especially in the Japan Alps, and for hiking and skiing, you couldn't ask for better.

Getting around is fairly easy. If you don't take a tour, you can fly to all the major cities here, or to Sendai and take the Shinkansen (Bullet Train), which also serves Niigata and Morioka. I recommend flying to Kanazawa and taking the train for Takayama from Nagoya or Kyoto.

The routes to Nikko are several. Fastest is the Limited Express of the private Tobu Railways, departing Asakusa Station in Tokyo and taking 1 hour 50 minutes. Runs every 30 minutes or 60, costs ¥2,000 ($12.12). Ordinary express takes 20 minutes longer, runs every hour, costs ¥1,000 ($6.06). On JNR, from Tokyo's Ueno Station, regular trains take 2 hours 50 minutes, run every hour, cost ¥2,300 ($13.94). This is recommended only if you have a Japan Rail Pass and thus can ride free.

PACKAGE TOURS

JTB tours including Nikko. There are four such JTB tours.

Nikko Full-Day Tour: Operates daily, taking nearly 12 hours, costing ¥17,500 ($106.06). Train to Nikko, see the Toshogu Shrine, lunch at Kanaya Hotel, sacred dance at Futaarasan Shrine, lots of scenery.

Nikko and Bonsai Tour: Operates daily, with some exceptions, March through November, costing ¥20,000 ($121.21). Bus to Nikko, less scenery, but otherwise same as Full-Day Tour, with stop at Japan's biggest *bonsai* garden.

Nikko and Mashiko Tour: Operates same days as Nikko and Bonsai Tour, costs ¥22,500 ($136.36), and instead of the *bonsai* garden, takes you to the town of Mashiko to visit a kiln of this world-famous pottery place. Also visits handmade-paper factory, and takes you back to Tokyo on the Bullet Train (short ride).

Two-Day Nikko and Mashiko Tour: Operates daily (except 9 days a year at holidays), costs ¥41,100 ($249.09). Same as Nikko and Bonsai Tour, staying at Nikko Kanaya Hotel. After lunch the 2nd day, much more sightseeing, then back to Tokyo.

Tobu. This railway company has a 1-day trip costing same as JTB, but lunch at Lakeside Hotel. Its 2-day trip is much cheaper, costing only ¥24,000 ($145.45), with accommodations at Lakeside Hotel, a bit far from Toshogu Shrine (you'd need taxi service). A free McDonald's breakfast is included on both tours! Free hotel pickup service, of course, as with JTB, above.

Fujita. Japan's largest coach operator has a 1-day tour for ¥15,000 ($90.91), operating from March to November. Same itinerary as others, lunching at Kanaya Boathouse Restaurant.

The Gray Line. Visits both Nikko and Mashiko on its 1-day tour, similar to JTB's third offering, but charges only ¥14,800 ($89.70). Lunch also at Kanaya Hotel. A movie is shown in bus en route back to Tokyo, and light snack served.

JTB tours of northern Japan. There are three tours you might want to look into.

One-Day Tohoku Trail: Bullet Train to Koriyama, drive to farmhouse and cruise on Lake Inawashiro, visit a former imperial villa. Operates Monday, Wednesday, Friday (except certain holiday periods) from March through November, costing ¥45,000 ($272.73), no lunch. A long day, but very relaxing nonetheless.

Two-Day Tohoku Trail: After lake cruise (see 1-day tour, above), drive to Bandai Atami Spa for Japanese dinner and overnight at Ichiriki *ryokan.* Next day, to Aizu Wakamatsu, see old castle, *sake* brewery, then two more small towns (one a pottery center), then back to Tokyo. ¥83,000 ($503.03), 1 dinner, 1 breakfast included.

Three-Day Tohoku tour: Train takes you to Sendai, then excursion to Matsushima (including cruise on bay), visit Zuiganji Temple. Overnight at Sendai Plaza or similar hotel. Day 2, to Togatta Spa for folkcraft collection, beautiful mountain scenery, Okama Crater Lake, then Kaminoyama Spa, where you have dinner and stay at Hotel Koyo or similar. Day 3, drive to Yonezawa to visit old temple, woodcarving workshop, old mansion, then train it back to Tokyo. ¥200,000 ($1,212.12), 1 dinner, 1 breakfast included.

NIKKO

You come here to see the Toshogu Shrine ♛ ♛ ♛ ♛ ♛ first of all, anything else being secondary. If you are on your own and don't want to take a taxi, which I recommend unless you have plenty of time, take bus 5 from in front of (and across street from) the JNR Nikko Station. Toshogu Jinja is the place you're going.

A marvelous progression of gates, halls, towers, pagodas, and outer buildings leads you from the entrance, especially if you start at the Shinkyo Bridge near the Kanaya Hotel. It's a gentle uphill climb, culminating in the mausoleum of Tokugawa Ieyasu, founder of the shogunate that bears his name, and model for *Shogun* in the novel and TV series. Although he died in 1616, the shrine was not completed until 20 years later. Many of the buildings are National Treasures, as the finest artists and craftsmen from all over the country were dragooned into working on this edifice. It only took 2 years to build, but 15,000 men were on the job.

The Sacred Bridge is a reproduction (1907), flood having carried off the original, and has been halfway open to the public only since 1936. There is a small entrance fee to the shrines, which are open from 8 A.M. to 5 P.M., closing 1 hour earlier in winter. You pass by Rinnoji Temple, where General Ulysses S. Grant stayed for a week when he visited in 1879. But if time is important, press on to the Toshogu Shrine itself, just beyond.

The moment you pass under the granite *torii* gate, you are going where no commoner could pass until after the Meiji Restoration. Passing by the pagoda (1818), look for the Sacred Stable, with the world-famous sculptures of the Three Monkeys who hear no evil, speak no evil, see no evil. Next to the second bronze *torii* is a marvelous Sutra Library. The Yakushido, the large building on the far left, is a 1968 reproduction of the original, destroyed by fire 7 years earlier.

Finally you reach the first gorgeous gate, Yomeimon (Gate of Sunlight), beyond which lower-ranking *samurai* were not permitted to pass in feudal times. Higher-ranking nobility could enter, but only after surrendering their swords. Spend as much time as you can looking at the carvings, of children, animals real and imagined, flowers, and trees. Next are two smaller structures, a Sacred Stage and Sacred Palanquin House. Next is Karamon (Chinese Gate), almost as breathtaking as Yomeimon.

The inner sanctum, the Haiden (Oratory), is less inspiring than the gates, but impressive enough, and contains the sacred mirror, which Shinto believers feel represents the spirit of the deceased shogun. The shrine's holy of holies is the Nai-Naijin of the Naijin (the innermost chamber of the inner chamber), in the Honden (Main Hall), and it is here that the shogun, now become a god, is enshrined. Out the gallery to the east, then up a steep hill behind the Honden, you can find the actual tomb. It is worth the climb for lovers of history, but is nothing to write home about from an artistic or architectural point of view.

More gods are enshrined down the hill and to the west,

at Futaarasan Shrine ♛ ♛, where you may see *kagura* sacred dances being performed by the shrine virgins. (This is done for a fee, so inquire if you want to see dancing and have the money for it.) Just to the south is Daiyuinbyo ♛, the mausoleum of Iemitsu, grandson of Ieyasu. Built only 17 years after Toshogu Shrine, it is smaller and much less colorful, but thoroughly beautiful in the way it harmonizes with its natural surroundings.

A "Japanese Williamsburg" called Nikko Edo Mura Village opened in 1986 in Nikko, displaying 82 houses from the Edo Period (1603–1867). You can see how the *samurai* lived, inspect a *ninja* (master spy) house, go through a haunted house (Japanese ghosts have no legs), and attend abbreviated *kabuki* performances. Just by chance, there are 16 restaurants (all Edo-style) and 16 souvenir shops (all no-style). Ersatz festivals will be held from time to time to jazz up the scene, too. Admission ¥1,500 ($9.09).

Nikko's natural beauty is the reason why many Japanese come here, to boat and fish on Lake Chuzenji, up in the mountains just to the west of town, or to go a bit farther to the hot springs and ski resorts up in the valleys beyond. Some of the tours will take you to the lake anyhow, and I can recommend the trip if you have plenty of time. Otherwise, get on with your tour of northern Japan.

SENDAI AND SIDE TRIPS

The capital of northern Japan, by any standards, Sendai is a surprising place, all bustle and boom around its station area and Ichiban-cho business district, but still homespun and unspoiled. Flattened by air raids in World War II, it is completely rebuilt, and has many fine parks. The nearby hills also seem to nestle the city in their leafy embrace, somewhat making up for the undistinguished architecture all around.

Use the town primarily for side trips (see below). Sightseeing here is highlighted by the Date family mausolea ♛ ♛ on a hill in the southern part of the city. Recently reconstructed, in imposing Momoyama Period style. Nearby is the Gokoku Jinja Shrine ♛, on the site of the ruined Sendai Castle. The most famous of all sights, however, is Osaki Hachiman Jinja Shrine ♛ ♛, about 15 minutes by bus from Sendai Station, with a black lacquer exterior of exquisite beauty, a National Treasure.

The most famous side trip from Sendai is to Matsushima ♛ ♛ ♛, a group of islands in a bay of the same name. Considered by the Japanese to be one of the three prettiest spots in Japan (the other two are Miyajima Island and Ama-no-hashidate), Matsushima is gorgeous, and sometimes more so in snowy weather or mist than in bright sunlight. The tiny islands and deep blue Pacific make for a striking combination, so much so that Toyotomi Hideyoshi built a Wave-Viewing Pavilion the better to enjoy it. This could be a perfect place to unravel if you have the time for a leisurely boat trip among the islands, or even for hiking to the various spots around the bay where the best views can be had (the "four grand sights," as the corners of the bay are designated). Don't miss Kinkazan Jinja Shrine ♛ ♛, at the eastern end of the bay.

The other side trip is to Hiraizumi, 1 hour north on the Bullet Train, where Chusonji Temple ♛ ♛ ♛ is located. A few minutes by bus from the station, Chusonji is the tutelary shrine of the Fujiwara family, one of Japan's most powerful groups. Dating back to the founding of the temple (1102) is Konjikido, a marvelously decorated hall, famous for its images of Buddha and the lacquered and mother-of-pearl-inlaid pillars. Dating from 1108 is the Kyozo (Sutra Hall), which has a splendid Monju Bosatsu, *bodhisattva* of wisdom and learning. Both buildings are National Treasures. The other structures here are more recent, fire having taken its usual toll over the years.

NIIGATA

Niigata, across the island of Honshu from Sendai and on the Sea of Japan, is headquarters of Snow Country, the Japan that is sometimes cut off from everywhere just because so much of the white stuff accumulates on roads, railways, and even airport runways. You would be visiting here because of nearby Sado Island ♛ ♛, a short hop from Niigata.

If you came here to escape, you'd be following in the footsteps of several great men of the past, exiled from

Kyoto to the most inaccessible part of Japan the shoguns could imagine. The rare *toki* (crested ibis) is found here, and you should ask for a performance or two of the famous Sado *okesa* dances. (Come to think of it, one is enough.)

KANAZAWA

Kanazawa, down the coast of the Sea of Japan and a 1-hour flight from Tokyo, is worth a special trip. In my opinion, it's up there right after Kyoto and Nara as a suitable target for sightseeing. Hardly ever visited by foreigners, Kanazawa has a rare grouping of *samurai* houses ♛♛♛, just down the hill from the new Tokyu Hotel, in the Nagamachi district. Although some are only Meiji Period houses, there are a few genuine feudal ones, such as that owned by the Yonekawa family. The Maeda family were feudal lords here, and the townspeople made their livings from gold lacquer work, silk fabric making, *kutani* pottery making, and woodworking, among other crafts.

More famous than the *samurai* houses is Kenrokuen Park ♛♛♛, classified by the Japanese as one of their "three best" (the other two being Korakuen at Okayama in western Japan, and Kairakuen at Mito, north of Tokyo). The name means "Six Combined," so the designers tried to get all of the following virtues into the garden—coolness, vastness, sobriety, alignment, antiquity, and beauty. The garden dates to the late 17th century.

Across the street from the New Grand Hotel is Oyama Shrine ♛, noted for the stained-glass windows of its Dutch-style gate (1875). South of the Tokyu Hotel in Teramachi is the Ninja-dera Temple ♛, famous for its secret tunnels, trick doors, and other devices connected to the clandestine arts of the *ninja*. The real name of the temple is Myoryuji, and reservations are necessary. Telephone 0762-41-2877, daily.

TAKAYAMA

Somewhat inland, in the heart of the Japan Alps, lies Takayama, which likes to call itself "little Kyoto." Although the town's business district is relentlessly vulgar, there is a section of gorgeous old houses which demands that you visit. From the station, get yourself by taxi or bus (no. 2 stop) to the Kusakabe House ♛ ♛, one of the best examples of these Edo Period structures. It and the Yoshijima House ♛ ♛ are both excellent examples of the large homes of prosperous merchants, who conducted their business from their family hearths. Next, get a taxi (or the same bus back to the station, then from stop 4 on another bus) to the opposite side of town, to see the Folklore Museum and Village ♛ ♛ ♛, two separate complexes near each other. The Hida-no-Sato Village is a lovely collection of about 30 buildings grouped around a pond. Many are old farmhouses once slated for destruction but moved here as part of an open-air village (what the Europeans call a Skansen, after the prototype outside Stockholm). A little bit like all of its kind, because there are demonstrations of papermaking and other crafts. The same ticket for this place gets you in to the Hida Minzoku-kan (Folklore Museum) ♛ ♛ ♛, just down the hill (note the wonderful old Hida Goten ♛ ♛ building on the right-hand side). The museum buildings are of the *gassho-zukkuri* style, or praying-hands mode, once common in the deepest valleys of central Japan, but now all disappearing. Some were 4 floors high.

INSIDERS' INFORMATION FOR NORTHERN JAPAN

HOTELS
Kanazawa

Tokyu ♛ ♛ ♛ ♛
2-1-1 Korinbo, Kanazawa, Ishikawa-ken 920, tel. 0762-31-2411
Two persons in twin, $86
Beautiful new (1985) hotel near famous *samurai* houses, also new shopping center of town. Larger rooms than usual these days, 250 of them. Several restaurants, the Japanese one being excellent. Nice top-floor sky lounge.

Miyako ♛ ♛ ♛
6-10 Konohanacho, Kanazawa, Ishikawa-ken 920, tel. 0762-31-2202
Two persons in twin, $75 and up
Best-sited for business travelers, just opposite big new

Sendai rail station. Coffee shop, 2 restaurants, 193 medium-sized rooms.

New Grand♛ ♛ ♛

1-50 Takaoka-machi, Kanazawa, Ishikawa-ken 920, tel. 0762-33-1311

Two persons in twin, $98

Great location across street from city cultural center and concert hall, near famous Oyama Shrine, 4 restaurants, 112 rooms, mostly Western-style.

Holiday Inn♛ ♛

1-10 Horikawamachi, Kanazawa, Ishikawa-ken 920, tel. 0762-23-1111

Two persons in twin, $80

Conveniently sited next to rail station, with 181 smallish rooms, 4 restaurants, most interesting of which is the Kitano Shoya "Japanese pub" in basement.

Sky♛ ♛

15-1 Musashi-machi, Kanazawa, Ishikawa-ken 920, tel. 0762-33-2233

Two persons in twin, $75

Halfway between railway station area and new shopping center of town, with 4 restaurants, nice sky lounge on top floor, about 100 rooms.

Garden♛

2-16-16 Honmachi, Kanazawa, Ishikawa-ken 920, tel. 0762-63-3333

Two persons in twin, $55

Small hotel, nicely done, about 100 tiny rooms, convenient location opposite rail station.

Murataya Ryokan♛

1-5-2 Katamachi, Kanazawa, Ishikawa-ken 920, tel. 0762-63-0455

Two persons in room, $40 (no meals)

Only 8 rooms available, some with bath, some without. Small garden, homey atmosphere. Dining room for breakfast.

Niigata

Okura♛ ♛ ♛

6-53 Kawabata-cho, Niigata 950, tel. 0252-24-6111

Two persons in twin, $80

On main drag from station to town center, 303 medium-sized rooms, 3 restaurants, shops. Good taste, as would be expected from parent hotel in Tokyo.

Italia-Ken ♛ ♛
7-1574 Nishibori-dori, Niigata 951, tel. 0252-24-5111
Two persons in twin, $105
Nothing very Italian about this establishment, best suited for business travelers. Fairly elegant, 101 smallish rooms, 2 restaurants.

Onoya Ryokan ♛ ♛
981 Furumachi-dori, Rokuban-cho, Niigata 951, tel. 0252-29-2951
Two persons in room, $155, breakfast and dinner included
Nice little inn, with 24 rooms, all with private bath, the usual amenities of classic *ryokan*.

Niigata ♛
5-11-20 Bandai, Niigata 950, tel. 0252-45-3331
Two persons in twin, $85
Garden, 126 smallish rooms, 3 restaurants, beer garden in summer.

Nikko

Prince ♛ ♛ ♛
Shobugahama, Chugushi, Nikko, Tochigi-ken 321-16, tel. 0288-55-0661
Two persons in twin, $105
Up away from town center on Lake Chuzenji, so perhaps better for vacation than sightseeing. Has 78 pleasant rooms, with pool, tennis, skating, skiing, boating, cycling, the works.

Kanaya ♛ ♛
1300 Kami Hatsuishi-machi, Nikko, Tochigi-ken 321-14, tel. 0288-54-0001
Two persons in twin, $90
The traditional place to stay, nearest to shrines, where the tour bus may stop to disgorge deluxe passengers for lunch on their 1-day outings from Tokyo. Fine old hotel, 83 large rooms, and an experience to stay here, as in Fujiya in Hakone area, Nara in that city. Pool and skating.

Konishi Ryokan Bekkan ♛ ♛
1115 Kami Hatsuishi-machi, Nikko, Tochigi-ken 321-14, tel. 0288-54-1105
Two persons in room, $150, breakfast and dinner included

Beautifully located for visiting the shrines. Charming little *ryokan*, very old, with 24 rooms, only 4 of them with private bath.

Pension Turtle Ryokan 👑

2-16 Takumi-cho, Nikko, Tochigi-ken 321-14, tel. 0288-53-3168

Two persons in room, $70, breakfast and dinner included

Near the Toshogu Shrine, a small (6 rooms, only 1 Japanese-style) pension with full restaurant service. Pleasant, cozy, almost like staying in someone's home.

Sendai

Plaza 👑 👑 👑 👑

2-20-1 Hon-cho, Sendai, Miyagi-ken 980, tel. 0222-62-7111

Two persons in twin, $95

Superb service in this hotel, run by same family for three generations. Just off main business area, quiet, 201 good-sized rooms, 3 restaurants, including excellent Maple Sky Lounge on top floor.

Sendai 👑 👑 👑 👑

1-10-25 Chuo, Sendai, Miyagi-ken 980, tel. 0222-25-5171

Two persons in twin, $90

Nicely sited, with direct access across plaza to Sendai Station, 7 restaurants, including Japanese, Chinese, and French-style (latter with garden view). Big shopping arcade. Has 123 rooms; sizes vary for twin, some 50 percent bigger than others, so ask for "big twin."

Tokyu 👑 👑 👑 👑

2-9-25 Ichibancho, Sendai, Miyagi-ken 980, tel. 0222-62-2411

Two persons in twin, $100

In middle of business district, recently built, 302 fair-sized rooms, 4 restaurants, shopping arcade, bars.

Koyo Grand 👑 👑 👑

1-3-2 Hon-cho, Sendai, Miyagi-ken 980, tel. 0222-67-5111

Two persons in twin, $86

You have to see this. It has the Most Best-Worst-Taste Hotel Lobby in the world. (The title, and its syntax, I am putting up for copyright.) Reproductions of every famous statue you ever heard of crowd the area, competing for attention with huge birdcages (plus inhabitants) and stained-glass copy of David's *Coronation of Napoleon,* if my memory is correct (my nerves were so jangled, I'm not sure). It's like attending a convention of statues. Has 3 restaurants, none outstanding, 149 average-sized rooms. You can't miss the hotel, as more statues adorn the front.

Rich ♛ ♛ ♛

2-2-2 Kokubun-cho, Sendai, Miyagi-ken 980, tel. 0222-62-8811

Two persons in twin, $75

A good-bargain chain hotel, 242 small rooms, 2 restaurants, plus 7 more in basement. Latter include Aster, which has Chinese lunch (5 items) for only ¥730 (about $4), and Riko, preparing French cuisine in the Japanese *kaiseki* manner, beautiful to look at, and expensive.

Washington ♛ ♛

2-3-1 Omachi, Sendai, Miyagi-ken 980, tel. 0222-22-2111

Two persons in twin, $60

A real find, though the 271 rooms are small. Good location, best view of nearby hills. Good dining in Japanese restaurant on top floor, 2 additional restaurants, sauna and bar in basement. Washington I has better view, Washington II is newer, like an annex, next door.

Miyagi Dai-Ichi ♛

112 Higashi, 7 Ban-cho, Sendai, Miyagi-ken 980, tel. 0222-97-4411

Two persons in twin, $70

Do not confuse with other Dai-Ichi Hotel, not nearly as good. Back side of Sendai Station, connected by elevated walkway, 121 smallish rooms, 2 restaurants.

Shiga Heights

Shiga Heights ♛ ♛ ♛

Hirao, Yamanouchi-machi, Nagano-ken 381-04, tel. 0269-34-2111

Two persons in twin, $80

Big (150 largish rooms) and old, as well as famous, skiing resort, also good place for Japan Alps hiking and flower-picking in summer. Mini-golf, boating, fishing, skating, among other sports.

Takayama

Green👑 👑 👑
2-180 Nishino Isshiki-cho, Takayama, Gifu-ken 506, tel.
0577-33-5500
Two persons in twin, $110
Out at edge of town near Hida Folklore Village, peaceful
and quiet, 184 average-sized rooms.

Hida Plaza👑 👑 👑
2-60 Hanaoka-machi, Takayama, Gifu-ken 506, tel. 0577-
33-4600
Two persons in twin, $80
Two buildings (ask for new one), 137 rooms, small (old
building) to spacious (new building) in size. Indoor pool,
health club, 4 restaurants, local dishes.

RESTAURANTS
Kanazawa

Goriya👑 👑 👑
Tel. 0762-52-2288
Average dinner, $35
Fish specialties, including *gori*, a local river fish.

Tsubajin👑 👑 👑
Tel. 0762-41-2181
Average dinner, $30
Famous local dish, kind of chicken stew, called *jibuni*.
Often has crab, too.

Zeniya👑 👑 👑
Tel. 0762-33-3331
Average dinner, $30
Traditional food at the counter. Ask for cheaper lunchtime
donbori dishes.

Jimbei👑 👑
Tel. 0762-31-4303
Average dinner, $18
Overlooking river in Century Plaza Building. Traditional
Japanese cuisine.

Kitama👑
Tel. 0762-61-4387
Average dinner, $24

Traditional cuisine and decor, fabulous fish courses, set courses.

Miyoshian ♛
Tel. 0762-21-0127
Average dinner, $7 up
Sushi in the garden, the famous Kenrokuen, that is.

Takanoha ♛
Tel. 0762-21-2118
Average dinner, $20 up
Jibuni (chicken stew), local specialty, after or during your shopping spree.

Takenoan ♛
Tel. 0762-61-3993
Average dinner, $8
Homemade noodles, with *soba* (buckwheat noodles) the specialty.

Nikko

Kanaya Hotel ♛ ♛
Tel. 0288-54-0001
Average dinner, $20
Only place to eat in town, unless you want cheap noodles somewhere. Trout, caught in Lake Chuzenji, the specialty here.

Sendai

Isahachi ♛ ♛
Tel. 0222-22-3532
Average dinner, $18
Robata yaki (food grilled over open fire and passed to you on a paddle) is the game they play here. Lots of fun.

Kurumaya ♛ ♛
Tel. 0222-65-1131
Average dinner, $13
Sukiyaki and *shabu shabu,* near Hotel Rich.

Tachibana ♛ ♛
Tel. 0222-64-2746
Average dinner, $20
Sushi, the best in Sendai, is what you'll find here.

Robata ♛ ♛
Tel. 0222-23-0316
Average dinner, $12
Famous old drinking place, decorated with folkcraft and large phallic symbols (part of the folklore). Try *nisshin* (herring), and it will come in a variety of ways with your beer. Near Hotel Rich.

Matsuribayachi ♛
Tel. 0222-64-3205
Average dinner, $25
Traditional, and local, cuisine, but you'll need help finding place and ordering. Near Hotel Washington.

Takayama

Kakusho ♛ ♛ ♛
Tel. 0577-32-0174
Average lunch (no dinner), $50
Teahouse where you can meditate while eating exquisite *shojin ryori* (vegetarian food), including wild vegetables and roots, noodles. If you're not going to Kyoto, you should try this cuisine here.

Susaki ♛ ♛ ♛
Tel. 0577-32-0023
Average lunch (no dinner), $50
Traditional *kaiseki* cuisine, heavy on vegetables. Elegant surroundings, service.

Kanenbo ♛ ♛
Tel. 0577-33-0776
Average lunch (no dinner), $35
Shorenji Temple itself offers this vegetarian meal, in spartan but oh-so-authentic surroundings.

Kitchen Hida ♛ ♛
Tel. 0577-32-5406
Average dinner, $40
Beef is featured here, in steak, *sukiyaki,* and other forms.

Mikado ♛
Tel. 0577-34-6789
Average dinner, $15
Near Kokubunji Temple. More *teishoku* (vegetarian food), but meat if you want it.

BEST SHOPPING
Kanazawa

Kaga yuzen silk. Watch it made at Saihitsuan in Naga-machi. Buy it at Erihana, Tatemachi, or Kiguraya in Oawari-cho.

Kutaniyaki pottery. Watch it made at Ace Kanazawa or Kanko Bussan-kan. Buy it at Moroe-ya, opposite Daiwa Department Store.

Maki-e lacquerware. Watch it made at Kanko Bussan-kan (near Kenrokuen Garden). Buy it at Nosaku on Hirosa-ka-dori or Ishida on Katamachi Hondori.

Nikko

Antiques. At three neighboring shops: Nakamura, 1004 Kami-hatsuishi-cho, tel. 0288-40320; Takemoto at 1015 same street, tel. 0288-40829; Kimura at 1017 same street, tel. 0288-40550.

Sendai

Local handicrafts. At Craft Corner, 2-4-8 Chuo, tel. 0222-21-3488.

Tamamuchi-nuri lacquerware. At Tohoku Kogei, 44-3-3 Kamisugi, tel. 0222-22-5401.

For a look at a huge arcade complex, just stay inside Sendai Railway Station and the adjoining S-Pal Department Store, especially in the basements.

FESTIVALS

Note: See also National Holidays listings, pages 21–22.

January 14	Sendai: Dondo Matsuri (Fire Festival) ♛ at Osaki Hachimangu Shrine.
January 17	Akita: Benten Matsuri ♛ ♛, Miyoshi Jinja Shrine. Large decorated poles carried around.
February 15–16	Yokote: Kamakura Matsuri ♛. Children build *kamakura* (igloos) and have tea parties. Great photos.

April 14–15   Takayama Sanno Matsuri ♛♛♛ in that town's Hie Jinja Shrine. Parade of gorgeous floats.

May 17–18   Nikko: Grand Festival of Toshogu Shrine ♛♛♛. Palanquins, *samurai*.

August 1–7   Nebuta Matsuri ♛♛♛ in Aomori and Hirosaki. Big effigies on parade, hundreds of dancers, children also.

August 5–6   Nikko: Waraku Odori (Laughing Dances) ♛♛, O-Bon dances, but among biggest in Japan.

August 5–7   Akita: Kanto Matsuri (Long Pole Festival) ♛♛. Young men try to balance long poles on parade.

October 9–10   Takayama Matsuri ♛♛♛ again in that town; see April above.

October 17   Nikko: Aki Matsuri (Autumn Festival) ♛♛ of Toshogu Shrine.

December 2–3   Chichibu City, Saitama prefecture: Huge floats ♛♛ which serve as stages for daytime performances of *kabuki* and dancing. Then they are illuminated with lanterns and pulled through streets in evening.

HOKKAIDO

Almost forgotten by the most experienced traveler visiting Japan, Hokkaido is the place to go if you want to ski in exotic places. The scenery is splendid, the mountains full of game, and facilities for sports abound. I can recommend coming here if you like scenery, sports, or hot springs. Or if you've seen all the other major sights in Japan and long for something different, something, well, less Japanese.

Getting here is no problem. It's the airplane for you, unless you want a long train and ferry ride. When the world's longest rail tunnel underneath the Tsugaru Straits is ready to take the Shinkansen railroad line, you'll be able to whisk here on the Bullet Train in only a few hours. Until then, land transport is not recommended. Japan's three major airlines (JAL, ANA, and TDA) all fly to Hokkaido. Once here, take JNR between cities.

The most important event of the Hokkaido Year is the Snow Festival♛♛♛, held every February. Volunteers, including students and lots of troops from the Self-Defense Forces (the Japanese army, navy, and air force), pitch in to build huge figures of fantasy, carved from ice blocks and lining the main street of Sapporo. All types of winter sports activities, concerts, and parades combine to make the celebration a kind of Japanese Oktoberfest, with icicles. Americans from newer cities of the U.S. should find Sapporo familiar, as it was laid out on the grid system with streets and avenues numbered and with compass directions (West 1, North 5, etc.). The American influence was strongly felt during the early days of development in Hokkaido, and the slogan of the university is still "Boys, Be Ambitious," a saying of one of its founders, Dr. William S. Clark.

About 50 miles southwest of Sapporo is Noboribetsu Spa♛♛, famous for its mammoth public baths. The hotels are relatively spartan, but if you are a fan of the spa system, you'll love it here. As indicated in the hotel listings, the Daiichi Takimoto-kan ♨ ♨ is the place to go, having about 40 different pools, with about 10 different kinds of mineral waters, making it unique in Japan (or perhaps anywhere else).

The natural wonders of Hokkaido are many, but I'll mention only one, the *marimo* (Lake Akan Disappearing Duckweed). A disappearing form of vegetation, it is now protected, and you'll be lucky if you see it. The stuff grows on the bottom, then comes to the surface in a ball shape, emits gas (yes, it smells like something rotten), soaks up sunlight for a while, then settles back to the bottom. It's not as exciting for the observer as for the duckweed, however, and like Mt. Fuji, you may not see it at all on the day you're there.

INSIDERS' INFORMATION FOR HOKKAIDO

HOTELS
Asahikawa

New Hokkai ♨ ♨
6 Gojo-dori, Asahikawa, Hokkaido 070, tel. 0166-24-3111
Two persons in twin, $75
Shops, 4 restaurants, beer garden, barber and beauty shops, 207 rooms.

Noboribetsu Spa

Takinoya Ryokan ♨ ♨ ♨
162 Noboribetsu Onsen, Noboribetsu City, Hokkaido 059-05, tel. 01438-4-2222
Two persons in room, $150, breakfast and dinner included
Has 70 rooms, own hot spring bath in half of them. Big public bath, too. Not the gentility and elegance of typical inn, but comfortable and fun.

Dai-Ichi Takimoto-Kan Ryokan ♨ ♨
55 Noboribetsu Onsen, Noboribetsu, Hokkaido 059-05, tel. 01438-4-2111
Two persons in room, $155, breakfast and dinner included
Huge place with biggest public bath in Hokkaido, sometimes gets unsegregated if big parties push their way in

after too much drinking. Has 340 rooms, mostly Japanese-style and mostly with private bath.

Sapporo

Keio Plaza ♛ ♛ ♛ ♛
7-2 Nishi, Kita 5, Chuo-ku, Sapporo, Hokkaido 060, tel. 011-271-0111
Two persons in twin, $150
Branch of famous Tokyo hostelry, convenient to everything, 525 smallish rooms, indoor pool, gym, sauna, several restaurants.

New Otani ♛ ♛ ♛ ♛
1-1 Nishi, Kita 2, Chuo-ku, Sapporo, Hokkaido 060, tel. 011-222-1111
Two persons in twin, $160
Also branch of leading Tokyo hotel, this one with 340 medium-sized rooms, 3 restaurants, access to skating, skiing, other winter sports.

ANA Sapporo ♛ ♛ ♛
1 Nishi, Kita 3, Chuo-ku, Sapporo, Hokkaido 060, tel. 011-221-4411
Two persons in twin, $100
Big airline hotel, 5 restaurants, 470 fair-sized rooms, sauna, shops, access to skating and skiing.

Grand ♛ ♛ ♛
4 Nishi, Kita 1, Chuo-ku, Sapporo, Hokkaido 060, tel. 011-261-3311
Two persons in twin, $115
A favorite with business travelers and groups, the Grand has 558 smallish rooms, sauna, shops, 4 restaurants, access to skating and skiing.

Prince ♛ ♛
11 Nishi, Minami 2, Chuo-ku, Sapporo, Hokkaido 060, tel. 011-241-1111
Two persons in twin, $95
Outside Tokyo, this chain calls its hotels "resorts," even if in a city such as Sapporo. Has 345 fair-sized rooms, 5 restaurants, shops, access to golf, skiing, skating.

Tokyu ♛ ♛
4 Nishi, Kita 4, Chuo-ku, Sapporo, Hokkaido 060, tel. 011-231-5611

Two persons in twin, $100
Usual facilities of this chain, 263 medium-sized rooms, several restaurants, shop, access to winter sports in area. Near rail station. Prices 40 percent cheaper from October to May.

RoyalW
1 Higashi, Minami 7, Chuo-ku, Sapporo, Hokkaido 060, tel. 011-511-2121
Two persons in twin, $86
Smaller hotel, 88 small rooms, restaurant, access to winter sports.

RESTAURANTS
Sapporo

Ten IchiW W W
Sogo Department Store, 10th floor, tel. 011-213-2705
Average dinner, $22
Branch of famous Tokyo original. *Tempura,* best on island of Hokkaido.

EzogotenW W
Tel. 011-241-8451
Average dinner, $15
Local specialties, including Hokkaido king crab. Cutely quaint rustic atmosphere.

HyosetsumonW W
Tel. 011-521-3046
Average dinner, $12
Crab, served in wide variety of ways. At these prices, you can be sure *surimi* (imitation crab) is what you're getting in some cases.

IkoiW W
Tel. 011-521-0918
Average dinner, $15
Fish is king of the sea and land here, and you couldn't do better.

Lorelei Lion Beer HallW
Keiai Building, tel. 011-251-3843
Average dinner, $7
You don't come here for the food, but for the beer, with something to eat, maybe. Watch the "salarymen" off duty.

Sapporo Beer Garden ♛
Tel. 011-742-1531
Average dinner, $15
In old brewery. Grill your own Genghis Khan lamb on barbecue, or ask for salmon or another fish. Just like a German beer hall, only more polite. Garden drinking in summer.

BEST SHOPPING
Sapporo

Handicrafts, including Ainu carvings, at Hokkaido Mingei (Folkcraft) Center Maruwa, 6 Tanuki-koji, tel. 011-261-3611; or Eibansha Craft Shop, Nishi 4, Minami 7-jo, tel. 011-251-7749.

FESTIVALS

Note: See also National Holidays listings, pages 21–22.

February 1–5	Sapporo: Yuki Matsuri (Snow Festival) ♛ ♛ ♛; see page 313.
May	Last Sunday, Rairakku Matsuri (Lilac Festival) ♛.
June 14–16	All towns: Hokkaido Jinja Matsuri (Shrine Festival) ♛, with parades and dancing everywhere.
Autumn	Sapporo: Kiku Matsuri (Chrysanthemum Festival) ♛, in late autumn, probably November.

OKINAWA (RYUKYU ISLANDS)

If you're in Okinawa on business, try to make the most of it by dining out Ryukyuan-style. Sad to say, Okinawa is a perfect example of a land whose territory has been trod heavily upon too long and too often, so that little of its own particular culture remains. It is, as it has been for years, a Japanese prefecture, and proud of it. But the differences in regional cuisine, folklore, and customs are rapidly disappearing. Direct American postwar rule for 27 years didn't help preserve the old culture, which had been under some strain since the islands became an integral part of Japan in 1872. Although closer in every way to Japan than China for its entire history, Ryukyuan leaders had tried to play off one country against the other.

For "mainland" Japanese, Okinawa and the other islands to the south (Yoron, etc.) are for vacationing, lying on the beach, water sports, and perhaps a little shopping. For some older Japanese, visiting Okinawa means paying respects to the dead on one of the islands' many battlefields. Americans visiting here have the same options, unless they have business with the giant U.S. bases still operating. I can recommend a beach holiday here if you live in Japan and the cold gray weather of winter is getting on your nerves. If you're not in that situation, however, I can suggest a visit to Okinawa only if you are a student of history, particularly of World War II.

Several battlefield monuments dot the landscape. The most famous is Hill 89, where the Japanese commanders committed suicide (some by *seppuku*, or *hara-kiri*) rather than surrender to American forces. The same tragic confusion of identity with status caused hysterical teachers to lead their students to suicide also, at a place now known as Kenji-no-to. Two memorials at caves commemorate the deaths of innocent schoolgirls, and you might wish to visit them—Shiraume-no-to and Himeyuri-no-to (White Plum and Lily towers, respectively).

If you're in Okinawa when one of its famous festivals takes place, count yourself lucky. The Naha Tsunahiki ♛ ♛ (October 8–10) features a giant tug-of-war. The Eisa dances ♛ of July 14–16 are the biggest festivities, but don't miss the August Moon Festival ♛, mid-August (lunar calendar). You might even want to celebrate it at the Teahouse of the August Moon, which is now a fixture on the Naha scene. The capital, Naha, has about as much charm as any dull provincial town.

INSIDERS' INFORMATION FOR OKINAWA

HOTELS

Harbor View ♛ ♛ ♛ ♛
2-46 Izumizaki, Naha, Okinawa-ken 900, tel. 0988-53-2111
Two persons in twin, $165
Good location plus view, as name says, 402 smallish rooms, pool, sauna, 3 restaurants.

Miyako ♛ ♛ ♛
40 Matsukawa, Naha, Okinawa-ken 902, tel. 0988-87-1111
Two persons in twin, $100
High on a hill, outside town, not for business travelers. Pool, Sky Lounge on revolving top floor, 4 restaurants, 318 average-sized rooms.

Tokyu ♛ ♛ ♛
1002 Ameku, Naha, Okinawa-ken 900, tel. 0988-68-2151
Two persons in twin, $90
Also up on hill outside town, and for vacationing travelers. Shop, pool, 280 fair-sized rooms, 2 restaurants.

RESTAURANTS

Naha ♛ ♛
Tel. 0988-68-2548
Average dinner, $30
Local specialties. Ask for *awamori* to drink, if you have the guts for it. (Remember *Teahouse of the August Moon?*)

TRAVELER'S GLOSSARY

Here are just a few words and phrases you'll find useful, as well as some warning and other vital signs. The romanized Japanese is followed by the correct pronunciation. Japanese vowels are pronounced like Italian: a=ah, e=ay, i=ee, o=oh, u=oo. The Japanese order of vowels, however, is a, i, u, e, o.

English	Japanese (pronunciation)
Please (when requesting something)	. . . *kudasai* (ku-dah-sai)
Please (when offering something)	. . . *dozo* (doe-zoh)
Thank you	*Arigato* (ah-ri-ga-toh)
You're welcome	*Do itashimashite* (doe-etah-she-mahsh-tay)
Excuse me	*Sumimasen* (sue-me-mah-sen)
Yes	*Hai* (high)
No	*Iie* (ee-yeh)
Maybe	*Tabun* (tah-boon)
I, me	*Watakushi* (wah-tahk-she)
You	*Anata* (ah-nah-ta)
He	*Kare* (kah-ray)
She	*Kanojo* (kah-no-joe)
Do you understand English?	*Eigo o wakarimasuka* (eh-go-o-wah-kah-ree-mas-kah)
Yes, I understand	*Hai, wakarimasu* (high, wah-kah-ree-mas)
No, I don't understand	*Iie, wakarimasen* (ee-yeh, wah-kah-ree-masen)
Good morning	*Ohayo gozaimasu* (Ohio go-zai-mas)
Good afternoon	*Konnichiwa* (kohn-nitchi-wah)
Good evening	*Kombanwa* (komb-bahn-wah)
Good night (on retiring)	*Oyasuminasai* (oh yah-su-mee-nah-sai)
Goodbye	*Sayonara* (sai-oh-nah-rah)

How do you do?	*Hajimemashita* (Hah-jee-may-mahsh-ta)
How are you?	*O genki desuka* (oh gen-key-des-kah)
Just a moment, please	*Chotto matte kudasai* (cho-toe-mah-teh ku-dah-sai)
I don't speak Japanese	*Nihongo o hanasemasen* (nee-hon-go-o hah-nah-say-mah-sen)
Please show me . . .	*. . . wo misete kudasai* (woe me-seh-tay ku-dah-sai)
Please show me a cheaper one	*Motto yasui no wo misete kudasai* (moh-toe yah-soo-ee noh woe mee-seh-tay ku-dah-sai)
What is this?	*Kore wa nan desu ka* (koh-ray-wah nahn des-kah)
How much?	*Ikura desu ka* (ee-koo-rah des-kah)
I'll take this	*Kore o kudasai* (koe-ray oh ku-dah-sai)
Expensive	*Takai* (tah-kai)
Cheap	*Yasui* (yah-sue-ee)
This	*Kore* (koh-ray)
That	*Are* (ah-ray)
Where is . . .	*. . . doko desu ka* (doe-koh-des-kah)
the restroom?	*Otearai* (oh-tay-ah-rye) *wa doko desu ka*
the police station?	*Koban* (koh-ban) *wa doko desu ka*
the rail station?	*Eki* (eh-key) *wa doko desu ka* (also "station," as in English)
the subway?	*Chikatetsu* (chi-kah-teh-tsu) *wa doko desu ka*
When?	*Itsu* (ee-tsu)
Hotel	*Hoteru* (hoe-teh-roo)
Inn	*Ryokan* (ree-yoh-kan)
Right	*Migi* (me-ghee)
Left	*Hidari* (hee-dah-ree)
Straight	*Massugu* (mah-sue-goo)
Stop	*Tomete* (toe-meh-tay)
Corner	*Kado* (kah-doe)
Go slowly	*Yukkuri* (you-ku-ree)
Which track (rail station)?	*Nam ban sen desu ka* (nahm-ban-sen-des-kah)
Number One	*Ichi ban* (ee-chi-ban)
Number Two	*Ni ban* (knee-ban)

Number Three	*San ban* (san-ban)
Number Four	*Yon ban* (yon-ban)
Five	*Go* (go)
Six	*Roku* (roe-ku)
Seven	*Shichi* (shee-chi)
Eight	*Hachi* (hah-chi)
Nine	*Ku* (ku)
Ten	*Ju* (joo)
Eleven	*Juichi* (joo-ichi)
Twenty	*Niju* (knee-joo)
Thirty	*Sanju* (san-joo)
Hundred	*Hyaku* (hyah-ku)
Two hundred	*Ni hyaku* (knee hyah-ku)
Thousand	*Sen* (sen)
Two thousand	*Nisen* (knee-sen)
Ten thousand	*Man* (mahn)
Twenty thousand	*Ni man* (knee mahn)
Million	*Hyaku man* (hyah-ku mahn)
Ten million	*Sen man* (sen mahn)
Hundred million	*Oku* (oh-ku)
Two hundred million	*Ni oku* (knee oh-ku)

MENU TRANSLATOR

This should be called a Menu Interpreter, since you can't expect to learn to read Japanese easily, so you may just hear the words spoken. Conversely, you may decide what you want, find it here, and order without bothering to look at the menu. Of course, there are plenty of menus which have English translations right on them, even in French or Chinese restaurants.

English	Japanese
Restaurant	*Restoran,* or *ryoriya*
Dining room	*Shokudo*
Dining car	*Shokudo-sha*
Japanese restaurant	*Nihon ryoriya*
Chinese restaurant	*Chuka ryoriya*
European restaurant	*Seiyo ryoriya*
Menu	*Menyu*
Table d'hote	*Teishoku*
A la carte	*Ippin ryori,* or *à la carte*
Rice	*Gohan*
Bread	*Pan* (pahn)
Soup	*Supu*
Toast	*Tosto*
Butter	*Bata*
Cheese	*Chizu*
Egg	*Tamago*
Fish	*Sakana*
Meat	*Niku*
Beef	*Gyu niku*
Pork	*Ton niku,* or *buta niku*
Chicken	*Tori*
Salt	*Shio*
Pepper	*Kosho*
Sugar	*Sato*
Soy sauce	*Shoyu*

Mustard	*Karashi*
Fruit	*Kudamono,* or *frutsu*
Salad	*Sarada*
Vegetable	*Yasai*
Knife	*Naifu*
Fork	*Hoku*
Spoon	*Saji,* or *supun*
Napkin	*Napukin*
Chopsticks	*Ohashi*
Bowl	*Chawan,* or *wan*
Plate	*Osara*
Cup	*Koppu*
Beer	*Biru*
Coffee	*Kohi*
Tea (black)	*Kocha*
Tea (green)	*Ocha*
Iced . . .	*Hiyashi,* or *aisu*
Milk	*Gyunyu,* or *miruku*
Soda water	*Sodasui*
Cold water	*Ohiya*
Hot water	*Oyu*
Whiskey	*Uisuki*
Wine	*Budoshu,* or *wain*
Sake	*Osake,* or *nihonshu*

TEISHOKU (COMPLETE MEAL) HAS THREE GRADES, FREQUENTLY:

Regular	*Nami teishoku*
Choice	*Jo teishoku*
Special	*Tokujo teishoku*
Today's Special	*Higawari*
Lunchbox	*Obento*

KAISEKI (TRADITIONAL JAPANESE)

Soybean soup	*Miso shiru*
Raw fish	*Sashimi*
Clear soup	*Wan mori*
Broiled(fish/meat)	*Yakimono* (*sakana/niku*)

Salty soup	*Hashi arai* (lit. washing chopsticks)
House specialty	*Hassun* (lit. small square dish)
Pickled vegetables	*Konomono*
Dessert (sweets/fruit)	*Okashi* (*okashi/kudamono*)
Frothy green tea	*Matcha*

SHOJIN RYORI (VEGETARIAN)

Soybean curd	*Tofu*
Soybean paste	*Miso*
Mountain vegetables	*Sansai*
Eggplant	*Nasu*
Radish	*Daikon*
Tofu, daikon, eggplant with sweet *miso* sauce	*Dengaku*
Devil's-tongue root	*Konnyaku*
Mushrooms	*Shiitake, matsutake, nameko*
Fermented soybeans	*Natto*
Burdock root	*Gobo*
Leek	*Negi*
White onion (Spanish)	*Tama negi*
Mandarin orange	*Mikan*
Carrots	*Ninjin*
Green pepper	*Piman*
Seaweed, dried	*Nori*
Ginger	*Shoga*
Potato	*Imo*
Beefsteak plant	*Shiso*
Sweet potato	*Satsuma imo*
Rice vinegar	*Su*
Pickles	*Tsukemono*
Radish pickle	*Takuan*
Horseradish (Japanese-style)	*Wasabi*
Rice gruel	*Zosui*
Soybean sauce	*Shoyu*

SUSHI

There are some special words used only in *sushi* shops. If you use them, you'll be treated as an expert. They are given following the polite Japanese term.

Chopsticks	*Ohashi* (*otemoto*)
Ginger in vinegar	*Shoga* (*gari*)
Horseradish	*Wasabi* (*namida*, lit. "tears" from the eyes)
Soy sauce	*Oshoyu* (*murasaki*, lit. "purple")
Green tea	*Ocha* (*agari*, lit. "the end")
Regular *sushi* (fish on rice ball)	*Nigiri zushi*
Rolled *sushi* (inside roll of seaweed)	*Maki zushi*
Bean-curd *sushi*	*Inari zushi*
Sushi on bowl of rice	*Chirashi zushi*
Tuna	*Maguro*
Fatty tuna	*Toro*
Sea urchin roe	*Uni*
Salmon roe	*Ikura*
Horse mackerel	*Aji*
Conger eel	*Anago*
Abalone	*Awabi*
Yellowtail	*Hamachi*
Flounder	*Hirame*
Scallop	*Hotategai*
Shrimp	*Ebi*
Turbot	*Karei*
Horse clam	*Mirugai*
Herring	*Nishin*
Mackerel	*Saba*
Sea bass	*Suzuki*
Sea bream	*Tai*
Octopus	*Tako*
Squid	*Ika*

TEMPURA

Most of the vegetables and fish mentioned above are cooked in *tempura* style. Here are a few more:

Lotus root	*Hasu*, or *rinkon*
Crab	*Kani*

Oyster	*Kaki*
Sea smelt	*Kisu*
Sweet smelt (often called river trout)	*Ayu*
Trout	*Yamame*
Whitefish	*Shirauo*
Asparagus	*Aspara*
Ginger root	*Shoga*
Ginkgo nuts	*Ginnan*
Lemon-mint leaf (also called beefeater's plant)	*Shiso*
Squash	*Kabocha*
Fried prawn	*Ebi furai*

TONKATSU (PORK CUTLETS)

| Pork fillet | *Hi-re katsu* |
| Pork loin | *Rosu katsu* |

NABE (STEWS)

Chicken in pot	*Tori no mizutaki*
Chicken/fish with vegetables	*Yose nabe*
Oyster nabe	*Dote nabe*

UNAGI (EEL)

| Eel on rice in lacquer box | *Unaju* |
| Broiled eel | *Kabayaki* |

YAKITORI (GRILLED CHICKEN), OTHER FOWL

Breast meat	*Yakitori*
Legs	*Momo yaki*
Wings	*Tebasaki yaki*
Giblets	*Motsu yaki*
Heart	*Hatsu yaki*

Liver	*Reba yaki*
Chicken meatballs	*Tsukune yaki*
Duck	*Kamo yaki*
Quail's eggs	*Uzura yaki*
Sparrow	*Suzume Yaki*

KAMAMESHI (STEAMED RICE CASSEROLE)

Steamed in pot encased in wooden box. Delicious and cheap, with many ingredients already listed as fish or vegetable, etc. Here are a few more good orders:

Bamboo shoots	*Takenoko*
Chestnuts	*Kuri*
Five Specials (vegetable, peas, carrots, dried gourd, mushroom)	*Gomoku*
Salmon	*Sake*

ROBATA YAKI (HEARTH GRILL)

Order any kind of meat, fish, or vegetable, as on previous lists, but ask for it to be grilled in a specific manner, if you wish:

Grilled with *miso* sauce	*Misoyaki*
Grilled with salt	*Shioyaki*
Grilled with soy sauce	*Teriyaki*
Pan-roasted	*Okaribayaki*

SOBA AND *UDON* (NOODLES)

Buckwheat noodles	*Soba*
Wheat noodles	*Udon*
Cold Chinese noodles	*Hiyashi Chuka soba*
Cold vermicelli	*Hiyamugi, or somen*
Flat, wide *udon*	*Kishimen*
Chinese egg noodles	*Ramen*
Bean sprouts topping on *soba/udon*	*Moyashi* (*soba/udon*)

Chicken and egg topping	*Oyako namban* (*soba/udon*)
Five Kinds (chicken, radish, etc.)	*Gomoku* (*soba/udon*)
Fried bean curd topping	*Kitsune* (*soba/udon*)

DOMBURI (RICE BOWL MEALS)

On the large bowl of rice come many different toppings, a few of which I list:

Beef topping	*Gyudon*
Omelette topping	*Tamagodon*
Pork cutlet topping	*Katsudon*
Shrimp *tempura* topping	*Ten don*
Curry (not hot)	*Kare raisu*, or *kare don*
Beef, *sukiyaki*	*Sukiyaki domburi*
Eel	*Unagidon*, or *unadon*

SNACKS

Rice crackers	*Senbei, arare*
Dried squid	*Ika no kunsei*
Roasted navy beans	*Edamamme*

SOME USEFUL PHRASES

English	*Japanese*
May I see the menu, please?	*Menyu o misete kudasai.*
May I have . . . please?	*. . . o kudasai.*
Bring me a selection, please. (Especially for *sushi*)	*Moriawase o kudasai.*
What do you recommend?	*Osusume wa nandesu ka.*
The *table d'hôte* special, please.	*Teishoku o kudasai.*
Your most popular dish, please.	*Ichiban ninki no mono o kudasai.*

I'll let you choose.	*Omakase shimasu.*
It's delicious.	*Oishii desu.*
No more, thanks, I'm full.	*Mo kekko desu.*
I'll have the same again, please.	*Onaji mono o kudasai.*
That was a delicious meal.	*Gochisosama.*
May I have the bill, please.	*Okanjo o onegai shimasu.* (Instead of *okanjo*, *okaikei* in Kyoto, *owaiso* in Tokyo, but all recognized everywhere.)
Do you use this credit card?	*Kono kado wa tsukaemasu ka.*
I would like a receipt, please.	*Ryo-shu-sho o kudasai.*
(To catch waiter's attention)	*Sumimasen* (lit. excuse me). Also, *chotto* (less polite)
One (dish or order)	*Hitotsu* (not *Ichi*)
Two (dishes or orders)	*Futatsu* (not *Ni*)
Three (dishes or orders)	*Mittsu* (not *San*)
Four (dishes or orders)	*Yottsu* (not *Shi*)

INDEX